# HOW DID IT REALLY HAPPEN?

# HOW DID IT REALLY HAPPEN

Reader's Digest

THE READER'S DIGEST ASSOCIATION, INC.
PLEASANTVILLE, NEW YORK / MONTREAL

A Reader's Digest Book produced by
The Reference Works, Inc. and Hopkins/Baumann

**TEXT AND CAPTIONS**
The Reference Works, Inc.
DIRECTOR  Harold Rabinowitz
EXECUTIVE EDITOR  Lorraine Martindale
EDITORS  Cassandra Heliczer, Geoffrey Upton
COPY EDITOR  Diane Lane Root

**WRITERS**
Adam Green, Jason Grote, Cassandra
Heliczer, Doug Heyman, Lorraine Martindale, Daniel
Mulligan, Brian Phillips, Harold Rabinowitz, Jake
Silverstein, Benjamin Soskis, Chanan Tigay, Geoffrey Upton,
Charles Wilson, Marcy Zipke

**DESIGN**
Hopkins/Baumann
DESIGNERS  Mary K. Baumann, Will Hopkins,
Amy Bohr, Guillermo Nagore
DESIGN COORDINATOR  Jennifer Dixon
COVER DESIGN  Reader's Digest Books

**PICTURE RESEARCH**
Carousel Research, Inc.
EDITORS  Laurie Platt Winfrey, Max Miller
RESEARCHERS  Van Bucher, Matthew Connors, Christopher
Deegan, Mary Teresa Giancoli, Robin Sand, Jill Tatara

**READER'S DIGEST PROJECT STAFF**
EDITORIAL DIRECTOR  Fred DuBose
SENIOR DESIGNER  Judith Carmel
PRODUCTION TECHNOLOGY MANAGER  Douglas A. Croll
EDITORIAL MANAGER  Christine R. Guido
ART PRODUCTION COORDINATOR  Jennifer R. Tokarski

**READER'S DIGEST ILLUSTRATED REFERENCE BOOKS**
EDITOR-IN-CHIEF  Christopher Cavanaugh
ART DIRECTOR  Joan Mazzeo
OPERATIONS MANAGER  William J. Cassidy

# HOW DID IT REALLY HAPPEN?

Address any comments about How Did It Really Happen? to
Editor-in-Chief, Illustrated Reference Books, Reader's Digest,
Reader's Digest Road, Pleasantville, NY 10570

To order additional copies of How Did It Really Happen?
call 1-800-846-2100.

You can also visit us on the World Wide Web at:
http://www.readersdigest.com

Library of Congress Cataloging in Publication Data
How did it really happen?/Reader's Digest.
    p.cm.
    Includes index.\
    ISBN 0-7621-0277-2
    1. History—Miscellanea.
    2. Curiosities and wonders.
    I. Reader's Digest Association.
D24 .H69 2000
902—dc21                              00-031083

Printed in China

# ABOUT THIS BOOK

THIS IS A BOOK ABOUT THINGS WE KNOW AND THINGS WE DON'T know. Putting the emphasis on whodunits and mysteries, we've sifted through historical events to assemble a collection of episodes that, to a degree, confound our efforts to completely understand what happened. Sometimes we are confronted with a story without an ending. Sometimes there are pieces missing—moments when no one else was around to record an eyewitness account. Sometimes a received view or a myth clouds our vision or leads us astray, and we have to rub our eyes and look carefully once again at the evidence.

This book doesn't confine itself to man-made history and famous personalities. How life arose, where human beings came from, what happened to the dinosaurs, what happens when we die—these are mysteries enough. As for our conclusions—well, it would be surprising if any reader agreed with all of the statements contained in this book. In putting it together, we discovered two things: how little we really know about the world we live in; and how much fun it is investigating these puzzles and finding out more about them.

THE EDITORS

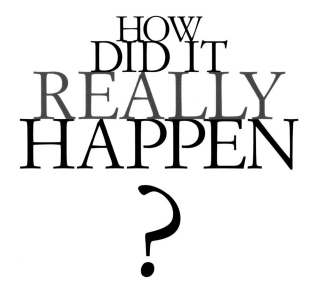

# HOW DID IT REALLY HAPPEN?

# PART 1

# THE DAWN OF TIME

So many of the elements of the world we confront in everyday life are easy to take for granted. It's sobering to think, for example, that the dramatic events of the 20th century may soon become part of the distant past simply because a new century and a new millennium have dawned. Yet the world we know today came about as a result of events that go back to the very beginning of time, events that failed to be recorded by history because early human beings did not have the tools.

These beginnings are lost in the dark recesses of time, but recently some light has been shone on those shadowy areas, leading us to deduce, surmise, and guess at how things happened. What explains the origin of the universe? Why did the dinosaurs become extinct? Then there are legends and traditional wisdom, which have often been found to have some basis in fact, ringing through time like the reverberating echoes of a bell.

# Was There a Big Bang?

### Did a violent explosion billions of years ago shape the universe?

HOW DID THE UNIVERSE BEGIN? IS THERE ANY question that has been asked more often, longer, and with greater wonderment than this one? Philosophers have spent centuries arguing one view or another—or arguing that an answer was beyond the grasp of human intellect. As the line of demarcation between science and philosophy became clearer, scientists appropriated the question from the 1920s onward, addressing it with bold conjectures.

As a new century dawns, the first among these is the Big Bang theory—a vision of a universe that emerged violently from compressed primordial material no bigger than the period at the end of this sentence. Compelling evidence for the Big Bang came in 1964, while Arno Penzias and Robert Wilson, two scientists at Bell Labs in New Jersey, were investigating radio emissions of the Milky Way. As they sought to eliminate radio noise from other sources, they discovered a background signal that seemed to come from every direction. The signal's frequency matched predictions made by astrophysicists who had advanced the theory of the universe's explosive birth.

## THE COSMIC HUM

Penzias and Wilson had discovered the "hum" of the universe, known as cosmic background radiation, which is a remnant of the primal explosion. For their discovery, Penzias and Wilson shared the 1978 Nobel Prize in physics.

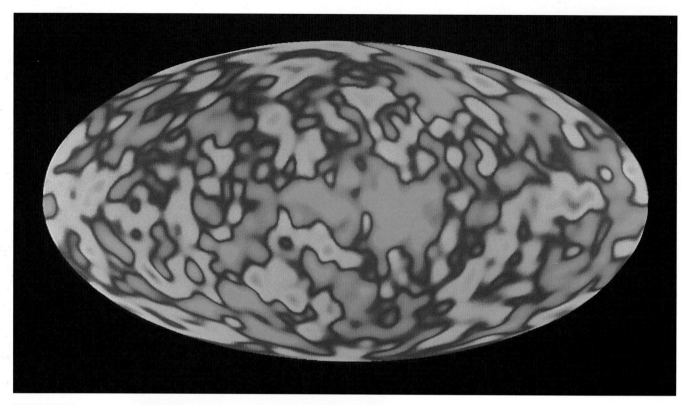

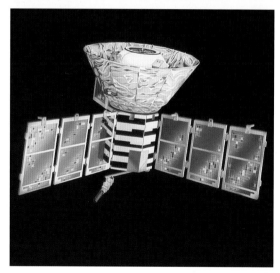

The discovery of the cosmic background radiation was only one of several observations that supported the idea that the universe began at a singular moment in time. The idea was first proposed by Belgian priest and astronomer Abbé Georges Lemaître in 1927. His prediction that galaxies would be found to be speeding away from each other as if from an explosion was confirmed by American astrophysicist Edwin Hubble when he discovered that celestial objects were indeed racing away, and the farther they were from us the faster they were going—again, a phenomenon one would expect in a Big Bang universe.

## A DIFFERENT UNIVERSE

As astronomical instruments were able to peer farther and farther to the edge of the universe, it became apparent that the universe out there was different from the one we know in our corner of space. For example, quasars—extremely bright objects that emit enormous amounts of energy—are found only at the edge of the universe, with none in our vicinity. Since what we're seeing when we observe the distant universe is how it was some 10 to 20 billion years ago, it seems the universe was a different sort of place in the very distant past than it is now—and this is an essential view of the Big Bang.

The Big Bang was not an easy theory to accept, even for some scientists, and it has its opponents. For one thing, it leaves untouched the fundamental question of how (and why) the Big Bang happened. Furthermore, the notion that the universe may not have existed at some point in the past—or that if it did exist, it existed in a way utterly outside our comprehension—challenges a basic scientific principle: The laws of nature are independent of where or when one examines them. A universe that has a singular and particular history—one that obeys a different set of laws depending on the cosmological time frame—is not one that obeys universal laws of physics that are supposed to be valid all the time and everywhere.

LAWYER-TURNED-
ASTRONOMER
EDWIN HUBBLE IS
PICTURED AT
CALIFORNIA'S MT.
WILSON OBSERV-
ATORY. A KEY
FIGURE IN FORMING
OUR CURRENT
PICTURE OF THE
UNIVERSE, HUBBLE
DISCOVERED THE
EXISTENCE OF
GALAXIES OUTSIDE
OUR OWN IN
THE 1920S.

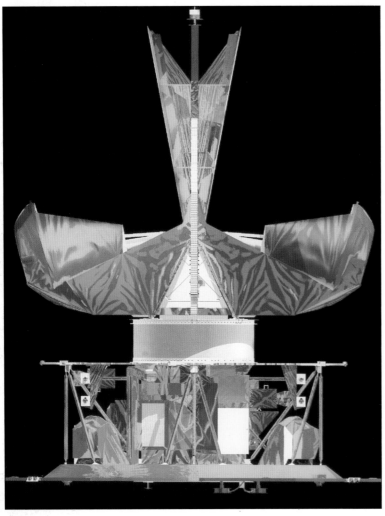

THE MICROWAVE ANISOTROPY PROBE (MAP) REPRESENTS THE LATEST TRY TO OBSERVE THE FARTHEST REACHES OF THE UNIVERSE. EQUIPPED WITH HIGH-POWERED TELESCOPES AND AMPLIFIERS, MAP WILL MAKE ITS OBSERVATIONS MILLIONS OF MILES FROM EARTH AND ANALYZE ITS READINGS BEFORE SENDING THEM BACK. OPPOSITE: THE CONE-SHAPED RECEPTORS AT THE CORE OF MAP ARE CAPABLE OF CAPTURING AND RECORDING SINGLE PHOTONS FROM 15 TO 18 BILLION LIGHT YEARS AWAY.

## THE VAST AND THE VERY SMALL

A powerful reason that the Big Bang theory is accepted by most astronomers and astrophysicists is that it provides a connection between current particle physics (defined as the physics of the very small) and cosmology (the science of the universe as a whole).

In our everyday world, we routinely come into contact with two forces: the force of gravity that keeps us planted on the ground, and the force of electromagnetism that runs our machines and keeps solids from falling apart. But in the realm of the atom, there are two other forces. There is the force that keeps the particles of an atomic nucleus together, called the "weak force" even though it is able to overcome the repulsive electrical force that the electrically-positive protons in the nucleus exert on one another. Far stronger is the so-called "strong force," which allows the particles (quarks) that make up the proton and neutrons in the nucleus to adhere together. There are, then, four forces we know about in nature.

Throughout the history of science, people have tried to show that the universe is governed by a simple scheme, with one force governing all of nature rather than four. So just as electricity and magnetism were shown in the 19th century to be two forms of a single force, science has looked favorably at any attempt to coalesce or unify the four forces of nature into a single force—a "grand unified force." Much of the theoretical work in modern physics has been to derive mathematically and experimentally what that force is like.

## COUNTDOWN TO CREATION

The Big Bang theory paints a picture of the early universe in which the energy in a small space is so high that all the forces of nature we experience are compressed into a single force. This force operates within the highly energetic "stuff" the universe consists of. This "stuff" would not be matter, because the universe had not cooled down enough for particles to form; nor would it be energy or radiation, because quarks and other particles were in a constant state of creation and annihilation.

As the universe expanded and cooled in the first instants of the Big Bang—during the incredibly and unimaginably brief time of $10^{-43}$ seconds—the gravitational force separated out of the grand unified force. At precisely $10^{-35}$ seconds, the strong force separated. Then, at $10^{-10}$ seconds, the weak force separated from the electromagnetic force. By the time the universe was a ripe old age of $10^{-4}$ seconds (one ten-thousandth of a second), the universe was cool enough for quarks to form, and then combine to form particles. The first nuclei were formed at the 100-second mark, but the universe did not cool down enough to become transparent until the 300,000-year mark. Galaxies began to form a billion years after the Big Bang.

The Big Bang theory presents a compelling picture of the evolution of the universe using what has been learned about nature at the smallest and most energetic levels. But will it remain the orthodoxy of science in the future? Perhaps, but we have learned that orthodoxies have a way of not remaining orthodoxies for very long. For instance, recent images from a telescope 40 times sharper than those obtained by COBE showed that the universe was "flat," not curved as previously believed. The truth, or just another step toward it?

# • Life's •
# Beginnings

**How did life originate? Scientists have searched for the answer for centuries, and continue to ponder how life began.**

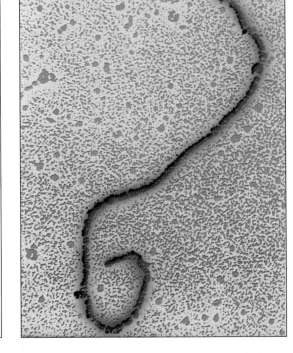

SEEN FIGURATIVELY, THE STORY OF LIFE'S BEGINNINGS AS TOLD IN THE BOOK OF GENESIS (NEAR RIGHT, FROM THE GUTENBERG BIBLE) IS NOT NECESSARILY CONTRADICTED BY SCIENTIFIC DISCOVERIES OF LIFE'S INTRICACIES, EVIDENCED BY THE AMAZINGLY COMPLEX STRUCTURE OF THE DNA MOLECULE (FAR RIGHT). BELOW IS SHOWN A TRILOBITE FOSSIL. THIS MARINE ARTHROPOD WAS COMMON ON OCEAN FLOORS FROM 600 MILLION TO 65 MILLION YEARS AGO.

ONCE RELEGATED TO MYTH AND RELIGION, THE origin of life on earth confounds and mystifies anyone who has ever wondered how human life came into existence. It is difficult to imagine how life could have developed without the aid of a divine being, and for many centuries it was considered inconceivable that life could have evolved from the inorganic matter that made up the earth and its atmosphere.

### IN DARWIN'S FOOTSTEPS

Adherents to Charles Darwin's theory of evolution believed that it explained the development of different species, but they were still hard-pressed to articulate how life began. In the early 1800s, while those in mainstream science were just beginning to accept the cell as the basic unit of life, Darwin had already been developing the idea that the cell was not only the basic unit but also the beginning of life.

When his *The Origin of Species* saw light in 1859, it was immediately bombarded with criticism. But ten years later, as more evidence of living organisms materialized, the idea of evolution led people to think that life could possibly have begun many eons ago, originating in a simple form. Darwin, in an 1871 essay, sketched the beginnings of a theory of the origins of life: "If (and oh! what a big if!) we could conceive in some warm little pond, with all sorts of ammonia and phosphoric salts, light, heat, electricity, etc., present, that a protein compound was chemically formed ready to undergo still more complex changes?"

Thus was born the cornerstone of evolution—the idea of the self-organization of simple molecules into the precursors of organic compounds. These simple organic molecules further organized themselves into proto-cells, and then ultimately into true organisms.

However, while this concept was believed to be sound, the idea was too complex for anyone to determine how the process might have occurred. The matter was left untouched until A.I. Oparin and J.B.S. Haldane independently published essays describing an earth millennia ago without oxygen (in the form of ozone) to shield it from the sun's ultraviolet radiation. The primitive compounds that existed on the earth would be besieged with huge amounts of energy in the form of radiation—energy that would promote the formation of organic compounds. Even more energy would be contributed by the abundant lightning storms that are known to have taken place on the primitive earth. After millions of years, more complex compounds would have formed until chance intervened, and a compound formed that was able to replicate itself. Here, in the soupy "Oparin ocean," was the beginning of life.

## MILLER'S EXPERIMENT

It wasn't until the early 1950s that scientific knowledge and technology caught up to Oparin's and Haldane's theory. Stanley Miller, a Ph.D. candidate at the University of Chicago, abandoned his doctorate thesis when his advisor left the university. Desperate for a new project, he came upon the Oparin/Haldane theory and settled on it as a promising topic.

Miller designed an experiment that he believed would closely approximate the conditions found on the earth in its early history. He combined methane and ammonia in a flask with a tiny amount of water, and then applied

electricity. The methane and ammonia gases acted as an "atmosphere" circulating over a "pond" of water, while the electrical sparks played the role of the lightning storms.

A day later, Miller came back to his experiment to discover that about half of the carbon that was originally methane gas had combined with the ammonia to form amino acids and other organic molecules. Further experiments have shown that almost all the different types of amino acids, and even the bases that form the building blocks of DNA, can be formed under the right conditions. However, it is still a long way from complex molecules to life, and science is only beginning to unlock its secrets.

STANLEY MILLER (ABOVE) WORKED WITH HAROLD UREY TO APPROXIMATE PRIMITIVE EARTH'S CONDITIONS IN THE LABORATORY. THERE, ELECTRICAL SPARKS STOOD IN FOR LIGHTNING.

# Earth's Moon

## How did it get there, and why?

LUNAR EXPLORATION AND RESEARCH IN THE 20TH century have expanded our knowledge of our natural satellite and nearest celestial neighbor, the moon. Since the dawn of human history, the moon has influenced myth, religion, and much poetry. But as the moon's radiant presence looms over us in the sky, we wonder of its creation. Why, indeed, is it there?

The moon is so close (some 240,000 miles away) that, with the help of ordinary binoculars, it is easy to see a profusion of detail on the near side of the moon that is always facing the earth. The moon is airless because its gravity is too weak to capture and retain atmosphere; hence, there is no weather—and no life. It is also waterless. The moon's dark plains, once believed to be stretches of water and still known as *maria* ("seas"), are really vast flat basins, created by congealed volcanic lava. The surface—despite the radiance of a full moon— is made up of dark gray rock that reflects only a tiny fraction of the sunlight that hits it.

Lunar exploration has stripped away some of the moon's mysteries. In 1959, the Soviet probe *Luna 3* revealed the far side that is hidden from the earth's view. In 1969, *Apollo 11* astronauts on the first manned flight to the moon brought back rock samples some 3,700 million years old—older than any rocks on earth. Samples from later missions indicate the moon may have been formed at about the same time as the rest of the solar system—4.6 billion years ago. Analysis of the moon rocks suggests an end of intensive meteor bombardment of the surface about 4 billion years ago, and an end of volcanic eruption about a billion years ago. The moon appears cold and dead—yet it still may be active. Observers report the flickering glow of what could be eruptions at the edges of the maria and in certain craters.

## A QUESTION OF ORIGINS

A fundamental question remains unanswered: What is the origin of the moon? Before the advent of the lunar probes, scientists had proposed three theories. The first claimed the moon was a fragment spun off from a rapidly rotating early earth. This theory, advanced by the 19th-century British astronomer Sir George H. Darwin, was dismissed in 1930. A second origin theory posited that the moon and the earth formed side by side from the condensation of primordial gases and particles.

A third theory said the earth and the moon originated at widely separate points in the solar system but, as they came into close proximity, the moon was pulled into orbit around the earth. Eventually, both the side-by-side and capture theories fell from favor because supporting evidence proved inconclusive.

In 1975, after studying moon rocks and close-up photographs of the lunar surface, scientists proposed another, more probable theo-

U.S. ASTRONAUT JOHN YOUNG OF THE *APOLLO 16* CREW SALUTES AN AMERICAN FLAG ON THE SURFACE OF THE MOON IN 1972. THE STUDY OF SAMPLES BROUGHT BACK FROM THE MOON BY ASTRONAUTS HAS CONTRIBUTED TO OUR UNDERSTANDING OF THE EARTH, THE MOON, AND INDEED THE ENTIRE SOLAR SYSTEM.

ry: "planetesimal impact." According to this theory, a giant object—known as a planetesimal—struck the earth more than 4 billion years ago. At first, scientists estimated the object was about the size of the planet Mars. But, in 1997, a U.S. computer simulation showed it must have been at least two-and-a-half to three times Martian size. The cataclysmic impact, the theory goes, propelled portions of the earth and this giant object into space, where the debris eventually coalesced to create the moon.

By the 1990s, this theory had become the most widely accepted explanation of the moon's origin. But it still poses a major problem: Where on the earth's surface is the crater created by the planetesimal's impact? Some scientists believe the crater may have been erased because of a major meltdown throughout the earth after the impact. But the geochemistry of the earth shows no such radical melting. So, even though a mighty impact is probable, the theory still contains holes.

## AN EVOLUTIONARY ROLE?

The chances of life evolving in the universe are unimaginably small, so small that scientists have begun to wonder what is so unique about the earth that made it suitable for life to flourish. Apart from the obvious—proper temperature, atmosphere, and water—it is now believed that the moon has played an important role in the evolution of life on earth. When the earth first formed, a full day was only 10 hours long and sunlight lasted only 5 hours. Since

then, the tidal drag of the moon slowed the earth's rotation and created the 24-hour day.

How has this affected us? For one, sunlight plays a critical role in ecology: A longer day exposes plant life to more sunlight, encouraging photosynthesis and generating more $CO_2$. The moon also acts as an asteroid shield, saving the earth from the impact of many asteroids. Evidence for this can be seen by comparing the ratio of

**TENDRILS OF TIME** ▼

craters on the moon's craggy surface to those found on the earth.

With the moon in place as a shield, life was able to evolve mostly undisturbed by possible cataclysmic impacts from space. Accordingly, some astronomers believe that the existence of a large, close moon is required for life to evolve. This has led to a search for planets that have large moons, in the hope of discovering life on other planets in the universe.

CALCULATIONS INDICATE THAT THE EARTH HAS HAD ITS SHARE OF METEOR AND ASTEROID IMPACTS, THOUGH NOT AS MANY AS IT WOULD HAVE HAD WITHOUT A MOON.

# Was Mars Ever Inhabitable?

**A century ago, some astronomers believed they had proof that life dwelled on the red planet.**

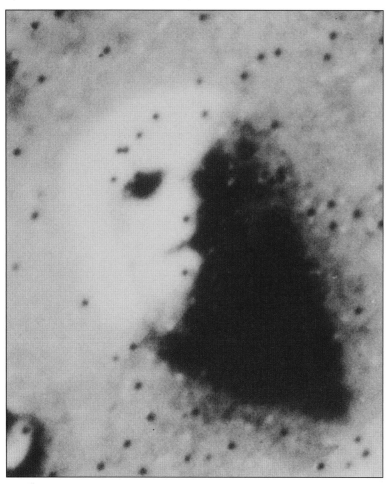

THIS PHOTOGRAPH OF THE FACE ON MARS WAS TAKEN ON JULY 25, 1976. THE LAND FORMATION IS ABOUT ONE MILE ACROSS AND DISPLAYS FACIAL FEATURES ONLY WHEN IT IS HIT BY THE SUN AT A SHARP ANGLE.

WERE THEY PLACED END TO END, THE COUNTLESS science fiction stories, books, and movies spawned by the question of life on Planet Mars would reach to the moon—figuratively, at least. But does life on Mars, and possibly on other planets, exist beyond the imagination?

Humans have searched for life on Mars for hundreds of years—not surprising, since the red planet is the most earthlike of the other planets in our solar system. It has polar caps, an atmosphere with meteorological activity, seasonal variations, and a 24-hour length of day similar to that of the earth. One man, the late-19th-century Italian astronomer Giovanni Schiaparelli, believed he saw seasonal color changes on Mars, signaling the arrival of spring. Italian scientists also believed they saw *canali*, or canals, crisscrossing Mars's surface.

In the early 20th century, astronomers saw what they thought were still more canals. American astronomer Percival Lowell wholeheartedly believed the canals indicated the existence of an advanced civilization on Mars. He wrote a number of books on this subject and theorized that the canals carried water from the wet polar regions to the dry equatorial deserts. But his theory failed to hold water, so to speak: as telescopes improved, astronomers found it difficult to locate the canals.

Then, in 1965, photographs of Mars's surface taken from the *Mariner 4* spacecraft finally proved that the canals didn't exist. It turns out that windblown dust causes color changes on the planet's surface, which from a distance create the appearance of lines. The canals, then, were an optical illusion.

## THE "FACE" ON MARS

The so-called face on Mars—the planetary counterpart of "the man in the moon"— was also believed by some to show that intelligent life once dwelled on Mars. Even the pictures taken by the *Viking* space probe in 1976 showed features that resemble a human face in the planet's Cydonia region. Geologists, however, see the face differently. The Cydonia region lies near the boundary of the southern highlands and the northern plains; it contains a large number of isolated hills, the eroded remnants of the edge of the highland terrain. Geologists explain that in the *Viking* photographs, the resemblance of these topographical features to human faces and pyramids is due to the low resolution and dark areas of missing data in the images, and to tricks of light and shadow. The Mars Global Surveyor took several photographs of the region in 1999, revealing that the "face" was merely a hill.

A part of the *Viking* lander's mission was to look for evidence of life on Mars. The search found no trace of organic molecules, and three biological experiments tested soil samples for evidence of metabolism, growth, or photosynthesis. None of these experiments showed substantial evidence for the presence of life. Furthermore, most of today's scientists believe that no life can exist on Mars because of the planet's incredibly hostile conditions. One reason is its thin atmosphere, which allows ultraviolet radiation to reach the surface, where it can wipe out living matter. Another is that the planet is so cold that liquid water cannot exist on its surface during the Martian night.

Case closed? Not yet. Pictures taken by the Mars Global Surveyor in June 2000 suggest that reservoirs of water exist under the icy surface. If real, the discovery "doesn't tell us that life exists on Mars," says Dr. Bruce Jakosky, director of the Center for Astrobiology at Colorado University, "but it is the smoking gun that tells us Mars has all the elements for life."

## WHAT ABOUT VENUS?

Because of its location and its protective cloud cover, Venus was the only other planet where it was thought life could exist. But Venus is extremely volatile, with a high level of volcanic

# A CLUE FROM ANTARCTICA

Evidence for past life on Mars came in the form of rocks from above. On August 6, 1996, scientists from NASA and Stanford University announced the discovery of a Martian meteorite which was recovered from Antarctica in 1984. They believed that the meteorite contained evidence—in

PIECES OF THE PUZZLE ▼

the form of microfossils—of the existence of primitive life on Mars. One year later, Mars *Pathfinder* and its small robotic rover *Sojourner* discovered evidence for the abundance of water on ancient Mars, lending support to the possibility that life once existed on the planet.

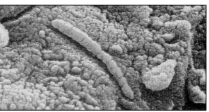

**THE MICROFOSSILS IN METEORITES FROM MARS MEASURE ONE ONE-HUNDREDTH THE WIDTH OF A SINGLE HUMAN HAIR.**

activity on its hidden surface—a hostile environment that is rugged and arid. Since 1932, it was known that the atmosphere contained large amounts of carbon dioxide, but only recently was it learned that the gas made up 96 percent of the atmosphere. It is thought that Venus resembles the earth as it was about 4.6 to 2.5 billion years ago. So, although no life exists on Venus now, the planet could progress to a stage where life might develop there.

**THE SURFACE OF MARS CONTAINS MANY FEATURES THAT COULD HAVE BEEN CAUSED BY FLOWING WATER— BUT ALSO BY METEOROLOGICAL, GEOLOGICAL, AND VOLCANIC ACTIVITY. FAR LEFT, TOP: A DUST DEVIL STORM IS CAPTURED BY THE MARS ORBITER CAMERA (MOC), DECEMBER 1999. LEFT, TOP: THE CANYONS OF THE NONDES VALLES SYSTEM SHOW MANY CHARACTERISTICS OF EARTH'S RIVER BEDS. LEFT, BOTTOM: VALLES MARINERIS (MARINER VALLEY), IS A HUGE CANYON THREE TIMES LONGER THAN THE GRAND CANYON—SO LONG IT STRETCHES A QUARTER OF THE WAY AROUND THE WHOLE PLANET.**

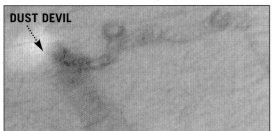

DUST DEVIL

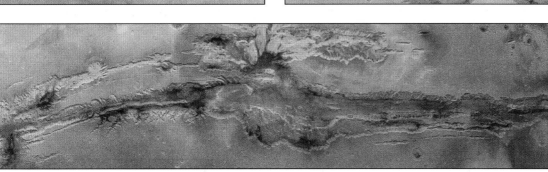

# Death of the Dinosaurs

IN THE ARTIST'S IMPRESSION ABOVE, A GIANT DINOSAUR WATCHES THE FILMY TAIL OF A COMET APPROACHING THE EARTH. OPPOSITE: WHEN VIEWED FROM AN ALTITUDE OF 100 KILOMETERS, THE IMPACT OF A METEORITE AT CHICXULUB, ON THE YUCATAN PENINSULA, MEXICO, MAY HAVE LOOKED LIKE THIS.

FOR NEARLY 140 MILLION YEARS, dinosaurs ruled the earth. Many were big, lumbering creatures, though some were small and agile. Dinosaurs managed to fill almost every ecological niche that the earth provided. Still, 65 million years ago all of the dinosaurs began to die out; over the course of the next few hundred thousand years, the fossil record shows, three-quarters of all the species alive on the earth would become extinct. What could possibly have caused the extinction of thousands of species of flora and fauna in so little time? Scientists hate gaps—and this was a rather big one.

A number of competing theories have been put forth, some reasonable and others that could be described as outrageous. Among the former are climate changes, volcanic ash, tectonic movement, floods, ice ages; the latter include alien invasion and abduction, and the disappearance of an ancient and nourishing species of ferns. Any explanation would have to account for the sudden cataclysmic demise of 75 percent of the earth's creatures.

## SUPERNOVA OR ASTEROID?

One interesting (and not altogether implausible) theory, proposed by scientist Dale Russell in 1979, suggests that the explosion of a star— a supernova—might have caused the extinctions of 65 million years ago. The massive amounts of radiated energy from these explosions can be equal to the energy generated by 10 million of our suns—as much as every star in the galaxy combined. A supernova even 50 million light years away would have had drastic effects on the earth. Within hours, the earth would have been bathed by the initial burst of

**Could it have been an asteroid impact, erupting volcanoes, or the earth's changing climate that led to sudden mass extinctions ?**

electromagnetic radiation. Between 3 and 30 years later, a second wave of cosmic rays and extreme levels of radiation would have reached the earth and lasted for about 10 years. However, the best calculations estimate that such an explosion occurs within 50 million light years of the earth, on average, every 70 million years. Since the dinosaurs managed to survive and thrive on earth for a period of approximately 140 million years, it does not seem likely that radiation from a nearby supernova killed the dinosaurs.

Then what did? In 1980, two scientists at the University of California at Berkeley proposed a theory that has been widely accepted since. Walter Alvarez and his father, Luis, had been studying a layer of clay in 65-million-year-old rock strata that exhibited a curious phenomenon. Concentrations of the extremely rare metal iridium were found to be, in some cases, 30 times the normal levels. This pattern was found repeatedly in similar studies of different samples found around the world. Where could such high levels of this scarce iridium have come from?

The answer, the two Alvarezes proposed, was from outer space. The main source of the earth's iridium is from the meteorites and micrometeorites that constantly pelt the earth. Still, such high concentrations of iridium would have required the simultaneous arrival of about 500 billion tons of material from space. The Alvarezes believed that this could be explained only by the impact of a huge asteroid. An asteroid with this mass would have been 10 miles in diameter and would have crashed into the earth with a speed of approximately 100,000 miles per hour. An impact like

A PTEROSAUR FROM THE MESOZOIC ERA IS MODELED IN THE CALGARY ZOO'S PREHISTORIC PARK. IT IS NOW BELIEVED THAT "FLYING" DINOSAURS WERE A COMMON FEATURE OF THE EARTH'S EARLY HISTORY.

this would be so cataclysmic as to wipe out much of the life on the planet.

Massive shock waves would have convulsed the land, and vast, dense clouds of ash and dust would have blocked out sunlight, throwing all into darkness. This decades-long period of darkness has been dubbed Meteorite Winter, and probably caused the extinction of most plant life on which most dinosaurs fed. If the asteroid had hit the earth in one of its oceans, tidal waves caused by the impact might have reached an incredible five miles in height.

All in all, the combination of effects would have proved devastating and could have resulted in the extinction of the dinosaurs and most every other living thing. Though the asteroid theory is widely accepted today, it is not with-

out its problems; some scientists are still working on an explanation that agrees more closely with the evidence they have gathered. Several of these theories are based on the notion that an extinction cycle exists that repeats itself approximately every 60 to 70 million years.

## THE CLIMATE QUESTION

The cause of the proposed cycle is in dispute; some researchers attribute it to volcanic action, others to a drop in sea level. Scientists at NASA and the United States Geological Survey have been using the United States' GOES satellite system to compare weather and water levels over periods of millions of years.

The data shows a significant worldwide drop in ocean levels approximately 65 million years ago. Such a drop in sea levels resulted in a dramatic climate change worldwide, and this drastic change forced living creatures to either adapt or die. The higher temperature and increased levels of carbon dioxide would have made the environment difficult for the dinosaurs to dwell in. In time they became extinct, allowing mammals—better adapted to warmer climates—to arise and thrive in the new environment. The cause of mass extinctions of the past is therefore far from settled.

---

# THE ALVAREZ THEORY...FACT OR FICTION?

One of the criticisms of the asteroid theory of extinction has been that such an impact would have been too cataclysmic to recover from. In other words, the death toll of species would have been too great. Little, if anything, could have survived the impact of a 10-mile asteroid, and the few surviving species would not have had the time to reproduce to allow for the earth's rapid repopulation.

The Alvarezes' theory also fails to properly explain the length of time that the extinction is believed to have taken. Their theory holds that the ensuing so-called Meteorite

Winter would have laid waste to the earth for mere decades or even for centuries. However, fossil records indicate the mass extinction of the dinosaurs occurred over a much greater span—approximately 140,000 years. Walter and Luis Alvarez based their

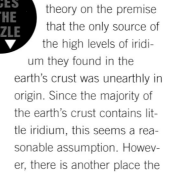

PIECES OF THE PUZZLE ▼

theory on the premise that the only source of the high levels of iridium they found in the earth's crust was unearthly in origin. Since the majority of the earth's crust contains little iridium, this seems a reasonable assumption. However, there is another place the

curious layer of iridium may have originated—the earth. Though iridium is scarce on the earth's surface, the earth's mantle is rich in iridium. More recent studies have shown that the iridium content of emissions from a highly active Hawaiian volcano, Kilauea, more closely matches the patterns found in the planet's iridium-rich clay layer than that in any meteorite known today.

WAS THIS THE ALVAREZES' ASTEROID? AN ARTIST'S RENDERING SHOWS WHAT THE CRATER FORMED BY AN ASTEROID THAT LANDED AT CHICXULUB, ON THE YUCATAN PENINSULA, WOULD HAVE LOOKED LIKE.

# Did Birds Descend from Dinosaurs?

One of the earliest birds was a creature called *Archaeopteryx,* which lived 150 million years ago. It had teeth and a long tail like a reptile, as well as feathers. The sternum, where flight muscles are attached, was small, so it may have been more of a glider than a flyer.

The first *Archaeopteryx* fossil was discovered in Germany in 1855 and was originally thought to be a type of flying lizard known as a pterodactyl. Another specimen was found in 1861 and identified for what it truly was: A transition animal between dinosaurs and birds.

As important as its discovery was, *Archaeopteryx* is only one important link in the evolutionary chain. Birds were not accepted as dinosaur descendants until the early 1970s; instead, they were believed to have possibly descended from a class of non-dinosaur reptiles like crocodilians. Today, the issue mostly boils down to *which* dinosaurs were the closest ancestors of birds—not whether birds descended from dinosaurs.

Many questions still remain regarding the dinosaur/bird link. These questions include the earliest function of feathers; how endothermy (warmbloodedness) evolved; which group of theropods are the actual direct ancestors of birds; and why some bird groups survived the Cretaceous extinction of dinosaurs.

**SINOSAUROPTERYX (IN A MODEL, TOP), THOUGH WINGLESS, IS A LIKELY ANCESTOR OF MODERN BIRDS. A MODERN ORIOLE (LEFT, TOP) IS COMPARED TO CONFU-CIUSORNES, THE EARLIEST BIRD WITH A TOOTHLESS BEAK.**

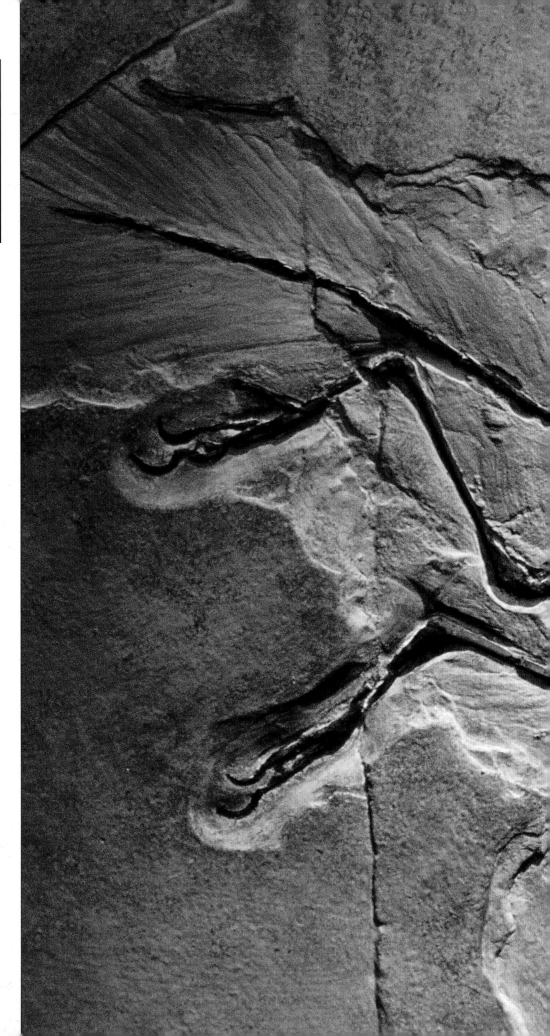

THE *ARCHAEOPTERYX* FOSSIL
FOUND IN GERMANY IN 1861
(RIGHT) WAS ONE OF THE MOST
STUNNING FOSSIL FINDS OF THE
LAST 150 YEARS. THE CREATURE,
CAPTURED IN LIMESTONE,
APPEARS TO HAVE HAD BOTH
FEATHERS AND TEETH. SEVERAL
RECENT FOSSIL FINDS IN CHINA
HAVE SUPPORTED THE THESIS
THAT BIRDS DESCENDED FROM
DINOSAURS. A RECONSTRUCTION
OF *CAUDIPTERYC ZONI* (ABOVE),
A 120-MILLION YEAR OLD
DINOSAUR THAT STOOD ONLY
ABOUT THREE FEET TALL, IS
SHOWN HERE IN A COURTSHIP
DISPLAY OF ITS FEATHERS.

# Who Were the First Humans?

**The details of human origins may be clouded in mystery, but they are known to reach back many, many thousands of years.**

PROCONSUL HAMILTONI
(23-15 MILLION YEARS AGO)

AUSTRALOPITHECUS AFARENSIS
(MORE THAN 4-2.5 MILLION YEARS AGO)

HOMO HABILIS
(1.5 MILLION YEARS AGO)

WHERE DID WE COME FROM? HOW DID HUMAN beings come to walk the earth? One wonders if there could be any greater mystery, and any question more important or more vexing. It seems that we can abide uncertainty regarding almost any riddle but this one; perhaps we hope that if we can determine how we came to be, we might gain some insight into that even more confounding question: Why are we here?

The kinds of answers we have historically entertained reveal a great deal about us. A scant 200 years ago, the prevailing opinion was that the earth was no older than about 5,000 years, and that no human existed earlier than 4004 BC, the date favored by biblical scholars as the year of the Creation. Cambridge cleric John Lightfoot pinpointed the advent of human beings even more precisely: The world, he claimed, was created at 9 A.M. on the 23rd of October of that year, and humankind came on the scene on the afternoon of the 28th. Educated people at the dawn of the 19th century who had long made peace with the Copernican system of the heavens still believed in the literal truth of the Book of Genesis.

## THE DAWNING

But then three developments made it increasingly more difficult to maintain this view—in the literal sense, at least. First, it became clear that the earth was much older than had previously been thought. Even before precise dating methods were developed, it was obvious from the observation of rocks and earth formations

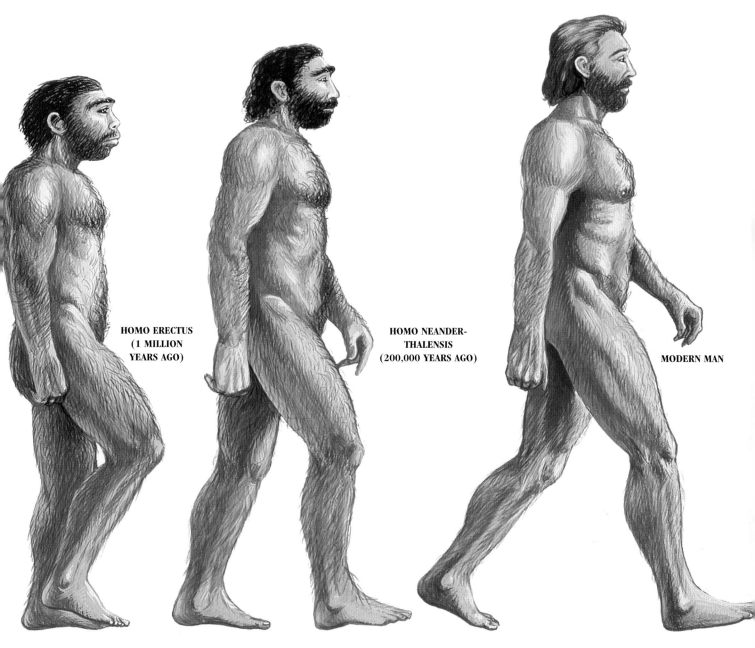

HOMO ERECTUS
(1 MILLION
YEARS AGO)

HOMO NEANDER-
THALENSIS
(200,000 YEARS AGO)

MODERN MAN

that the earth was very old. The layers, or stra-ta, of earth deposits and the forces at work in the creation of mountains, valleys, and other formations showed that processes were at work for many thousands, even millions, of years in shaping the world as we found it.

A great deal of human ingenuity was applied to dismiss this evidence—from theories that the earth only appears to be very old because of its past catastrophes (including the biblical Flood) to the notion that the world was creat-ed to appear *as if* it were millions of years old—but the weight of observation and evi-dence dealt a crushing blow to any thought of the earth being only some 300 generations old. Sedimentary deposits in West Virginia, for example, show the cycle of the land being

THIS SEQUENCE OF
HUMAN EVOLUTION
OMITS MANY OTHER
HOMINIDS THAT
ONCE POPULATED
THE EARTH. ALSO,
NEANDERTHAL MAN
(SECOND FROM
RIGHT, ABOVE) MAY
NOT HAVE BEEN IN
THE DIRECT LINE TO
MODERN HUMANS.
BUT HE WAS SO
CLOSELY RELATED
TO HOMO SAPIENS
THAT SOME SCIEN-
TISTS THINK THAT
INTERBREEDING
BETWEEN THE TWO
SPECIES MIGHT
HAVE OCCURRED.

## THE OMPHALOS HYPOTHESIS

The book *Omphalos,* by English naturalist Philip Gosse (the creator of the first institutional aquarium) appeared in 1857, providing food for thought for biologists and philosophers alike. A staunch opponent of evolution, Gosse was nevertheless aware of the fossil and geological evidence in support of it. To fend off critics, he came up with an answer to a question: Did Adam and Eve have navels (Greek *omphalos*)? Since the navel is a vestige of a birth—the cutting of the umbilical cord—Adam should have been created without one. But if Adam and Eve were both the model of the human being, they should each have had one.

Gosse concluded that Adam and Eve both had navels because they were created as if they had been born from a womb. He even suggested that Adam may have been created with memories of a childhood that never happened so that he would

**VIEW FROM THE FRINGE**

be a "normal" human being. This speculation raised the possibility that all the physical evidence for

the earth's antiquity found in the ground—fossil remains; geological formations; prehistoric habitation sites; and even dinosaur fossils—was created in 4004 BC so that the earth would appear to be millions of years old.

Why such a thorough and elaborate ruse would have been perpetrated by the Creator was never made clear—Gosse attributed it to a test of faith—and neither was Gosse ever able to respond to the simplest question critics asked: How do we know that the entire universe wasn't created five minutes ago with all of human history, including the Biblical account of Creation, embedded in our memories as if it really happened?

**THIS 16TH-CENTURY PAINTING SHOWS ADAM AND EVE WITH NAVELS, EXPLAINED AWAY BY PHILIP GOSSE.**

under water, then above water as the sea level rises and falls with each successive ice age—hundreds of times over the past 4 million years.

Then came the fossil evidence. At first, a few isolated bones were regarded as anomalies—perhaps remnants of creatures that existed before the Flood or some other catastrophe. But the spectacular find in 1856 of a human-like fossilized skeleton in Germany's Neander Valley, by workmen blasting in a limestone cave, brought the field of fossil archeology to bear on the question of human origins. Here was a being that was not like us, but also not like the apes and primates we knew.

The early views of what came to be called Neanderthal Man were, as it turned out, mistaken in describing him as brutish and dumb. Neanderthal Man walked upright as we do (the particular specimen unearthed in Neander was stricken with debilitating arthritis and walked in a labored stoop) and was intelligent. How intelligent is not clear, though to the surprise of paleontologists he had a brain size slightly larger than ours. What happened to Neanderthal Man and whether we are his descendants are questions still being investigated, but many of the other gaps have been tentatively filled by assiduous digging around the world and by the development of many dating techniques to accompany radiocarbon dating.

## THE STORY OF US

With spans of time so immense, there are bound to be gaps. To appreciate the time scale involved, imagine that the history of the earth were a book a thousand pages in length. Within this book, the Swiss Alps would have been formed at the top of page 997. The first hominid toolmakers and the ice ages would appear at the top of page 1,000, the book's last. Neanderthal Man would not appear until the last line on that last page, and the first civilizations of Mesopotamia would not appear until the last eight letters. The Age of Rome and the 1066 AD Norman conquest of England would not appear until the last two letters of the last word in the book. And the past 100 years would scarcely take up the book's final period.

The early years of research were difficult—the gaps were so large, the evidence so meager, and the debates were so heated (both within the field of paleontology and between paleontologists and conservative society) that at times

extravagant claims were made that later had to be recanted. Even dedicated scientists were ripe to be taken by hoaxsters, like those who "created" Piltdown Man. But as the 20th century wore on, more and more specimens were found—thousands, in fact—that pointed to the line that stretched back to our ancestors.

It is now possible to trace the steps taken in the development of our evolutionary lines through many stretches of time and in particular areas of the globe. In each case, some physical trait or adaptation (a modification of an organism that makes it more fit for the conditions of its specific environment), allowed an ancestor to survive more easily. It also happened that an adaptation that was advantageous for one environment suddenly became a liability when climate or conditions changed, meaning that not every step in the story represented progress or improvement.

IN 1978, MARY LEAKEY ACHIEVED FAME IN HER OWN RIGHT WHEN SHE DISCOVERED AND ANALYZED THE FOSSILIZED FOOT-PRINTS OF HOMI-NIDS THAT WALKED UPRIGHT ACROSS A BED OF TANZANIAN VOLCANIC ASH MORE THAN 3 MILLION YEARS AGO.

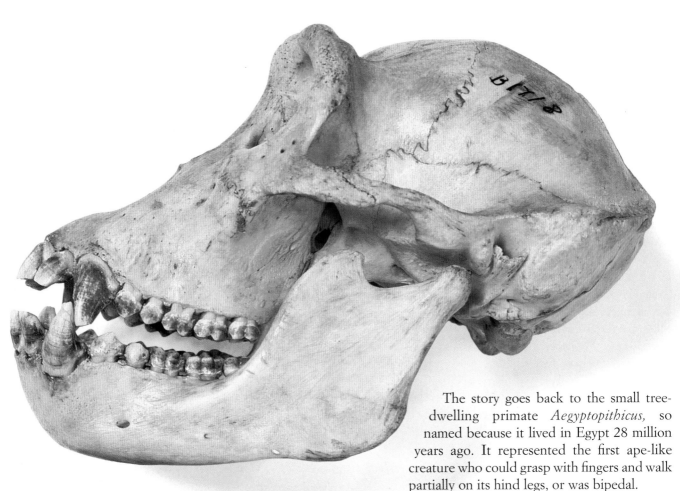

The story goes back to the small tree-dwelling primate *Aegyptopithicus,* so named because it lived in Egypt 28 million years ago. It represented the first ape-like creature who could grasp with fingers and walk partially on its hind legs, or was bipedal.

Some 10 million years pass—during which some interesting things no doubt happened, though we don't know very much about them—and a more clearly bipedal primate, *Dryopithicus* (who nevertheless is gamboling about on all fours much of the time) emerges. By now several physiological abilities are entrenched: The hands not only have fingers that grasp, but the thumb is able to swing around and "oppose" the other fingers, creating a more effective grabbing tool. Soon—in, say, 3 or 4 million years—this creature is making tools and is nearly ready to walk upright all the time instead of sporadically.

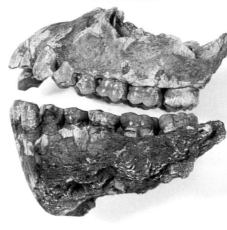

**THE JAWBONE OF *AUSTRALOPITHECUS AFARENSIS* (MIDDLE), A HOMINID THAT ROAMED THE AFAR VALLEY IN ETHIOPIA SOME 3.3 MILLION YEARS AGO, BEARS A CLOSER RESEMBLANCE TO A CHIMPANZEE JAWBONE (TOP) THAN TO THAT OF A MODERN HUMAN (BOTTOM). THIS SHOWS HOW EARLY HOMINIDS STILL HAD A LONG WAY TO GO ON THE ROAD TO SPECIES *HOMO SAPIENS.***

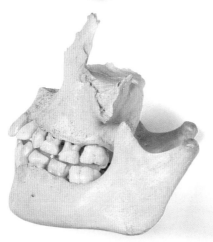

When, after a period of 6 million years cloaked in darkness, we next find a hominid he is *Ramapithecus,* fully bipedal and with an opposing thumb not unlike ours—a toolmaker with a rounded-tooth arrangement that enables him to broaden his diet over the squared-tooth arrangement characteristic of apes. With this creature, adaptive opportunities suddenly open up: Thumb-opposed hands capable of precise manipulation and efficient grabbing foster the development of hunting skills and upright walking. A more delicate hand fosters toolmaking abilities, and this means more inventiveness and resourcefulness, which in turn means increased size and capacity of the brain. The use of tools allows for a reduction in the size of canine teeth—sharp flint knives now do the cutting and chopping—and that, along with a brain with more convolutions (which serves to integrate the senses), leads to a greater capacity to enunciate sounds—and possibly to communicate in a way that permits the coordination of hunting, and courting, and living. Like all primates, these creatures uttered sounds and tried to make themselves understood as best they could for the sake of their survival and for the good of their brood.

### THE HOMINID LINE

Creatures that are looking more and more like modern humans from the neck down begin to appear about 4 million years ago, the first being *Australopithecus.* Then, some 2 million years ago, a creature with a still more human torso, *Homo habilis* ("Hand Man"), appears. He is followed by *Homo erectus* just a half million years later. These creatures had mastered the technology of fire and buried their dead amid ceremony and, it appears, had some beliefs in an afterlife. Not much separates *Homo erectus* and Neanderthal Man on the evolutionary scale, with barely a third of a million years between them. But the world of *Homo neanderthalensis* was one that has a richness and complexity that we can immediately appreciate as having more in common with us than with the animals. Many animals use tools, but none conduct commerce in tools; many animals communicate to others of their species, but none communicate myths handed down from bygone generations—as the persistence of mythical aspects of burial ceremonies across many generations indicates.

> **Our lineage has been drawn and redrawn by scientists, and has yet to be fully understood.**

### HOMO SAPIENS

And, in the short period of some 170,000 years, a new arrival emerged in Europe, an immigrant hominid who gradually replaced the original European species. This creature arrived with some kind of an adaptation, a physical characteristic that gave it an astounding advantage over Neanderthal Man. This was Cro-Magnon Man, also known as *Homo sapiens,* a version of hominid that has, in the course of the last 32,000 years, spread across the earth and numbers in the billions. For *Homo sapiens* is really the modern human.

While other hominid lines on the evolutionary process have come and gone—none, from all the evidence, ever doing much better than the best ape line that typically numbered in the thousands even in their heyday—humans have thrived to the point where Neanderthals were pushed aside and crowded out of existence. In truth, the lineage of hominids that eventually evolved into modern humans has been drawn and redrawn, over and over again. Until a few years ago, for example, the species *Ramapithecus* was considered a part of the direct lineage to humans, but now is considered part of a branch that parted from the trunk of our evolutionary tree.

The key to unlocking the mystery of what happened to other hominids (Neanderthal Man included) and how modern humans replaced them lies in a surprising place—in another area that points to an answer to the question of human origins: our increasing ability to manipulate, measure, and analyze our genetic material or DNA. The answer may well lie in our genes.

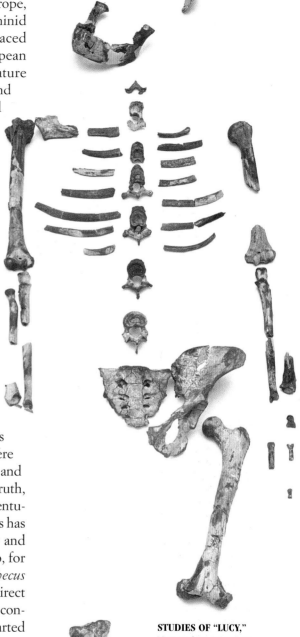

STUDIES OF "LUCY," THE FOSSIL REMAINS OF AN *AUSTRALOPITHECUS AFARENSIS* HOMINID WHO LIVED 3.3 MILLION YEARS AGO AND IS CONSIDERED THE EARLIEST LINK IN THE HUMAN EVOLUTIONARY RECORD, SHOWED HER TO BE PROBABLY FEMALE, ONLY 4 FEET TALL, AND ABOUT 20 YEARS OLD AT HER DEATH.

# What Happened to Neanderthal Man?

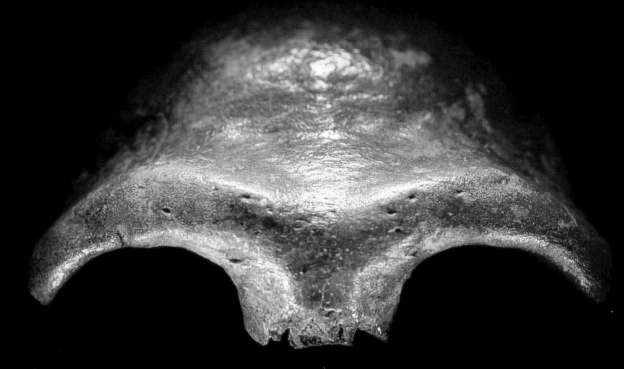

THERE IS AN IMAGE OF NEANDERTHAL man so pervasive that it is part of our culture: He is pictured as brutish, hairy, dumb, violent, and primitive. He walks with a kind of lumbering, ape-like hop as he swings a club over the head of an animal or another Neanderthal. This was the view that emerged in the early 20th century, and it was in large part created by the famed French paleontologist Marcellin Boule, dean of French paleontology and editor of the influential journal *L'Anthropologie*.

It turns out that Boule's picture of *Homo neanderthalensis* was wrong. The particular specimen he studied was that of an old Neanderthal male suffering from acute arthritis, which accounted for his stooped posture. Other Neanderthal bones found since (and even several others found earlier, but not identified until later) confirmed that Neanderthal Man walked perfectly upright. In many ways he was

**He wasn't so very different from us, and his brain was probably larger. But for some reason our ancestors succeeded, while he failed.**

much like people today; in other ways he was burdened with disadvantages that made surviving and thriving difficult, especially during the period 40,000 to 30,000 years ago, when Cro-Magnons (*Homo sapiens*), and Neanderthals occupied the same area and vied for the same resources. In still other ways, the Neanderthal had clear advantages over us *Homo sapiens* in the fight for survival. This is why the fate of Neanderthal Man is such a vexing problem.

## A SPECIES SUPPLANTED

After eons of success in conditions more hostile than existed 40,000 years ago, Neanderthals vanished over the course of seven to ten millennia. Then modern humans emerged, covering the earth in a scant 30,000 years. What happened to our predecessors? Did we evolve from them or absorb them? Or did they die out, losers in the contest for earth's bounty?

By any meaningful measure, Neanderthals were a successful chapter in the story of hominid evolution, thriving in many areas of the earth for over 60,000 years. In fact, Neanderthal Man was as capable as Cro-Magnon Man would become. They hunted with weapons shaped from flint and exhibited the same dexterity and ingenuity that the Cro-Magnon displayed 30,000 years ago. They displayed the same level of socialization and family structure, the same manipulative dexterity and ingenuity in tool-making, the same organization of hunting parties, and the same ability to process and store food. Neanderthals also engaged in rituals and mythologizing (as evidenced by their burial practices), and they could communicate with one another much as Cro-Magnons did (as evidenced by their hunting strategies). They had large brain capacities—larger on average than our own—though some subtle but important differences may have existed in our respective brain structures.

## THE SLIGHTEST EDGE

Today, anthropologists have gained a deeper understanding of the time needed for a genetic mutation to take hold in the mechanism of natural selection. From an evolutionary point of view, 10,000 years is the blink of an eye. So if something happened 40,000 years ago to create a hominid with greater survivability than Neanderthal's, it would have to be a subtle mutation expressed as a minor physiological change. At the same time, that change would have such an effect on the robustness of the species that the species would supplant Neanderthal, not simply cohabit with it.

Whatever it was that Cro-Magnon Man had that his Neanderthal neighbor didn't, it had to be so slight as to be hardly noticeable, yet decisive in their mutual struggle for survival.

We have also gained, in the last 50 years, an appreciation of how strict the barriers are to interspecies breeding. We know that creatures do not breed with creatures who are different, and these barriers extend to the last level of speciation. This means that in spite of the fact that the difference between Cro-Magnons and Neanderthals was too slight for either of them to have noticed, they would have had a difficult time mating and absorbing one another.

## A MATTER OF SPEECH?

In the 1970s, American anthropologists Philip Lieberman and Edmund Crelin noticed a subtle difference between Neanderthals and Cro-Magnons in the structure of their voice boxes. As with other vertebrates, the vocal area of modern humans consists of two parts: the larynx (which contains the vocal cords) and the upper or supra-laryngeal tract (which consists of the pharynx, that part of the trachea just above the larynx). But in Neanderthals, this configuration is more like that of earlier hominids—that is, the vocal tract follows a simple curve that does not separate the larynx and the supra-laryngeal tracts.

The difference is small, to be sure, but computer models of the kinds of sounds that could

possibly be produced by the Neanderthal vocal tract reveal something quite startling: An entire range of sounds—especially vowels, out of which much of our language is constructed—were beyond Neanderthal capabilities.

The findings related to language suggest what happened. Being able to enunciate a wider variety of syllables gave Cro-Magnons the capacity to name many more things and to communicate with others of its kind verbally—and this might account for Cro-Magnon's success and Neanderthal's disappearance.

# Who Invented Writing & Counting?

**The invention of writing and counting by the Sumerians turned society away from oral tradition and gave birth to our ability to permanently record the past.**

TABLETS WITH ANCIENT SUMERIAN MATHEMATICAL TEXT ARE ON VIEW AT BAGHDAD'S IRAQ MUSEUM. SIMPLE ARITHMETIC NOW EASILY MASTERED BY A SCHOOLCHILD WOULD HAVE BEEN CONSIDERED SHEER WIZARDRY IN THE ANCIENT WORLD.

WHAT IS CIVILIZATION? IS IT THE ABILITY TO record history? Expertise at tool-making? Or is civilization just a term used to describe groups of people with highly developed systems of belief, culture, and skill? Scholars and writers have long debated this question. Although no consensus has been reached, there is no question that writing and counting were fundamental to civilization's development.

### A SYSTEM TAKES SHAPE

The earliest known civilization was created by the Sumerians in Mesopotamia, present-day Iraq. Between 3500 and 3000 BC, the Sumerians took possession of the land near the Persian Gulf, where they drained the swamps and established agriculture on a permanent basis. They developed trade with surrounding areas and built up an industrial economy. Many Sumerian villages were transformed into walled cities. This change reflected complex social organization—another indication of civilization. At the same time as the shift from villages to cities took place, the Sumerians developed a system of writing in which important items were represented graphically with simple drawings. This rudimentary system evolved into the script now known as cuneiform.

Cuneiform, later used by other peoples of Mesopotamia, comprised an unwieldy number of symbols representing an infinite number of ideas, objects, and sounds. These characters were drawn in clay with a wedge-shaped instrument known as a stylus.

The birth of writing introduced a new mode of communication, convenient for business transactions and other forms of personal contact. Moreover, it signaled the beginning of a completely new enterprise: the writing of history. Before the emergence of the written symbol or word, history was the domain of human memories, as fallible as man himself.

Until the Sumerians developed cuneiform, history was an oral tradition, in which one generation regaled the next with stories of the past; that generation then assumed responsibility for informing their successors. The stories gradually changed during this prehistoric form of "whisper down the lane," and after many generations had been so frequently altered that they hardly resembled the original versions. The advent of writing, however, changed this process by creating a permanent record of the past for the benefit of future generations.

### WRITING'S ROOTS IN COUNTING

Actually, the Sumerian writing system seems to have developed from a more ancient system of counting that may date back as far as 8000 BC. Many small clay tokens have been discovered from this period that are thought to have represented common agricultural goods, mainly for the purposes of bookkeeping.

During the 4th millennium BC, this system was updated to a significant degree. These simple tokens, now shaped like the objects they represented, were often stored in clay envelopes, which were inscribed on the outside with likenesses of the tokens they held.

These markings showed users what was contained within the envelope without their having to open it. As the number of goods used in Sumerian society increased, so did the number

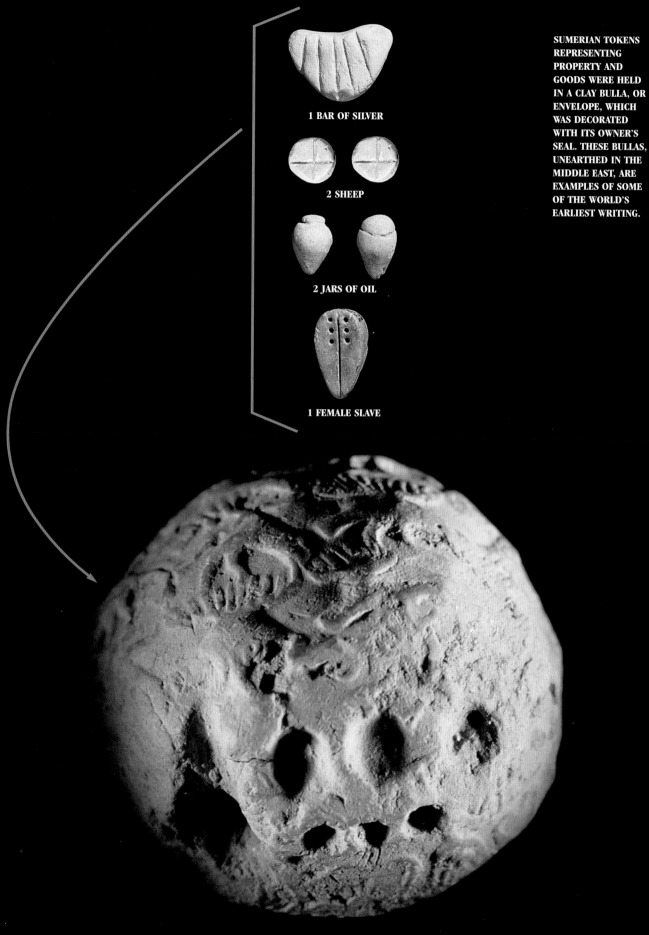

1 BAR OF SILVER

2 SHEEP

2 JARS OF OIL

1 FEMALE SLAVE

SUMERIAN TOKENS REPRESENTING PROPERTY AND GOODS WERE HELD IN A CLAY BULLA, OR ENVELOPE, WHICH WAS DECORATED WITH ITS OWNER'S SEAL. THESE BULLAS, UNEARTHED IN THE MIDDLE EAST, ARE EXAMPLES OF SOME OF THE WORLD'S EARLIEST WRITING.

CLAY ENVELOPE

A SUMERIAN SCRIBE WITH A STYLUS WRITES ON A CLAY TABLET. HIS FELLOW SCRIBES PREPARE CYLINDER SEALS USED TO MARK GOODS OR OFFICIAL DOCUMENTS. CARVED IN STONE, THE SEALS PRODUCED RAISED IMAGES WHEN ROLLED ON CLAY (BELOW).

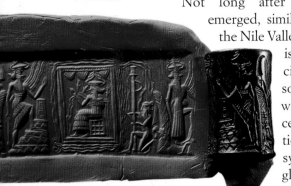

of tokens and their representative envelope-markings. By 3100 BC, as many as 1,200 different stamps were in use. As the system for marking the envelope contents grew more elaborate, the Sumerians realized that actually putting the tokens in the envelope was unnecessary. As a result, envelopes and tokens gradually fell out of use, and the clay engravings themselves became the primary method for accounting.

### CUNEIFORM EVOLVES

After 3200 BC, archeological evidence points to the development of a more universal script, helpful not only in representing specific items and events but also for recording more general ideas. It was this script, rooted in the use of symbols for accounting, that eventually developed into cuneiform writing.

Not long after Sumerian civilization emerged, similar cultures appeared in the Nile Valley and the Indus Valley. It is apparent that these new civilizations engaged in some form of commerce with their Sumerian predecessor. From these civilizations emerged the writing system known as hieroglyphics. Like cuneiform,

the system was made up of numerous symbols representing words, syllables, and sounds, though they were a great deal more pictographic. This difference is primarily a result of the methods utilized in writing each script: The brute pressing of a stylus into clay, as practiced by cuneiform scribes, was far less nuanced than the drawing or painting of symbols employed by the writers of hieroglyphics.

How did the breakthroughs leading up to Sumerian civilization occur? According to scholars, a managerial class—priests or overlords—directed the labor of the majority of the people, who may have been enslaved by conquest. The priests, who had to explain why the gods had chosen some men to be their slaves, also collected huge quantities of grain and other food from the populace as offerings to the deity. With this wealth, the priests were able to employ artists, architects, carpenters, clothmakers, and others with special skills who worked full-time to assure the divine pleasure. In this way, far-reaching changes in architecture and other fields took effect, paving the way for Sumerian civilization to blossom.

OPPOSITE: A DETAIL OF HIEROGLYPHIC INSCRIPTIONS FROM A RELIEF ON THE TOMB OF QUEEN NEFERTARI, WIFE OF RAMSES II (REIGNED 1304-1237 BC.)

# Piltdown Man

BETWEEN 1911 AND 1913, CONSTRUCTION WORKERS AT Barkham Manor, a sprawling English estate on Piltdown Common near Lewes, often found bone fragments in a gravel pit and turned them over to Charles Dawson, a local lawyer and the executor of the estate. An amateur paleontologist and fossil collector, Dawson had alerted the workers to keep an eye out for such bits and pieces. Dawson loved to dabble in the art of fossil preparation, which included ways to make fossils appear much older than they really were.

In February 1912, Dawson sent his collection of bone fragments to Arthur Smith Woodward, chief geologist of what would become the Natural History Museum of London. In June, Woodward and his friend, the famed French priest-paleontologist Pierre Teilhard de Chardin, accompanied Dawson to the gravel pits at the estate. There, the group found additional fragments—including, amazingly, a jawbone fragment lying on the ground, even though workers at the site later swore they had thoroughly cleaned the site earlier.

RENDERINGS OF PILTDOWN MAN (TOP AND RIGHT) OFTEN APPEARED IN BRITISH NEWSPA-PERS, SOME EVEN 40 YEARS AFTER THE "DISCOVERY."

The trio came out of Piltdown with a virtually complete skull that, when reconstructed, appeared to be the top half of a human skull (the cranium) and the jaw of an apelike creature. (That there was very little else of the skeleton should have sounded some alarms.) In 1913, Dawson was invited to present a paper published in the respected scientific journal *Nature* to the Geological Society of London. In the paper, Dawson claimed to have found the "missing link" in the chain of the evolution of human beings, something that had been predicted by Charles Darwin some 70 years earlier.

Dawson was hailed for the discovery—Woodward prevailed upon the British Museum to name the find *Eoanthropus dawsoni*—and "Piltdown man" entered the language. The town of Piltdown soon became a tourist attraction, and a number of celebrities lent their prestige to the find. One was Arthur Conan Doyle, creator of Sherlock Holmes, who accompanied Dawson on a public lecture tour.

### THE DOUBTS BEGIN

Many anthropologists pointed out as early as 1913 that the jawbone Dawson found looked remarkably like the jaw of a modern chimpanzee. Also arousing suspicion was the fact that the missing piece of jawbone was the condyle (the area where the jaw is connected to the cranial section), which would have identified the skull as either a modern ape's or that of an ancient hominid. Despite the doubts, it would be decades before the true circumstances surrounding the "find" were revealed.

The hoax did not begin to unravel until methods of dating fossils became more reliable. The earliest inquiries were conducted in 1949 by Kenneth Oakley, a geologist at the British Museum. By measuring the amount of ground-water fluorine that had been absorbed by the bones, he showed them to be less than 50,000 years old; he also stated that the jaw and the cranium were not from the same creature. Further investigation by Oxford anthropologist J.S. Weiner showed that the teeth of the jaw had been mechanically filed down and that the bones had been treated with potassium dischromate, a chemical often used to forge ancient remains.

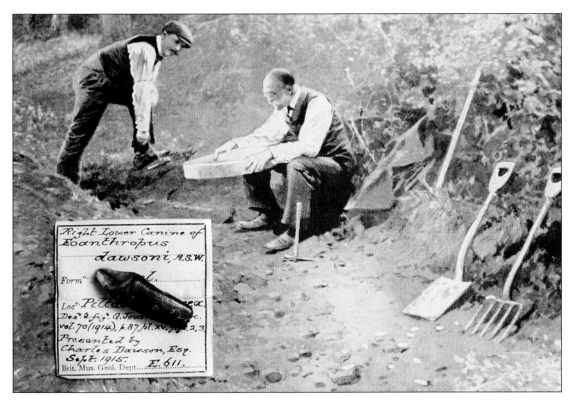

Right Lower Canine of
Eoanthropus
    dawsoni, A.S.W.

Form"............L...........

Loc? Pilt.................ex.
Des? & fig. Q. Jour............
vol. 70 (1914), p.87, pl. XV.......2,3,
Presented by
Charles Dawson, Esq.
Sept. 1915.    E. 611.
Brit. Mus. Geol. Dept....E. 611.

A COMPOSITE PICTURE SHOWS THE PERPETRATORS OF THE PILTDOWN MAN HOAX: CHARLES DAWSON (LEFT), WHO DIED IN 1916, AND ARTHUR SMITH WOODWARD. THE BONES DAWSON "FOUND," AMONG THEM A CANINE TOOTH (INSET), TODAY ARE ON VIEW IN A DISTANT CORNER OF THE NATURAL HISTORY MUSEUM OF LONDON.

By the mid-1950s, there was no doubt that the Piltdown bones were phony, and that they were an elaborately planned and sophisticated hoax. And though it was probably Dawson who placed the bones in the pits, where he knew they would be found, the hoax had to be perpetrated by individuals with greater knowledge and expertise than Dawson.

## A RELUCTANCE TO DISBELIEVE

Over the years, nearly everyone associated with the episode has been accused of being involved in the hoax, but suspicion has focused on two men who championed Piltdown Man long after the rest of the scientific community recognized that it had been duped: Grafton Elliot Smith and Arthur Keith. These two British anatomists knew how the fragments would have to be altered to fool the experts; they were in contact with Dawson before, during, and after the Piltdown finds; and they had proposed theories of human evolution that were momentarily advanced by Piltdown Man. In fact, for 50 years a large segment of British paleoanthropology stood behind Piltdown Man. While the rest of the field forged ahead, the fragments were kept under lock and key until the late 1940s, largely because of national pride. Only in the last decades of the 20th century has it been asked, how could so many scientists have been fooled for so long?

The answer may lie in looking at what scientists were expecting to find in the first decades of the 20th century. The latter half of the 19th century was a cauldron of controversy as Darwin's theory of evolution was debated across Europe, particularly in England. British paleontologists had hoped to find physical evidence of human evolution on British soil, but the early finds were in France, Gibraltar, the Middle East, and the Far East. When the finds in Germany's Neander Valley were discussed at an 1864 meeting of the British Association for the Advancement of Science, Thomas Henry Huxley, who as Darwin's most vociferous defender should have been uncontained in his enthusiasm, coolly agreed that the new find—dubbed Neanderthal Man—might indeed be a preliminary stage in human evolution.

Further hurting England's pride, the French anthropologist Marcellin Boule did the initial work on Neanderthal man, reconstructing a very apelike version of a modern human: It walked on all fours most of the time, had poor tool-making skills, and had a heavy overhanging eyebrow-ridge and a receding forehead. (We now know that Boule was mistaken: Studies in the 1950s of the many newly-discovered Neanderthal remains showed that Neanderthal men walked completely upright.)

Yet British paleontologists, eager to find a human ancestor on British soil and laboring under the misapprehension that a primitive apelike Neanderthal ancestor walked the earth just 50,000 years ago, were primed to accept Piltdown as a near-relative of Neanderthal and a missing link between Neanderthals and modern humans. So it was that the apelike jaw was not seen as a problem. As a result, some British paleontologists accepted Piltdown Man and created a theory of human evolution in which this fraudulent piece of "evidence" made sense.

# PART 2

# THE ANCIENT WORLD

Civilization was humanity's greatest work of art, born in what we call ancient times, amid the sand and the stone of the valleys of the Tigris, the Euphrates, and the Nile, and later on the shores of the Aegean and Mediterranean seas. How did it happen? As we marvel at the grandeur of the pyramids and the splendor of the Parthenon, we can easily lose sight of the genius of civilization—clearly a work in progress.

Stonehenge was built and rebuilt on England's Salisbury Plain. Rome created the largest empire the world had ever seen, then watched its western sector fall as military and financial systems collapsed. Unknown scribes were writing the book that would become the most influential in Western history, the Bible. In legend, the Trojan War was fought, the Queen of Sheba traveled from the south to visit King Solomon, and the Greeks told of a society of women warriors called the Amazons.

# Who Built Stonehenge?

CENTURIES AGO, A VISITOR might have attributed Stonehenge's construction to magical powers; a typical 12th-century British legend asserted it was built "not by force but by Merlin's Art," and the site has long been associated with Druid assemblies. More recently, its design has so impressed archeologists that they have insisted it could only be the product of an advanced, colonizing population. Mycenae, a flourishing citadel culture on the Greek mainland, and Brittany, in northwestern France, were suggested as possibilities for this invading force, because each boasted similar, if less impressive, gigantic structures made of stone.

**Since time immemorial, travelers on Salisbury Plain have felt a need to discover Stonehenge's origins.**

So the archeological world was shocked when, in the 1960s, carbon dating revealed that the original building of Stonehenge occurred possibly as early as 3000 BC, centuries before the Mycenaean period. In fact, the tests confirmed that Stonehenge was built in stages, spanning a period of up to 1,500 years, as later immigrants renovated the original site. Stonehenge I, the earliest version, was little more than a raised bank with a ring of 56 shallow pits just inside. Stonehenge II, begun in about 2000 BC and more sophisticated in its design, consisted of a double circle of huge bluestones; some time before 1500 BC, these were replaced in Stonehenge III by a 100-foot diameter ring of 30 larger sarsen sandstone monoliths. On top of some of these stones were set huge lintels, with peg and socket joints used to secure them in place, forming a vast horseshoe of trilithons.

## THE BEAKER FOLK

The first builders of Stonehenge were probably members of a prosperous, warlike group of people called Beaker Folk, known for their use

SALISBURY PLAIN (ABOVE, GLIMPSED THROUGH THE MONOLITHS), IS THE SITE OF STONEHENGE. THE PONDEROUS STONE COMPLEX (RIGHT, PICTURED DURING THE SUMMER SOLSTICE) HAS BEEN ENVELOPED IN MYTH FOR CENTURIES ON END.

of pottery drinking vessels. Even so, one can sympathize with the archeologists who remained incredulous that a primitive Stone Age people, lacking initially both metal tools and a system of writing, could build such a complex structure. The ultimate success of the builders depended on a combination of ingenuity and sweat. Stonehenge contains some marvelous, delicate touches: the upright stones, for example, were fashioned with a central bulge (as in the columns of many classical Greek temples), so that a circular perspective was preserved when viewed from below. But much of its grandeur is due to the bluestones' sheer size—and that, of course, translates into back-breaking labor.

The bluestones used in the first ring came from the Preseli Mountains in Wales, some 240 miles away, transported by water with rafts and on land in wooden sleighs. (Recently, a team from the BBC demonstrated that this was possible; a group of able-bodied young men moved stones of a similar size using a sleigh tied to log rollers.) The larger sarsen stones, weighing as much as 50 tons apiece, were found loose in a region 20 miles away. They were dragged, one by one, by teams of up to 1,000 men. These stones, pounded into shape with smaller rocks, were placed into deep pits on the site, sloping to one side and later raised by using a primitive rope-operated lever.

### ASTRONOMICAL ALIGNMENTS
What was Stonehenge's purpose? Scholars have long assumed the site had a religious significance, a theory supported by the absence of debris such as broken pottery. Quack theories proliferated until 1963, when British astronomer Gerald Hawkins introduced what is now the most widely accepted explanation. Hawkins noted that when a person stands in the center of Stonehenge, certain celestial bodies appear over various stones with a regularity that defies coincidence. Hawkins recovered astronomical data from the time of Stonehenge's construction and, with the help of a computer, confirmed a number of these astronomical alignments. Most spectacularly, during the summer solstice—an important date for an agricultural community—the sun seemed to rise directly over one of the larger stones. It seems as if Stonehenge functioned as

## A DRUID CONNECTION?

The theory that associated Stonehenge's origins with Druid festivals was first popularized by John Aubrey, a 17th-century English antiquary who discovered many of the site's more prominent features, including the ring of 56 shallow pits, which were named after him. The Druids, ancient Celtic priests, lent the site an added dose of **DID IT REALLY HAPPEN?** ▼ hooded mystery. Unfortunately, however, this alluring legend clashes with archeological fact. The Druids emerged in England in the waning years of the pre-Christian era, more than two millennia after Stonehenge was first constructed. By 300 BC, as Celtic culture flourished on the island, Stonehenge lay in ruins.

**FOLLOWERS OF THE ANCIENT DRUIDS GATHER AT THE MONUMENT IN JUNE AND DECEMBER TO CELEBRATE THE SUMMER AND WINTER SOLSTICES.**

a giant calendar and observatory, one of man's first great efforts to keep track of time.

In the wake of this discovery lay unanswered questions. Some archeologists suggest that Stonehenge was also used to predict solar eclipses. Its social function, as opposed to its religious or calendrical purposes, has yet to be fully understood. These mysteries may very well endure as long as the ponderous stones themselves. As Henry James remarked about the mysteries of Stonehenge, "You may put a hundred questions to these rough-hewn giants…but your curiosity falls dead in the vast sunny stillness that enshrouds them."

# How Were the Pyramids Built?

**The magnificent Pyramids are testaments to the power of man's ingenuity.**

On the west bank of the Nile stand the astonishing pyramids. The very shape of the pyramid, with its sturdy, earthbound base and its apex reaching for the heavens, articulates the combination of technical skill and spiritual commitment that their construction required.

The golden age of construction in Egypt occurred during the Third Period, from 2868 to 2613 BC. For the most part, the pyramids were meant to serve as burial chambers for pharaohs and other high officials. The foundation of the Egyptian monarchy relied on the immortality of the pharaoh, and thus was predicated on a devout belief in an afterlife.

The pyramid not only glorified the pharaoh but served as a sort of antechamber in which he would wait until he entered the next world. The Egyptians perfected the art of embalming to preserve the buried body, and often stocked the pyramids with royal amenities the pharaoh would want with him in the afterlife. In one tomb, for example, archeologists found some 40,000 stone vessels, enough to satisfy even the most regal of mummies, as well as a retinue of servants, often buried close by the pharaoh.

## THE PYRAMID AT GIZA

The most magnificent pyramid standing today—the only surviving structure of the Seven Wonders of the Ancient World—is the pyramid at Giza, built during the reign of Cheops, the Greek name for King Khufu (2545–2520 BC). At the time of its construction, the pyramid rose some 482 feet, covered 13 acres, and weighed at least 6.5 million tons. Napoleon calculated that the material from which it was built—over 2,300,000 blocks— would form a wall around France 10 feet high and 1 foot wide. The grand scale of the Cheops pyramid is matched by its precise design. Each side of its base measures some 776 feet, and the sides vary by only 7.9 inches; the pyramid's stones are placed so accurately that it is impossible to fit a sheet of paper between them. The sides of the pyramid run, with an error of a little more than 4 degrees, almost exactly from north to south and from east to west.

**THE SPHINX STANDS GUARD BEFORE THE PYRAMID OF KHEPHREN.**

THE WALLPAINTING IN THE TOMB OF REKHMERE, A HIGH GOVERNMENT OFFICIAL IN 15TH CENTURY BC IN LUXOR, SHOWS WORKERS HEWING STONE FOR A PHARAOH'S TOMB.

THE PYRAMIDAL BURIAL TOMBS OF CHEOPS AND CHEPHREN LOOM OVER THE LANDSCAPES OF MODERN EGYPT, LOOKING JUST AS THEY MUST HAVE MORE THAN 3,500 YEARS AGO.

In the 19th century, as archeologists mapped out the pyramids, the wonder induced by these details encouraged a whole new pseudo-scientific discipline. "Pyramidology" sought to discover the "pyramid inch," a standard unit that allowed the Egyptians to build with such uncanny precision. Standards such as *pi*, the mass and circumference of the earth, and the distance of earth to sun were suggested. Others proposed the theory that the pyramids were great stone texts, in which details of the entire history of the world had been encoded.

Pyramidologists stretched to even greater imaginative lengths to explain how these stone marvels were constructed. In the 20th century, one widely held theory held that the pyramids were carried to earth by aliens, and dropped into their current positions by UFOs. And yet the real story behind their creation—which took place over a period of about 30 years—is no less impressive, if less fantastic.

The building process began with the hewing of the rocks, which were removed from quarries—some as far as 600 miles away, in Aswan. Most historians think the rocks were probably floated on rafts down the Nile in flood season, even though there is no archeological evidence of rafts large enough to float rocks of such enormous size. At the site of the pyramid, workers would first establish a level building surface by flooding the area with water, cutting a system of channels, and then digging until the water was level. A perimeter was then established and cut to the appropriate level, with the occasional large chunk of rock preserved.

A massive stone causeway was built on the banks of the Nile, facilitating the unloading process. The stones were dragged on wooden sledges resting on rollers for the half mile to the building site. Here, a team of masons and stonecutters worked at the rocks, smoothing them and preparing them for use.

Once ready, the huge stones were rolled into position, a process complicated by the fact that the wheel did not arrive in Egypt for another 800 years. Some scholars have suggested that the Egyptians built enormous ramps, lengthened as the building progressed, but with a constant slope; others have suggested a spiral ramp that snaked its way up the pyramid. The stone would be pushed to the tip of the ramp, then placed on a bed of liquid mortar. It was then left to set. The ramps would be dismantled when the workers reached the top of the pyramid, as masons worked their way downward and smoothed the stones.

And who made up this massive labor force? The Greek historian Herodotus put the number of workers at 100,000 men, replaced every three months for a period of 20 years, though this is probably an exaggeration. An ancient barracks found nearby housed around 4,000 men, and there were most likely several barracks in the area. The workers were not slaves, and the work was not coerced, casting doubt on the biblical stories of cruel taskmasters brandishing whips. An inscription on the tomb of one pharaoh boasts that he never struck a worker hard enough to knock him down.

In fact, prisoners of war performed much of the heavy work, while peasants did much of the skilled labor. Paid in food, the peasants worked during the flood season, when farming was impossible. The pyramids can be said to have granted these workers a certain immortality, just as they have the pharaohs buried within.

## THE MUMMY'S CURSE

**KING TUT'S COFFIN**

The legend of the mummy's curse might never have arisen if archeologists had used a little more insect repellent. In November 1922, Lord Carnarvon, a respected British Egyptologist, and Howard Carter, an archeologist, entered the sealed tomb of the boy-king Tutankhamun and uncovered one of the most spectacular treasures ever found. But Lord Carnarvon did not have long to relish this discovery. A few months later he died of an infected mosquito bite, and at a press conference held soon after, a French occultist declared that Carnarvon's death was the price for desecrating the tomb. This curse held the public's attention, but it loses

**PIECES OF THE PUZZLE**
▼

much of its bite in the face of statistics: Of the 22 people present when the tomb was discovered, only 6 had died by 1934, a natural percentage considering that foreigners in Egypt often succumbed to local diseases. Carter, in fact, lived to the ripe age of 66, no doubt mildly amused by the curse as the years rolled by.

**LORD CARNARVON**

# The Roots of
# Greek Culture

**In which Bronze Age culture lie the origins of ancient Greece, whose thinkers and dramatists were among the world's most influential?**

A 6TH-CENTURY VASE PAINTING SHOWS THESEUS SLAYING THE MINOTAUR, A BULL. ANCIENT GREECE'S RICH TRADITION OF MYTH-MAKING PROMOTED SOCIAL COHESION AT THE EXPENSE OF THE HISTORICAL RECORD. BELOW, THE MINOTAUR ON A GREEK COIN.

AWED BY THE GRANDEUR OF CLASSICAL Greek culture, people today find it tempting to imagine Sophocles, Socrates, and Archimedes bursting into the world in the manner of their mythological gods and goddesses, fully-formed like Athena, emerging from the head of her father, Zeus. In truth, until a little more than a century ago scholars had very little idea about the origins of Greek civilization. Herodotus, Thucydides, and other ancient historians did speak of a previous "age of heroes," but it is difficult to extract the truth from the haze of legend and fable.

Who were those heroes? One legend told of a mythical race inhabiting the nearby island of Crete and ruled by Minos, a son of Zeus. So powerful were the Minoans that the ancient Greeks were required to send seven youths each year to sacrifice to the Minotaur ("Minos' bull"), a fierce creature that lived in a gigantic underground labyrinth. In the late 19th century, excavations in Crete uncovered massive, labyrinthine palaces dating to the 2nd and 3rd millenniums BC; they also found festive wall paintings depicting elaborate ceremonies involving bulls. Scholars now believe that the Minotaur myth was an imaginative refashioning of these raw materials.

Another legend told of a tremendous fortified city at Mycenae, on the Greek mainland,

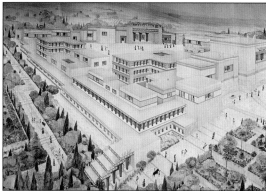

built by Perseus and the one-eyed race of giants called Cyclops. The Mycenaeans were believed to have been the major power of prehistoric Greece; it was there that mighty Agamemnon, the king who led the Greek forces in the Trojan War, ruled. Homer called the Mycenaeans "Acheans" and celebrated them for their bravery in battle. But after the Mycenaean civilization crumbled around 1200 BC, their history, like that of the Minoans, took on an epic and heroic character.

## INTRIGUING EXCAVATIONS

In the 19th century, discoveries shed some light on the legends of prehistoric Greece. In the 1870s, excavations led by Heinrich Schliemann on the Greek mainland uncovered evidence of a people who flourished there from between 2800 and 1200 BC. Archeologists were also able to link these people (who Schliemann named after the town of Mycenae, where one of the largest fortifications was discovered) to the conquest of the Minoan civilization in the 15th century BC. Some historians have even suggested that the conquest was responsible for the great flowering of Mycenaean culture in the 16th century BC, which would mean that the ancestors of the Greeks actually borrowed much of their cultural inspiration.

The Minoans were a peaceful people, and had few military fortifications on their island;

most of their great wealth derived from foreign trade. Despite frequent contact with their neighbors, the Minoans remained illiterate long after other nations in the region. They eventually created their own system of pictographs, which they then transformed into linear signs around 1600 BC, a language called by archeologists Linear A.

One of the strongest links between the Minoan and the Mycenaean cultures is that the latter adapted a system of writing based on Linear A, which we now label Linear B. Tablets of Linear B were found on the isle of Crete around the time of its destruction, and so scholars assume that the Mycenaeans not only borrowed the Minoan's language but also took their land. Indeed, this theory corresponds to everything we know of Mycenaean culture; they were a fierce, warlike people, whose martial heroes were buried in colossal tombs, which quite possibly inspired Homer to write of them so grandly in the *Iliad*. The massive

Treasury of Atreus in Mycenae, for example, which was erected some time between 1300 and 1250 BC, is 48 feet in diameter and 44 feet tall; its entryway is topped with a lintel stone weighing nearly 120 tons. The Mediterranean world would not witness a building as monumental as this one until Hadrian built the Pantheon in Rome some 1,300 years later.

## WHO ARRIVED WHEN?

Even though scholars now know more about the Bronze Age Greeks, they are still struggling to understand exactly why these people arrived on the Greek mainland in the first place. Was it through another invasion? Or through a gradual migration? And at what time precisely was the Greek mainland first populated by the ancestors of Aristotle and Hippocrates? By examining Bronze Age sites that contain evidence of destruction with subsequent levels of technological and cultural advancement, some scholars have placed the date of the infiltration

THE TREASURY OF ATREUS IN MYCENAE WAS BUILT SOMETIME BETWEEN 1300 AND 1250 BC. IT AND OTHER COLOSSAL BUILDINGS OF THE TIME INSPIRED HOMER TO WRITE OF THEM IN THE *ILIAD*.

HIPPOCRATES (TOP, IN A 14TH-CENTURY AD IMAGE) AND ARISTOTLE—TWO TOWERING FIGURES OF ANCIENT GREECE WHOSE BRONZE AGE ANCESTORS ARE OPEN TO QUESTION.

at about 2200 BC. Other scholars dispute this, cautioning that, in the words of one scholar, "a burned palace can be the work of a careless cook as well as a ruthless enemy." These archeologists believe that there is no real evidence of interruption from the earliest traces of settled communities in Greece in 6000 BC to the end of the Mycenaean civilization.

Yet another camp has put the date of the first arrival to the mainland at 3000 BC, and has traced these immigrants, through their languages, to Asia Minor. The scholarly consensus is still forming. Even today, historians experience that same awe and puzzlement when approaching the "age of heroes" as did their respectful Greek counterparts.

## THE AFROASIATIC THEORY

Is our traditional conception of Greek civilization a myth? One scholar, Martin Bernal, in his daring work *Black Athena: The Afroasiatic Roots of Classical Civilization*, proposes that Greece was invaded, conquered, and civilized by Egyptians around the 16th century BC, and that Classical

**VIEW FROM THE FRINGE** ▼

civilization has deep roots in Afroasiatic cultures. Bernal claims that these influences were disregarded or suppressed during the 18th century because of racism. Classical Greeks believed, Bernal says, their political institutions, science, and philosophy to be derived not from Indo-

European speakers or Aryans from the North but from the East, especially from Egypt. "The political purpose of *Black Athena* is, of course, to lessen European cultural arrogance," he explains.

THE GODDESS ATHENA WAS THE PROTECTRESS OF ATHENS.

# Jason and the Argonauts

THIS PAINTING OF THE LEGENDARY JASON AND THE ARGONAUTS WAS BY THE ITALIAN LORENZO COSTA. THEIR TALE IS ONE OF THE OLDEST IN THE GREEK TRADITION, BUT IS THERE ANY TRUTH BEHIND THE LEGEND?

ONE OF THE OLDEST TALES RELATED FROM GREEK TRADITION involves the reluctant hero Jason and his not-so-merry band of Argonauts. The ancient legend met with the usual embellishments along its passage through the mouths of Greek story weavers from as far back as 1300 BC.

The myth recounts the adventure of Jason and a carefully hand-picked crew of men who set sail on the *Argo* to the farthest reaches of the known eastern waters to bring back the illustrious Golden Fleece, the golden wool of a ram. But what truth, if any, lies behind the Argonauts' legend? With such vivid descriptions of rivers conquered and battles waged, are there any morsels of fact that can be culled from Jason's quest?

Indeed, the tricky part of reading ancient myths is extracting those tidbits of information based on reality, however mundane they tend to make the glorious pictures of life in antiquity. Putting aside the fantastical creatures and wars the heroes faced, much can be discovered about Jason's adventures on the high seas.

From the very date of the story and from uncovered artifacts, we know that ancient Greece had established itself as a maritime power long before most civilizations. In fact, proof of Mediterranean nautical expeditions by the pre-Hellenic people (whom ancient Greece would eventually incorporate) date as far back as 6000–7000 BC.

## JASON'S ADVENTURES

Most experts date Jason's quest to 1289 BC, when shipbuilding was a relatively simple process. Although the characteristics of the divine ship the *Argo* are often boasted of, it actually had no deck. Most likely, when the Argonauts (and other explorers of the time) reached land, their ship was disassembled, its parts were carried to the next shore, and they were reassembled, good as new. However, the depth to which the story goes to affirm a boat's superiority shows not only the bonds between the Greeks and the adventure, but also between the Greeks, the rough sea, and its unruly master, Poseidon.

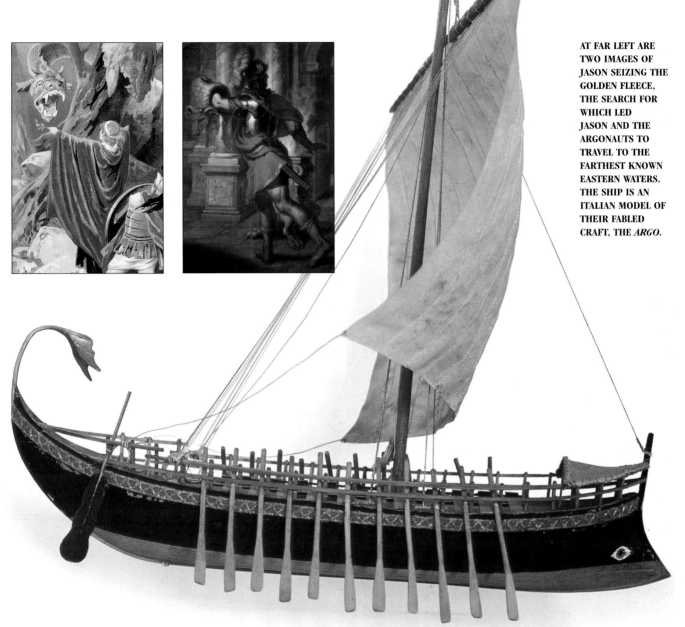

Chances are, the real Jason and his cronies were little more than glorified treasure hunters. The legend of gold in the rivers of Colchis was quite common in the 12th century BC, and that precious metal was in all probability the actual impetus of the Argonauts' journey. Seamen of old were most moved by the promise of finding great rewards on the high seas—not by the spirit of adventure.

But perhaps more significant than their mission and exaggerated battles with monsters is the Argonauts' wild ride through European waters. Based on astronomical observations made throughout their tale, it is clear that Jason and his men weren't just chancing it on the open waves; they had a deep understanding of navigational techniques, all the way back 3,500 years ago.

Their escapade carries the men far to the east through the Black Sea, toward the base of the Caucasus Mountains in an area that today is part of Georgia. As far as Greek navigators knew at the time, the Black Sea was a gulf into an infinite ocean, not bounded as it is by the towering mountains of Asia. This discovery no doubt showed their place in respect to Eastern nations.

## THE FIRST EXPLORER

The Argonauts' return route, according to various historians, took them north toward Scandinavia, west to the British Isles, and then south along the western coast of Europe, where they gently slipped back into the Mediterranean. Others theorize that the return route took them through the heart of Europe, west along the Danube, and farther west along smaller rivers to the Adriatic, where they went south down to the Ionian Sea and Greece. Either way, the Argonauts' journey, spurred on by the promise of booty, inadvertently revealed much about the geography of European waters.

The Argonaut legend was the first tale of a groundbreaking nautical expedition, thereby making Jason the first explorer. Perhaps Jason's real reward was his contribution to the Greeks' knowledge of the physical world.

# Was there a
# Trojan Horse?

## An amateur archeologist uncovered the city where the Trojan War took place, but is there any evidence that the battle was won by an imaginative ruse?

THE *ILIAD*, HOMER'S MAGISTERIAL TELLING OF THE Trojan War, stands as the preeminent epic of antiquity. Generations of schoolchildren have sat enraptured by its catalogue of heroes, its recitation of bloody battles, and its vivid portrayal of victory and defeat. It is undoubtedly a grand story, but is any of it true?

Many ancient writers vouched for the tale's authenticity; the great historian Thucydides claimed that there was indeed a Trojan War, but since he was born in 460 BC, some 800 years after the war was supposed to have occurred, his testimony is somewhat unreliable. Ultimately, Homer remains our only source for the story, but no one knows who he is or how he came to know so much about Trojan history. And even if Homer was an actual person, he lived between 900 and 700 BC, four centuries after the war was supposedly fought.

Scholars even wondered whether there was a historical city of Troy. No one knew exactly where the city was, and many suspected that it was a figment of the imagination, a convenient foil against which to pose the glory of Athens.

### HERR SCHLIEMANN'S QUEST
One man—a morose but fabulously rich German businessman with a passion for archeology—was responsible for solving this mystery.

After amassing a fortune in the California Gold Rush and in international trading, Heinrich Schliemann dedicated himself to finding proof of Homer's great epics, first searching for the castle of Ulysses, and then for the city of

**THE STORY OF THE TROJAN HORSE IS PART OF WESTERN CULTURE, BUT IS IT FACTUAL? SOME SUGGEST THE STORY IS BASED ON THE USE OF A BATTERING RAM OR A SIEGE TOWER TO CONQUER THE CITY OF TROY —AND ELABORATED BY IMAGINATIVE STORYTELLERS.**

Troy. Using ancient Greek texts as guides and with the help of nearly 100 workers, Schliemann began excavating the tell of Hissarlik in Turkey near the Aegean coast, in 1871.

Schliemann's faith in Homer's narrative served him well; digging downward, he actually found nine "Troys," the remnants of cultures dating back to the end of the Early Bronze Age of 2500 BC, buried one on top of the other. And then Schliemann struck gold.

On June 14, 1873, the day before he had decided to pack up for the season, Schliemann uncovered one of the greatest treasure troves ever discovered, including some 8,700 jeweled cups, rings, and bracelets. Schliemann called his discovery "Priam's Treasure," after the famous Trojan king featured in the *Iliad*. But in actuality, Schliemann's zeal had gotten the better of him; he had dug past the level representing Priam's Troy to a habitation some 1,000 years earlier. The Troy of the *Iliad* was already scattered among the excavation's rubbish heaps. Still, his discovery of the multi-layered tell proved convincingly that a historical Troy did indeed exist.

But the existence of Troy did not guarantee that a war was fought there between the city and Greece. Archeologists have uncovered high walls surrounding the city, suggesting that it was a militaristic society, but there is no evidence that an army camped outside those walls, let alone the huge Greek force described in the *Iliad*, numbering some 110,000 men. Moreover, historians have pointed out that if there was a war, it certainly did not last 10 years, as the *Iliad* claims. In those days, army discipline was lax, and wars lasted only a few months before the bonds that held the forces together disintegrated, and soldiers returned home.

### NEITHER HORSE NOR HELEN?

And then there is the famous myth of the Trojan Horse, the giant wooden equine by which the Greeks managed to smuggle themselves into Troy when the Trojans accepted the horse as a gift. There is no evidence that the horse ruse was based on a historical event, nor have objects appeared in excavations to substantiate the legend. The role of Helen, the Greek beauty whose elopement with the Trojan prince Paris instigated the war, is also doubtful. Her face may have launched a thousand

## SEARCH FOR THE REAL HOMER

Walter Bagehot, the famous British editor, once wrote, "A man who has not read Homer is like a man who has not seen the ocean." But for a man so celebrated, little is known about antiquity's greatest poet. Until the middle of the 5th century BC, Greeks sited his birthplace on the little island of Chios, off the western coast of Asia Minor, where his epics were sung by the Homeridae, a tribe claiming to be Homer's direct descendants.

As Homer's stature grew, other towns, including Athens, claimed him as a native son. But local references in the *Iliad* suggest Homer actually hailed from the eastern Aegean. Additionally, grammatical, stylistic, and metrical elements of the *Iliad* suggest a date for its

**HOW DO WE REALLY KNOW?** ▼

composition of approximately the 8th century BC, as do references to certain distinctive and time-specific fighting methods. Some scholars disagree as to Homer's authorship of both the *Iliad* and the *Odyssey*, the tale of Odysseus's circuitous voyage home after the Trojan War.

THIS BUST OF HOMER IS ON DISPLAY IN ROME. HOMER PROBABLY RECORDED, NO DOUBT WITH HIS OWN EMBELLISHMENTS, STORIES THAT HAD BEEN HANDED DOWN FOR GENERATIONS BEFORE HIM.

ships in Homer's tale, but there is no record of such a queen in the records of antiquity.

Homeric apologists suggest that even if some of the details were invented, the basic facts of the war are correct. They point to artistic elaboration practiced by poets, explaining that the story was told and passed on orally through the generations. Storytellers would change the story with each narration, adapting the tale while using a repertoire of traditional themes and heroes. If a particular elaboration was popular, it might have stuck to the story and been propagated by thousands of retellings. Eventually, one of these oral narratives was recorded in writing and became the standard version of the Trojan War. Ultimately, as with so many mysteries of antiquity, the best we can do in the face of these historical uncertainties is to simply enjoy the story.

# Noah
## and the Great Flood

**In the past century, archeological and historical evidence has revealed that the archetypal tale of a Great Flood may be rooted in fact.**

**ARTISTS THROUGH THE AGES HAVE GRACED CANVASSES WITH THE STORY OF NOAH AND HOW HE SAVED THE ANIMALS. THE AMERICAN PAINTER NATHANIEL CURRIER TOOK HIS TURN IN 1855.**

IT IS A TRUISM OF THE CRIMINAL JUSTICE SYSTEM that the more witnesses corroborate a certain event, the more likely it is that the event actually occurred—especially if the witnesses are of different perspectives and backgrounds. This principle can easily be applied to the fields of archeology and comparative anthropology as well. If a single story appears in the traditions of many cultures, there is a good chance that the story reflects historical fact.

The Great Flood is such an archetypal tale, the story of a tremendous deluge from which only a single family is spared and left to repopulate the world. The most familiar Western articulation of this story appears in the Book of Genesis. Noah, a man of virtue, is commanded by God to build an ark 300 cubits long (about 450 feet) and 50 cubits wide (75 feet), which would float above the waters as God pours down His rainy wrath on a sinful world. A similar tale appears in the mythologies of many other ancient cultures, including those of Mesopotamians, Scandinavians, Greeks, and American Indians. The most famous nonbiblical narration of the Great Flood myth was discovered in 1872, engraved on the Gilgamesh tablet of Babylonia. The tablet tells the tale of a man named Ur-Napishtim, who survived a flood sent by the gods to punish mankind.

Segments of the same story have since been found on hundreds of cuneiform fragments and were possibly the source for the Noah story. The stories share many details: the large ark, the animals taken on board, the sending out of birds to find land, and the symbol of divine remorse to signal the end of the cataclysm (Noah saw a rainbow; the Gilgamesh tablets cite a goddess's necklace flung to the sky).

The constant struggle fledgling civilizations everywhere waged against the flooding of arable land may account for the appearance of flood tales in nearly all ancient cultures.

## DIGGING THROUGH MILLENNIA

As more references to a great flood accumulated, archeologists became determined to find physical evidence of this cataclysmic event. The search culminated in the excavation led by Sir Leonard Woolley in the late 1920s, which succeeded in unearthing the lost city of Ur, in southern Iraq. Digging through the millennia, Toolley found alternating layers of ruins and river deposits. At one site, Woolley dug down 65 feet, through a Babylonian potter's workshop, then through an 11-foot-deep stratum of alluvial clay, reaching a primeval level of human occupation. From this layering, Woolley concluded that the region underwent several periods of massive flooding, and after each, civilization gradually reasserted itself.

In Woolley's own words, "It was not a universal deluge. It was a vast flood in the valley of the Tigris and Euphrates which drowned the whole of the habitable land between the mountain and the desert; for the people who lived there that was indeed all the world."

Another compelling piece of evidence was Woolley's discovery of a large hill that at the time of the flooding would have been the only natural outcrop in the plain standing above water. Excavating it, he found layers of civilization extending downward uninterrupted, suggesting that the place had served as a refuge as the waters rose. It was on that lonely hill that the Flood myth was born, Woolley suggested, as the waters subsided and the next, drier generations tried to make sense of their lost world.

## A SECOND RIDDLE SOLVED

Recently, scientists have come closer to solving another riddle of the deluge. Through geological and oceanographical analysis, they have concluded that a Great Flood (though not necessarily Noah's flood) occurred some 7,600 years ago. At that point, melting glaciers increased the water level of the Mediterranean Sea, causing it to overrun a natural dam that separated it from an inland lake (now the Black Sea). Every day for two years, the channel known as the Bosporus was flooded, and the water entered the lake. Each day the water

advanced a mile inland, transforming the entire region into a giant sea, one where the water could not circulate, and where the wrecks of generations of ancient ships lay preserved. It is possible that this was the first Great Flood, and its survivors took the story with them as they spread out across the Mediterranean basin.

MT. ARARAT (*AGRI DABRI* IN TURKISH) LOOMS ABOVE THE MIST (BELOW). THE HIGHEST PEAK IN TURKEY, IT IS SUPPOSED BY SOME TO BE THE LANDING SITE OF NOAH'S ARK.

## SEARCH FOR THE ARK

The Bible gives no specific geographic location for Ararat, the mountain where the ark rested as the waters subsided. Nevertheless, generations have searched for the mountain in an effort to find the ark.

The Greek version of the Old Testament translates Ararat as Armenia, as do ancient Assyrian versions of the flood narrative. But the Mt. Ararat in northeastern Turkey has long been revered as the holy site.

The mountain was first explored in the early 1800s, and over the next 50-odd years several expeditions had returned with "proof" of the ark. These included sodden timbers of a type that does not grow anywhere on the mountain and that seem to

**PIECES OF THE PUZZLE** ▼

have been cut approximately 4,000 years ago from trees in Mesopotamia (Noah's home). More impressive developments have recently occurred. In 1952, Ararat was reconnoitered from a helicopter, and a photograph was taken of a structure protruding from the ice near the peak. In 1974, photographs taken by a satellite revealed a formation a little lower on the mountain's northeast side. It was described as "clearly foreign to anything else on the mountain, about the right size and shape to be an ark." However, to continue with the excavation would mean moving a large amount of ice; and so we await conclusive proof of the ark's whereabouts.

# Moses and the Exodus

**The Exodus from Egypt is not only the central story of the Jewish tradition but a consoling narrative for all those in need of hope.**

THE BIBLICAL LEGEND OF THE EXODUS FROM Egypt has brought great meaning to many cultures. For example, black slaves incorporated the story of the Exodus from Egypt into their plantation songs and imagined themselves as latter-day children of Israel, waiting to travel to the Promised Land. It comes as somewhat of a

THE STORY OF MOSES AND THE EXODUS HAS INSPIRED ARTISTS AND WRITERS FOR THOUSANDS OF YEARS. THESE THREE PAINTINGS FROM THE SCHOOL OF THE ITALIAN MASTER RAPHAEL DEPICT MOSES RECEIVING THE TABLETS OF THE LAW (TOP); THE PILLAR OF CLOUD (CENTER); MOSES STRIKING THE ROCK (BOTTOM).

surprise then, that for all the event's historical import, there is little consensus among scholars as to its authenticity. Surprisingly, the only true scholarly agreement about the Exodus is that there is no definitive evidence available to corroborate it—no ancient tablets referring to it specifically, no revelatory hieroglyphic illustrations, no remains of temporary dwellings haunting the Judean wilderness. In fact, no record of Moses or of the Exodus is contained in all of ancient Egypt's chronicles.

## LOST OR FOUND?

This historical silence troubles many archeologists, who point out that artifacts from even late Stone Age cultures have emerged from the area. A mass exodus and a 40-year sojourn through the Sinai would certainly have reverberated through the region, they argue, leaving some imprint. They often explain the story as a latter-day political fabrication, invented to unite the disparate tribes living in Canaan.

But other archeologists are quick to defend the possible authenticity of the Exodus narrative. The lack of historical records could be explained by the ancient Israelites' use of perishable papyrus for their documentation (unlike many of their neighbors who used the more durable clay). They explain the lack of Egyptian documentation by pointing out that history's losers often neglect to record events unfavorable to them. They also point out that the Bible does not explicitly refer to the pyramids, but no one doubts their existence.

These scholars also have some fragmentary nonbiblical material in their arsenal. There is the legend described by the first century BC Greek historian Strabo of an ancient army drowning on the coast of Canaan, "near Egypt." There is also a Phoenician legend of a hero named Danaos, who led his followers out of Egypt after a series of disasters befell the land, eerily echoing the biblical tale. Another theory suggests that there were actually multiple oppressions and expulsions, and that the Exodus narrative is a compilation of these events.

## THE TREASURE CITIES

Even if we accept that the Exodus did occur, plenty of controversy persists. To start, scholars disagree on the correct dating of the event. In I Kings 6:1, the Exodus is said to have occurred some 480 years before Solomon began building the Temple, which would place it at around 1446 BC. But this date conflicts with others included in the Old Testament. The Book of Exodus contains a passage that claims the Israelites were building "treasure cities, Pithom and Raamses," for the Egyptian pharaoh. Scholars believe that Raamses was Pi-Ramesse, a Nile delta city built by Ramses II, in the late 13th century BC.

This date for the Exodus is in accord with the earliest known reference to the people of Israel outside of the Bible—a granite monument found in a temple to Pharaoh Merneptah,

the son of Ramses II. The hieroglyphs on the monument commemorate the military victories of the pharaoh, and include a line boasting of vanquishing the Israelites during a campaign in Canaan in 1210 BC. For the Israelites to have been established by that time in Canaan, observers point out, the Exodus must have occurred at least a half century before.

Some scholars have approached the Exodus story not from a historical perspective but from a scientific one, attempting to explain the naturalistic mechanisms behind Moses' miracles. Scientists have also tried to explain the parting of the Red Sea (which is actually a mistranslation of the Hebrew for "Reed Sea"). One of the more popular theories points to tidal waves that would have swept through the region after the explosion of a massive volcano.

The scientific basis to the story mattered little to the generations who found comfort in the Exodus story. They cared little about the mechanism that parted the waters, but only that the waters parted at all, and that a promised land lay somewhere on the other side.

# The Ten Lost Tribes

THE EXILE OF THE TEN LOST TRIBES OF ISRAEL AND THEIR unexplained disappearance is a story shrouded in mystery, not to mention historical significance. Until recent times, the history of the Jewish people was by and large a tale of wandering and displacement. Exiled from one land or driven by famine or persecution from another, the Jews became a diasporic nation, settling in lands throughout the world but with a steady, vigilant eye cast toward Zion. Such an uprooted culture finds great solace in stories—especially those that feature redemption, reunification, and a return to its ancestral homeland.

The legend of the Ten Lost Tribes is perhaps the most poignant of these stories, a tale of the loss of more than three quarters of the Jewish people and of the hope that someday they will be found. In fact, the story is based more on this hope than on any historical truth. The Ten Tribes of Israel were indeed "lost," but the secret of their disappearance is much more mundane than the fantastic tales traditionally associated with them.

## THE TRIBES DIVIDE

The story begins with the reign of King Solomon (circa 970–931 BC), and of his prodigal son Rehoboam, whose rule was so odious that it split Israel into two hostile kingdoms. Ten of the original twelve tribes, descendants of Jacob's sons, moved north, while the remaining two, led by Benjamin and Judah, established the southern Kingdom of Judah. For the next 200 years, the two kingdoms squabbled and fought each other, paving the way for an enterprising king to conquer the region.

In 732 BC, the Assyrian king Tiglath-pileser III conquered Damascus. In 722–721 BC, his successors, Shalmaneser V and Sargon II, defeated the northern Kingdom of Israel, sending its people into exile. And then they vanished from the pages of history, seemingly without a trace. The Kingdom of Judah remained intact.

**AN 18TH-CENTURY DRAWING DEPICTS THE ENCAMPMENT OF THE TWELVE TRIBES OF ISRAEL IN THE WILDERNESS.**

Although these Jews were exiled by the Babylonians in 586 BC, they were allowed to return to their homeland by the Persian ruler Cyrus, who conquered Babylon in

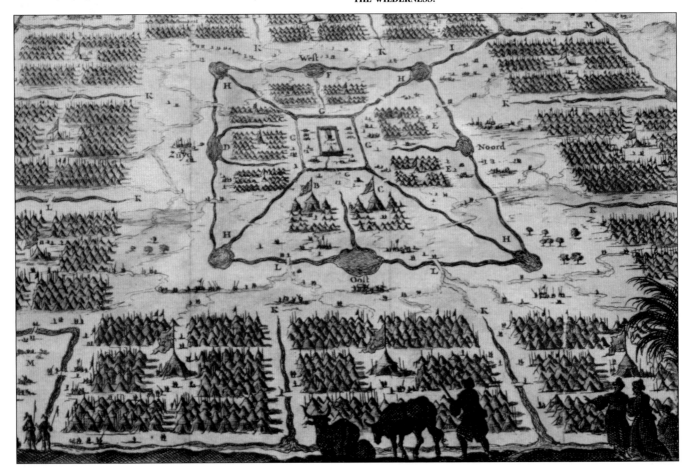

The most likely explanation behind the disappearance of the ten tribes (and the one most widely embraced by historians) is that after their exile from Israel at the hands of the Assyrians, the people of the Kingdom of Israel simply assimilated into the nearby regional cultures. This vanishing is perhaps less dramatic than an ancient crossing of the Atlantic, but in the grand view of history, just as fascinating.

**THE BATTLE OF LACHISH (BELOW) WAS FOUGHT IN THE ASSYRIAN CAMPAIGN TO CONQUER ISRAEL.**

539 BC. The known history of the Jews after this point is essentially that of the Kingdom of Judah, home to only two of the original twelve tribes.

**THE CISTERN OF SHILOH (ABOVE) WAS THE RELIGIOUS CENTER OF THE KINGDOM OF ISRAEL, WHERE ELI AND HIS SONS OFFICIATED.**

The first hint of the lost tribes' whereabouts appears in the Bible (II Kings 17:6), placing them in upper Mesopotamia. Josephus, the Jewish historian, believed they were dispersed even farther—"beyond the Euphrates." According to another Greek text written at around the same time, the tribes set off for a place called "Azareth." But this name has not been attached to any known location, and it is likely that it is merely a corruption of the Hebrew phrase *erez aharet*, meaning "another place."

## THE LOST TRIBES FOUND?

Historically, interest in the whereabouts of the Ten Lost Tribes has revived at times of disaster, when the Jewish people were in need of an inspiring legend. During the Crusades, while the Jews were suffering terrible persecution, they took hope in the prophecy that promised the entire House of Israel would soon be reunited.

New and unfamiliar lands have also frequently been suggested as the location of the lost tribes. For instance, when the New World was discovered, many explorers thought that the native peoples of the Americas were descended from one or more of the tribes. Europeans claimed the "natives" had semitic features and that their language bore some phonetic similarities to Hebrew. Too, a traveler returning from South America told the rabbi in Amsterdam that the Indians in Peru practiced Jewish rituals. And after seeing his first American native, William Penn, the founder of Pennsylvania, declared, "I imagine myself in the Jewish Quarter of London."

The implicit claim was that the lost tribes had somehow managed to cross the Atlantic and to pass their culture on to the native population. Similar claims linking a cultural, religious, or ethnic group to the lost tribes have been made by the Mormons, the Afghans, the Falashas of Ethiopia, the Tatars, and even by the Britons.

## THE RIVER SAMBATYON

One of the most imaginative stories about the Ten Lost Tribes was advanced by Eldad ha-Dani, a 9th-century Jewish traveler. He claimed to have seen the lost tribes beyond the River of Sambatyon, the legendary "Sabbath River." The river was an impassable torrent of stones, which ceased only on the Sabbath. Since for Jews, travel is proscribed on the Sabbath, the lost tribes were **VIEW FROM THE FRINGE** forever guarded behind the river. Throughout the ages, historians have sought out the location of this magical river. The Jewish historian Josephus (AD 37–100) claimed it was in Syria, and Pliny asserted it was in Judea; others searched for it in India, Africa, China, Japan, and Spain. Like the Ten Lost Tribes, to this day it has never been found.

# The Tower of Babel

**An authentic history surrounds the legend of the mighty Tower of Babel.**

WHEN FLEMISH PAINTER PIETER BRUEGEL THE ELDER PUT THE TOWER OF BABEL ON CANVAS IN THE 16TH CENTURY, HE HAD NO KNOWLEDGE OF THE RUINS OF BABYLON'S ZIGGURATS. WHY? BECAUSE THEY HAD NOT YET BEEN UNEARTHED. WAS IT MERE COINCIDENCE THAT BRUEGEL IMAGINED THE TOWER AS STEPPED?

AMONG BIBLICAL LEGENDS, THE STORY OF THE Tower of Babel has much of the archetypal morality tale about it, warning readers against hubris, or exaggerated pride. (Noah's descendants, who spoke one language, tried to build a tower reaching to heaven.) It also serves as an explanatory fable, in that it elucidates the origins of the world's languages. (For their presumption, the builders lost the ability to speak intelligibly to each other.) But it also has what many biblical stories lack: an historical episode that archeologists believe inspired the tale.

Along the riverbanks of Mesopotamia, in the fertile strip between the Tigris and Euphrates rivers, a succession of city-states emerged some 5,500 years ago. Among them were Sumer and Akkad. Their violent, inventive people created the first system of writing. Their most impressive architectural achievements were the ziggurats, spectacular stone structures with a series of platforms that decreased in size as they rose,

some to 300 feet. Each was dedicated to a local god, and was topped with a temple meant to serve as the stopping point for the god on his journey to earth. The greatest of these, the ziggurat of Etemenanki, was built beside the Euphrates in Babylon, the capital of Nebuchadnezzar II (630–562 BC). It was almost certainly the model for the Tower of Babel.

In fact, Etemenanki means "the foundation house of heaven and earth." The name Babel, normally assumed to derive from the Hebrew word "confuse," originally came from the Babylonian "Bab-ilu," meaning "Gate of god." Thus, the entire legend of linguistic confusion thwarting the Tower's construction was most probably itself the result of a word mix-up.

## HOUSES OF BRICK

The ziggurats were built of brick because there was little timber available in the region, and there were few stone quarries nearby. The reliance on brick is faithfully recorded in the biblical account of the Tower of Babel's construction: "And they said one to another, Go to, let us make brick, and burn them thoroughly. And they had brick for stone, and slime had they for mortar." This "slime" was bitumen, a binding and coating material imported from the Iranian plateau and widely used in the region. Both archeological evidence and written records suggest that many of the ziggurats were painted in magnificent hues and were decorated lavishly with enamel tiles and gilded sculptures. A Babylonian inscription states that the Etemenanki ziggurat was built with "baked brick enamel in brilliant blue."

In all, there are some 30 known ziggurats, dating from between 2200 and 500 BC and built by the Mesopotamian city-states. But whereas the pyramids of Egypt still stand proud and defiant against the years, most of the ziggurats have long since succumbed to the ravages of time. The bricks of the ziggurats were pilfered by local residents to build houses; what remained faced the even greater threat of erosion from weather and dust. All that is left of the Etemenanki ziggurat is the outline of its huge stone base, swathed by earth embankments and choked by weeds and vegetation.

### THE TOWER'S GLORY AND DEMISE

At the time of its construction Etemenanki was one of the world's most astonishing creations. And modern excavations and biblical records have enabled scholars to reconstruct something of its grandeur. It was built and rebuilt a number of times, most spectacularly by Nebuchadnezzar II in the late 6th century BC. According to testimonies from Nebuchadnezzar and other Babylonian kings, the ziggurat's sides were each 295 long, as was its height, rising up seven stories. When modern archeologists explored the foundations of Etemenanki, they found its base dimensions to be around 300 feet, confirming the ancient measurements.

According to ancient records, at the top of the tower was a splendid temple to the great god Marduk, with a golden sculpture weighing some 22 tons. Marduk's association with Etemenanki helps to explain why the ziggurat was so much larger than many of the towers built in nearby cities. Originally, Marduk was only

## FIT FOR A KING

After the Assyrian king Sennacherib sacked Babylon in 689 BC, the Babylonian king Nabopolassar (625–605 BC) undertook the task of rebuilding the ziggurat of Etemenanki. An inscription from the time contains his account of the reconstruction: "Gold, silver and precious stones from the mountain and from the sea were liberally set into its foundations. . . Oils and perfumes were mixed into the bricks . . . I made a likeness of my royal person carrying the brick basket, and I carried it into the foundations. I bowed my head before Marduk."

**EYE-WITNESS** ▼

**THE BUILDING OF THE TOWER OF BABEL (ABOVE) WAS DEPICTED BY VENETIAN PAINTER LEANDRO BASSANO. AT LEFT, THE REMAINS OF A ZIGGURAT BUILT ABOUT 2100 BC LOOMS OVER THE IRAQI DESERT. IT FORMED THE CENTER OF A STRONG FORTRESS IN THE 2ND CENTURY AD. CROWNING IT IS A HOUSE AMERICAN EXCAVATORS BUILT AROUND 1900 AS A REFUGE FROM THE LOCAL TRIBESMEN.**

the local deity of Babylon; however, as the city grew to become the most powerful in the region, Marduk became Mesopotamia's dominant god. The ceremonies of Marduk worship were long, verbose, and contained passages from many languages. To visiting nomads, the Temple indeed must have seemed the home and source of myriad languages.

But even Marduk's prominence could not prevent the ziggurat from falling into neglect when Babylon became a Persian province in the late 5th century. In 331 BC, Alexander the Great visited the ziggurat and decided to rebuild the ruin, just as a string of Babylonian kings had done; but just to clear the land took 10,000 men two months to complete, and Alexander was forced to give up the project. As with those original, haughty builders of the biblical Tower of Babel, who wished to build a tower "whose top may reach into heaven," some higher power had other plans.

# The Ark of the Covenant

THE ARK OF THE COVENANT FIRST gained notoriety in the best-selling book of all time—the Bible. In the intervening years, the ark has been the topic of numerous books and films, including the 17th highest-grossing American movie in history, *Raiders of the Lost Ark*. While its religious import is second to none and its historical significance profound, the ark is best known for its mystifying disappearance.

The ark was constructed by the biblical artisan Bezalel, and measured approximately 4 feet 2 inches in length and 2.25 feet in both width and height. Fashioned from acacia wood and coated inside and out with pure gold, it was well-suited for its task: to hold the tablets upon which God had inscribed the Ten Commandments. Four golden rings adorned the ark's bottom corners where posts were inserted to carry the vessel. Its cover was sculpted

**Scholars and archeologists are still searching for this significant icon of biblical history.**

entirely of gold, with two cherubs (winged sphinxes) guarding each end. The space between the cherubs was thought to be God's throne and the ark his footstool, a symbol of the pact between Yahweh and the people of Israel; hence, the ark of the "covenant."

## LEGENDS OF THE LOST ARK

From the moment Solomon's temple was built, the ark was housed there in the sanctuary known as the Holy of Holies, which the high priest entered but once a year, on the Day of Atonement. Earlier, the Jews carted the ark along with them from place to place because it was thought to possess potent power with which no mortal could contend—most notably when it was taken into battle. On one occasion, when the ark was carried before the people of Israel, the waters of the Jordan River are said to have dried up. The ark is also supposed to have played a role in reducing the storied walls of Jericho to rubble.

Curiously, after its account of the first temple's destruction (586 BC), the Bible makes no further mention of the ark. What, then, happened to it? When the temple was rebuilt, why did it no longer house the ark? Where is the ark now? These questions have perplexed scholars and lay people for centuries.

One legend holds that the ark was hidden by the prophet Jeremiah on Mount Nebo, in present-day Jordan, where it remains to this day. Interestingly, this mountain is also rumored to be the site of Moses' death. (How fitting it would be for the father of the law to be buried by the base of the mountain where the Ten Commandments found their final resting place!) Another tradition has King Josiah hiding the Ark under an unspecified wood shed.

Two prominent Israeli rabbis have asserted that the ark is hidden in a cave beneath the Temple Mount in Jerusalem, directly under the site where the Holy of Holies stood during the temple periods. In fact, one of these rabbis claims to have come within 40 feet of the hiding-place when he was forced to stop his search because of tensions with Jerusalem's Muslims.

## ETHIOPIA? OR EGYPT?

Perhaps the best-known theory for the ark's disappearance has the fabled chest ending up in Ethiopia. When King Solomon's dalliance with the Queen of Sheba led to his siring a son, Menelik, the elders of Israel were forced to compete for the king's attentions. None too pleased with this situation, the elders demanded that Menelik return to his mother in Ethiopia. Solomon concurred, but on one condition: that the elders of the land each send their first-born son to Ethiopia along with

Menelik. And so it came to pass that Azarius, son of Zadok the high priest, got up and left the promised land with Menelik, son of Solomon. But he did not leave empty-handed. Before departing, Menelik crept stealthily into the temple, made his way silently into the Holy of Holies, and greedily stole the Ark of the Covenant from under his father's nose. And, some say, the ark remains hidden away in an Ethiopian church's chapel until this day, displayed publicly only once a year, during the Christian festival known as Timkat.

A similar theory places the ark in Elephantine, Egypt. The Jews from this region petitioned Jerusalem for permission to build a temple of their own. The nature of this request was highly controversial—and it is therefore hardly surprising that it took a whole two centuries for it to come to fruition. But it did: The son of the high priest at the time carried out the request and built a temple at Aswan.

THE BEST-KNOWN THEORY OF THE ARK'S DISAPPEARANCE HOLDS THAT IT ENDED UP IN ETHIOPIA. THE ARK WAS ONCE HOUSED IN A CHAMBER OF THE TEMPLE OF SOLOMON (ABOVE). A RENDERING OF THE ARK OF THE COVENANT (BELOW LEFT) IS IN THE ETHIOPIAN STYLE.

## WHAT IF...?

**PIECES OF THE PUZZLE** ▼

Theories about the Ark of the Covenant are many, and it is interesting to speculate about the effect its discovery might have on everything from Middle East politics to the separation of Church and State. Would the discovery of the fabled ark discredit certain religions? Create accord or discord among those groups which place faith in the Old Testament? Engender a legion of converts to Judaism? Christianity? Islam? If the ark truly possesses the powers attributed to it, could it become the ultimate implement of war? If so, who would be imbued with these powers? All of these questions, and many more, will have to wait. In the meantime, the search for the ark continues.

# Who Wrote the Bible?

**Scholars have debated for centuries about who wrote the most famous book in world history.**

THE BIBLE IS, FAR AND AWAY, THE MOST INFLUENtial book in the history of Western civilization. Its effects can be seen and felt every day in fields as diverse as politics and literature. Between 1777 and 1957, more than 2,500 English-language editions of the Bible were published. In 1982 alone, Americans spent $172 million on Bibles. The first English dictionary ever published (in 1530) was a glossary of biblical terms. Finally, and most ironically, the Bible is the book most frequently stolen from libraries and bookstores worldwide.

And yet we do not know who wrote the Bible. The question itself is actually misleading, given that "the Bible" is not one book but rather a compilation of dozens. In the case of the Old Testament, the question "who wrote it" generally refers to the Pentateuch, or the Five Books of Moses, which present the greatest difficulty in ascertaining authorship.

## THE OLD TESTAMENT

Traditionally, authorship of the Pentateuch was attributed to Moses himself. In the past, numerous scholars, researchers, and men of the cloth were excommunicated and excoriated for proposing that Moses was not the writer—this, despite the fact that the Pentateuch itself never claims Moses' authorship. In fact, ever since Talmudic times (135 BC–500 AD) certain sages have doubted that Moses wrote the entire Pentateuch alone.

These scholars noted that the section in Deuteronomy that describes Moses' death and its immediate aftermath could hardly have been written by Moses himself. Another such passage refers to a saying chanted at the temple mount which "is recited nowadays"—but the temple mount didn't exist until centuries after Moses had died. In the late 17th century, the Jewish scholar Spinoza postulated that the Pentateuch was not written by Moses but rather by Ezra the Scribe, who used Moses' writings as a basis for his book.

Spinoza was excommunicated for his views, but his theories provided the basis for modern critical scholarship of the Bible. His shift away from attributing at least most of the Bible to

Moses served as the springboard for further discoveries about the book's origin.

The most dominant of these theories is the "documentary hypothesis," which holds that the Pentateuch was written by four people with different backgrounds and distinctive voices. The documentary hypothesis took form based on discoveries regarding biblical doublets. (A doublet is the repetition of the same story in two or more locations within the Pentateuch.)

Scholars realized that while these doublets were often remarkably similar, important distinctions existed. The most notable difference concerned how the deity was named.

Scholars noted that within each version of a doublet's story, the Lord was referred to consistently as either Jehovah or Elohim, which is the Hebrew word for God. From this they deduced that the Pentateuch was, in fact, written by two separate authors. These scholars

A 14TH CENTURY DEPICTION OF ST. JEROME, AN EARLY CHRISTIAN SCHOLAR WHO, IN 378, BEGAN A NEW VERSION OF THE BIBLE AT THE REQUEST OF POPE DAMASUS I.

referred to the writer who called God Jehovah "J," and the author who called God Elohim was dubbed "E." Later, scholars noticed that within the narrative attributed to E, a good portion of the text had to do with priests and their functions. A third author, therefore, was assumed to have contributed to the writing of the Pentateuch; he was called "P," for priest. Finally, the book of Deuteronomy seemed to have a style unto itself, wholly separate from that of J, E, and P. A fourth author was therefore discerned by scholars and called "D," for Deuteronomy.

### THE NEW TESTAMENT

Mystery also surrounds the authorship of the Gospels of the New Testament, which tell of Jesus' birth, baptism, teachings, crucifixion, and resurrection. The word "gospel" means "good news," and it is these portions of Jesus' life upon which the gospels focus. Despite attributions of each gospel to the apostle whose name it bears, scholars are not at all certain whether Matthew wrote the Gospel According to Matthew, Mark wrote the Gospel According to Mark, and so on.

The Gospel According to Matthew, known as the First Gospel, is a handbook of rules and instructions for Christians. Composed sometime during the late first century, Matthew is noteworthy for its levelheaded tone. During the period of its composition, the Christian community was rife with what eminent New Testament scholar Burton L. Mack calls "the fantastic flight of early Christian mythic imagination...[and] apocalyptic temper." Despite this environment, Matthew is a decidedly down-to-earth rendering of Jesus' biography.

What first-century author, with his feet so firmly planted on the ground, penned Matthew? One thing seems certain: it wasn't Matthew. This first gospel is of anonymous authorship. And while it is possible that whoever wrote it used a collection of Jesus' sayings, assembled previously by Matthew himself, as a source, all we know for sure about him, says Mack, is that he considered himself "a scribe trained for the kingdom."

The Gospel According to Mark was probably written prior to any of the other gospels, though it follows Matthew in the New Testament. It is more biographical, and seems to be an elaborated compilation of the stories about—and quotations attributed to—Jesus that existed in the period leading up to its writing. Like Matthew, Mark is anonymous. Some scholars, however, think it probable that Mark indeed wrote this book in Rome, summarizing the teachings of Peter. Others, though, assert that Mark is merely legendary, and therefore could not have written this book.

The Gospel According to Luke was composed during the final third of the first century. It emphasized the importance and activity of the Holy Spirit in Jesus' life as well as the compassion he displayed toward the destitute. In Jesus, Luke found the embodiment of the Holy Spirit. Similarly, Luke emphasized the significant role women were to play in Christianity. But did Luke write the book which bears his name? There does seem to be significant evidence that this doctor, a friend of Paul's, indeed wrote the Third Gospel. But that evidence is by no means universally accepted. There are some who maintain that, for historical reasons, Luke simply could not have been the author of this work. As in the cases of Matthew and Mark—and many other nonbiblical texts from the period—the name of an apostle, or friend of an apostle, was likely added to this gospel at a date after its writing to impart it with an added air of legitimacy.

## JOHN'S ACCOUNT

While the first three Gospels—Matthew, Mark, and Luke—are often referred to as the "synoptic Gospels," in that they share so much in common that it may be instructive to read them as a unit, the Gospel According to John is different. John is a far more mystical account of Jesus, a cosmic rendering of his life and teachings. While John presents historical events as such, it interprets these events in metaphorical, mystical terms.

What metaphoric mystic wrote the Gospel of John? Possibly John, although many scholars agree that John himself could not have composed the text and that it is more likely the work of one of his disciples. Until relatively

recently, this Gospel was thought to have been written in about 90 AD. While many scholars still hold this to be the case, there are those who would ascribe an earlier date to this book.

Despite questions about the origins of the New Testament, the power and extraordinary beauty of its 27 books still moves and astounds anyone who reads and studies its teachings.

**THIS BELGIAN BIBLE MANUSCRIPT, CIRCA 1440, SHOWS FOUR EVANGELISTS AT WORK, AS DESCRIBED IN THE BOOK OF HOURS.**

---

## WHO WERE J, E, P, AND D?

Just who were the biblical authors that scholars have labeled with a mere initial? Examining those portions of the text attributed to each author gives a sense of their backgrounds. Each writer presents his own, subjective view of events, and by noting his various biases and focuses we learn something about him. E, for example, seems to have been a Levitical priest from the city of Shiloh; it is also possible that E was a descendant of Moses. P was probably an Aaronid priest

**PIECES OF THE PUZZLE** ▼

from Jerusalem who lived and wrote prior to the city's sacking in 587 BC. D, like E, was likely a priest from the tribe of Levi who lived in Shiloh. Finally, it seems clear that J hailed from the tribe of Judah, and probably lived sometime between 1200 and 722 BC. Something else of interest: Unlike the other authors, who were priests, J seems not to have been one. And because J placed a greater focus on female characters, one cannot rule out the possibility that J was a woman.

# The Shroud of Turin

THE ANCIENT, WATER-STAINED LINEN WITH THE FAINT imprint of a bearded man, his hands folded across his groin, had already been venerated for at least 200 years as Jesus' burial shroud when in 1578 it was brought to Italy for safekeeping. For nearly 500 years—except for a brief period during World War II—the shroud has been locked away in an ornate silver casket in a Turin cathedral. However, the tranquility of its repose has frequently been disturbed by those who doubt its authenticity, and their clamoring has grown louder in recent years as science and faith clash over the shroud's cryptic origins.

## A MYSTERIOUS IMAGE

The cloth's defenders do have some substantial evidence on their side. The imprint on the cloth shows a man with what appear to be wounds in his wrists and at his waist—possible marks of the crucifixion. In medieval iconography, Christ's wounds were traditionally depicted on his hands, complicating the charge made by skeptics that the cloth is the work of a medieval forger.

The print on the cloth is in the form of a negative photographic image, depicting both the front and rear views of a man. Many of the shroud's anatomical details were not discernible until the shroud was photographed and a positive version was created. More recently, one Israeli scientist performed tests on the shroud that revealed traces of two pollen species that coexisted only in one place and at one time in world history: first century Palestine, which would fit Jesus' time and place.

So, if the shroud is authentic, how was the ghostly image created? Sindonologists (from the Greek word for shroud, *sindon*) have proposed a number of solutions. Some claim that the imprint was caused by a stain produced by embalming oils smeared on the body. Others contend that gases leaving the pores of the body acted chemically on the cloth to produce the image, while another group suggests that Jesus emitted a certain form of radiation, a result of his personal agony, that acted on the cloth as light does on a photographic plate.

None of these theories have convinced the more skeptical scientists and archeologists, however, who insisted

A COMPUTER-ENHANCED IMAGE OF THE SHROUD OF TURIN MAKES CLEARER THE CHARACTERISTICS OF THE FIGURE.

CARBON DATING FOUND THE SHROUD IS NO MORE THAN 725 YEARS OLD, BUT SOME SINDONOLOGISTS DIFFER.

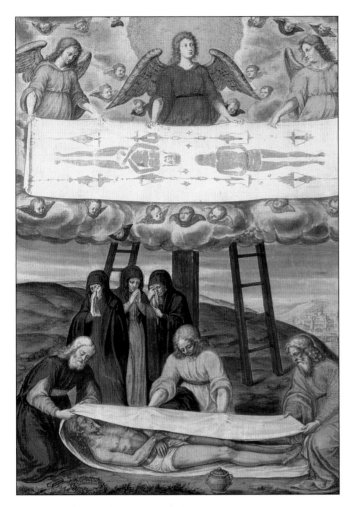

on subjecting the cloth to rigorous scientific testing. Finally, in 1988, scientists at the University of Arizona carbon-dated the cloth and concluded that it was no more than 725 years old and of European origins. These results were duplicated by three studies at three different labs. The Shroud of Turin, it seems, was a hoax.

## FINAL ANSWER?

This "final" verdict was not widely accepted by those who believed in the shroud's authenticity. Brother Bruno Bonnet-Eymard, a French priest, asserted that it was the carbon dating, and not the Turin Shroud, that had been falsified. Another startling theory claimed that the results had been altered by the Church. Authors Holger Kersten and Elmar R. Gruber argued in *The Jesus Conspiracy* (1992) that Christ had been alive when he was laid in the tomb. To defend the religious doctrine of the Resurrection, the authors argue, the Vatican had decided to dismiss the shroud as a phony artifact. Their theory notwithstanding, both authors believe that the shroud is the genuine article.

Even if the divine cloth is not, many mysteries linger. In the 14th century, false relics were ubiquitous, and the making and selling of them was big business. Could the shroud have been forged for money-making purposes in the marketplace of the past? Perhaps, but this seems unlikely, as the figure on the shroud is thought too naturalistic to have been painted by medieval painters.

"BLOOD" IMAGE

RUST LEFT BY OLD TACK

BURN MARK

A 16TH-CENTURY PAINTING (ABOVE LEFT) SHOWS HOW THE SHROUD MIGHT HAVE BEEN DRAPED. AT LEFT, PHOTO-MICROGRAPHS USED TO EXAMINE POSSI-BLE BLOOD, RUST, AND BURN MARKS ON THE SHROUD.

## THE WORK OF LEONARDO DA VINCI?

Scholars have speculated that if the shroud were a forgery the artist must have been a genius. In the quest for the authentic creator of the shroud, the name Leonardo da Vinci has surfaced.

Reflecting on his artistic brilliance, the 1982 film *The Silent Witness* concludes that da Vinci was the only individual who could have created such a forgery. Supporters of this theory include Lynn Picknett and Clive Prince, whose book *Turin Shroud: In Whose Image?* (1994) examines the theory that da Vinci transformed the ancient forgery.

**PIECES OF THE PUZZLE** ▼

Was an entirely different man enclosed within the shroud?

Some believe the holy cloth contained the body of a 14th-century Crusader who, in a blasphemous parody of the death of Christ, was crucified by the Saracens. This, at least, would account for the crucifixion-like wounds. Whether one defends the authenticity of the cloth or not, new studies and tests and increasingly complex theories are being proposed by both sides. Jesus' most important relic, like almost everything about him, seems destined to remain a mystery.

# Dead Sea Scrolls

## It is widely assumed today that many of these ancient manuscripts were written by the sect known as the Essenes. But why?

**WHEN DISCOVERED IN 1947, THE 800 SCROLLS WERE STORED IN CLAY URNS (ABOVE). A CONSTITUTION OF SORTS FOR THE ASCETIC ESSENE SECT WAS CALLED THE MANUAL OF DISCIPLINE (BELOW).**

THE UNEARTHING OF THE DEAD SEA SCROLLS, hailed as the greatest discovery of an ancient manuscript in modern times, has provoked as much controversy as progress in the various fields it has affected. Although these texts were discovered more than 50 years ago, many of them lay unpublished until recently.

The first set of Dead Sea Scrolls was discovered by a Bedouin shepherd in 1947, along the northwestern shore of modern-day Israel's Dead Sea. While leading his goats to water, Muhammad edh-Dhib tossed a stone toward a nearby cave where one of his herd had wandered. Something in the cave shattered, and his curiosity was piqued. Edh-Dhib returned the next day to investigate, and on entering the cave he discovered seven Hebrew scrolls, wrapped in linen and stored in clay jars. These

were the first of thousands of scrolls and scroll fragments discovered at Qumran—the Arabic name for the area. Today the scrolls are known collectively as the Dead Sea Scrolls.

### THE AUSTERE ESSENES

Although some debate persists over who wrote the Dead Sea Scrolls, they are widely assumed to have been the work of the Essenes, an ascetic sect of Jews who had journeyed south toward the desert in the middle of the 2nd century BC to distance themselves from the urban Jews who, they believed, practiced an illegitimate brand of Judaism. So austere were the Essenes that they are said to have been celibate. The Essenes are also thought to have shared their personal belongings with the community as a whole, much like a commune.

Several explanations have emerged regarding why these scrolls might originally have been deposited in the caves. It is possible that some of the caves were Essene homes, and the scrolls were remnants of personal libraries. Some scholars believe that the Qumran caves actually served as the communal library for the Essenes who dwelled nearby. Because of the haphazard fashion in which the scrolls were deposited in a number of the caves—11 caves with scrolls were discovered in the Qumran region—it has also been postulated that they were hidden hastily to avoid their destruction prior to the Roman onslaught in 68 AD .

army manual in sections, and seems to have been intended to prepare the Essenes, on a practical level, for an inevitable Armageddon.

## NON-ESSENE SCROLLS

Among the imported scrolls, books of the Bible are prominent. These scrolls, in fact, account for over a quarter of the 800 manuscripts found. The Qumran community clearly adhered to Scripture and thought it important. The book of Psalms is the most frequently found biblical manuscript at Qumran, with 36 copies. Deuteronomy and Isaiah lag slightly behind, at 29 and 21 copies respectively.

The popularity of the biblical works at Qumran shed light upon some of the prime concerns of Essene life. Those books of a legal nature—the final four books of the Pentateuch—probably served as a basis for the life style outlined in the Manual of Discipline. The book of Psalms may have been the foundation for several forms of worship.

The Dead Sea Scrolls also run parallel to portions of early Christian history. Some scholars postulate that Jesus' brother James was the Teacher of Righteousness described in the scrolls, an unnamed priest who was leader of the Essenes. Similarly, the Man of the Lie, the Teacher of Righteousness's historical enemy, is sometimes equated with Paul the Apostle.

Others theorize that the Teacher of Righteousness was John the Baptist, and Jesus of Nazareth was his nemesis. References to crucifixion are also cited as possibly connecting the Dead Sea Scrolls to early Christianity, although most scholars agree that such readings contradict archeological and scientific data that date many of the scrolls' composition prior to Jesus' birth. It does seem clear, however, that many ideas and phrases later included in the New Testament originated in these scrolls—documents that may never have come to light were it not for a shepherd tossing a stone.

THE CAVES WHERE THE SCROLLS WERE DISCOVERED ARE GENERALLY ON THE FACE OF CLIFF WALLS, AND HARD TO REACH. INSIDE, THE DARK CAVES ARE OFTEN INHABITED BY SNAKES AND SCORPIONS, MAKING THEIR EXPLORATION DANGEROUS. MOST OF THE CAVES WERE THEREFORE NOT EXPLORED FOR CENTURIES, SAFEGUARDING THE WRITTEN TREASURES THEY HELD.

The texts discovered at Qumran can be divided into manuscripts written by the Essenes themselves and those that were imported by the Essenes from elsewhere. The former are instructive in revealing how this group lived and what its members believed. The Manual of Discipline—discovered in the first cave by the Bedouin shepherd—was a strictly sectarian work, written by the Essenes themselves. It included a statement of who they were and what they believed; a guide for entrance into the group; a list of communal rules; a penal code; a discussion of their theology; and a hymn praising God.

The War Scroll, another document particular to the Essenes, describes a 40-year war that is to ensue at the end of the world, when the Sons of Light (the Qumran community) will battle their nemeses the Sons of Darkness, culminating in a final, crushing victory for the Sons of Light. This manuscript reads like an

# The Rise of Rome

**Romans believed their city originated with gods and heroes, but what were the real origins of its greatness?**

ANCIENT ROME GLORIED IN ITS MYTHIC ORIGINS. According to legend, the city was founded in 753 BC by twin brothers, Romulus and Remus, offspring of the god Mars and a vestal virgin named Sylvia. A villainous usurper threw the twins in the River Tiber, but they were washed ashore and cared for by a she-wolf. After many vicissitudes, the twins were returned to their grandfather. Later, Romulus killed Remus in a dispute over the best site for a settlement, then established the city that still bears his name.

Seven centuries later, Virgil adapted another legend about Rome's origins for his epic poem *The Aeneid*. It told the story of Aeneas, who fled from Troy after it had been destroyed by the Greeks. Aeneas's adventurous wanderings led him to Italy, where he received a prophetic vision of Roman history from the spirit of his dead father, Anchises. Aeneas's mother was the goddess Venus, and he was a forebear of Romulus and Remus. Virgil's version of this story satisfied Rome's dream of a link with the divine world. It was also a paean to the Emporer Augustus and the newly created Roman Empire.

## BEYOND LEGEND

In reality, Rome had humble beginnings. About 1000 BC, herdsmen settled in the region of present-day Rome. By the 7th century BC, their settlements combined into larger communities, of which Rome became the dominant center. At this time, the city fell under the benign control of Italy's chief power, the Etruscans, whose culture and language had a vital impact on the city. Greek culture, also introduced by the Etruscans, cast an even more enduring spell over the Romans. Despite these influences, Rome developed its own institutions. In 509 BC, the Romans created a republican form of government that lasted 500 years.

The early Republic preserved the Romans' simple rural way of life. Unlike their neighbors, they were a hard-working people who resisted the corrupting effects of ease and luxury. Their disciplined attitude helped them to assert control over the weaker states in the rest of Italy.

In a conflict over Sicily, Rome clashed with the North African power Carthage, waging intermittent warfare with the Carthaginians from 264 to 146 BC. The worst time came when invading Carthaginians, led by Hannibal, wreaked havoc throughout Italy. But Rome would survive, crush Carthage, and gain control of the western Mediterranean.

### PATRICIANS AND PLEBIANS

The Republic was initially controlled by the patricians (aristocrats). But the plebians (commoners) acquired their own elected leaders. The plebian leaders were discredited after their defeats during the Carthaginian invasions, and patrician generals, who saved Rome, took over as political leaders. The Senate, which made the republican system work, retained the right to appoint generals, but found it best to have these bellicose commanders fighting wars abroad in order to avoid conflict in Rome.

With its relentless war machine, Rome conquered Greece and the eastern Mediterranean, and its boundaries soon stretched from Egypt to the English Channel. Fabulous plunder poured into the capital, but its effect was disastrous: It opened up a vast gap between rich and

AN ANCIENT ROMAN BATH IN PLOMBIERS, FRANCE IS SHOWN IN A MID-16TH CENTURY WOODCUT.

poor. Troubles grew as the Republic gave way to civil strife and military dictatorship. Julius Caesar seized power, but his plans to reorganize the government alarmed the Senate.

The assassination of Caesar by a senatorial clique in 44 BC was supposed to bring about a return to republican government. Instead, it sparked a civil war, in which Caesar's adopted son, Augustus, triumphed. Although he kept some republican forms, he set up an empire with himself as emperor in 27 BC. As foretold in *The Aeneid*, Augustus gave Rome peace—a despotic peace—which lasted two centuries. When it ended in the late 2nd century AD, Rome's decline and downfall began.

## VIRGIL THE INFLUENTIAL

Virgil, the great Roman poet who wrote of Rome's legendary founding in *The Aeneid*, gained even greater influence after the Roman Empire had crumbled. In some of his poems, titled *The Eclogues* and published 30 years before the birth of Jesus, he wrote about the birth of a divine baby who would usher in a new age.

Considered by Christian scholars to be a prophet, Virgil and his works became a cornerstone of education up through the Renaissance. Writers would practice prophecy by interpreting Virgilian passages. The Roman poet also had an influence on writers throughout history: Dante used him as his guide

**TENDRILS OF TIME ▼**

through Hell in the *Inferno*, and John Milton imitated his style in his own epic writing. Thought to be more than a prophet—also a magician and necromancer—the poet's original name, Vergil, was changed by his loyal students to the common spelling Virgil— meaning soothsayer.

A ROMAN MOSAIC CAPTURES THE GREAT POET VIRGIL (OR VERGIL), WHO LIVED DURING THE REIGN OF AUGUSTUS.

# Caesar & Cleopatra

THE UNTIMELY DEATHS OF THOSE TWO GREAT LOVERS AND superstars of antiquity, Caesar and Cleopatra, undoubtedly amplified their celebrity. But the facts of his assassination and her suicide, mythologized by Shakespeare and by countless novels and films, can get lost in the glare of the legend.

To start, neither Caesar nor Cleopatra was especially attractive; when he met Cleopatra, Caesar was full-faced and balding, while the beauty of the great Egyptian queen, in the words of the ancient historian Plutarch, "was by no means flawless or even remarkable." What each had—and recognized in the other—was a vigorous charm, and a gift for amassing power.

BOTH GAIUS JULIUS CAESAR AND THE DAUGHTER OF PTOLEMY IX, QUEEN CLEOPATRA, WERE IMMORTALIZED IN STONE AND LEGEND.

When he met Cleopatra, Gaius Julius Caesar was, in fact, the most powerful man in the world, the ruler of the Roman Empire from 59 to 44 BC. After returning from a victorious military campaign in the East, on Feb. 14, 44 BC, Caesar declared himself *dictator perpetuus,* dictator for life. But several senators grew concerned that Caesar's power would threaten the republican nature of the Roman government. They were also concerned about his developing relationship with Cleopatra, who was then feuding with her siblings for Egypt's throne. Though she now might be associated with Egypt, Cleopatra was actually considered Greek. Her family, the Ptolemies, had ruled Egypt for three centuries and cloaked a largely Greek administrative and legal system with a veneer of Egyptian customs to satisfy the natives.

Many of the senators objected to a union between Rome and her traditional enemy, the Greeks. Their discontent grew strong enough to cause a cadre of senators to turn conspiratorial—and for a plan to assassinate Caesar, led by his main rival Cassius, to emerge.

## MURDER AT THE SENATE

The Senate had scheduled a meeting for March 15, purportedly for routine business, and the conspirators chose that date, known as the Ides of March, for an attack. They were able to recruit a few of Caesar's close friends into the scheme, including Cassius's brother-in-law, Marcus Brutus, by suggesting that Caesar was going to declare himself king on that day. In all, the conspiracy attracted about 60 people, with 20—all senators—to do the killing; the collective responsibility implicit in the act would allow them to transfer power to the senate.

The tradition of the Ides of March notwithstanding, Caesar actually heeded personal premonitions and his wife's advice to stay home that day (each had had disturbing dreams the night before). But Cassius recruited a friend of Caesar's to persuade him to come to the Senate meeting. As he left his house, someone—we do not know who—thrust a note into his hand. It went unread.

Caesar arrived at the Senate at around 11 A.M. He almost immediately received a petition and as he read it, the senators crowded around him. At the signal, one of them grasped Caesar's robe and pulled it down at the neck, and the designated first striker (a tribune of the people,

PAINTER NEROCCIO DE LANDI WAS ONE OF MANY ARTISTS TO RECORD THE VISIT OF CLEOPATRA TO MARC ANTONY.

named Casca) made a poorly executed stab that barely grazed Caesar's chest. But as Caesar tried to defend himself, he opened himself up to attack by the others.

Blinded by blood, Caesar covered his head with his robe. He said nothing until he saw Marcus Brutus make a thrust; his response was not *Et tu, Brute* ("You too, Brutus"). What he actually said was "You too, my child?". Caesar had a long affair with Brutus's mother and suspected he might be Brutus's father. Caesar received 23 wounds, only one of which could be called fatal. The note, which they found in his hands after his death, fully

**ARTISTS THROUGH THE AGES HAVE BEAUTIFIED QUEEN CLEOPATRA, WHO SUPPOSEDLY WAS RATHER PLAIN. THIS PAINTING IS BY FRENCH ARTIST A. CABANEL.**

disclosed the conspiracy. Had it been read, history would have been deprived of one of its most famous episodes.

### CLEOPATRA IN CHAINS

Meanwhile, Cleopatra was busy consolidating her power. Two years after Caesar's assassination, she took Mark Antony, one of the triumverate who now ruled the eastern part of the Roman Empire, as her lover. At Cleopatra's behest, Antony murdered the last of Cleopatra's Ptolemy rivals, and the two devoted themselves to a life of debauchery. Antony even left his Roman wife and married the Egyptian queen. His infatuation with Cleopatra began to incense those back in Rome, and eventually, Octavian, Caesar's heir, declared war on her. Antony and Cleopatra marshaled their troops, but they were no match for the might of the Roman army and navy; Cleopatra was taken prisoner by Octavian, who planned to march her through the streets of Rome.

However, the defiant Cleopatra committed suicide in her chamber to foil Octavian's plan—not out of grief over the death of Antony, who had himself committed suicide days before. Plutarch, the first-century Greek historian, is responsible for the story that her death was caused by the bite of an asp, smuggled into her room in a basket of figs. However, the tale cannot be substantiated. The asp was traditionally a symbol of the Egyptian royalty and would have added a nice touch. But, then again, witnesses did notice two marks on her arm.

## CLEOPATRA FOR THE AGES. . .IN HOLLYWOOD

Hollywood has romanticized the story of the sultry Egyptian Queen on film, featuring some of the movies' most famous actresses. Theda Bara starred in the 1917 version of *Cleopatra*.

Cecil B. DeMille's lavishly produced *Cleopatra* in 1934 featured Claudette Colbert as the Egyptian Queen; she played Cleopatra as a saucy coquette.

Apparently, DeMille thought he should have a chat with Colbert before casting her, thinking the final scene—Cleopatra committing suicide by clutching an asp to her breast—might frighten her. Before the scene, in which Colbert would mount the throne of Egypt for the last time, DeMille coiled an enormous snake around himself and walked onto the set. "Oh, Mr. DeMille, don't come near me with that!" she

**THE STUFF OF LEGEND**

exclaimed. "Well," said DeMille, "how about this?" He showed her a snake the size of an Egyptian asp. "That little thing? Give it to me!" she

cried, and played the scene flawlessly. The 1962 version of the story, starring Elizabeth Taylor, was a box office disappointment but a remarkable role for the actress. It had a huge budget and was a feast for the eyes, but left something to be desired in terms of historical accuracy.

# The Wrath of Mt. Vesuvius

**There's more to the volcano's story than the burial of Pompeii.**

**THE ANCIENT CITY OF POMPEII WAS BURIED IN ASH WHEN MT. VESUVIUS ERUPTED IN 79 AD. SOME OF THE DEAD WERE CAPTURED IN THE SETTLED ASH, ALLOWING ARCHEOLOGISTS TO MAKE PLASTER CASTS OF THE DECEASED (BELOW).**

FOR MOST PEOPLE, MT. VESUVIUS CALLS TO MIND the devastation of Pompeii, the ancient jewel of a city buried in ash when the famous volcano erupted in 79 AD. But two other sizable cities, Herculaneum and Stabiae, were destroyed at the same time. Vesuvius has, in fact, been erupting for the last 17 millennia—there have been about three dozen eruptions since Pompeii—producing devastating explosive eruptions every few thousand years and medium-force eruptions every few hundred.

An estimated 3,360 people were killed in Pompeii, Herculaneum, and other towns near

southern Italy's Bay of Naples. A deadlier eruption came more than 600 years later, in 1631. Though small by comparison, that eruption killed at least 3,500 people because there was a far larger population living in the mountain's shadow. It also signaled a new cycle of explosions, all damaging, and two of which were catastrophic. In 1794, the town of Torre del Greco was destroyed, and in 1944, San Sebastiano was the target of Vesuvius's wrath.

There was a considerable difference between the kinds of devastation visited upon Pompeii and Herculaneum, a difference that had to do with both geography and weather. Pompeii lies to the southwest of Vesuvius, whereas Herculaneum lies to the northwest. More significant is that Herculaneum had been built on a promontory between two streams that flowed down the slopes of Vesuvius—a propitious site as far as scenery and cool climate were concerned (the city's setting was the envy of the region), but one that lay in harm's way.

On the day of the eruption the prevailing wind was toward the southwest; this meant that when Vesuvius literally blew its top Pompeii was subjected to a rain of ash and pumice stone, or lapilli, while Herculaneum was swallowed by advancing waves of mud.

## TERROR IN TWO FORMS

No lava flowed over Pompeii, but ashes and lapilli settled over the city of 2,000 to a depth of at least 10 feet. The ash covering the bodies of the dead made it possible for modern archeologists to fashion plaster casts of the displaced space, yielding eerily lifelike sculptures of people in their final moments. Most appear to have been asphyxiated by lethal gasses. Many seem to be fleeing, but drop when they can no longer breathe: A father lifts himself on one arm as he tries to crawl toward his children; down the street, a man sits in a corner with his hands clasped over his nose and mouth.

But Pompeii's end was almost gentle compared to Herculaneum's. Rivers of hot volcanic mud (created when escaping steam mixed with earth, ash, and pumice) followed the stream beds and submerged the town to depths of 65 to 85 feet. Because the mud took longer to deluge the town than the ash and pumice did at Pompeii, the citizens had more time to escape.

But, unlike at Pompeii, where bodies were left intact, people who hesitated were caught in the hot mud and left as skeletons.

## WHAT NEXT?

Since 1944, Vesuvius has been in a state of repose, its longest sleep since the cycle that ended in 1631. But it has the potential to be even more dangerous and deadly today, since the surrounding area supports a population of some 2,000,000 people—one of the highest densities in the world. Given such density, vulcanologists believe that roughly three million people in outlying areas could be affected to some degree if Vesuvius were jolted awake.

FRENCH ARTIST JEAN BAPTISTE GENILLION DEPICTED THE ERUPTION OF VESUVIUS (BELOW), WHICH DESTROYED POMPEII AND HERCULANEUM. ONE PAINTING (LEFT) SURVIVED THE RAIN OF ASH.

## PLINY THE YOUNGER'S ACCOUNT

Pliny the Younger, who witnessed the eruption that destroyed Pompeii in the first century AD, described it to Tacitus:

EYE-WITNESS ▼

"You might hear the shrieks of women, the screams of children, and the shouts of men; some calling for their children, others for their parents, others for their husbands, and seeking to recognize each other by the voices that replied; one lamenting his own fate, another that of his family; some wishing to die, from the very fear of dying; some lifting their hands to the gods; but the greater part convinced that there were now no gods at all, and that the final endless night of which we have heard had come upon the world.

"The fire fell at a distance from us: then again we were immersed in thick darkness, and a heavy shower of ashes rained upon us, which we were obliged every now and then to stand up to shake off, otherwise we should have been crushed and buried in the heap."

# The Fall of Rome

**Rome wasn't built in a day, nor did it crumble in a day. In a sense, the empire had begun to fall as soon as it began to rise.**

ROME WAS AWARE OF THE ROLE OF POMP IN MAINTAINING CONTROL OF ITS FAR-FLUNG LANDS. A 19TH-CENTURY ENGRAVING SHOWS EMPEROR NERO, WHO RULED FROM 54–68 AD, AT A GLADIATOR CONTEST. BELOW, A ROMAN COIN BEARS THE FACE OF NERO.

HISTORY HAS ATTRIBUTED ROME'S DOWNFALL TO numerous causes, not the least of which was the relentless pressure exerted by barbarian tribes along its frontiers. From the time of its founding, Rome had successfully repelled myriad attackers and, by the 2nd century AD, the security of its European borders required little military effort. But this was not to last. When those many Vandals, Huns, and miscellaneous ruffians began arriving in ever greater numbers, Rome was growing smaller and weaker, making defense decidedly more difficult.

Stretching from northern England to the Middle East, the Roman Empire fluctuated in extent but it always encompassed the Mediterranean, which the Romans called *mare nostrum* ("our sea"). But Rome found that the gigantic and extraordinary empire it had so successfully created was too unwieldy to administer and protect. Its size awakened ambitious dreams of power in megalomaniacal generals and senators who waged wasteful internal wars to gain imperial control.

## A GOLDEN AGE ENDS

Until the late 2nd century AD, the smooth succession of emperors had ensured the stability of the empire. But this golden age ended with the death of the emperor and Stoic philosopher Marcus Aurelius (161–180 AD), who bequeathed the throne to his foolish son Commodius, whose assassination provoked a civil war. The Roman legions proclaimed their candidates as successors, but Septimius Severus, the commander of the largest battalions, was the winner. During his reign (193–211 AD), he diminished Rome as the imperial center and initiated a military despotism. His campaigns secured the imperial borders, and his last years were spent fighting in Britain. After his death at Eborcum (present-day York), the empire passed to his relatives, notable for their cruel and dissolute behavior. The last of his successors was assassinated in 235 AD.

There followed three decades of anarchy as one emperor after another briefly came to power. The army chose an emperor for benefits he might bestow. His short reign was spent fighting his rivals, and his life ended in battle or at the hands of his erstwhile supporters. These struggles weakened imperial authority, bankrupted the empire, and left the frontiers poorly defended. In western Europe, barbarians crossed the Rhine, overran Gaul, and penetrated as far as Spain and Italy. In the East, they invaded the Balkans and Turkey, while the rival Persian Empire conquered Armenia.

After 270 AD, Rome crushed all rebels, rivals, and barbarians, restoring unity in the empire. But the military was not what it had been. The troops, firmly rooted in their provincial bases, were reluctant to serve elsewhere. The emperor's presence was required to maintain his authority with his troops and, at the same time,

THE WESTERN
SECTOR OF THE
ROMAN EMPIRE
WOULD FALL LONG
BEFORE THE BYZAN-
TINE, OR EASTERN,
EMPIRE. RUINS OF
THE TEMPLE OF
JUPITER IN TUNISIA
ARE REMNANTS OF
BYZANTINE GLORY.

THE COLOSSEUM, ORIGINALLY THE FOCUS OF A MILITANT SOCIETY, DEGENERATED INTO AN ARENA FOR DIVERTING ENTERTAINMENT. WHEN ROME WAS ATTACKED BY SUCH BARBARIANS AS THE HUNS OF CENTRAL ASIA, LED BY ATTILA (BELOW), THE ROMAN ARMY WAS INCAPABLE OF DEFENDING IT.

he was expected to fight barbarians all along the frontier from England to Egypt. To ease this burden, the Emperor Diocletian (284–305 AD) divided the empire into eastern and western sectors, each with its own emperor, and in 285 AD moved the western capital to Milan to be closer to the northern frontier.

So began the empire's internal breakup. In 330 AD, Constantine, a Christian convert, made a Turkish city founded by Greeks, Byzantium, the East's capital. Rebuilt by Constantine, the city was renamed Constantinople. Constantine's new faith quickly took root and, despite religious disputes, strengthened a state destined to survive a thousand years more.

### THE DECLINE OF THE WEST
In the Western Sector, the collapse of the military and financial systems was more damaging than the barbarian threat. Diocletian, seeking to reestablish the currency, ordered balanced budgets and higher taxes. When defense spending outran revenues, the government devalued the coinage to hide the deficit. The resulting inflation destroyed the government's credit and crippled its power. When Diocletian moved the capital to Milan, Rome became provincial backwater. With the division of the

empire, Rome lost the wealth of the East, which flowed instead to Constantinople. As trade and industry dwindled away, people reverted to subsistence living. Towns were abandoned. Wealthy townspeople, weary of taxes and martial law, retreated to country estates. Impoverished rural folk left their own small farms to find work on these estates or in the fortified, if increasingly empty, towns.

### BARBARIANS AT THE GATES
By the late 4th century, many barbarians had converted to Christianity. At the same time, barbarian turmoil beyond Rome's frontiers

drove Visigoths, Vandals, and others to seek sanctuary within the empire, where they were permitted to settle. As a defensive measure, the Romans employed the new arrivals as mercenaries, and barbarian generals soon assumed military and political control.

In 402 AD, Rome's army led by Stilicho the Vandal beat back the Visigoths' invasion of Italy. But when Stilicho was murdered by the Emperor Honorius, the Visigoths poured in unopposed, demanding land and subsidies. Rome's refusal to negotiate signaled its ruin.

The Visigoths besieged the walled city, where plague and famine had already run rampant through the citizenry. Finally, in August 410 AD, the Visigoths, with help from slaves within the city, marched through its gates. Their sack of Rome was mild, almost respectful. But it dimmed Rome's prestige, and the city became prey for more ruthless barbarians.

The year 476 is usually given as the date for the fall of the Roman Empire. In that year, the barbarian general Odoacer deposed the last western emperor and, refusing to acknowledge the power of the emperor in the East, proclaimed himself King of Italy.

The event passed almost unnoticed. By this time, the regions in the West had been swallowed up by belligerent barbarians.

### THE ETERNAL CITY TODAY
Rome—often called "the eternal city"— revived, of course, and survives in much of its glory. In the Dark Ages, the Papacy established its importance as a spiritual center, and Roman ruins and monuments that include the Pan-

theon—a church for 1,000 years—now dominate the cityscape. In the Middle Ages and the Renaissance, Rome's citizens recycled stones and statues from ancient structures to build beautiful palaces and churches.

Whither Rome today? At the beginning of the 21st century, the city is engaged in a massive effort to renovate its ancient structures, piazzas, and multifaceted treasures. When the scaffolding is pulled down, Rome may be revealed as the true *caput mundi*—the head of the world— if not in power, then certainly in splendor.

## OMEN IN THE SKY

Some scholars say the struggles between Rome's new Christianity and the old atheism contributed to the fall of the Roman Empire. If so, the seeds were sown when Constantine the Great's Edict of Milan officially approved Christianity. But how was Constantine supposed to have been converted?

**WE MAY NEVER KNOW** ▼

Legend has it that on October 27, 312 AD, the night before a decisive battle with his rival, the soon-to-be Roman emperor saw a golden Chi-Rho cross, the sign of Christ, in the skies near the Milvian Bridge. On the cross were emblazoned the words, *In Hoc Signo Vinces,* or "With this sign, you will win."

Constantine embraced the prophetic miracle, and the next day handily defeated his opponent, crediting his victory to Christ and urging Rome to embrace the Lord. Constantine became the first Christian emperor and, in 313, gave Christians full freedom to practice their religion.

How likely was that evening occurrence? Con-

stantine did not seem too affected by it overall—he himself converted to Christianity only on his deathbed, and even that is disputed. Christianity did not even become the official religion under Constantine's rule—that happened 60 years after his death, about six emperors later.

Modern scholars theorize that the "vision" he had in the sky was the rare conjunction of Venus, Mars, Jupiter, and Saturn, which occurred around the October 27 date. In an attempt to rally his troops, the quick-thinking Constantine may have turned a possible bad omen into a prophecy of victory.

CONSTANTINE THE GREAT REBUILT THE CITY OF BYZANTIUM AND NAMED IT CONSTANTINOPLE, WHICH WOULD BECOME ISTANBUL. MANY OF THE CITY'S TREASURES, LIKE THE HAGIA SOPHIA ("CHURCH OF HOLY WISDOM"), DATE FROM THE ERA OF CHRISTIANITY.

# Did the Amazons Exist?

"WE ARE TOLD, NAMELY, THAT there was once in the western parts of Libya, on the bounds of the inhabited world, a race which was ruled by women and followed a manner of life unlike that which prevails among us. For it was the custom among them that the women should practice the arts of war, and be required to serve in the army for a fixed period, during which time they maintained their virginity; then, when the years of their service in the field had expired, they went in to the men for the procreation of children, but they kept in their hands the administration of the magistracies and all the affairs of state." The

**Did the women warriors of legend have real-life counterparts before the time of Christ? Or were they little more than a fantasy?**

quote is from Diodorus Siculus, the first-century BC historian, and it nicely describes the allure of the Amazons legend, part of the Greek mythology canon since the earliest days. But scholars have largely come to believe that the longevity of the legend is not so much a tribute to its truth as to that aspect of human imagination which it satisfies.

## AN INVERTED WORLD
Scholars point to our imaginative tendency to reverse familiar social roles and conventions. The Greeks lived in a male-dominated society where descent was traced through the paternal line, and the Amazon legend is a topsy-turvy

version of that world, where women were warriors and magistrates and its men were submissive, domestic males.

For such a legend to be credible, it would have to be located at the fringes of the world known by the Greeks. Indeed, the Greeks originally placed the Amazons' habitat in the region around the Caucasus mountain range, on what is now the Black Sea coast of Turkey. But when the geographic horizons of the Greeks expanded and the Black Sea was colonized, no Amazonian culture was found there.

Consequently, the legend was revised, and the Amazons' domain was moved farther out into the fringes. Of course, another legend would have to be created to reconcile this discovery, a task that was fulfilled by the Hercules myth. The hero was said to have traveled to the Amazonian kingdom, bested their queen Hippolyte in combat, and taken her belt to complete his ninth labor. He then banished the rest of the tribe, driving them farther east.

Early storytellers went to great imaginative lengths to explain how a society of women could produce offspring. In many versions of the legend, the society consisted completely of women—but in the more biologically feasible versions, the men were submissive rather than absent. Other variations of the legend had certain Amazons mate with deities, such as Ares, god of war, or Greek heroes, including Theseus, the slayer of the Minotaur.

## ROOTED IN CULTURE?

Is there any truth to the legend? There were some ancient cultures in which women were treated, to some extent, as equal—the Kurgan nomad society in Russia, for one—and it is possible that the Amazon myth evolved from early, exaggerated reports of such societies. And though there is no archeological evidence for the Amazon customs described by historians like Diodorus, there are indeed some ancient cultures in which women have had a military role. At an ancient grave in the southern Ukraine, for example, several female skeletons have been found buried with weapons, suggesting some martial involvement.

Ultimately, the greatest element of truth in this legend of women warriors is of the self-fulfilling sort. Throughout history, women, perhaps subliminally inspired by the Amazonian legend, have taken up arms themselves; there

# WARRIORS ON HORSEBACK

In many versions of the legend, the Amazons were the first people to ride horses into battle. Myrene, the legendary Amazon founder of the

ancient city of Smyrna, was said to have had a cavalry of some 30,000 women. There might even be some archeological proof to this theory: In an ancient burial site in what is now Kazakhstan, the curved leg bone of a female suggests a life spent on horseback. Some historians have also suggested that an early female tribe riding on horseback might have been the origin of the centaur—the mythic beast that is half human, half horse.

**AN 18TH-CENTURY GERMAN WOODCUT SHOWS AMAZONS, MEN, AND HORSES TANGLED IN BATTLE.**

are examples of Roman women gladiators as well as women crusaders and more than 8,000 females who defended the barricades during the French Revolution. In this way, the legend of the Amazons has broken free of its mythic confines and entered the world of history.

**THIS BATTLE DETAIL IS FROM THE SARCOPHAGUS OF THE AMAZONS, ON DISPLAY AT THE MUSEO ARCHEO-LOGICO, FLORENCE.**

# Who Was the Queen of Sheba?

## The mysterious visitor to King Solomon's court won him with her wisdom and her beauty— but who was she?

AN ETHIOPIAN MINIATURE SHOWS KING SOLOMON (AT LEFT) AT A BANQUET HONORING THE QUEEN (SEATED AT UPPER RIGHT). FOR MANY CENTURIES, THE SITE OF THE LAND OF SHEBA WAS UNCERTAIN, WITH SEVERAL COUNTRIES LAYING CLAIM. NOW, YEMEN—HOME TO RUINS THOUGHT TO BE MARIB—APPEARS TO HAVE GAINED THE EDGE OVER ETHIOPIA, SAUDI ARABIA, AND OTHER POSSIBLE LOCATIONS.

ALL SHE NEEDED WAS 25 LINES TO CAPTURE THE world's imagination. We know of the queen of Sheba, embodiment of a wise and exotic sensuality, from the tenth chapter of the Book of Kings in the Old Testament as well as the ninth chapter of the Book of Chronicles. But in neither book are we given any of the details that would satisfy our curiosity: her appearance, her history, even her name. She exists as a vague yet alluring historical phantom.

Assuming that the biblical account is correct, what we do know is this: On hearing about the fame of King Solomon, the wisest and most wealthy king of Israel, who ruled during the middle of the 10th century BC, the Queen of Sheba traveled to Jerusalem to meet him. She arrived with a very long caravan. Hundreds of camels bore spices and large amounts of gold as well as precious stones. Once within his court, she confronted the king with difficult questions, all of which he was able to answer.

Impressed with his wisdom, the queen presented him with magnificent gifts. Solomon in turn gave her whatsoever she asked and part of his royal bounty. After the exchange, the queen returned to her own land.

Some scholars have suggested that the trip was actually made for the purpose of negotiating trade routes, and especially for Sheba's use of Israel's ports on the Mediterranean. But the Bible remains silent about the reasons for the queen's visit. Nor have archeological investigations been any more helpful in filling out the tale. There are no other references to this mysterious queen in the annals of antiquity.

There is a rich folkloric tradition that fills in these historical gaps, though it is unclear how solidly these legends are based on historical fact. The queen of Sheba was a favorite subject of medieval Christian myths, where she sometimes appears as sorceress or is endowed with mystical properties. She is also, for some unclear reason, often associated with animals: One French Gothic sculpture presents her as the *reine pédauque*, the web-footed queen, while a German sculpture transforms her into a goose. In Islamic and Jewish texts, she is often associated with the magical hoopoe bird, and is even shown with hairy feet.

### THE QUEEN'S HOMELAND
Although we know very little about the queen herself, archeologists have been able to discover a great deal about Sheba, the land from which she hailed and one of the Arabian kingdoms bordering the Red Sea. It is referred to several other times in the Bible, and the name itself actually derives from a descendant of Shem, one of Noah's sons.

Sheba was a green and flowering land, watered through the use of a giant dam built at its capital, Marib. It derived much of its wealth from the trade in such spices as frankincense and myrrh, which grew on its verdant mountain slopes. The Shebans used the secret of the desert winds—which from February to August blow to the east—to navigate the treacherous desert terrain, and were able to monopolize trade in the region until the Greeks learned the secret sometime near the first century AD.

The Shebans were geographically isolated, allowing them to avoid invasion by the large armies, including Alexander the Great's, that ravaged northern Africa, and they resisted foreign attack until the end of the 4th century AD. However, their land was well known to classical historians such as Herodotus and Pliny, and references to it appear frequently in their works. It is interesting to note, however, that despite these references we first hear of the place only in the 8th century BC, about two centuries after the queen's visit to Solomon. Those earlier years, when the legendary queen might have ruled over the land, still lie hidden beneath her dark veil of silence.

## ETHIOPIAN ECHOES

**TENDRILS OF TIME** ▼

One of the most fascinating elements of the queen of Sheba myth is that of her child by King Solomon, named Menelik.

According to a 14th-century myth, Solomon seduced the queen during her visit with a cunning strategy: He threw a banquet for her but warned her that she must not take anything of his without his permission. When later in the night the queen, tormented by the spicy foods, took some water, Solomon accused her of violating their pact and demanded her favors in return. When the queen left Israel after converting to Judaism, she bore her son, Menelik.

When he grew older, Menelik became the first emperor of Ethiopia. The legend even goes so far as to claim that Menelik stole the Ark of the Covenant from Solomon's temple, and believers contend that it is buried with Menelik in his tomb at Aksum.

For more than a millennium, Menelik has played a crucial role in the coronation of Ethiopian kings. At the climax of the coronation of Haile Selassie, the nation's last emperor, Selassie stood under a magnificent Coptic cross and declared, "I am the son of David and Solomon and Ibna Hakim"—the Son of the Wise, or Menelik.

# Did Aliens Visit the Ancients?

### Mysterious artifacts and etchings in the earth pose the question of whether civilizations of the past encountered aliens.

THE FIGURES OF THE NAZCA LINES WERE CREATED BY DIGGING NARROW DITCHES THAT EXPOSED LIGHTER SOIL, THEN OUTLINING THE DITCHES WITH DARK GRAVEL. A BIRD FIGURE WAS INTERPRETED BY ERICH VON DANIKEN AS AN INTERSTELLAR LANDING STRIP.

IT IS A FANTASTIC IDEA—EXTRATERRESTRIAL LIFE coming to earth and influencing the development of past civilizations. But did aliens pay us a visit? Some Bible readers note the similarities that the visions of Ezekiel share with modern-day UFO sightings—airborne flaming wheels carrying "living creatures." Is it possible that the miracles described in the Bible and other ancient texts could have been no more than the reaction of primitive peoples to machines and advanced technology? (Imagine how mysterious a television or other modern devices would be to anyone even a hundred years ago.)

Pure speculation, or a basis in reality? In two cases—giant figures etched into a plain in Peru and the appearance of several mysterious crystal skulls—it appears we have the answer.

## THE NAZCA LINES

On a Peruvian desert plain between the Inca and Nazca valleys, the Nazca people left their legacy—a series of figures of birds, strange beasts, and unusual symbols engraved into dry earth. In an area that measures about 37 miles long and 15 miles wide, a set of perfectly straight lines forms a spectacular bird pattern

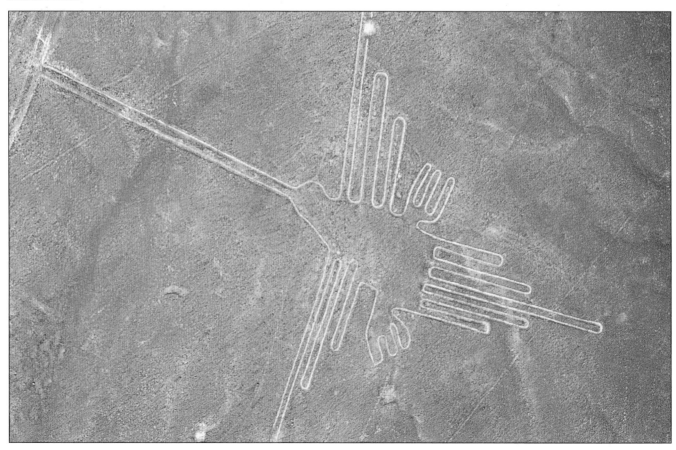

that captured the attention of the Swiss writer Erich von Daniken. So strikingly similar is the pattern to the interconnecting landing strips of a modern airport that von Daniken firmly believed the lines had been etched in the earth to function as an interstellar spaceport.

Although the ground upon which the figures are drawn is soft earth—unsuitable for the continued landing of either aircraft or space-craft—the speculation was fueled by the fact that it is impossible to view these figures from the ground. (This explains why the figures weren't discovered until the 1930s, when a pilot spotted them while surveying for water.)

Engineers studying the lines concluded that the terrain should have made it virtually impos-sible to construct such precise patterns from the ground. But skeptics who dismissed the notion that the plain was visited by aliens were soon to find the alternative nearly as difficult to believe—that ancient civilizations were some-how able to view the lines from a height.

In the early 1970s, Jim Woodman, the author of *Nazca: Journey to the Sun,* demon-strated that the Nazca people might indeed have been able to see the lines from on high—by flying. All they needed, he showed, was rope and tightly woven textiles, and they would have been able to construct a hot-air device powered by bonfires on the ground.

Duplicating samples of cloth found on the bodies of pre-Columbian Nazcans, Woodman built such a balloon. On November 28, 1975, his balloon rose over the plain, demonstrating that it was possible for the ancient inhabitants of Peru to be airborne. Moreover, many of the ground patterns are repeated on Nazca tex-tiles, and as glyphs on pottery, confirming that the lines had meaning to the inhabitants of the plains. It now remains for archeologists to find physical evidence that ancient Peruvians had taken man's first flight, centuries before it had been previously thought possible.

## THE CRYSTAL SKULLS

Speculation also swirled around a group of crystal "skulls" that mysteriously came to light in the late 19th century. Because some experts insist that only 20th-century power tools and diamond-coated bits could have shaped a material as hard as crystal, believers in alien visitations were quick to attribute an extrater-restrial origin to the strange artifacts.

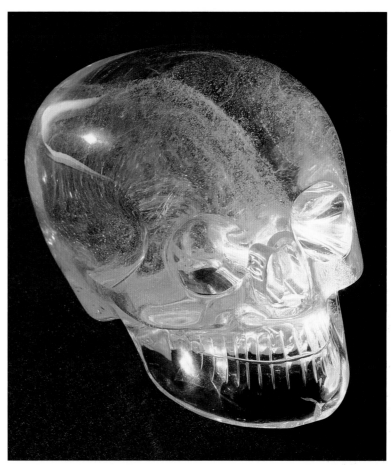

Two of the most famous skulls belong to the Smithsonian Institution and to London's Museum of Mankind, which purchased theirs from Tiffany's in the 1890s. (Tiffany's had obtained it from a Monsieur Baubin, a French-man who dealt in antiquities.) The most con-troversial crystal skull is another—the Mitchell-Hedges skull, named for its Canadian owner. While Anna Mitchell-Hedges of Kitchener, Ontario, has always claimed that she found the skull in 1924 while on an archeological expedi-tion with her father in Central America, some researchers have cast doubt on her story.

Scientists at Hewlett–Packard examined the crystal skulls in their materials laboratory but could not explain how these objects were cre-ated by ancient civilizations, which lacked the tools required to carve quartz crystal. Some speculate that during long periods of time, gen-erations of devoted workers may have finished the shaping of the skulls by painstakingly rub-bing the crystal with an abrasive substance like sand. Others point to a group of 19th-century German craftsmen who specialized in crystal ornaments, identifying them as the more likely, and conclusively earthbound, explanation.

THE QUARTZ OF THE CRYSTAL SKULLS SHOULD HAVE BEEN VIRTUALLY UNCARV-ABLE BEFORE THE DIAMOND-COATED BIT ARRIVED IN THE 20TH CENTURY. COMPOUNDING THE MYSTERY, NO TOOL MARKS ARE FOUND ON THE SKULLS.

# Did Atlantis Exist?

THE MYSTERY OF THE SUNKEN CITY OF Atlantis, lost and glittering somewhere on the ocean floor, has fascinated people for centuries. But few realize that the source of the legend isn't some crackpot dreamer but the father of Western thought, Plato, the Greek philosopher (c. 427–347 BC). Indeed, the only extant references to Atlantis from antiquity occur in two of Plato's dialogues: *Critias* and *Timaeus*. In them, Plato (through the character of Critias, Plato's cousin) describes a vast island paradise, rich in metals and dotted with luxurious gardens, that existed somewhere off the coast of the Straits of Gibraltar. The city, which had conquered the surrounding regions with its mighty navy, was protected by Poseidon, the god of the sea. However, when the island's inhabitants became corrupt and began to worship other gods, Poseidon punished them with "a single

**Did the lost city of Atlantis, protected by Poseidon, the mythical god of the sea, exist on a lost island in the Aegean Sea?**

day and night of misfortune in which the island of Atlantis disappeared into the depths of the sea."

### A PHILOSOPHICAL DEVICE?

Plato reveled in allegories and fables, and some scholars—including Plato's student, Aristotle—have speculated that the legend of Atlantis was merely a philosophical device, a way to highlight the dangers of national conceit. But some historians believe otherwise and have searched antiquity for signs of an actual event that might correspond to this devastating cataclysm. The search reached a peak of intensity during the 15th century, the age of European exploration; any newly discovered territory was a candidate to be the Lost City. In fact, when America was first discovered, many considered it Atlantis—although there was no evidence that the New World was ever submerged in water.

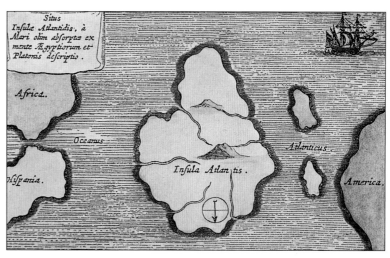

In fact, the United States itself has harbored more than its share of Atlantis fanatics. Congressman Ignatius Donnelly published his best-selling *Atlantis: The Antediluvian World* in 1882, which posited that Atlantis was an island continent that existed between the Old and New Worlds. Donnelly claimed that the existence of Atlantis explained the similarities between the pre-Columbian civilizations of America and ancient Egyptian culture, including the building of pyramids and the 365-day year. Both cultures originated on Atlantis, said Donnelly, and moved to their respective continents when the island was submerged.

## THE THEORIES MULTIPLY

In the decades that followed, more theories bubbled to the surface, placing Atlantis everywhere from Tibet to the Amazon basin to the Bahamas. But the most plausible account situated the island in the vicinity of Greece.

Modern day seismologists and vulcanologists have scoured the historical record to find an event of such cataclysmic proportions that it could literally destroy an entire civilization, and the most promising match occurred on an island in the Aegean Sea. Some 3,500 years ago, a tremendous explosion rocked the island of Kallisté, now known as Santorini, the southernmost of the Cyclades Islands. The eruption had the force of 500–1,000 atomic bombs and deposited ash over an area greater than 300,000 square miles. Kallisté was an outpost of the larger island of Crete, which was then at the height of its decadence. In fact, archeologists have excavated the ruins of magnificent cities that seem to match the ones described by Plato in his dialogues. The eruption on Kallisté created tidal waves that quickly spread to Crete, destroying many of its ports, including its magnificent capital, Knossos—in its time, the largest city in the eastern Mediterranean. Crete never recovered and soon waned in power—interestingly, a trajectory of rise and fall quite similar to that of Atlantis.

So how did the legend emerge? In the dialogues, Critias claims he heard the tale from his

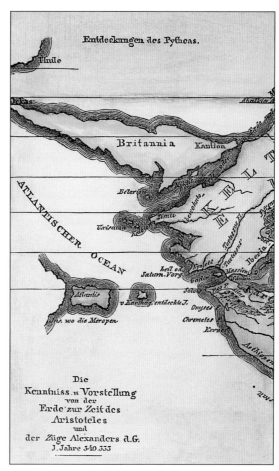

ATLANTIS APPEARED ON MAPS AS LATE AS 1831 (LEFT, BY THE BERLIN MAPMAKER IGNACY LELEWEL). A 1678 MAP FROM KIRCHER'S *MUNDUS SUBTERRANEUSAS* (ABOVE) SHOWED ATLANTIS SITUATED BETWEEN AFRICA AND AMERICA.

great-grandfather, who traces the story back to Egypt. Egyptians were not themselves a seafaring people, but they did trade extensively with the Cretans and had no doubt heard tales of Crete's grandeur. After the eruption, when the Cretan ships suddenly disappeared, it might have seemed to Egyptians as if Crete simply vanished. It is quite possible that over time, that idea amassed the barnacles of narrative embellishment and was transformed into the legend of the Lost City of Atlantis.

# PART 3

# THE MIDDLE AGES

DURING THE RENAISSANCE, THE MIDDLE AGES WERE LOOKED BACK ON AS A time of disaster and pain. If peasants weren't being oppressed by the manorial lords, they were being slaughtered by Crusaders, pillaged by invading bands of barbarians, tortured by inquisitorial zealots, or ravaged by plague or by the many epidemics that flared during the period. But in the past hundred years, our view of the Middle Ages has changed.

This was also a time when great ideas took shape, despite the usual clashes. Why was it the Church, not the British, who burned Joan of Arc at the stake? Who, and what, made printing possible? And who were the legendary figures of King Arthur, Robin Hood, and Lady Godiva? Just as the elaborate illuminations in the manuscripts that have survived the medieval period become entwined with the words in those works, so have the fables that survive illuminate history's shards of evidence.

# Was there a Robin Hood?

### "Robyn was a proud outlaw," sang balladeers of the intrepid woodsman. But did Robin Hood even exist? And why has his legend persisted?

THE LEGEND OF ROBIN HOOD HAS CAPTURED THE WORLD'S IMAGINATION FOR THE PAST FOUR CENTURIES. SHOWN HERE IS A LATE 19TH-CENTURY ILLUSTRATION OF ROBIN AND A BOWMAN.

IT SEEMS ALMOST AN INJUSTICE TO QUESTION THE Robin Hood legend, such is our innate appreciation for the celebrated champion of the underdog and the common man. Scholars who seek to debunk parts of the legend are practically accomplices to the evil Sheriff of Nottingham; and yet it is the historian's duty to examine the past, however entertaining the legend handed down to us. In the 19th century, scholars who had grown up with the beloved chivalric tales of Sir Walter Scott reexamined the Robin Hood stories and found them wanting in historical foundations. In his 1882 *English*

*and Scottish Popular Ballads,* scholar Francis James Child declared Robin Hood a fiction, "absolutely a creation of the ballad genre." But in later years, more research has suggested there may be some truth to the legend.

The first known, extended version of the Robin Hood story is the 15th-century ballad collection *Lyttle Geste of Robyn Hode.* It contains the familiar cast of characters: the sheriff of Nottingham, Robin, Little John, and the rest of his "merrie men" who steal from the rich and give to the poor in their forest lair. In many of the early versions of the tale, the sylvan locale is Barnesdale forest, in Yorkshire. But references to Robin Hood appear in stories and ballads from as early as the mid-14th century, so historians speculate that if there was a historical "prince of thieves," he lived sometime before then. In the manorial rolls and similar local records from 1228 and 1230, the name Robert Hood appears, and he is described as a fugitive from justice, who stole "for the benefit of the many." But the name Robert Hood was actually a quite common one at the time, making the census evidence inconclusive.

## CLAIMS AND CONTRADICTIONS

One of the greatest difficulties in dating the hero is the contradictory historical references within the legends; various suggestions within the ballads place him in the reign of four separate English kings, from Richard the Lionheart (r. 1189–1199) to Edward II (r. 1307–1327). The monarch with the strongest link to Robin Hood is Richard, who ruled in the late 12th century and was opposed by his brother and eventual successor King John. But Robin has also been linked to a 1265 revolt against King Henry III, led by his brother-in-law Simon de Montfort. According to the early historian Walter Bower, after the rebellion against Henry, "the famous robber Robin Hood. . . rose to prominence among those who had been disinherited and banished on account of the revolt." However, modern historians have pointed out that the longbow, which features so prominently in many of the Robin Hood legends, was not in general use at the time of King Henry III, casting doubt on Bower's claim.

The candidate with the most plausible claim to Robin's identity is a tenant of Wakefield, Yorkshire, in the early 14th century, who was probably involved in an uprising against the Earl of Lancaster in 1322. The 1320 Manor Rolls of the town list a Robert Hood who had been charged with breaking "forest laws," resisting the lord of the manor, and negligence in fighting against the Scots. There is also some indication that Hood's home was confiscated because of this dereliction of duty, which might account for his move to the forest. The Wakefield Robin would place the story in the reign of King Edward II, and indeed, there is a record of the king taking into his service one "Robert Hood" as a court valet.

## A LITERARY STEW

Despite the effort historians have spent searching for the first historical Robin Hood, most agree that the legend has evolved so dramatically over the centuries that its original inspiration might very well be unrecognizable, even if discovered. Maid Marian, the story's love interest, did not appear until the 16th century, nor did the earliest versions of the tale feature the portly Friar Tuck. In other versions of the story, Robin is actually motivated less by righting injustices than by national pride, fighting for the Saxon people against the conquering Normans. Some scholars have even contended,

with much controversy, that Robin Hood and his "merrie men" were actually members of a gay community forced to live outside the city, beyond the reach of the law and the Church.

What is not disputed is that the story of Robin Hood, the archetypal outlaw-hero, took on the characteristics and details of many outlaw ballads, becoming a sort of literary stew of local lore and contemporary events. In fact, the story was so susceptible to adaptation and interpolation that in 1773, the lexicographer Samuel Johnson claimed that he could fabricate a Robin Hood legend that readers would swear they had known their entire life.

Those who enjoyed the Robin Hood legend, with its colorful cast of characters in pursuit of justice for the common man, didn't mind if it had evolved through the centuries; they expected no less, for so powerful is the love of justice that heroes who champion it necessarily become larger, greater, and more entertaining than anything history could produce.

ON THE SCREEN, ERROL FLYNN PLAYED ROBIN IN 1938 (ABOVE). THE AMERICAN PAINTER N.C. WYETH'S COLOR ILLUSTRATION FOR A 1917 COLLECTION OF TALES (BOTTOM LEFT) SHOWS THE QUILL-TOTING BANDIT MEETING MAID MARIAN FOR THE FIRST TIME, AT A ROYAL TOURNAMENT.

## A HOST OF HOODS

Many other rebels, outlaws, and miscellaneous outcasts have been suggested as the historical Robin Hood. Among them are Sir Robert Thwing, who led a movement where he and his devotees raided monasteries, stealing grain and distributing it to the poor; and Robert Fitzhooth, claimant to earl of

**THAT NAME AGAIN?** ▼

Huntington, who was born about 1160 and died in 1247. Fitzhooth is a more likely candidate, as some historical documents actually cite these particular dates for Robin Hood's birth and death. But critics point out that more recent records do not mention a defiant nobleman bearing the Fitzhooth name.

# The Legend of King Arthur

**A MEDIEVAL IMAGE OF ARTHUR, RULER OF 30 BRITISH KINGDOMS, GLORIFIED THE KING WITH 30 CROWNS AT HIS FEET.**

WITH NO CERTAIN PROOF THAT KING Arthur ever existed, some historians have concluded he is only a legend. Yet if he never lived, why did people believe for so many centuries that Arthur was a real person?

The answer begins with a book. Somewhere between 1135 and 1139, Geoffrey of Monmouth, an ecclesiastic and chronicler, published a Latin tome called *Historia regum Britanniae* ("The History of the Kings of Briton"). This mixture of fact and fancy portrays King Arthur as a monarch of truly heroic proportions. In its own time, the book was dismissed by the historian William de Newburgh, who called Geoffrey the "father of lies" and derided him for "cloak[ing] fables about Arthur under

the honest name of history." Despite William's carping, there is archeological support for some of Geoffrey's stories. For instance, he claims that Arthur was born on the island stronghold of Tintagel on the northern coast of Cornwall. Modern archeologists have discovered the remains of a stronghold there, which suggests that Geoffrey was not being purely fanciful.

## A WARRIOR IN DARK TIMES

Before the publication of Geoffrey's book, Arthur's name had already appeared briefly in early chronicles. The *Historia Brittonum* of the 9th-century Welsh monk Nennius describes Arthur as the *dux bellorom* ("leader of troops") who crushed invading Saxons at Mons Badonicus (Mount Badon), a site that has never been identified. Gildas' *De excidio et conquestu Britanniae,* dating from the middle of the 6th century, makes no reference to Arthur but suggests this battle was fought about 500 AD. The Mons Badonicus victory is mentioned in the 10th-century *Annales Cambriae,* which also records a battle at Camlann where Arthur reputedly fell.

From these tenuous sources, some historians believe Arthur may have been a 5th-century Christian British warrior who defended his country against Saxon invaders in the turbulent days after the departure of the Romans. Unable to stem the invaders, Arthur's followers fled to the mountains of Wales where, through many long and turbulent centuries, they told tales that transformed an obscure warrior into a world-class hero, who fought not only in Britain but also abroad.

Geoffrey's sources for Arthur were these tales, which he had probably heard in his Welsh homeland. The *Historia regum Britanniae* describes Arthur's beautiful wife Guinevere, his treacherous nephew Mordred, and the powerful magician Merlin. It also mentions a popular belief that Arthur was not dead, but would return to deliver his people from their enemies. To this day, Arthur is called "the once and future king."

In the Middle Ages, when most people confused legend and history, English monarchs used Arthurian symbolism to promote patriotism and enhance their own prestige. By the early 17th century, however, skeptical historians had extinguished the legend's hold on the populace.

Geoffrey's vision of Arthur spread to the Continent, where the story enjoyed tremendous popularity during the 12th and 13th centuries. French writers such as

Most modern historians have doubts about King Arthur's existence, but this has not always been so. During the Middle Ages, it was thought to be good for Britain's morale that royalty should be heirs of such a famous king. English kings not only believed in Arthur's existence, but some claimed kinship: Edward I (in a medieval portrait, right) claimed that, as Arthur's heir, he had a right to rule Scotland as well as England.

**PIECES OF THE PUZZLE**

Chrétien de Troyes and Marie de France added some of the legend's enduring elements, such as the love story of Lancelot and Guinevere, the Knights of the Round Table, and the quest for the Holy Grail. In 1469, the first English printer William Caxton issued Sir Thomas Mallory's *Morte d'Arthur,* which told Arthur's story as we now know it. The legend has continued to inspire writers, notably the poet Alfred Tennyson, whose *Idylls of the King* revived Victorian interest in Arthur.

**A 15TH CENTURY MINIATURE SHOWS "THE ONCE AND FUTURE KING" PRESIDING OVER THE KNIGHTS OF THE ROUND TABLE.**

### THE MYSTERIOUS RIOTHAMUS

The search for the real Arthur continues. Some historic documents lend support to Geoffrey's claims that Arthur left Britain to fight abroad. Although most historians doubt this, the British historian Geoffrey Ashe believes otherwise. Ashe is co-founder and secretary of the Camelot Research Committee, which was responsible for the 1966-70 excavation of Cadbury Castle—a strong possibility for the site of King Arthur's Camelot. Ashe decided to take Geoffrey seriously. In his search for clues outside Britain, he discovered records of a "king of the Britons" who led an army to France around 470 AD. In one document, a king who could be Arthur is referred to as Riothamus, which translates as "supreme royal."

Until archeologists or historians turn up something truly conclusive, King Arthur will remain a tantalizing, shadowy figure. He is the stuff of legend—a heroic portrait, possibly assembled from lives of several kings. As yet, no one is ready to forget his story, which has fascinated so many for centuries.

**KING ARTHUR, SHOWN ON HORSEBACK IN A 14TH CENTURY FRENCH WORK, HAS LONG INSPIRED WRITERS AND ARTISTS THE WORLD OVER.**

# The Rise of the Catholic Church

**The influence of the Catholic Church on world history is tremendous, but in the midst of war and bloody Crusades, the Church faced much conflict in its rise.**

THE CATHOLIC CHURCH, ESTABLISHED NEARLY 2,000 years ago, is the oldest institution in the Western world. There is, simply put, no way to estimate the immense influence the Church has had in determining the course of history. We are all familiar with certain trappings of the Catholic Church—the white-clad Pope waving to an adoring crowd from the confines of the "popemobile" or the gorgeous vision of the Sistine Chapel in the Vatican City—but how did the Church become what it is today?

## GROWTH IN ROME

The Catholic Church began in Jerusalem shortly after the crucifixion of Jesus and by the middle of the first century AD was centered at Rome. Initially comprising a small group of Jesus' disciples, the Church rapidly expanded throughout the Roman Empire. The term "the Catholic Church" was introduced by St. Ignatius (d. 110 AD), a Syrian Bishop.

Christianity's swift expansion through pagan Rome did not go unchecked; Roman emperors harshly persecuted the early Catholics for their opposition to the Roman moral code, or, as the Christians perceived it, the lack thereof. As is often the case, however, this subjugation, culminating frequently in Christian martyrdom, only served to fortify Christianity and hasten its spread across the length and breadth of Europe.

The oppression of Christians subsided in 312 AD when the Roman Emperor Constantine I

converted to Christianity after having had a vision of the cross with the words, "By this sign, you will conquer." Constantine marked his soldiers' shields with the cross and proceeded to stampede his brother-in-law and rival Maxentius at the Milvian Bridge. The cross, he believed, had secured his victory.

In 313 AD, Constantine, in coalition with Licinius, Emperor of Rome's Eastern empire, issued the Edict of Milan, ushering in a period of religious tolerance. The edict came to have an enormous impact on both the Church and the Roman Empire. By making Christianity an officially sanctioned religion, it brought all aspects of the Church to the forefront of Roman life. The spread of Christianity was

**CONSTANTINE'S VISION MAY HAVE BEEN THE MOST INFLUENTIAL DREAM IN HISTORY. IT IS DEPICTED IN A LATE 14TH CENTURY FRESCO BY THE FLORENTINE ARTIST AGNOLO GADDI.**

CONSTANTINE THE GREAT CONVENED THE COUNCIL OF NICAEA (325 AD) TO RESOLVE DISPUTES THAT HAD ARISEN BETWEEN CHURCH AND STATE. BISHOPS PRESENTED THE EMPEROR WITH A LARGE BUNDLE OF GRIEVANCES; WITHOUT READING IT, CONSTANTINE SET ALIGHT THE ENTIRE BUNDLE, BURNING IT BEFORE THEIR EYES. SO IT WAS THAT THE SQUABBLING CAME TO AN ABRUPT HALT. IN A SYMBOLIC 4TH-CENTURY MOSAIC (ABOVE AND BELOW) A ROOSTER REPRESENTS LIGHT AND A TORTOISE REPRESENTS DARKNESS.

encouraged, and it was given a magnificent home by Constantine with the erection of the Lateran Palace in Rome, where the Bishop of Rome ruled. In 320 AD Licinius reinstituted the persecution of Christians in his realm and was later ousted from power by Constantine.

Having consolidated leadership of the empire, Constantine encouraged the Church to flourish even further. By the end of the 4th century, Christianity had become the official religion of the Roman Empire, establishing what is known today as Roman Catholicism.

During the reigns of Constantine and his successors, the line between Church and State became blurred. The Roman emperors saw themselves as both heirs to the traditions of the caesars of yore and forebears of the apostles' mantle. In such a capacity, these leaders were involved not only in political decision making but also in sacred matters. Emperors frequently participated in affairs of church administration, doctrine, and liturgy. When a controversy erupted in Egypt over the nature of the relationship between the Father and the Son, Constantine convened the Council of Nicaea to resolve the disagreement. On May 20, 325 AD, approximately 220 bishops joined the Emperor in a spirited debate on this issue. The result was the well-known formula stating that Christ was "one in being with the Father"; that is, both were of the same essence. While this compromise did ease tensions, the argument smoldered on long after Constantine's death.

That is not to say that the Church did not maintain some degree of autonomy; it did. During the 8th and 9th centuries, a number of emperors (most in Rome's East) attempted to remove icons from church worship. Their efforts were resisted, and eventually defeated, by those who believed that the functions of Church and State ought to be more rigidly differentiated. Chief among the proponents of autonomous legislative power for the Church were monks and empresses. Their successes eventually led to a severe abridgment of the emperors' ability to influence church doctrine.

The coming of the Middle Ages heralded a shift in the seats of power for the Roman Empire as a whole, and for the Church in particular. When the imperial capital moved to Constantinople (modern-day Istanbul), the papacy overtook the empire, and the bishops of other nations became paramount in determining the course of Christianity in terms of religion and doctrine. The establishment of the pope's primacy reflected the culmination of the papacy's gradually expanding influence, which had occurred over the course of many years.

## TWO MEDIEVAL EPISODES

Along with the ascendancy of the pope, the Middle Ages are well known for two events that might be categorized today as "public relations blunders." The Crusades and the Inquisition were attempts by the church to assert the Church's supremacy both within its domain and against the newly emerging realm of Islam.

Following the death of Mohammed, the founding prophet of the Muslim faith, Islam spread with dizzying speed—more quickly, in fact, than Christianity had expanded. Among Islam's territorial acquisitions during this phase were several of Christianity's holy places, including Jerusalem. To recapture the holy sites themselves and to diminish the prestige Islam seemed to have usurped from it, the Church launched eight Crusades, beginning in 1096 AD. Only the first of these military expeditions proved successful, with the capture of Jerusalem in 1099. Nearly 90 years later, under the leadership of the sultan Saladin, the Mus-

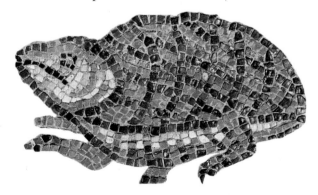

lims won Jerusalem back.

In the early Middle Ages, non-believers came to be regarded by Christendom as enemies of society. The emergence of heretical groups such as the Waldenses and the Cathari in France during the 11th and 12th centuries prompted Pope Gregory IX to institute the first Inquisition to locate and try heretics.

Once apprehended, suspected apostates were given the opportunity to confess their heresy and repent. Barring a confession, the disbeliever was brought before the inquisitor. In accordance with the dictates of the bull Ad Extirpanda, issued by Pope Innocent IV in 1252, the suspect was sometimes tortured to obtain a confession. The decree sanctioned torturing a heretic only once; but inquisitors interpreted this to mean once per session, leading to torture on multiple occasions.

Although the Inquisition was initiated and developed in northern Europe, it soon spread south, where it entered its most notorious phase—the Spanish Inquisition. Starting in Seville, this Inquisition became too brutal for the tastes of several popes who were compelled to intervene. Pope Sixtus IV's mitigating efforts failed, and in 1483 he was induced to appoint Tomás de Torquemada the Grand Inquisitor for Castile. During Torquemada's reign, some 2,000 convicted heretics met their death, often in public and gruesome spectacles; a large percentage were Jews, who were burned at the stake. Pope Alexander VI, troubled by Torquemada's excesses, appointed four special

inquisitors to restrain him, to no avail.

Once found guilty, heretics were paraded at an "auto-da-fe" ceremony, at which sentences were pronounced for the condemned. This spectacle was a source of celebration in Spain; cheering crowds looked on as the prisoners, heads newly shaven, were burnt at the stake.

## THE REFORMATION

With the 16th century came the advent of the Reformation, a movement reflecting dissatisfaction with the strictures of papal authority and the corruption of this institution. In the past, reform movements within Christianity had fallen decidedly within the rubric of Catholicism; reform was expressed through a

MARTIN LUTHER ATTACHES THE THESES AT THE CASTLE CHURCH OF WITTENBERG IN 1517 (ABOVE RIGHT). MARGIN AND BOTTOM RIGHT: DETAILS FROM AN 18TH-CENTURY ENGRAVING OF AN INQUISITION TORTURE CHAMBER.

deepened adherence to monasticism and a tighter bond with the papacy. By contrast, the Protestant Reformation railed against these very things which had previously been the vessels of reform. The Catholic Church and its pope, they believed, were not legitimate sources of religious authority. The only such authority was the Bible, and it was to scripture that Protestants were to turn for answers to their religious inquiries.

The founder of the Reformation movement, Martin Luther, was himself a former monk. His brand of Protestantism, known as Lutheranism, was not the only branch of Christianity to grow out of the Reformation. The Protestant movement consisted of manifold groups spanning a wide spectrum of beliefs and ideologies. Some Protestants resembled Catholics more closely than they resembled each other. What these groups shared were belief in the Holy Trinity, original sin, and salvation through Christ's death. They rejected all but two of the Catholic sacraments, regarding only baptism and the Lord's Supper as a Biblical requirement.

The Counter-Reformation, the popular term for the Catholic Church's reaction to Reformation, incorporated responses to the Reformers' ideologies and resulting practices. The Council

of Trent (1545–1563) issued decrees which became the basis of the Catholic reaction and sharply differentiated the two movements.

While the Catholics agreed that scripture was a necessary authority on religious matters, they stressed, additionally, the import of tradition—specifically, the papacy—regarding such issues. That which the Protestants denied was reaffirmed at the Council, and the issue of corruption was addressed. Having suffered this difficult period of self-examination, the Catholic Church emerged religiously strengthened, if numerically depleted.

## THE CHURCH TODAY

The history of the rise of the Catholic Church reveals that even the oldest institution in the Western world, believed by its followers to be sanctioned by God himself, experienced significant growing pains—dramatically acknowledged in March 2000 when Pope John Paul II delivered a sweeping papal apology for the Church's past sins, including the Crusades and the Inquisition. "We cannot not recognize the betrayals of the Gospels committed by some of our brothers, especially during the second millennium," he announced.

The Church's turmoil today is benign by comparison: Debates persist, and the technological advances the 21st century promises are certain to raise new questions and challenges for the Catholic world. It will be the Church's ability to deal with such challenges that determines the extent of its influence into the next millennium of Christendom and beyond.

IN HIS HOMILY OF MARCH 12, 2000, POPE JOHN PAUL II STATED, "IN THIS YEAR OF MERCY, THE CHURCH, STRENGTHENED BY THE HOLINESS THAT SHE RECEIVES FROM HER LORD, KNEELS BEFORE GOD AND BEGS FOR FORGIVENESS FOR PAST AND PRESENT SINS OF HIS SONS."

# The Crusades

The catalyst for the Crusades was the conquest of Jerusalem by the Seljuq Turks in 1070 AD. Christian pilgrims returning home brought alarming news of Turkish desecration. Commercial interests also had a hand in raising the battle cry. Italian merchants were eager to advance their empire eastward, and the downtrodden serfs desired any chance to improve their lot.

In 1095 Pope Urban II announced that an "accursed race, wholly alienated from God" had taken control of Christian lands. And so the 200-year-long war known as the Crusades began. Urban set August 1096 as the departure date, but an unruly throng of 12,000 set off in March. Their zeal overran their preparations, and they resorted to pillaging along their route for provisions and food. They arrived in Constantinople penniless, their ranks decimated. Imprudently, they advanced on Nicaea, where a force of skilled Turkish bowmen wiped them out.

By 1097, another wave of nearly 30,000 Crusaders had gathered in Constantinople. It was more successful by far. Infighting among the Muslims aided their efforts, and the jubilant Christian army entered Jerusalem on July 15, 1099. What followed was a brutal massacre, with 70,000 Muslims slaughtered, and Jews herded into synagogues and burned alive.

### SECOND AND THIRD

In 1144, a Muslim uprising roused Europe to the Second Crusade, which departed three years later. When the crusaders, weakened by starvation and disease, reached Jerusalem they could do very little. Still, some formed a small unit and marched on Damascus. But, intimidated by rumors of a gigantic Muslim army, the Christian forces retreated, and the Second Crusade ended in disgrace.

In 1187, the Egyptian sultan Saladin conquered Jerusalem, where he allowed Jews and Christians to worship so long as they were unarmed. This stirred a dejected Europe and led to the Third Crusade, led by the English king Richard the Lionheart. Ultimately, Richard was defeated, but Saladin then proposed a treaty—though Jerusalem would stay in Muslim hands, Christian pilgrims would be permitted to visit it.

### THE BLOODY FOURTH

The Fourth Crusade was the most dreadful. French Crusaders gathered in Venice, but with too little money to pay for the crossing to Egypt. The Venetians suggested the conquest of Constantinople, then Europe's richest city, to pay the balance. There, the crusaders engaged in an orgy of murder and pillaging, and most quickly returned home with their booty; almost no one continued on to fight the accursed Muslim infidels. Europe was scandalized. The Church was beginning to find it difficult to explain what was so "holy" about the wars.

The Fifth Crusade restored little faith, ending again in Muslim triumph. The Sixth resulted in a bloodless treaty that ceded most of Jerusalem to the Christians, but the Seventh accomplished nothing.

King Louis IX of France launched the Eighth. Few Frenchmen were interested by now, and Louis's recruitment drive had meager results. In 1270 he landed in Tunisia with a pitifully small army, contracted dysentery, and died. With this, the Holy Wars came to an end.

**A MEDIEVAL ARTIST DREW THE BATTLE OVER JERUSALEM OF RICHARD I AND SALADIN (LEFT). THE CAPTURE OF JERUSALEM IS SHOWN IN A 15TH CENTURY PAINTING FROM THE FLEMISH. SCHOOL (ABOVE).**

# Did St. Patrick Drive the Snakes from Ireland?

**Much of the popular legend about Ireland's patron saint is fanciful myth, but the real story of St. Patrick is the stuff of high drama.**

**ST. PATRICK IS OFTEN DEPICTED CRUSHING A SNAKE BENEATH HIS FOOT.**

NO CULTURE TREASURES ITS MYTHS MORE THAN the Irish, but their most prominent legend is actually of foreign provenance. St. Patrick, Ireland's second bishop and the man largely responsible for Christianizing its pagan tribes, is also credited with banishing its snakes. The legend derives from a Norse mistranslation of Patrick's name. When the Norse invaders arrived in Ireland in the 9th century, they noticed that the island had no toads. The Norse word for toad is "paud," and when they heard of Paudrig, as Patrick was called, they understood his name to mean "toad expeller." Toads soon became snakes—undoubtedly because the snake has traditionally been a symbol of evil—and a legend was born.

### PATRICK'S LIFE AND LEGEND

The story that Patrick introduced the shamrock to the Irish as a visual explanation of the Trinity is also spurious. It seems the Christian Irish had valued the shamrock before Patrick's arrival as a natural representation of the Cross. But even after these colorful legends are dispensed with, there is still much that is fascinating about Patrick's life.

Scholars debate his exact date and place of birth. The general consensus was that Patrick was born in the early 5th century AD in western Britain. In ancient manuscripts, his birthplace appears as "Bannavem Taburniae," but scholars have been unable to locate the site, and many believe the name to be a copyist's error. Patrick was a Roman Briton, who came from a respected family; his grandfather was a priest and his father a deacon.

At the age of 16, before Patrick was able to complete his education, he was kidnapped by Irish raiders who took him back to their island homeland as a slave. It seems that he served a master in the country's north, but once again, historians dispute the exact location.

Six years into his captivity, Patrick began hearing voices telling of his imminent escape and seeing visions of a great ship that would be the instrument of his freedom. How Patrick escaped is not clear. But encouraged by his visions, he made his way some 200 miles to the port city now known as Wicklow. Sure enough, Patrick found a waiting ship and, according to legend, convinced the captain to let him join the crew. A few scholars suggest that he may have been taken on board as a captive.

Some legends claim that Patrick sailed to Gaul (France), then to Italy, where he disembarked on the French-Italian Mediterranean coast. It is said he spent a number of years in a monastic community near present-day Cannes.

After returning briefly to Britain, Patrick traveled again to Gaul, where he was ordained as a priest, dedicating himself to ministering to the Irish Christians. Patrick claimed that his decision was once again prompted by a striking dream, in which he was given a bundle of letters which were labeled "The Voice of the Irish." He also heard this solemn plea: "We ask you, holy boy, come back again and walk among us once more."

Patrick was motivated by a concern for his fellow Roman Britons: They had been taken as captives to Ireland, and their descendants had established small Christian communities that were struggling to survive in a pagan land. Also, in keeping with the Catholic Church, Patrick believed that bringing Christ to "the remotest parts of the land beyond which there is nothing and nobody" would quicken the coming of Christ's return.

## ORIGINS OF A PARADE

**TENDRILS OF TIME** ▼

March 17—St. Patrick's Day—was designated a holy day, devoted to the worship of St. Patrick. In Ireland in the 19th century, pubs normally closed on that day, only serving travelers, but many got around this proscription by walking in groups to the next town.

It was the Americans who held the first official St. Patrick's Day parade in 1737 in Boston. The event spread to New York in 1762, when Irish military units were recruited to serve in the American colonies.

The parade itself began as a short walk from breakfast to church. But it did not make it to Ireland until the 19th century, and there it still exists more as a day for prayer, family gatherings, and sport—not green beer and mass-produced trinkets.

### THE BISHOP'S LEGACY

Though Patrick came to Ireland to be its bishop in 457, he was passed over for the position—the church instead chose a senior prelate named Palladius. But after Palladius's death, Patrick, then in his mid-forties, was named bishop. Until his death in 492, he spent the rest of his life establishing churches and developing a native clergy. Tradition has it that Patrick impressed and then converted Ireland's pagan High King, Laoghaire.

Patrick was hampered both by feelings of inadequacy—in his *Confessions,* he describes himself as an ignorant country bumpkin—and by the fierceness of the pagan kings, who resented his ministering and often killed his converts. And yet one has only to consider the deep commitment to Catholicism of the Irish to appreciate how successful he was. Before Patrick, Ireland was considered by the Church a land *ubi nemo ultra erat*—"beyond which no man dwelt." Through his efforts, Ireland became part of Christian Europe.

ANOTHER TYPICAL PORTRAYAL HAS THE SAINT HOLDING A SHAMROCK IN HIS HAND (LEFT). A ST. PATRICK'S DAY PARADE HELD IN 1837 WAS SKETCHED BY AN AMERICAN ARTIST (TOP). THE EARLY PARADES WERE SOLEMN EVENTS, BECOMING BIG AND CELEBRATORY—AND OFTEN POLITICAL—ONLY IN THE 20TH CENTURY.

# William Tell & Lady Godiva

SOME LEGENDS ARE SO INTERTWINED WITH A NATION'S SENSE of pride that regardless of their veracity, they graft on to a place's identity like a tenacious vine. For example, in Switzerland a lime tree once marked the spot where legend says William Tell's son stood bravely as his father shot the apple from his head. Now the site is marked by a fountain, and camera-laden tourists flock to pose in front of this "birthplace of Swiss independence." To the north, citizens of Coventry, in central England, were for centuries treated to a solemn reenactment of Lady Godiva's ride through the town (her part played tastefully by a young boy). Today tourists visit these sites more out of respect for the myth than for historical accuracy, rarely asking whether these events happened at all.

In the case of Tell, the answer is probably no. The story now known around the world was popularized by the dramatist Friedrich von Schiller in his 1804 drama *Wilhelm Tell,* one of the classics of the German stage.

The time of the legend is the late 13th century, and its setting is the forest cantons of Uri, Schwyz, and Unterwalden. For centuries, the cantons had been ruled from Vienna by the monarchs of the Holy Roman Empire, whose representatives alienated the populace with autocratic, heavy-handed governance. The Uri governor, Hermann Gessler, was one such tyrant. He required that every last citizen salute a hat placed on a flagpole in the marketplace. This hat represented his authority whenever he was absent from the town.

## THE SCORNFUL PEASANT TELL

William Tell, so the legend goes, was one of the peasants who toiled in the nearby valleys—and who scorned Gessler's rule. One day, while walking by the pole with his young son, he refused to give the mandatory salute and was quickly confronted by soldiers. The governor was alerted and brought to the marketplace, where a crowd had formed. Tell's young son, unaware of the danger, bragged to the crowd of his father's skill as an archer, and Gessler, seizing on an opportunity to humiliate

REAL LIFE OR FROM THE STAGE? THE SWISS PEASANT WILLIAM TELL AIMS AT AN APPLE ATOP THE HEAD OF HIS SON, AS GESSLER AND THE TOWNSFOLK OF URI, A FOREST CANTON, LOOK ON.

MARSHALL CLAXTON PAINTED A BARE AND VOLUPTUOUS LADY GODIVA IN 1850.

the insubordinate, asked Tell to demonstrate his prowess by shooting an apple off his son's head.

Tell pleaded for another task, to no avail. Grabbing his bow and loading it with two arrows, he warned Gessler, "If my first arrow had my dear child struck, the second arrow I had aimed at you. And be assured, I should not then have missed." Tell managed to hit the apple, but was promptly taken into custody. He soon after escaped, then ultimately ambushed and killed the governor. His act was said to be the first shot of Swiss independence.

Doubts began to arise over the story's truthfulness as early as the 16th century, when Swiss historians suggested it was probably invented in order to stir the hatred of neighboring Austrians. Even the dramatist Schiller admitted taking liberties in assigning Tell a central role in the fight for Swiss independence. But the legend suffered its most crushing blow in the middle of the 19th century, when the historian Joseph Kopp, after scouring the archives of the early forest cantons, concluded that Tell never existed.

Historians have now traced the story back to the late 15th century and say it was probably based on earlier oral traditions. The first print reference to Tell occurs in four stanzas of a 1477 ballad, *Song of the Origin of the Confederation*; mentions are made of archery, but not of Gessler, the hat,

**CHALLENGED BY HER HUSBAND, AN EARL, LADY GODIVA TOOK HER RIDE IN THE INTEREST OF LOWER TAXES.**

or the pole. Those elements do, however, appear in other works, such as *The White Book*. Published sometime between 1467 and 1474, it names Gessler as a bailiff and the skilled archer as Thall (not Tell) but fails to link them to Swiss independence.

So how did the story gain such stature? Historians can only point to the prevalence of tested marksmen in European legend, who appear in the oral traditions of Germany, Denmark, Norway, Iceland, and England. It is possible that whoever first told the Tell story in the context of Swiss independence was adapting one of these foreign tales to the cause.

## LADY GODIVA'S RIDE

And what of Lady Godiva? According to the story, she was the matriarch of Coventry who rode naked through the town to save it from paying taxes. There are indeed records of a Godiva who married Leofric, the 11th-century earl of Mercia. Leofric was required by King Edward the Confessor to raise a large tax from his populace in Coventry, and the distraught citizenry turned to the earl's wife for help. Godiva begged her husband to lower the levies, and he responded by saying that he would do so after she rode through the town naked on a horse—probably a medieval version of "fat chance."

Yet so dedicated was Godiva to the townspeople that she took up her husband's challenge, mounting a horse and riding through town unclothed, her body cloaked by her flowing hair and the townsfolk staying respectfully indoors. Leofric had little choice but to keep his word.

It is a moving legend, combining civic virtue with the slightest hint of prurient fascination. And it may very well be true. The story is first referred to in the chronicles of a 13th-century historian, Roger of Wendover, who relied on documentation since vanished. But there are plenty of historical records of a Godiva, who throughout her life showed an impressive dedication to the people of Coventry. She founded a Benedictine monastery in the city in 1043, which through her generosity became one of the richest in the land. Up until the 17th century, Coventry also boasted a number of tax exemptions, which some claim to have derived from Leofric's concession.

This is not to say that the legend hasn't evolved through time. In the early 18th century, the tale included a tailor named Tom, who peeked through the shutters of his home at the naked Godiva and was struck blind—the origin of the phrase "peeping Tom."

# Genghis Khan
## and the
## Mongol Empire

**How did a ruthless Mongol tribal leader establish the largest empire in the world, the likes of which we probably will never see again?**

SO WROTE GENGHIS, THE GREAT KHAN: "THE GREATEST PLEASURE IS TO VANQUISH YOUR ENEMIES, AND CHASE THEM BEFORE YOU, TO ROB THEM OF THEIR WEALTH AND SEE THOSE DEAR TO THEM BATHED IN TEARS, TO RIDE THEIR HORSES AND CLASP TO YOUR BOSOM THEIR WIVES AND DAUGHTERS." THE 13TH-CENTURY MONGOL LEADER IS SHOWN ABOVE ON A SILK ALBUM LEAF.

THE MONGOLS WERE A GROUP OF NOMADIC ASIAN tribes that emerged as a cohesive nation at the beginning of the 12th century, their ancestors having come from the northern Siberian forests. Skilled as hunters, trappers, fishermen, and herdsmen, the Mongol tribes were a relatively prosperous people. The area they roamed, in what is today Mongolia, was divided into three states ruled by tribes of Turkish descent. In the far west were the Naimans; in the central region dwelt the Kereits; and in the west lived the warlike Tatars, who were often in alliance with the Chinese against the other Turkic tribes or the Mongol nomads.

The growth of the Mongol empire from these disorganized nomadic roots into a dominant power was largely, if not completely, the work of one man, known as Genghis Khan, or "Universal Monarch." His given name was Temuchin, celebrating the victory of his father Yesukai—a great and respected leader who had united a large number of Mongol tribes—over a Tatar adversary of the same name.

When Temuchin was nine, he left home to live with the tribe of his future bride. While he was away, Yesukai was poisoned by Tatars and died. Temuchin returned home. Almost immediately, the tribes his father had led disbanded, some helping themselves to Yesukai's possessions. Soon Temuchin and his family were destitute, subsisting on wild plants and roots—nourishment the Mongols thought shameful.

Slowly, Temuchin began to rebuild his father's empire. He was a violent and valorous youth, and tales spread of his exploits against the Taijiuts, an unfriendly neighboring tribe. Mongol youths began showing up to offer their services at Temuchin's burgeoning camp. They achieved a miraculous victory against the Taijiuts, whose army outnumbered their own by 17,000 men. Temuchin's political and military strength continued to grow, and at the start of the 13th century his power was great enough to attack the other Turkic tribes, beginning with the Tatars who had slain his father. By 1204, he had eliminated all three. In 1206 he was proclaimed supreme ruler of the Mongol peoples and received the title Genghis Khan, by which the world has known him since.

### RULE FROM THE SADDLE

These early conquests were a mere hint of what he would do next. For the rest of his life, Genghis Khan would rule the Mongol people from a horse's saddle, endlessly slaughtering, enslaving, and subjecting region after terrified region. He began with the Chin rulers of North China. In 1213, Mongol warriors poured through the Great Wall and seized all the land north of the Yellow River. After that, they turned and began to march west, crushing armies and sacking towns. They rarely knew defeat, and their emerging dominance was the source of considerable confusion in Europe. Beleaguered Christian crusaders thought

GENGHIS KHAN (ABOVE, IN A PERSIAN MINIATURE) UNITED DISCORDANT MONGOL TRIBES TO FORM THE MOST POWERFUL ARMY OF ITS TIME. SO EFFECTIVE WAS KHAN'S ARMY THAT IN ONE DAY HIS SOLDIERS COULD DEMOLISH LAND 60 MILES AWAY, RETURN HOME, AND THEN (OR SO IT IS SAID) COME BACK THE NEXT DAY. KHAN (LEFT, SHOWN IN BATTLE) WAS OFTEN BARBAROUS AND INHUMANE TOWARD HIS OPPONENTS: HE PUNISHED ONE OF HIS ENEMIES BY POURING MOLTEN SILVER INTO HIS EARS AND EYES.

(hopefully) that they were a mighty army led by a Christian king, come from the east to deliver the Holy Land from Muslim rule. Jews thought they might be one of the lost tribes of Israel.

In 1220, the Mongols attacked Merv, in what is now Iran, killing most of the inhabitants and sparing not even the dogs and cats. Three years later, after extending their empire all the way to the Indus River, Genghis Khan and his triumphant troops returned to their homeland.

Shortly after his return, on August 25, 1227, Genghis Khan died while resting in his summer quarters. The cause of death is unknown. Tenacious to the end, he made his last command: to delay the announcement of his death until all the garrisons were in place, a ploy that defended against opportunistic raiders.

### KHAN'S LEGAL LEGACY

Khan's death did not leave the empire in disarray. He had established the Yasak (legal code) of the Mongol government years before; it combined his rules and ideas and the traditional Mongol laws. Notably, the code decreed that the clergy of conquered peoples were exempt from taxation and conscription. Whether this was a testament to the respect Genghis Khan held for his enemies—or an example of his voracious need to increase the learning and power of his empire—is debat-

able. Whatever the reason, much of the Mongol government was made up of conquered officials. Muslims, Jews, and Christians held high office. Khan's prime minister was Chinese. His grandson, Kublai, even had a European, Marco Polo, among his administrators.

Following his death, Genghis Khan's third son Ogadai became the ruler of the Mongol nation. Ogadai was an able and powerful ruler, and the nation prospered under his command. He built the capital city of Karakorum and extended the empire toward Europe, capturing the Russian cities of Moscow and Kiev.

In 1241, Ogadai's armies surged through Poland, taking everything east of the Danube and invading Croatia. Europe braced for an attack—but it never came. Ogadai died in November 1241, and his armies withdrew. It had been the Mongols' westernmost campaign.

Following Ogadai's death, his son Guyuk became the khan, but died shortly after assuming the mantle. A council of Mongol princes chose Mangu, the eldest son of Genghis Khan's youngest son, as their next ruler.

Soon civil strife and disunity began to creep into the kingdom, with Guyuk's sons opposing the appointment of Mangu. A plot to overthrow Mangu was discovered, resulting in the loss of many princely heads. In the end, Mangu ruled successfully, adding several minor conquests to the still-powerful empire until his death during a battle in 1259.

Following the death of Mangu, the empire dissolved into many states. He is considered the last khan of the unified Mongol empire, the largest nation the world has ever known.

A DRAWING FROM
THE MING DYNASTY
SHOWS A MONGOL
ARCHER ON HIS
HORSE. THE IMPOR-
TANCE OF THE MON-
GOLS' POWERFUL
STEEDS CANNOT BE
OVERSTATED, WITH
HORSES KEY TO THE
SUCCESS OF MONGOL
MILITARY STRATEGY.

"GENGHIS KHAN," WROTE MARCO POLO, WHO AT ONE POINT IN HIS TRAVELS WAS THE GUEST OF KHAN'S GRANDSON KUBLAI, "WAS A MAN OF GREAT WORTH AND GREAT ABILITY AND VALOR." HERE IN A 13TH-CENTURY PAINTING, KHAN'S ROYAL TENT IS GUARDED BY FOUR OF HIS MINIONS.

## MONGOLIAN MILITARY STRENGTH

**THE STUFF OF LEGEND** The Mongol armies rarely outnumbered their enemies, but their organization and tactical skill were unparalleled. They were ruthless and merciless in battle, and their prisoners, if indeed there were any, made up the front lines of their next attack. In this way, wrote papal emissary John de Plano Caprini, "with the inhabitants of one country they would destroy another."

A favorite maneuver of Genghis Khan was to use his swift Mongol horsemen to sweep around an enemy's flank, which would disrupt their formation. He would then sneakily attack them from behind. On long campaigns, the Mongol armies would bring many more horses than warriors, which allowed each warrior to ride a fresh mount every day. The speed of the Mongol warriors atop these well-rested animals left many a foe floundering in disarray.

Another advantage the Mongols enjoyed over their adversaries was a collapsible boat, which allowed their troops to easily cross rivers that halted the progress of competing armies.

# Was Marco Polo a Fraud?

**In his sweeping adventures, did this legendary figure really travel to the Far East?**

**KUBLAI KHAN WAS SO TAKEN WITH HIS VISITORS THAT HE FUNDED THEIR TRAVELS THROUGH CHINA. KHAN PRESENTS HIS GOLDEN SEAL TO THE POLOS IN A 1413 PAINTING (TOP). MARCO ALONE IS FEATURED ON THE TITLE PAGE OF THE FIRST EDITION (1477) OF *THE TRAVELS OF MARCO POLO* (ABOVE).**

MARCO POLO'S ADVENTURE INTO THE HEART OF China and the Far East has long been a crowning achievement for the European Age of Discovery. The chronicles of his 13th-century journey became the definitive sourcebook for the customs and geography of Asia. Polo, with his father and uncle, had described in colorful, rich detail a vast region of the world, and his journeys became yet another feather in the cap of European ingenuity. But did Marco Polo actually make it to China?

## THE ADVENTURER'S TRAVELS

Just 17 years old when he began the journey towards China (then called Cathay) with his father and uncle, Marco and crew began what would become a three-year journey. Marco's accounts report how they sailed to Palestine, rode camels to Hormuz (in modern-day Iran), and entered Kublai Khan's magnificent capital of Cambuluc (now Beijing). The apparently lonely Khan enthusiastically welcomed his new visitors and began to show off his lands—fresh spoils in the Mongol military conquest of China. So taken with Marco's charms was the Khan that he supposedly asked the multilin-

gual lad to take tours of the new lands, and to then report back on his observations. Travel Marco did, for 17 years, all around China, noting his escapades and encounters.

## EXIT POLO, ENTER SKEPTICS

Toward the end of his expedition, Marco was also allegedly appointed to the position of governor of Yangzhou, a city in eastern China, acting as an objective foreign overseer. As the Polos grew weary of their stay, they requested their leave more often, but the clingy Khan was too enamored with them to allow it. They were finally granted departure in 1292. They reached Venice in 1295, whereupon Marco became an instant sensation for his fabulous tales of an unknown world. When Genoa went to war with Venice a few years later, Marco was imprisoned. He recounted his tales to Rustichello, an inmate and a romance writer who knew gold when he saw it. Exaggerating much in his friend's stories, Rustichello prepared Polo's adventures for release; it became a European hit immediately.

Yet no one can verify any of Marco Polo's tales. Skeptics of the Venetian merchant's journey have been quick to note his glaring omissions of Far East culture. The adventurer failed to mention the tea-drinking obsession; he overlooked the use of chopsticks; and he even neglected to point out the Chinese calligraphic written language. Perhaps more bizarre is Polo's lack of discussion on the art of binding girls' feet, which other explorers had found noteworthy. Or what about the oversight of the Great Wall, which, though not yet fully completed as it would be two centuries later, was undeniably impressive? Moreover, the versatile Marco, who by his own account was fluent in

EXPLORER MARCO POLO IS COSTUMED IN TATAR ATTIRE (LEFT). A CATALAN MAP SHOWS MARCO TRAVELING WITH HIS FATHER AND UNCLE IN A CARAVAN OF CAMELS (RIGHT).

four languages, didn't seem to pick up a word of Chinese in all of his time there. No documentation of the Polos' visit exists, despite a 17-year "official" stay in the region—and a government position to boot. Stir these omissions in with other errors and sprinkle in a poor sense of geography, and out comes what many skeptics call "bunk."

At the same time, the naysayers haven't offered any solutions to the truths that Polo's book related. One theory contends that Marco Polo just had a very good ear for stories: He made it no farther than his father's trading posts in Constantinople, and for close to two decades wandered around, meeting explorers who had visited the Far East. He took copious notes on their experiences, and subsequently produced his own "travels."

But Marco's accounts of China's large cities, the pleasant demeanor of Kublai Khan, and thousands of other observations are too personal and exact to be second-hand knowledge. Oversights may have been due to his preferential treatment; in the company of the nobility, he would not have been exposed to certain elements of society. And while it is difficult to prove that Marco Polo was in China, it's probably more difficult to prove he was elsewhere.

Chances are, Marco did make the journey, but because his prison mate Rustichello was a romance adventure writer, there was quite a bit of external editing and embellishment on points that weren't considered attention-worthy. Too, the glorious details recorded in Polo's tales are intricate enough to suggest an extensive journey in China. Exaggeration assuredly took place, but then again, what great autobiography hasn't had its share of hyperbole?

## POLO AND PASTA

The myth of Marco Polo introducing pasta to Italy from China is a puzzling one; it seems to have originated, or at least been popularized, in a 1920s magazine article, but there is no real basis for the claim.

Much like geometry, pasta has had more than its share of inventors. While the Chinese had been savoring noodle dumplings for centuries, the Arabian culture had not

**HOW DO WE REALLY KNOW?**

only been eating pasta but making it as a way of preserving flour on desert treks. But Italy is not to be overshadowed: Italians had been munching on ravioli for years before Marco Polo made his journey. In fact, it was the Etruscans of that region, way back in the 8th century BC, who began making noodles and lasagna from a Greek recipe for dough cakes (*laganon*).

# The Prophet Nostradamus

## Was this "prophet of doom" a visionary, or are his powers merely a myth?

**THE 16TH-CENTURY PHYSICIAN AND SOOTHSAYER MICHEL DE NOSTREDAME WAS BETTER KNOWN AS NOSTRADAMUS.**

THE PROPHECIES OF NOSTRADAMUS HAVE CAST a long shadow over mankind's collective psyche. Nearly 500 years after "the prophet of doom" was born, his predictions are still the subject of much research, speculation, and conjecture. Certainly as the 20th century drew to a close, Nostradamus's millennial prognostications were the subject of numerous heated debates in countries far and wide.

Despite their popularity and the animated discussion they continue to engender, Nostradamus's prophecies are widely misunderstood—and largely exaggerated. Much of the excitement over his storied ability to see the future is based on hearsay, and has been corrupted by erroneous reports of what he actually said. Although a number of Nostradamus's visions are remarkably accurate, many more are either vague or seem to have had their meanings imposed on them by some modern writer with the benefit of 20/20 hindsight.

### WHO WAS HE?

Nostradamus was considered unusually intelligent by his peers long before he began to prophesy. Born Michel de Nostredame in France to Jewish parents on December 14, 1503, Nostradamus was initially educated by both of his grandfathers; among other subjects, they taught him Hebrew and Latin. Soon, the future prophet was shipped off to the town of Avignon, where he pursued studies in other subjects before enrolling in medical school at the University of Montpelier. During each phase of his education, young Nostradamus was noted for his phenomenal memory.

During his tenure at Montpelier, Nostradamus won the admiration of many for his performance during a lengthy outbreak of the plague. His medical techniques, markedly different from those of his contemporaries, cured hundreds, perhaps thousands of ill French citizens. He refused to drain blood from the afflicted, as was the practice of the time. Medical science was still in its infancy in Nostradamus's day; many practices that worked (by design or by accident) must have seemed like magic to patients and observers alike.

Some years after leaving Montpelier, Nostradamus was married and sired several children. In an ironic twist of fate, however, his wife and children fell victim to the plague, and the renowned doctor could not save their lives. Some years after his family's death, Nostradamus wrote his first book of prophecies for the year 1550. This tome proved a best seller,

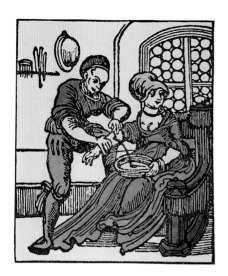

A 16TH-CENTURY WOODCUT SHOWS A PHYSICIAN PRACTICING VENESECTION—CUTTING OPEN A VEIN—IN ORDER TO ALLOW "BAD BLOOD" TO BE DRAINED. NOSTRADAMUS DECRIED THIS THERAPY, AN UNUSUAL STANCE AT THE TIME.

## ENCOUNTER WITH A PIG HERDER

**DID IT REALLY HAPPEN?**

During a brief sojourn in Italy, Nostradamus is said to have passed a young, unknown pig herder and proceeded to stop, bow, and address the man as "Holiness." At the time, witnesses to his odd show of respect were con-fused. After Nostradamus's death, however, those who had witnessed the incident were dumbfounded when the beneficiary of his courtesy that fateful day was elected pope in Rome. The young man turned out to be none other than Felice Peretti, later crowned as Pope Sixtus V.

and the budding prophet went on to write ten *Centuries*—that is, ten books of predictions, each containing 100 four-line prophesies. The publication of his books led to great fame for Nostradamus and, despite those who claimed he was an agent of the devil, he became a court physician to Charles IX. The demand for his services escalated all the more when Catherine de' Medici, the queen consort of France, invited him to prophesy in her royal court.

### PRESENT-DAY INTERPRETATIONS

But why all the fuss over Nostradamus? Following are two of his prophesies as translated and interpreted by Stewart Robb, an expert on the prophet, in his *Prophecies On World Events by Nostradamus*; and by Henry C. Roberts, in *The Complete Prophecies of Nostradamus*.

First, consider the prophecy said to foretell the rise of Hitler: "After victory over a raging tongue, The mind that was tempted shall be in tranquility and rest. The bloody emperor by battle shall make a speech, And roast the tongue the flesh and the bones." Roberts interprets it this way in his book: "Adolf Hitler was known to have had a raging tongue. Line 3 predicts the extermination ovens of Nazi Germany. A grim but true prediction."

Another of Nostradamus' prophecies is somewhat eerie: "The year 1999, seventh month, A great king of terror will descend from the skies, To resuscitate the great king of Angolmois, Around this time Mars will reign for the good cause." Author Stewart Robb's interpretation: "In this remarkable quatrain...we see that Armageddon is on in 1999." Given that the clock clicked safely past 2000, Nostradamus was off by at least a year.

In both cases, the language of Nostradamus allows for many interpretations. In fact, critics point out that nearly any collection of predictions, however vaguely worded, will usually conform in some imaginative way to world events. This parallels horoscopes in a newspaper, which can be made to apply to a reader's life only because they are so equivocal.

Nostradamus was a great doctor, but was he a great prophet? We may have to wait nearly 2,000 years to find out. Although he predicted Armageddon in 1999, Nostradamus did not foresee the world's end until the year 3797.

In the meantime, the soothsayer's advocates have had, and will likely continue to have, a field day injecting their own hopes and beliefs into his prophecies. Many of these involve little more than taking Nostradamus's words and describing the activities and feelings of modern personages in the same terms.

A FAVORITE MEDIEVAL THEME WAS ARMAGEDDON AND THE END OF THE WORLD. THIS PAINTING, BY HANS MEMLING, IS ABOVE THE ALTAR IN THE CATHEDRAL IN DANZIG. THE BELIEF INCLUDED A GREAT BATTLE BETWEEN GOOD AND EVIL, ON EARTH AND IN HEAVEN, THAT WOULD HERALD THE SECOND COMING OF CHRIST.

# Was there a Count Dracula?

IN THE WORLD'S MENAGERIE OF HORROR, the vampire has earned a preeminent place. Among all the monstrous creatures people have invented to frighten one another throughout history, none has terrified more or been more widely portrayed. Clad in a black cloak, his razor-sharp fangs glinting in the light of the full moon, the vampire—that living corpse who rises from his coffin at night to drink the blood of the living—has been a staple of fearsome folktales for more than a thousand years, in stories, books, and films pored over around the world.

Tales of vampirism were common to cultures as far-flung as ancient Greece, Egypt, and India. Present-day vampire myths, which emphasize the creature's aversion to garlic, sunlight, and the cross, and which instruct anyone hoping to kill a vampire to drive a stake through his heart, descend mostly from the folk legends of Romania and Eastern Europe. In the view of some regional religions, those who die under a curse—children, witches, and the excommunicated, for example—are doomed to become *moroi,* or walking corpses, until they are granted divine forgiveness. The moroi have the power to assume the form of a wolf or a bat and are doomed to drink the blood of the living until they can finally obtain absolution.

The reason that vampire stories today tend toward the Romanian variety is simple. Our most famous vampire story, Bram Stoker's *Dracula*, drew heavily on Eastern European sources. Today, Dracula is synonymous with vampirism. The tale of the ghoulish count, scheming in his ruined castle deep in the mountains of Transylvania, was a best-seller when it appeared in 1897. In the century since then, it gave rise to dozens of movies, books, cartoons, and television programs. But why has the legend of Dracula proved so compelling, and for so long? Perhaps because it is based, at least in part, on truth.

## A RULER NAMED VLAD

Around 1431 in Walachia (the region next to Transylvania in the Carpathian Mountains), the wife of Prince Vlad Dracul ("Vlad the Devil") gave birth to a son: Vlad IV, who in Romanian custom was also called Dracula ("Son of the Devil"). Vlad was not a vampire, but as the third name by which he was known suggests, he was one of the most astonishingly brutal rulers in the history of medieval Europe—and that name was "Vlad the Impaler."

IT WAS AUTHOR BRAM STOKER (RIGHT) WHO BROUGHT DRACULA INTO THE WORLD, BUT THE VAMPIRE FROM TRANSYLVANIA IS MORE OFTEN ASSOCIATED WITH THE HUNGARIAN ACTOR BELA LUGOSI (OPPOSITE), WHO PORTRAYED HIM IN THE 1931 FILM. STOKER'S *DRACULA* WAS SIGNIFICANT FOR THE MANY VAMPIRE STORIES AND MOVIES THAT FOLLOWED. THE CREATURE HAS MADE NUMEROUS APPEARANCES ON THE SILVER SCREEN, AS IN FRANCIS FORD COPPOLA'S 1991 ADAPTATION *BRAM STOKER'S DRACULA*.

The nocturnal creature known as Dracula—immortalized in legend and the written word—took his name from a brutal ruler who lurks in the dark corners of history.

Vlad lived during a time of unremitting war between Christian Europe and the Islamic Turks, who were attempting a wholesale invasion of the European continent. As a youth, he was taken prisoner by the Turks, and it was from them that he learned his favorite method of execution—impalement. The method is simple yet savage, bearing an eerie similarity to a certain aspect of the vampire myth: a sharpened wooden stake or an iron pike is driven through the body of the victim, and then hammered into the ground. That done, the victim is left there to die in agony.

In 1448, the Turks placed the adolescent Vlad upon the throne of Walachia, but he rebelled and fled to a Christian monastery.

Eight years later, after the Turks captured Constantinople—the capital of the Byzantine Empire in Christian Eastern Europe—Vlad returned to the Walachian throne in 1456 and began waging a savage war upon his Turkish enemies. He gained fame and notoriety throughout the region, marching his forces nearly to the Black Sea, reclaiming Christian fortresses along the Danube, and brutally punishing captured enemies. On one occasion, when a pair of Turkish emissaries refused to remove their turbans in his presence, he ordered the turbans nailed to their skulls.

## TERROR IN TRANSYLVANIA

Not surprisingly, Vlad treated his own people little better than he treated his enemies. With no provocation, he would often raid friendly towns, murdering and torturing thousands of his own subjects, sometimes burning, boiling, and skinning them alive. In his most brutal massacre, which took place on St. Bartholomew's Day in 1460, Vlad raided a town in Transylvania and killed 30,000 people by impalement. Woodcuts and paintings from the period show a sickly-looking prince enjoying dinner at an outdoor table, surrounded by dozens of impaled bodies, while a servant hacks apart the corpses of the victims with an axe.

When Vlad's forces were defeated by the Turks, his people finally rebelled against him, forging documents that suggested he was secretly allied to the hated Turks. He was then dragged to prison by Hungary's King Mathias, and was held there for 12 years. True to fashion, Vlad charmed the prison guards into

## A DRACULA DISEASE?

For almost as long as there have been stories about vampires, there have been attempts to prove them true by scientific explanation. Attempts to offer a medical explanation for vampirism have centered on a rare disease known as porphyria. In the 1980s, medical descriptions of a form of porphyria called CEP led to speculation that CEP might cause a "real" form of vampirism. Those afflicted with

**WE MAY NEVER KNOW** ▼

the disease develop pointed teeth, sensitivity to light, and a need for blood. CEP is extremely rare—only a few dozen cases have been reported worldwide. Could an ancient form of porphyria have accounted for the widespread vampire stories that circulated thousands of years before the publication of *Dracula*? The answer, like so much else about these creatures, is shrouded in mystery.

bringing him mice and small animals, which he would impale on little stakes in his cell.

Released in 1474, Vlad briefly reclaimed the throne in 1476. Two months later he was killed in a battle against the Turks, and his severed head was preserved in honey and sent to the Turkish sultan as a prize. The original Dracula, like the fictional vampire he inspired, met with harsh judgment at the hands of his enemies.

A 1499 WOODCUT (ABOVE LEFT) SHOWS THE RUTHLESS VLAD DINING AMID THE IMPALED BODIES OF HIS VICTIMS. VLAD USED BRAN CASTLE (BELOW) AS HIS TRANSYLVANIAN HEADQUARTERS.

# The Execution of Joan of Arc

A DISTINGUISHED HISTORIAN once noted that we know more about Joan of Arc than we do of Christ, Plato, or Alexander. Paradoxically, she was "saved" from obscurity by the transcripts of her heresy trial, at which she was found guilty and subsequently burned as a witch. But just 24 years later, in 1455, the Catholic Church revoked the verdict, convening a nullification trial that produced even more documentation. These court transcripts, rediscovered in France's national library in the 1840s, paint a picture of a girl full of contradictions, not the least of which was that she dressed like a man. Until the end, she remained unimpressed by the sagacity of the court-appointed interrogators, yet was awed by the material splendor of the court itself; courageous in battle, she was terrified of dying after her capture. In short, her heroism was amplified by her humanity.

Joan was born in 1412, during the dynastic conflict now known as the Hundred Years War, in which the English Plantagenets fought the French Valois dynasty over the control of France. By the 1420s, the Valois, under the corrupt Charles VII (the disinherited son of Charles VI, and known as the Dauphin), held most of the land below the Loire River, while the British, allied with the French Burgundians, controlled the lands above the Loire. Born in a village in the north controlled by the

**At the mere age of 17, she led France to victory in the siege of Orléans. A year later, she was burned at the stake by the French Church.**

British, the child Joan lived a simple life performing farm chores. According to trial transcripts, Joan testified that she first began hearing voices—"beautiful, gentle and humble, and speaking the language of France"—at the age of 13. When she was 17, those voices, which she believed to be St. Margaret and the Archangel Michael, called her to the aid of the Valois. A religious child, she did as she was told.

She did so none too soon. In the year 1428 the British seemed to gain the upper hand in the struggle. After capturing Paris, they made their way to Orléans, a crucial city on the border between the north and south of France; from here, the British would be able to cross the Loire and invade the Valois-held territories.

## THE BATTLE OF ORLÉANS

With an army of 4,000 men, joined by some 1,500 French Burgundians, the British surrounded the city, breaking through its outer defenses and laying siege. At this point, Joan's voices instructed her to come to Orléans's defense. They called for her to break through the blockades and vanquish the British, and then to take the Dauphin to Rheims to be crowned king of all France.

Somehow, the farm girl dressed in male clothing succeeded in convincing Charles to give her command of a relief force to send to Orléans. In all probability, the indolent Charles had given up hope of achieving victory through all nonsupernatural means, but Joan was still an unlikely candidate to lead France to victory. By all accounts, including her own, she was a provincial who had never been far from her small village and who had no military training. But the men were inspired by her example, if not convinced of her military and tactical genius. After a fierce battle on May 8, Joan led the troops, wearing white armor, and the British were driven from Orléans.

Two days later, Joan led a force against the British fortifications surrounding the town. Seriously wounded, she still continued to lead. This fortitude from a farm girl convinced the Burgundian French that Joan was a witch and the loyal Valois that she was an angel. Through her inspiration, the tide of the war changed; though it dragged on until 1453, the French were never in danger of losing much territory.

## TO THE CHURCH, A HERETIC

After her impressive showing at Orléans, Joan convinced Charles to allow her to lead a force to Paris. Charles agreed, and it was during that campaign that Joan was captured at Compiègne by the French Burgundians, allied to the British. The Burgundians were paid some 10,000 pounds by the British army to hand her over, and the British kept her locked up before giving her to the French church. This, then, is one of the central ironies of Joan's story: Even though she is hailed as a martyred French national hero, it was actually the French who presided over her trial and execution. The Catholic Church considered Joan's claims to direct and unmediated contact with God a heresy and wished to make an example of her.

The outcome of the trial, which lasted four months, was never in doubt. Joan's examiners were in league with the British, who did not want her released. She seemed to have a faint

understanding of her inevitable fate and pleaded with her captors for her release. In prison, she wrote that her voices told her she would be saved, but in a poignant admission of doubt, she claimed not to know whether this referred to heavenly or earthly salvation.

Indeed, Joan never embraced martyrdom or sainthood (which was finally granted to her in 1920 by Pope Benedict XV). Nor did she claim that she could heal the sick, as other visionaries through history have done. Once, when an ailing, powerful duke called her to ask how he might recover, she told him she had no idea, and lectured him on his shameful behavior.

The final days of Joan of Arc are especially revealing of the conflict between her powerful faith and her equally potent terror over her earthly fate. Just days before her execution, Joan's faith finally relented. She signed a statement denouncing her mission from God and, in an about-face, agreed to don women's clothing (like heresy, a woman dressing as a man was considered a capital offense in 15th-century France). Until then she had worn her hair short and dressed in a man's shift. Four days later, however, she withdrew her recantation and defiantly reappeared in her shift.

Two days later, at the age of 19, Joan was taken out to the marketplace at Rouen, tied to a stake, and burned alive. It is written that her desperate, sorrowful pleas to Jesus were barely audible above the crackling blaze.

AT LOCHES, JOAN OF ARC ANNOUNCES THE LIBERATION OF ORLÉANS TO THE DAUPHIN (ABOVE). INSPIRED BY JOAN, THE VALOIS HAD FOUGHT FIERCELY AND THE BRITISH HAD BACKED OFF, BELIEVING THAT JOAN WAS IN LEAGUE WITH THE DEVIL. IRONICALLY, IT WAS THE FRENCH CHURCH THAT CONDEMNED HER AS A WITCH; SHE WAS BURNED AT THE STAKE IN THE PUBLIC SQUARE OF ROUEN (LEFT).

# Who Invented Printing?

## Was Gutenberg the original inventor of the printing press, or can it be traced to earlier sources?

SHOWN AT RIGHT IS THE PRINTING PRESS INVENTED BY THE GERMAN JOHANNES GUTENBERG. BEFORE THE 15TH CENTURY, ONLY THE CHURCH CREATED BOOKS, AND SOLELY WITH WOOD ENGRAVINGS.

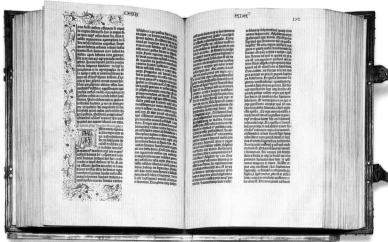

THE GUTENBERG BIBLE, ONE OF THE FIRST BOOKS OFF THE NEW PRESS, WAS PRINTED FROM MOVABLE TYPE IN 1455.

THE LATIN TEXT WAS PRINTED IN GOTHIC TYPE SIMILAR TO OLD ENGLISH. THE BOOK WAS ILLUMI-NATED, OR DECO-RATED, BY HAND.

CONSIDERED ONE OF THE MOST IMPORTANT, influential inventions of the last millennium, the printing press, along with the utilization of printing, changed the world. It has been argued that the advent of printing was the start of mass communication—that without it, the Protestant Reformation may not have taken place, nor the scientific and artistic advances leading to the Renaissance come to pass.

But where did printing really come from? Though the roots of printing are thought to lie in 15th-century Germany with Johannes Gutenberg, it can be traced back far before the Middle Ages and Western civilization.

### SIGNET STONES

As far back as ancient Babylon, civilizations would group signet stones together, wet them with tinted mud, and press them down on clay for simple impressions. While "printing" pictures on textiles was common all around Europe and Asia by the first century AD, it was the East that finally brought the art of printing text to the world. The Greek and Roman empires dabbled in stamping designs, but it wasn't practical for them to try stamping text—their "paper" was flimsy papyrus, too delicate to be subjected to a printing process. They did mass produce some of their writings: Using remarkable penmanship, literate slaves would painstakingly copy texts by the hundreds, even thousands. But it took the East to introduce the printed word to the world.

In the 2nd century, the Chinese began to put characters on wooden blocks for the reproduction of holy texts and prayers. What did the ancient Chinese have that the ancient Greeks and Romans did not? Paper. Stronger than papyrus, paper was able to withstand the pressure of wooden blocks. By the 10th century, printing text was in the form that it is today— movable type, or the arranging of characters in sequence to make an imprint. However, the complexities of the Chinese language—not to mention the almost limitless number of characters—made it relatively impractical for the Chinese to keep up the printing fad, so movable type gradually faded from use.

### ENTER EUROPEAN INGENUITY

Before the 15th century, only the Church created books, and these were produced by way of wood engravings. But in the 1400s, wooden wine presses began to be converted into rough printing presses, with a new format of movable type. This mechanical printing press seems to have originated independent of the Eastern presses of five centuries earlier, using oil inks and replacing the old wooden blocks with more reliable metal ones.

Rather than using clay or rods to hold the letters together, the Europeans held the metal blocks on a tray, applying pressure to keep them in place. The press took off like gangbusters; books were churned out more quickly than ever before. Religious pamphlets, intellectual works, and literature of all kind were mass produced, making knowledge and writings previously confined to the upper classes and the Church open to all members of society.

Claim to the invention goes, rightfully, to Johannes Gutenberg, from the German city of Mainz, in 1436 or 1437. Although skeptics

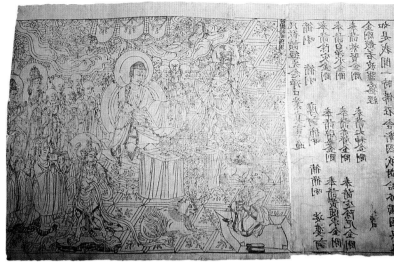

THE DIAMOND SUTRA (ABOVE), FROM 868 AD, IS CONSIDERED THE WORLD'S FIRST PRINTED BOOK. BY THE 10TH CENTURY, MOVABLE TYPE WAS IN USE IN CHINA. BELOW, A CLAY STAMP FROM 2280 BC USED TO MAKE INSCRIPTIONS ON BRICKS.

argue that no substantial documentation proves his ownership, enough citizens of the town and the provinces agreed that the press was Gutenberg's brainchild. French and Dutch descendants continue to assert that their countrymen were the originators, but Gutenberg's autograph on pages printed in 1450 precedes all others.

It was Gutenberg whose transformed wine press first utilized the new mold type lettering, screw press, and nonsmearing ink. And it was his new printing press design that would not change for years to come, as the machine spread to all parts of Europe. One of the first books from his press was, of course, the Gutenberg Bible, a pinnacle of craftsmanship that even now stands as the apex of printing press art.

## KOSTER'S CLAIM

As with any great invention, dispute over printing's father was to be expected. Though now lost in the tides of history, a Dutchman from Haarlem also claimed to have been the creator of the printing press. Laurens Janszoon Koster (or Coster) was one of the preeminent printers of the day. His design for

**THAT NAME AGAIN?** ▼

carved, reusable blocks of type was an integral part of the creation of the press, and without him, the press may have been unusable.

While his name may not have made its way into the history books as Gutenberg's has, Laurens Koster's role in the development of printed text cannot be ignored.

# PART 4

# THE EARLY MODERN AGE

MEMORIES ARE NOT INFALLIBLE, ESPECIALLY WHEN THEY HAVE BEEN PASSED down over generations and possibly amplified to suit the need for heroes. So, even as Americans appreciate the symbolic value to the nation of events like Paul Revere's midnight ride warning that the British were on their way, it is also interesting to ask what the real Paul Revere actually did and did not accomplish on that night in 1775.

Of course, speculating about the founding figures and events of early American history doesn't mean ignoring intriguing questions arising in Europe and elsewhere. In 1791, Wolfgang Amadeus Mozart was found dead in his Vienna home. Did the composer die of natural causes or was he murdered by a rival musician? Around the same time, Napoleon began to build an empire. But why did it fall so fast? Almost a century later, a wave of murders shocked Londoners and threw the city into a state of fear. Who was the serial killer known as Jack the Ripper? These and other mysteries await us as we look back at the Early Modern Age.

# Who Discovered North America?

**Christopher Columbus is regarded as the modern discoverer of the New World, but many historians disagree— and they have solid evidence backing them.**

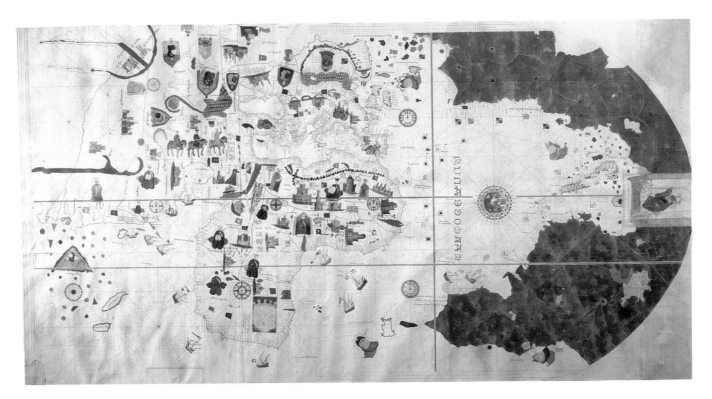

A 1493 WOODCUT (TOP) IS THE EARLIEST PICTURE OF THE DISCOVERY OF THE NEW WORLD BY COLUMBUS (ABOVE, IN A PORTRAIT BY THE ITALIAN RIDOLFO GHIRLANDAIO). A MODERN MODEL OF A NORSE SHIP IS SHOWN OPPOSITE.

FOR DECADES, HISTORIANS HAVE BEEN AMASSING evidence to prove that several other explorers predated Christopher Columbus's discovery by centuries. The Norseman Leif Eriksson supposedly made the journey to the New World 500 years before Columbus, but some scholars think that earlier mariners might have made a similar voyage. These scholars point out the anthropological similarities between various Mediterranean and Middle American peoples; like the Egyptians, the Olmecs and Mayas also built pyramid-like structures and used hieroglyphs. They also note botanical links between Middle America and North Africa. They suggest that visits by the ancients to pre-Columbian America might account for the complexity of the societies developed in Mexico, the Yucatan, and Peru.

## LEGENDARY ENCOUNTERS

The splendid navigational prowess of the ancient Phoenicians have made them natural candidates to have been early visitors to the New World. In 600 BC, Pharaoh Necho II of Egypt commissioned them to circumnavigate Africa; three years later, a fleet returned, claiming to have achieved the task. The Phoenicians also sailed the Atlantic in their vessels, reaching Iberia and the Canary Islands. Some historians claim they made it to the Azores, where a hoard of gold was found in the 18th century that many believed was of Phoenician origin. Given such evidence, we can only conjecture whether the Phoenicians might have sailed farther west and stumbled upon the New World.

Many Central American cultures have legends of encounters with godlike foreigners,

THE VIKINGS
DEVELOPED THE
ART AND SCIENCE
OF SAILING THE
SEAS AND USED IT
TO EXPAND THEIR
EMPIRE. ABOVE,
CHRISTIAN KROHG'S
DEPICTION OF
LEIF ERIKSSON'S
FIRST SIGHTING
OF NORTH AMERICA.

and several Eastern cultures have fables of journeys to a land across the eastern ocean. The Chinese called it Fu-Sang and record a trip made in 458 AD by a group of five Buddhist priests searching for an earthly paradise. The land they discovered bears some resemblance to the ancient metropolis of Teotihuacan, in central Mexico—the people there had a system of writing, unwalled cities, and cultivated a fruit that matches the description of the agave, native to the region.

It is also possible that Irish monks, in search of the contemplative isolation promised by remote islands, may have crossed the North Atlantic in tiny vessels called curraghs. Each vessel was made with ox hides sewn over a wooden frame, and driven by oars and a square sail. Timothy Severin, a writer and explorer, demonstrated the curragh's seaworthiness when he sailed in a replica from Ireland to Newfoundland in 1976. His ship was named for St. Brendan who, folklore says, explored the North Atlantic in the 6th century AD. It is certain that the Irish knew a great deal about the far Atlantic, and their knowledge appears in treatises as early as 825 AD.

LEFT, EXCAVATION
OF A NORSE SHIP
BURIAL (THIS ONE
IN THE ORKNEY
ISLANDS), A WAY
OF SHOWING THE
IMPORTANCE THE
NORSE PLACED ON
THEIR ABILITY TO
SAIL THE SEAS.

## THE NORSEMEN COMETH

The only conclusive evidence of a pre-Columbian visit to the New World involves the early Norse, who began settling Iceland in the late 10th century. In 982, Erik the Red, having been exiled for three years, sailed westward to the ice-clogged coast of an unknown land and eventually landed at a place of grassy meadows and sparkling fjords. He returned to Iceland, rhapsodizing about this newly discovered "Greenland," as he called it. Around 986 AD, he returned with 25 ships carrying more than 400 colonists; just 14 ships arrived safely.

Following Erik the Red was Bjarni Herjólfsson, a trader. Although he was blown off course while sailing from Iceland to Greenland, Bjarni probably saw what is now Newfoundland, setting eyes on the New World centuries before Columbus. Erik's second son Leif would continue his father's exploration. Around 1000 AD, Leif, who knew about Bjarni's sightings, bought Bjarni's vessel and sailed southwest with a crew of 35. The men landed on an island full of mountains and glaciers (Helluland, or Flat Rock Land). Leif then sailed farther, passing Markland (Wood Land) and finally docking at a cape jutting out from the mainland. The men settled by an inland lake, where they spent the mild winter feasting on salmon and on the grapes native to the region. When spring came, they loaded their vessels with grapes and timber, and left what they called Vinland (Land of Vines).

### FACT OR FABLE?

Over the next few decades, other Norse traveled to Vinland, including Leif's brother Thorvald and the Icelandic merchant Thorfinn Karlsefni. Snorri, a boy born to Thorfinn's wife Gudrid, is thought to have been the first European born in North America. In several other expeditions, the Norse were able to continue their explorations up and down the coast, trading with natives they called *skraelings,* Norse for "barbarian" or "pygmy." Relationships between the two peoples soured, however, and after a number of violent clashes, the Norse fled back to Greenland. The final attempt at colonization ended abruptly in 1014 when the exploration party fell prey to internal rivalries, and many of the men and women were murdered by Erik's illegitimate daughter, Freydis, a leader of the mission. The Norse appear to have made no more attempts to settle Vinland.

The Vinland story was preserved by word of mouth and written down some 200 years later as *The Saga of the Greenlanders* and *The Saga of Erik the Red.* Some scholars consider them fables, but most archeologists agree on the location of the main landing sites mentioned: Helluland is Baffin Island and Vinland is on the northern tip of Newfoundland. The case for the latter was strengthened in the 1960s, when excavations of the town of L'Anse aux

## THE VINLAND MAP

A map of Vinland, now belonging to Yale University, was produced in Germany some 50 years before Columbus' discovery. The Western European portion is recognizable, but the North Atlantic portion shows several islands, including a relatively accurate depiction of Greenland and another larger island—labeled "Island of Vinland"—that may represent Baffin Island, Labrador, and Newfoundland. Since publication of the scholarly edition of the map

**PIECES OF THE PUZZLE ▼**

in 1965, it has been the subject of scholarly controversy. In the 1960s, a Chicago firm analyzing the ink found a 20th-century substance (a titanium derivative known as anotase) and concluded the map was a forgery. Yet, at a recent conference at New Haven, other investigators from the University of California reported that this particular substance does appear in medieval maps. The original investigators reject this finding, and the controversy rages on.

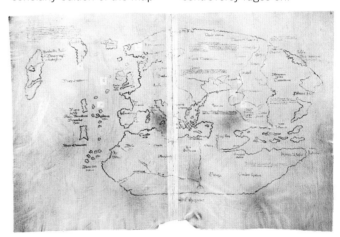

THE FAMOUS VINLAND MAP HAS BEEN THE SOURCE OF CONTROVERSY FOR DECADES. BUT THE CONTENTION IT SUPPORTS—THAT THE NORSE DISCOVERED NORTH AMERICA WELL BEFORE COLUMBUS—HAS BECOME MORE AND MORE ACCEPTED.

Meadows uncovered the sites of six houses built of turf and timber, the largest measuring 70 feet long and 55 feet wide. The houses are similar in structure to Norse dwellings found in Greenland, and have been carbon-dated to around 1000 AD. The only problem with Newfoundland's identification as Vinland is that the former has no grapes. Some scholars suggest that the Norse were actually referring to the gooseberries and cranberries that grow there.

For the next several centuries, there was probably sporadic contact between Greenland and Vinland, but by the beginning of the Age of Discovery, Europe lost contact with Vinland, and the stray ships that docked there reported that its people had vanished.

# Forgotten
# Native American Women

## Why are so many American Indian women missing from the history books?

**SARAH WINNEMUCCA BECAME THE FIRST NATIVE AMERICAN WOMAN TO PUBLISH A PERSONAL AND TRIBAL HISTORY BOOK, IN 1883.**

IF HISTORY BOOKS HAVE REDUCED NATIVE AMERI-can societies to a supporting role when telling the story of America, then they have reduced the role of the women within those societies to a bit part. But despite the neglect of some historians, Native American women have in fact made a number of significant contributions to their cultures. As in other societies, these contributions sometimes involved break-ing down their culture's gender boundaries. In most North American Plains tribes, for exam-ple, the duties of hunting and war traditionally belonged to men. Women were expected to perform other vital tasks, including the rearing of children and the fashioning of shelter and clothes from animal skins. It is known, howev-er, that among these tribes there were at least a few female warriors and hunters.

### "MANLY-HEARTED WOMEN"
Called "manly-hearted women" by some, these women rivaled the proficiency of their male peers on both hunting ground and battlefield. The Cheyenne produced some of the most dis-tinguished women warriors, including Buffalo-Calf-Road-Woman, who in 1876 stormed into the heart of a fierce battle to rescue her broth-er, the Cheyenne warrior Chief Comes-in-Sight. In honor of her heroic act, the victorious Cheyenne named the day's struggle the Battle Where the Girl Saved Her Brother. Another Cheyenne woman warrior, Island Woman, once helped her tribe raid the Pawnee. When rushed by an attacker on horseback, she is said to have wrested the enemy's hatchet from his grasp, toppling him from his steed in the process. Yellow-Haired Woman, the daughter of a Cheyenne chief, fought beside her tribesmen in the battle of Beecher's Island in 1868. In a bat-tle the next year, she saw action again, this time injuring one enemy and killing another.

In some Native American societies, women and men regularly hunted together. In the Blackfoot tribe, for instance, bison were hunt-ed by a method known as "the surround of the buffalo." When scouts located a herd, the chief would tell the men to get their arrows and lances, and the women to get their *travois* (a sled-like device fashioned from poles that was normally used to transport a load). The women would stand their travois upright, lashing them together to create a makeshift fence in the shape of a semicircle. A few men would then drive the bison toward the fence, behind which the women hid. As the herd neared the travois, the women would shout, keeping the animals at bay. The men then moved in from the flanks, surrounding and killing the bison.

## DIPLOMACY AND LETTERS

American Indian women have also excelled at that art typically aimed at the prevention of bloodshed: diplomacy. It was a woman—Pocahontas—who played the role of ambassador and interpreter at Jamestown. After a European education, Mary Musgrove, a Creek, handled relations and interpreting for James Oglethorpe, the founder of the Georgia colony. In another example, Molly Brant worked for more than 40 years as a liaison between her native Mohawk tribe and Sir William Johnson, a British Indian agent.

And then there was Sacagawea. If not for her skills as an emissary, history might very well have forgotten the Lewis and Clark expedition. The Shoshone woman's service as a guide for the expedition was limited, despite popular myths to the contrary; it was in her role as interpreter and diplomat that she most benefited the explorers. Besides conveying the group's peaceful intentions throughout the trip, Sacagawea managed to convince a Shoshone chief to provide guides and horses to the expedition for the difficult trek through the Bitterroot Mountains and Salmon River country.

History has also seen accomplished American Indian women of letters. In 1883, Sarah Winnemucca became the first Native American woman to publish a personal and tribal history. Her book was titled *Life Among the Paiutes: Their Wrongs and Claims*, and it argued for the restoring of lands to the people of the Malheur Reservation in Oregon—a subject that dominated the public lectures she began giving in 1879. Her lecture tour eventually took her east, where she lectured in the homes of supporters like Ralph Waldo Emerson and Senator Henry Dawes of Massachusetts. Though she was eventually promised her people would be allowed to return to their land, the promise was never kept.

Christine Quintasket, another literary pioneer, was one of the first American Indian women to pen a novel. In 1927, writing under the name Mourning Dove, she published *Cogewea, the Half-Blood*, a novel revealing a broad spectrum of emotions in its characters in an attempt to dispel the stoic, dispassionate stereotype of the Native American. Quintasket, an Okanogan from the Colville Reservation of eastern Washington, also preserved many of her people's tales; her collection, titled *Coyote Stories*, was published in 1933.

Hunters, warriors, diplomats, writers: In light of such accomplishments, the limited appearance of Native American women in the pages of history texts is hardly justified by claiming their impact on history has been limited. In truth, their roles have been diverse, their contributions of no small consequence.

ABOVE, A DETAIL OF THE DESIGN ON A NATIVE AMERICAN DRESS. WOMEN WERE RESPONSIBLE FOR FASHIONING CLOTHING AND SHELTER IN MOST TRIBES. BETSY, AN OMAHA INDIAN (LEFT), WAS AN EXPONENT OF WOMEN'S RIGHTS. SHE JOINED THE MEN OF HER TRIBE ON BUFFALO HUNTS AND SPOKE THREE INDIAN LANGUAGES BESIDES ENGLISH AND FRENCH.

# What Happened to Henry Hudson?

## The famed explorer's ultimate fate has fueled many haunting legends. Even more remarkably, the mutineers who set him adrift were acquitted. Why?

ABOVE, "HUDSON, THE DREAMERS, LANDING ON THE SHORES OF DELAWARE BAY, 1609." OPPOSITE, JOHN COLLIER'S "THE LAST VOYAGE OF HENRY HUDSON." BOTH ARE LATE 19TH-CENTURY DEPICTIONS OF THE EXPLORER, WHOSE ACCOMPLISHMENTS WERE UNDONE BY HIS FAVORITISM AND POOR LEADERSHIP.

ENGLISH NAVIGATOR HENRY HUDSON'S NAME endures in three bodies of water that he explored: the Hudson River, at the mouth of which lies New York City; Hudson Strait; and Hudson Bay, northern Canada's vast inland sea. Yet, despite this renown, Hudson's end was anything but glorious: He disappeared in 1611 after mutineers cast him adrift in a small open boat on ice-clogged northern waters.

During the late 16th century, a robust sea trade developed between western Europe and the Spice Islands and China. Because the route—south along Africa's west coast, around the Cape of Good Hope, and across the Indian Ocean—was long and often perilous, European mariners and merchants sought a shorter, safer, and cheaper route. Unable to find an inland route through North America, they sent their ships to find routes along Russia's north coast (which was called the Northeast Passage) and over the top of present-day Canada (called the Northwest Passage).

The search for the Northwest Passage inspired the voyages of Martin Frobisher in 1576 and John Davis in 1585. Along on the Davis voyage there may have been a young sailor whose family had invested heavily in the expedition's London sponsor, the Muscovy Company. His name: Henry Hudson.

### HUDSON'S FOUR EXPEDITIONS

Little is known about Hudson's early life; even the date of his birth is uncertain. But he was already an accomplished mariner when he captained his first expedition in 1607. Under the auspices of the Muscovy Company, Hudson sailed the *Hopewell* along Greenland's east coast, searching in vain for an opening that would lead to the Northwest Passage. Instead, he reached the Spitsbergen archipelago, north of Norway, where he found rich fishing grounds that would be exploited by British whalers and sealers for centuries.

The following year, the Muscovy Company sent Hudson and the *Hopewell* to Spitsbergen, where he began a search for the alternate Northeast Passage. When Hudson found the sea blocked by ice, he thought about sailing west to resume the previous year's explorations. The crew would hear none of this, however. Led by Robert Juet, the rascally master seaman, the irate crew forced Hudson to abandon his plan and return to England in late August.

This incident shook the Muscovy Company's faith in Hudson, and its backers refused to sponsor a third voyage. Instead, Hudson turned to the Dutch East India Company, which outfitted him with a new ship, the *Half Moon,* and instructed him to sail once again in search of the Northeast Passage. Hudson

explored the waters north of Norway for a month, but the crew—a mixed lot of English and Dutch sailors—grew weary and cold.

At the instigation of Juet—amazingly, still part of the crew despite his unruliness—Hudson set sail for North America, hoping to find a route across the middle of the continent. It was on this voyage that Hudson sailed upstream to a point near present-day Albany on the river that bears his name.

On his return to England in November, Hudson prepared a report for the East India Company, but before he could deliver it English officials accused him of "voyaging to the detriment of his country." As a result, the *Half Moon* was returned to the Dutch, who would rely on Hudson's records and maps when they settled the area at the mouth of the Hudson River. That should have been the end of Hudson's career, but the explorer still had many influential friends who backed one more attempt at finding the Northwest Passage.

In April 1610, Hudson set out in the ship *Discovery,* accompanied by his son, John, and a rough-and-tumble crew of nineteen who included Juet, Henry Greene, and William Wilson. The *Discovery* passed through Hudson Strait in July and, a month later, reached Hudson Bay. Hudson was the first European explorer known to enter this vast inland sea. His explorations established England's claim to the surrounding region, which would become an abundant source of furs.

The *Discovery* sailed down the desolate east shore into James Bay, where Hudson tacked to and fro searching for that elusive channel to the Far East. The crew began to suspect that irresolute Hudson was looking for a spot where he could beach the ship and spend the winter. Their fears were confirmed when Hudson ordered the ship's carpenter, Phillip Staffe, to build a house on shore. It was by now mid-November, and the crew realized that it was already too late for a return journey to England. December began with the *Discovery* still in James Bay; clearly they would have to spend the winter there and fight to survive.

The winter was a bitter one, and the crew subsisted on the occasional seagull they were able to kill or on soups made of pine needles and tamarack buds. The ice broke up in late May 1611, and the crew thankfully prepared to return home. But Hudson gave the order to continue the search for the Northwest Passage. He may have realized that this would be his last chance, and so did the crew. Determined not to spend yet another winter in this inhospitable region, the crew decided to take control of the ship and sail for England.

## THE HUDSONS CAST ADRIFT

The mutiny that would go down in North American history began on June 22. Led by Juet, Greene, and Wilson, the mutineers forced Hudson, his son, and seven loyal crewmen into a small open boat without food and water, then cast them adrift in icy James Bay. The mutineers offered to spare Staffe, but he insisted on remaining with Hudson. As the *Discovery* sailed away, the men in the boat desperately tried to keep up with it, shouting at the mutineers and begging for help. Soon, the small boat was lost in ice and fog. Hudson and the other castaways were never seen again.

Hudson's ultimate fate became the stuff of speculation and legend. In 1631, Capt. Thomas James found remains of a shack on Danby Island in the middle of James Bay. More than 30 years later, Capt. Zachariah Gilliam found similar remains. Fur trappers of the region reported seeing stones bearing the carved letters "HH," but these may have been native symbols. One legend claims Hudson and his son reached shore, where they were captured by the natives who enslaved and, later, killed them. Another legend says Hudson and his son sailed 3,000 miles across the Arctic to Spitsbergen, where they perished—but not before they had built a shelter, reputedly found by Capt. Douglas Clavering in 1823.

As for the mutineers, the ringleaders Juet, Greene, and Wilson died en route to England; the other survivors were arrested as soon as they docked on October 20. Four of the men were charged with murder—not mutiny—but were acquitted, spared because mercantile interests valued their knowledge of Hudson's voyages more than justice.

TOP, HENRY HUDSON IS PORTRAYED AS A BRITISH ARISTOCRAT AND A FOIL FOR HIS UNRULY MASTER SEAMAN, ROBERT JUET, IN WILLIAM HEATH'S 1825 ILLUSTRATION FROM WASHINGTON IRVING'S *KNICKERBOCKER HISTORY OF NEW YORK.* MIGHTY ICEBERGS MADE NAVIGATION HAZARDOUS FOR HUDSON IN THE ICY CANADIAN WATERS (BELOW).

# El Dorado & the Seven Cities of Cibola

"WHOEVER POSSESSES GOLD CAN ACQUIRE ALL that he desires in the world. Truly, with gold he can gain entrance for his soul into paradise." Christopher Columbus gave voice to the feelings of dozens of Spanish explorers when he made this statement more than 500 years ago. Of course, the pursuit of riches is a universal passion, transcending time and place; but the search for the legendary El Dorado, as well as the Seven Cities of Cibola, is part of the endlessly fascinating history of Spanish exploration in the New World.

El Dorado (Spanish for "the gilded one") was a South American Indian king who is said to have presided over a region so rich that he covered himself with gold dust. His name was also used by Europeans for the land where he dwelled. Stories of El Dorado first surfaced in the 16th century through the accounts of Inca kings from Peru. Encouraged by these anecdotes, Spanish explorers departed for South America, where most of their searches focused on the region near present-day Bogotá, Colombia. Here, they hoped to locate and conquer El Dorado and plunder its gold.

### DREAMS AND COLONIZATION

The Spaniards expected to enter a realm where palaces were constructed entirely of gold and where even the cooking utensils were fashioned out of the precious metal. And while they were able to loot enormous amounts of gold from the local Muisca Indians and their neighbors, hundreds of adventurers died in the effort, often by sinking into swamps, overloaded with booty.

Although the Spanish were the chief visitors to the region where El Dorado was thought to be located, there were other European explorers. The English explorer Sir Walter Raleigh made two failed expeditions to find the

THE ENGLISH EXPLORER SIR WALTER RALEIGH (ABOVE) MADE A MAP OF THE SUPPOSED SITE OF EL DORADO IN 1600 (RIGHT).

supposed site of El Dorado. It was the failure of his second expedition, in 1617, which led to his execution.

Several other European countries also attempted to set up colonies in South America. While colonization was supposedly the thrust of these expeditions, the explorers did not shy from treasure hunting in this fabled region of riches. In 1602, the French king Henry IV ordered the establishment of a colony in the Guyana area. The English tried again between 1602 and 1609, when John and Charles Lee attempted the establishment of an English presence on the River Oyapock, on Brazil's border.

### SEARCH FOR THE LOST CITIES

While the word "El Dorado" has come to symbolize any place where great wealth can be obtained quickly, the Seven Cities of Cibola acquired a less dazzling meaning. The story of the cities originated with the Spaniard explorer Alvar Nuñez Cabeza de Vaca, who had set out to conquer Florida in 1527. After many misfortunes, the explorer and three companions ended up wandering through Texas, New Mexico, Arizona, and northern Mexico, where they claimed they had seen the Seven Cities, reputed to possess fabulous riches.

In 1536, when Cabeza de Vaca reached Mexico City, his story of the Seven Cities excited official interest. In 1540, the viceroy of New Spain, Antonio de Mendoza, sent out a reconnaissance expedition of Fray Marcos de

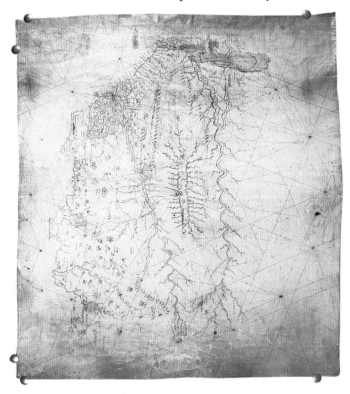

**CORONADO SET OFF THROUGH ARIZONA IN SEARCH OF THE LOST CITIES, BUT HAD TO SETTLE FOR THE GRAND CANYON —A DISAPPOINTMENT FOR HIM AND HIS PARTY.**

Niza, who also claimed to have glimpsed the Seven Cities.

Francisco Vasquez de Coronado, the governor of the province of Nueva Galicia, was called upon to provide military support for de Niza's expedition. Coronado and a small party marched northward into Arizona, until they reached one of the Seven Cities—a Zuni Indian community with adobe huts, but no palaces of gold. Undeterred, Coronado dispatched a band of men to search for other cities. Although the men found no riches, they discovered a natural treasure never seen before by Europeans—the Grand Canyon.

Bitterly disappointed, Coronado returned to Mexico City in 1542. He was coolly received by the authorities and, two years later, relieved of his position of governor. Thereafter he lived quietly in Mexico City, possibly musing on the whereabouts of the "lost" cities of Cibola.

**A TIMELESS LURE**

Explorers searched for El Dorado and the Seven Cities of Cibola, although no one has discovered the treasures said to be hidden there. Why have so many people made the journey, despite their predecessors' failures? Is it the mystery and glamour surrounding these destinations? The story of the Seven Cities of Cibola tells of vanished sites and the lure of gold. El Dorado has all the intrigue and glitter of an adventure movie. Both provided alluring destinations for larger-than-life explorers.

## LAKE OF GOLD

El Dorado (above) got his name because of a curious religious ritual he performed during certain Indian festivals. El Dorado is said to have plastered his nude body with gold dust as his subjects tossed gold and

**THE STUFF OF LEGEND ▼**

jewelry into Lake Guatavita. Upon completion of the ritual, the Golden Man would dive into the lake to wash off the gold dust. The treasures left in the water are still rumored to lie on the lake's bottom.

# What Happened at Jamestown?

**More than a few myths surround the history of America's ill-fated first settlement.**

A PORTRAIT OF POCAHONTAS HANGS IN THE NATIONAL PORTRAIT GALLERY IN WASHINGTON, D.C. THE NOTION THAT SHE THREW HER BODY IN FRONT OF CAPTAIN JOHN SMITH TO SAVE HIS LIFE IS CONSIDERED SUSPECT BY MANY SCHOLARS, AS ARE OTHER LEGENDS SURROUNDING THE FAMOUS NATIVE AMERICAN GIRL.

THE STORIES OF THE FIRST PERMANENT ENGLISH settlement in America—Jamestown—have often been subject to some "stretchers," as Mark Twain's Huck Finn would call them. Disney's 1995 animated hit *Pocahontas*, for example, would have us believe that the daughter of the American Indian Chief Powhatan married the dashing Captain John Smith of Jamestown, whereas in truth she married farmer John Rolfe of the settlement, who has the dubious distinction of being the first to export tobacco and was by all reports an "ardent smoker." Who was Pocahontas, then? What was life really like at Jamestown? And why did so many of the settlers die there in its early years?

Four hundred years after Europeans set their first permanent stakes in the New World, new evidence has undermined some assumptions about the first settlement. Of the 105 people who survived the five months at sea to arrive at "James' Towne" (named after the presiding English king James I) on May 13, 1607, only 38 of them remained alive after eight months. And when 400 new colonists arrived in the winter of 1609, there was so little food in storage that all but 60 died by spring. Scholars, using written records, had ascribed the deaths to many causes: dysentery, contamination of the drinking water by salt water, spoilage of the food brought from England, and early skirmishes with the local Algonquian Indians.

### A CASE OF BAD TIMING?

Until recently, historians assumed that a more versatile bunch of people might have been able to endure the hardships on the Virginia coast. But in 1998, archeological teams from Virginia's College of William and Mary and the University of Arkansas happened upon a startling discovery. In studying the width of tree rings of ancient bald cypress trees in southeastern Virginia, some of which date as far back as the 11th century, the scientists saw that from 1587 to 1589 there was a drought more extreme than any in the preceding 800 years. The years 1606 to 1612 accounted for the driest seven-year period in 770 years. No matter what the skill of the men involved, the climate at Jamestown would have presented difficulties in those early years. "If the English had tried to find a worse time to launch their settlements in the New World, they could not have done so," said Dennis Blanton, who directed the study.

In September 1996, a team of archeologists led by William Kelso announced the discovery of the remains of James Fort—built in 1607 to defend Jamestown—which was thought swallowed by the James River centuries ago. Perhaps the most fascinating discovery was the body of a young European male in his 20s, buried within the fort, with a musket ball lodged in a lower leg and a hole in his shoulder blade, suggesting gunshot wounds. As the local Indian population had limited access to guns (though they did acquire them through trading), the wounds suggest the man could have been shot by another settler.

Could there have been a revolt within the fort because of the drought and scarcity of

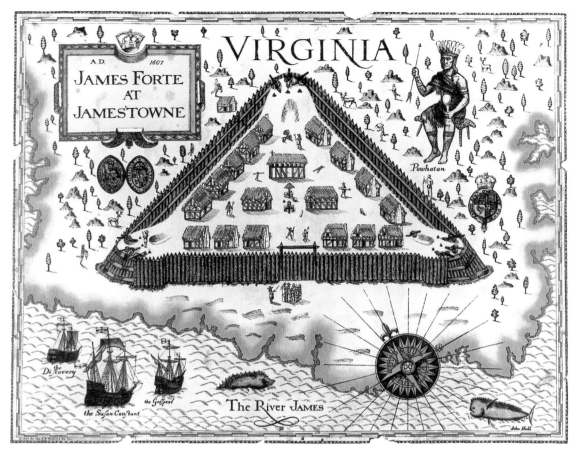

**VIRGINIA**

A.D. 1607
JAMES FORTE AT JAMESTOWNE

Powhatan

the Discovery
the Godspeed
the Susan Constant

The River JAMES

John Hull

food? Such a finding would undermine the picture of peaceful cooperation amid terrible hardship that the settlers wanted to paint for the Virginia Company, the group of investors back in England who financed the venture.

## THE INDIAN "PRINCESS"

Will the new finds be able to tell us any more about Pocahontas? Captain John Smith, who led Jamestown in its difficult early years, wrote that in December 1607 he was captured and forced to stretch out on two large, flat stones, with Indians standing over him with clubs. Then Pocahontas rushed in, took Smith's head in her arms, and "hazarded the beating out of her owne braines to save mine."

Some historians doubt the veracity of the story, as it was written some 16 years after the event; Smith made no mention of it in previous correspondence. Others wonder whether the scene could have been a set-up, intended to make Smith believe his life was spared, thereby tempering his attitude toward the natives.

Regardless, while still a little girl, Pocahontas would deliver messages from her father to Jamestown, bringing furs, hatchets, and trinkets to trade. When the boys of the colony

would spin cartwheels, "she would follow and wheele some herself, naked as she was all the fort over." But any romantic interest with John Smith, as storytellers would have it, is unlikely; he left the colony while she was still a girl of 14.

Only later, when taken as a hostage by the British and held for ransom, did Pocahontas meet tobacco farmer John Rolfe. Rolfe was piously religious, and struggled with the idea of interracial marriage. But his love for Pocahontas triumphed, and the marriage went forward, bringing a period of peace between the two populations. Pocahontas became Rebecca, had a son whose ancestry survives today, and braved a voyage to England, where she died of pneumonia or tuberculosis at 22.

# The Discovery of **Australia**

**Dutch navigators, not Captain Cook, were the first Europeans to discover Australia. But even they may not have gotten there first.**

CHINESE EXPLORERS (ABOVE) WOULD HAVE USED ASTROLABES TO NAVIGATE BY THE STARS. IN 1773, CAPTAIN COOK REFITTED THE *ENDEAVOUR,* ANCHORED AT A RIVER ON THE EASTERN COAST OF AUSTRALIA (BOTTOM).

IN THE AGE OF DISCOVERY, VAST LANDS OPENED UP to conquistadors, missionaries, and traders alike. But beyond the Americas, the Far East, and the African coasts, a gigantic land mass to the south loomed. Titled on maps *Terra Australis Nondum Cognita* (The Not Yet Known Southern Land), the enigmatic realm seemed to promise fertile land and future settlements. Little was known about it, and fables of fantastical creatures spurred interest in Europe.

## A SOUTHERN EDEN?

Many people mistakenly assume that English navigator Captain James Cook was the discoverer of Australia, but even he would not have been the first explorer to sight and set foot upon the land. China most likely poked around the continent in the early 15th century, when the Ming Dynasty sent an armada of ships out to explore the southern waters. They even had preliminary knowledge of the southern land when Marco Polo came on his well-wishing journey a hundred years earlier. After he returned from the Far East, talking of a southern continent, maps began to depict the unknown land. Magellan's expeditions also conveyed reports of a land at the base of the world that seemed to stretch forever.

By the early 17th century, fleets of ships were sent out to what promised to be a southern Eden. The Spanish charted some near misses of the land, seeing only the island that would become known as New Guinea. But the first European to set foot on the continent would be Dutch. In 1606, Dutch navigator Willem Jansz was sent by the East India Company to scout New Guinea for gold and spices. After coasting New Guinea, Jansz turned his ship

south and landed at a cape—the promontory known today as Cape York, the northernmost part of the present-day state of Queensland.

Later Dutch explorers reported unfavorably on the terrain they saw. Australia was considered to be a wasteland, devoid not only of fertile land but also of gold, silver, or any other trade commodities. It would remain uncolonized for the next century and a half.

Enter Captain Cook: On a mission in 1768 to explore uncharted waters, Cook sailed west from New Zealand and was nudged north by a gale—whereupon he encountered what other explorers had missed: Australia's fertile eastern coast. He named his first anchorage Botany Bay for its profusion of new plant species. After charting the entire eastern coast, he claimed it for Britain, naming it New South Wales. It was now 1770, and it wasn't long before Australia would be settled by Europeans, most against their will.

## PRISON COLONY TO OZ
"Wasn't long" came all of 17 years later. With English prisons full (after losing its war with the American colonies, Britain could no longer transport its criminals across the Atlantic), the British saw New South Wales as the answer to its problem.

In 1787, two navy ships and nine transports under the command of Captain Arthur Phillip sailed from Portsmouth with 649 crewmen, merchant seamen, and Marines and 770 convicts. The voyage took eight months. Arriving at Botany Bay, Phillip found the location wanting, and he sailed farther up the coast to find

what he described as "the finest harbour in the world." At sunset on January 26, 1788, he raised the Union Jack beside a deepwater inlet on the southern shore, naming it after the British home secretary, Lord Sydney.

Britain would transport as many as 162,000 convicts over the next 80 years. Soldiers and freed prisoners were given land grants, and Sydney and the lands beyond it began to flourish. More free settlers started to immigrate, founding both Adelaide and Perth, and a new country was born.

And 212 years later? Despite some unique problems (environmental degradation in a dry land where water is the most valuable natural resource, and the citizenry's efforts to come to terms with the mistreatment of the Aborigines by early settlers), Australia is one of the most livable industrialized countries in the world—a place whose seductive, sun-struck ambience has lent it the storybook nickname of "Oz."

THOUGH HE NOTED ITS ENTRANCE, CAPTAIN COOK (LEFT) FAILED TO INVESTIGATE SYDNEY HARBOUR, THE JEWEL IN AUSTRALIA'S CROWN. CAPTAIN PHILLIP, COMMANDER OF THE FIRST FLEET, FOUND BOTANY BAY UNPROMISING AND SAILED 7 MILES NORTH TO LAND AT SYDNEY COVE (ABOVE). THE FLEET'S SHIPS ANCHORED AT PRESENT-DAY CIRCULAR QUAY, NOW FLANKED ON EITHER SIDE BY THE SYDNEY OPERA HOUSE AND THE HARBOUR BRIDGE.

# How Pure Were the Puritans?

**The prevalent belief that the Puritans were pious churchgoers who frowned on immorality may be an American myth.**

THE CHURCH AND THE BIBLE MAY HAVE BEEN THE cornerstones of Puritan society in 17th and 18th-century New England, but that does not mean the Puritans were any too kind to their fellow man—especially if their fellow man happened to subscribe to a different religion. The Puritans fled England to protect their own religious freedom, but in America, they treated other religious groups shamefully.

In 1656, for example, the general court of the Commonwealth of Massachusetts passed a law stipulating that, for each of their first two offenses, Quakers should have an ear chopped off, and for their third offense, "they shall have their tongues bored through with a hot iron." When Quaker women were caught, they were tied to the back of horse-carts and paraded through several towns, being lashed across their backs all the while with a whip.

The 17th century was wracked by religious strife; throughout Europe and the American colonies, sects and denominations wrestled for control of the Christian faith, often with gruesomely bloody results. The Puritans' deep-seated anxiety in the face of competing religions was in many ways typical of its time—but just as the tenets of their religion were uniquely strict and demanding, so too was the fervor with which they sought out heresy.

## A FASCINATION WITH MYSTICISM

The most famous example of the Puritans' excessive zeal for uncovering "evil" is the Salem witch trials, during which 150 people were imprisoned, 19 were hanged, and one was crushed to death. But the town of Salem, Massachusetts, was only one of many places infected by the witch craze. Before the witch trials, some 200 similar incidents had taken place throughout New England, resulting in the executions of more than 25 people.

In many ways, the obsession with witches in Puritan New England was indicative of a strangely irreligious fascination with mysticism, black magic, and the occult. It was common for towns to have astrologers and fortune tellers who claimed to foretell the future by studying the stars. The almanacs people regularly consulted for advice also purported to reveal mystical knowledge. Many people made important decisions about farming and childbearing based on the predictions they read there. For a society supposedly obsessed with Christian spiritual piety, the Puritans were unusually attracted to this kind of decidedly un-Christian folk magic.

## SOCIAL PRESSURES

But the idea that they were obsessed with Christian spiritual piety may simply be the most obstinate myth about the Puritans. For all that religion-dominated public discourse, historical records reveal that shockingly few citizens of Puritan towns attended church regularly. The first generation of Puritan settlers were very pious indeed, but as time went by, the direct influence of the local churches seems to have waned. If the tax rolls are any indication, fewer than half the adult males in Boston were church members in the middle of the 17th century, and the numbers were even smaller in the outlying towns. Puritan records reveal that by the end of the 17th century, there was a general consensus that religious commitment was in decline, and the standards for church membership had to be relaxed to prevent even more people from slipping through the congregation's hands.

What no one will deny is that, especially in their early years in New England, the Puritans set a high standard for the exemplary Christian life, and people seemed to have been under considerable social pressure to live up to that standard. The psychological forces at work in such a society are difficult to fathom for anyone confronting the Puritans' history in modern times. The sexual and emotional repression, the nervous sense of unbreakable moral protocol, the obsession with appearances, and the lack of any acceptable outlet for any nonreligious feeling—all certainly contributed to

# H IS FOR HERESY

The persecution of those who subscribed to religious faiths the Puritans considered heretical was often a very public matter. Just as the witch crazes provided people with an outlet for resentment and aggression, so too did the spectacle of punishing heretics give Puritan communities an excuse to vent their pent-up hostilities.

The Scarlet Letter.

Such punishments sometimes took place in town squares. They typically featured some form of permanent disfigurement—often in such a way as to identify the victim with the sin of which he had been accused. Nathaniel Hawthorne's *The Scarlet Letter*, in which a Puritan community forces a woman convicted of adultery to wear a scarlet letter A, reads almost like a subdued echo of this 16th-century eyewitness account of the harsh treatment doled out to an unfortunate Quaker by the name of Norton:

"The Drum was Beat, the People gather'd, Norton was fetch'd and stripped to the Waist, and set with his back to the Magistrates, and given in their View, Thirty-six cruel stripes with a knotted cord, and his hand made fast in the Stocks where they had set his Body before, and burn'd very deep with a Red-hot Iron with H. for Heresie."

the violence, intolerance, and fascination with mystical alternatives that characterized Puritan life. The frenzy of the mob mentality, as exhibited in the witch trials, was one way to give voice to pent-up aggressions. The attraction to folk magic was a way to sidestep the solemn commands of biblical wisdom, and the paranoid fascination with the grotesqueries of paganism may have stemmed from a constantly present terror of eternal damnation.

Whatever the explanation, Puritan society was harsh and complex—and by the usual standards of Christian morality, which condemns hypocrisy, intolerance, and violence, the Puritans were oftentimes hardly pure.

# The Salem Witch Trials

**In the ignoble history of the persecution of religious heretics, the Salem witch trials stand out as a pinnacle of injustice and disgrace.**

THE SLAVE TITUBA, IDENTIFIED AS A WITCH, MENACES HER ACCUSERS IN A 19TH-CENTURY ENGRAVING. IN HER CONFESSION SHE TOLD A HORRIFIC TALE INVOLVING BLACK AND RED ANTS AND A DOG WITH A WOMAN'S HEAD. TITUBA LATER RECOUNTED HER CONFESSION WHEN THE TOWNSPEOPLE STOPPED BELIEVING THE CRIES OF THE ACCUSING GIRLS.

LED BY A COURT SPECIALLY APPOINTED BY GOVERnor William Phips, the so-called Salem witch trials were little more than the upwelling of petty rural animosities amplified by the religious fervor of 17th-century New England. Historians have shown that the demons, satanic visitations, and the terror that gripped Salem in 1692 can be adequately explained by referring to tax records, church documents, business and residence listings, and Puritan superstitions.

The whole shameful business began in the early months of 1692 in the kitchen of Samuel Parris, the village minister. A group of teenage girls had gathered to consult a crystal ball for clues regarding the identity of their future husbands. The Parris's slave, a West Indian woman named Tituba, oversaw their divinations. During the ceremony, one of the girls thought she saw something that looked like a coffin. Perhaps Tituba said something to frighten them; perhaps a dog howled. In any case, the entire group was frightened and began acting strangely. The unusual behavior

included speaking nonsense and "getting into Holes," according to one account. Their fits did not abate overnight, and the minister was alerted. He determined the cause of their torment to be witches, and the hunt began.

## WIDESPREAD WITCH-HUNTS

Witch-hunts were far from uncommon at the time; prior to 1692, more than 25 alleged witches had been put to death in greater New England. But the Salem trials are notable for their folly and scope. Over the course of ten months, 165 people were accused of witchcraft, 150 people imprisoned, and 19 put to death—because of a game of "Who-Will-I-Marry?" Community leaders pressed the girls, who had begun to see specters, to name their tormentors. At first the girls would not, but finally they identified two unpopular elderly women. One of the women, the slave Tituba, immediately confessed that she was a witch. Just what Tituba's motives were remains unclear, but her testimony spurred on the hunt.

At the behest of the girls, whose initial reluctance had passed and who were now naming witches all over town, the community brought in more women and men. In April, constables from Salem even went to Maine to arrest George Burroughs, Salem's former reverend, under suspicion of wizardry.

On June 2, the first case was heard, concerning tavern keeper Bridget Bishop. Bishop was found guilty and hanged. Accusations multiplied: July saw five hangings, August five more, and in September eight more were hanged. Finally, Increase Mather, a religious leader in the province, published a sermon condemning the legal techniques of the trials. The judges had permitted the girls to offer spectral evidence—that is, when they were visited by ghosts (a not infrequent occurrence) the courts would ask them to identify the spirit, then base their conviction upon this evidence. Mather

reasoned that if the specter was the work of Satan—a premise most could agree upon—the courts were taking the devil at his own word. Governor Phips was convinced by Mather's criticisms and disbanded the Salem courts, pardoning the remaining accused in May, 1693. The witch trials were over.

## A TOWN DIVIDED

How had it happened? Was it the cruelty of the girls? The religious fervor of their parents? Had the spirit world played a part? Compared to what the courts believed, the explanation favored by most historians is rather plain.

Salem Village was just barely a village in its own right. Salem Town, right down the road, was still the municipal center, and the Salem villagers paid taxes there. This did not sit well at all with the residents of Salem Village, who campaigned tirelessly for autonomy.

This type of dispute was common in 17th-century New England, but within Salem Village there were divisions. Those in the eastern section of the village were less concerned with autonomy; the road ran through their area, meaning the people who lived there had much more contact with Salem Town. The villagers in the western section were mostly farmers, and they distrusted the residents of the eastern side, many of whom were entrepreneurs.

There was a further dispute. After much argument, Salem Village was permitted to build its own church. Once the church was built, however, the villagers could not agree on a minister. Four ministers came and left without a consensus being reached. The disagreeing factions could more or less be divided into the same two groups—those from the east and those from the west.

In short, the Salem witch trials had their roots in a long-standing rural feud: Of the 32 adults who testified against witches during the trials, 30 lived on the west side of town; of the 14 accused witches who lived in the village, 12 were from the eastern section.

Of course, it is not quite as simple as that. Many of the accused lived in surrounding towns and had no part in the Salems' divisions. And it would be careless to suggest that the accusers followed a conscious plan to eliminate their political enemies. Rather, it seems that the highly superstitious residents of Salem Village's western half were alarmed at the inexplicable behavior of a group of teenage girls. Armed with a host of superstitions regarding witchcraft, they allowed their personal prejudices and neighborhood concerns—unconsciously, we assume—to become the basis for a campaign of persecution and murder that left 19 innocent so-called witches dead.

A YOUNG GIRL "TESTIFIES" AT A WITCH TRIAL. SUCH TESTIMONIALS LED TO THE INDICTMENT —AND OFTEN THE HANGING—OF THE UNFORTUNATE "WITCH" WHO WAS ACCUSED (TOP). THE SALEM MADNESS CAME TO AN END WHEN INCREASE MATHER PUBLISHED A SERMON CONDEMNING THE TRIALS. IN 1693 MATHER'S SON, COTTON, PUBLISHED AN ACCOUNT OF WITCH TRIALS IN NEW ENGLAND, PRESENTING IT AS *THE WONDERS OF THE INVISIBLE WORLD* (ABOVE).

# Who Wrote Shakespeare's Plays?

**The Bard's complex comedies and dramas are obviously the work of a brilliant wordsmith, but was Shakespeare himself the author?**

A GOUACHE BY ARTIST ERIC FRASER FEATURES BOTH THE PROLIFIC BARD AND, CURIOUSLY, SAINT GEORGE, WITH SHAKESPEARE'S BIRTHDAY BETWIXT THEM. SHAKESPEARE OFTEN ACTED IN HIS OWN PRODUCTIONS, APPEARING IN ELIZABETHAN THEATRES (OPPOSITE).

HE WAS A PROVINCIAL WITH NO MORE than a grammar-school education, but he somehow managed to compose works extraordinary for their erudition and depth of learning. He was the son of a glove maker from the small market town of Stratford-upon-Avon, but he wrote plays exhibiting an intimate knowledge of court politics, law, the habits of royalty, and the practice of warfare. Out of a life hemmed in by limitations of birth, wealth, access, and opportunity, the writer William Shakespeare created an art that lives on.

## THE MAN FROM STRATFORD

Or did he? Did "William Shakspere," the upstart actor from Stratford, really write the works the world knows as Shakespeare's plays? For more than 200 years, various doubters—encouraged by the lack of surviving biographical information about the man from Stratford—have sifted through the plays, the sonnets, and the annals of Elizabethan England for evidence of another author.

The search dates back to the early 1780s, when the Reverend Doctor James Wilmot traveled to Stratford and its surrounding environs, looking for information about the life of the man hailed as the greatest of all English writers. To his surprise and alarm, Wilmot found not a shred of evidence connecting the Stratford Shakespeare with the authorship of the plays. The available information was limited to a group of legal documents—on which are preserved the six signatures of Shakespeare, written in a wobbly and barely legible hand, that

constitute the sole surviving examples of his handwriting—and no sign beyond his gravestone memorial that he ever penned a poem, much less that he wrote *Hamlet* and *King Lear*. In the years that followed, small groups of scholars, writers, actors, and journalists began proclaiming candidates, claiming that they had discovered the "real" writer. In the early years, attempts to dethrone the man from Stratford centered on two alternative writers: Christopher Marlowe, a poet and playwright who was murdered (some say he disappeared) under mysterious circumstances in 1593, shortly before Shakespeare's greatest works were written; and Francis Bacon, the great scholar, philosopher, and scientist.

## FOCUS ON AN EARL

In the last century, the authorship question has centered increasingly around Edward de Vere, the Earl of Oxford during Shakespeare's day. "Oxfordians" (those who believe Oxford wrote Shakespeare's plays) have amassed an armada of suggestive evidence. A number of Shakespeare's sonnets hint that their author's true name has been obscured, and they are dedicated to a mysterious "Mr. W.H."—the reversed initials of Henry Wriothesley, the Earl of Southampton, whom Oxford urged to marry his daughter Elizabeth. A Bible known to have belonged to Oxford contains many marked passages that were alluded to in Shakespeare's plays. The sonnets contain hints of Shakespeare's bisexuality, and also of a mysterious public scandal that tarnished his name—

MOST OF SHAKESPEARE'S WELL-KNOWN PLAYS WERE PERFORMED AT LONDON'S GLOBE THEATER, WHICH WAS ERECTED IN 1598.

and Oxford was accused of the shameful crime of sleeping with young boys. After Oxford's death in 1604, there was an interruption in the publication of Shakespeare's plays. Twelve years later, upon the death of William Shakespeare, there seems to have been no public memorial ceremony in London, nor even in Stratford—a strange omission for a celebrated playwright. The original monument to Shakespeare in Stratford seems to have portrayed him as a grain merchant, and only later was it changed to show him holding a pen.

The Oxfordians claim that Oxford chose the pen name "William Shake-speare" because it was considered improper in Elizabethan England for noblemen to write plays. They claim that his choice of the name had nothing to do with the actor and theater-owner from Stratford, but that it referred instead to the spear held by Pallas Athena, the Greek goddess of wisdom and protector of the theatrical arts. They see biographical parallels between Oxford's life and many of Shakespeare's plays; the character of Polonius from *Hamlet*, for instance, bears a certain resemblance to Lord Burghley, Oxford's stepfather.

## THE STRATFORDIANS OBJECT

Although a number of prominent writers and thinkers—including Sigmund Freud—have been convinced that the Earl of Oxford was the real author of the plays, very few serious specialists have ever given credence to the idea. To start with, much of the evidence for Oxford is conjectural or circumstantial. Simply because Oxford experienced public disgrace does not mean that he wrote Shakespeare's sonnets; simply because *Hamlet* can be interpreted in such a way as to indicate parallels to Oxford's relatives does not mean that Oxford wrote the plays. And as much evidence as the Oxfordians have, the Stratfordians (those who believe Shakespeare was the writer) have an equally impressive bulk of evidence against Oxford's authorship. For one thing, Shakespeare is referred to as the author of the plays in the private notebooks of Ben Jonson, a contemporary playwright and friend of the poet. Perhaps most important of all, Oxford's death occurred before the last 12 of Shakespeare's plays had even been written.

Some of the charges against Shakespeare's authorship are compelling, but based on the

## SIGNS AND SYMBOLS

Some of the evidence offered by the Oxfordians that the Earl of Oxford wrote Shakespeare's plays may seem excessively circumstantial, but it is nothing compared to the evidence

**VIEW FROM THE FRINGE**

that has been presented by those advocating other candidates. Supporters of the theory that Francis Bacon (shown here) was the real author are legendary for the lengths to which they'll go to establish a connection between their candidate and the writer of the plays. They've searched for buried manuscripts and secret documents, and even scoured the plays for hidden codes, ciphers, and anagrams. For instance, in "unscrambling" a nonsense word from *Love's Labour's Lost*—"honorificabilitudinitatibus"—they claim to have found a Latin phrase, *hi ludi F. Bacon nati tuiti orbi,* which translates roughly to "These plays born of F. Bacon are preserved for the world."

## MR. WILLIAM SHAKESPEARES

COMEDIES,
HISTORIES, &
TRAGEDIES.

Published according to the True Originall Copies.

Martin Droeshout sculpsit London.

LONDON
Printed by Isaac Iaggard, and Ed. Blount. 1623.

THE FIRST BOOK OF SHAKESPEARE'S PLAYS CAME OUT IN 1623, EDITED BY J. HEMINGE AND H. CONDELL. THOUGH NOW A COLLECTOR'S ITEM, IT WAS NOT THE BEST EXAMPLE OF BOOKMAKING, EVEN BY LOW ELIZABETHAN STANDARDS: IT HAD SEVERAL OMISSIONS, POOR PUNCTUATION, AND OFTEN CONFUSED PROSE WITH VERSE. THE ENGRAVING ON THE FRONT, BY DROESHURT, IS ONE OF THE MOST AUTHORITATIVE PORTRAITS OF SHAKESPEARE—BUT IT, TOO, HAS ITS INACCURACIES. DROESHURT PLACED SHAKESPEARE'S HEAD ON A BODY TOO SMALL IN COMPARISON, AND DRESSED THE WORDSMITH IN A COSTUME MORE ORNATE THAN WHAT HE REALISTICALLY WOULD HAVE WORN.

available historical evidence, none are convincing enough to wrest history's mantle from William Shakespeare. It is remarkable that Shakespeare could have written such erudite works with no more than a grammar-school education, but it is hardly impossible to imagine: Jonson, in fact, was educated at the same level and wrote even more erudite works. There will always be doubters who believe Shakespeare from provincial Stratford could not have written the greatest dramas in the English language; but in the absence of reliable proof, theories of alternate authorship can never be considered more than beguiling myths.

# Newton
## and the Birth of Physics

THE HOUSE WHERE NEWTON WAS BORN, IN WOOLSTHORPE, ENGLAND, DISPLAYS SCIENTIFIC INSTRUMENTS THAT WERE ADDED WHEN IT WAS TURNED INTO A LANDMARK. BELOW, THE TITLE PAGE OF THE *PRINCIPIA*, WHICH IS ARGUABLY THE MOST INFLUENTIAL SCIENTIFIC WORK EVER WRITTEN, AND THE BOOK THAT WOULD MARK THE BIRTH OF MODERN PHYSICS.

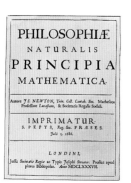

NEWTON AND THE APPLE: IT'S AN image as enduring as any in history. As the story goes, the 23-year-old Isaac Newton was sitting in his garden in his home in Woolsthorpe, England, when he noticed an apple fall to the ground. A moment's pondering, and he was inspired to postulate the law of universal gravitation.

Newton himself never put this story in writing, though he did recount it to his friend and biographer, William Stukeley, one evening in 1726. Yet, two other biographers of Sir Isaac—his physician Henry Pemberton and mathematician William Whiston—interviewed Newton extensively about the origins of his theory of gravity, and neither mentioned the apple.

The story comes to us through Voltaire, who recounted it in *Elements de philosophie de*

**When it comes to the law of gravity, just how much credit does Newton's apple deserve?**

*Newton*, claiming he had heard it from Newton's niece, Catherine Barton Conduitt, who lived with Newton and managed his household for 20 years. Some historians speculate that Catherine may have been telling the truth—but she mistook an example her uncle had used to explain gravity for an actual occurrence. Carl Friedrich Gauss, the great 19th-century mathematician, dismissed the entire story as an absurd insult to Newton's genius.

Whether or not the story is true, the impression it leaves—that Newton formulated his theory in isolation—is certainly misleading. In the late 1670s, Newton was already famous for his theories about light, his experiments in optics, his formulation of calculus, and his invention of the reflecting telescope. He climbed the academic ladder at Cambridge quickly but found himself embroiled in several disputes over who had thought of what scientific theory first. Newton had little patience for such squabbling and resigned from the Royal Society, calling science "a litigious lady."

But then, in 1679, one of Newton's earlier rivals, Robert Hooke, became secretary of the society. Hooke was stymied by several problems in mechanics and believed Newton was the only man who could help. So, in November of that year, Hooke wrote a gracious letter to Newton inviting him to correspond on subjects in physics of mutual interest. Newton accepted the invitation, but soon regretted doing so. And the reason? Hooke made public some of Newton's erroneous speculations, much to Newton's embarrassment.

## A QUESTION FROM HALLEY

It was in one of Hooke's letters, however, that Newton first heard the idea that the motion of an object under the influence of a force could be broken up into two composite motions: one in the direction of the force, and changing in accordance with Newton's second law (an object acted on by a force is accelerated by that force in proportion to the object's mass); and the other perpendicular to the force and moving uniformly, in accordance with Newton's first law (in the absence of an external force, an object at rest tends to remain at rest, while an object in motion tends to remain so at a constant speed). Unbeknownst to Hooke, this was the breakthrough idea that Newton needed.

Meanwhile, Hooke was engaged in discussions with two friends—the astronomer Edmond Halley (also a friend of Newton's) and the astronomer-turned-architect Christopher Wren—about what form the force between celestial bodies might take. Halley speculated that the law ought to resemble the law regarding how light intensity diminishes as one moves away from the source, which is inversely as the square of the distance. (At twice the distance, light is one-quarter as intense.) Hooke boasted that he was certain Halley was right, and Wren offered him a monetary reward if he could prove it. Hooke was stymied, so Halley decided to put the question to Newton.

Halley knew Newton was aware of his friendship with Hooke, and thus would be reluctant to answer such a question. So Halley couched the question in terms of Kepler's laws of planetary motion: What mathematical form would the force between celestial bodies have to be in order for Kepler's laws to be true?

Today, Kepler's laws are at the foundation of celestial physics, but in the 1680s they were not universally known or accepted. But Newton knew them and had, in fact, already worked out the answer to Halley's question. Indeed, the force would have to be an inverse-square law, as Halley had guessed; Newton had worked this out using his first two laws and his calculus. But he then took matters much further. Newton applied his third law—to every action there is an equal and opposite reaction—and concluded that the gravitational force between any two bodies must be the same for both of them. In one of the boldest strokes in the history of science, Newton formulated his law of universal gravitation: The force attracting any two bodies—be they the sun and the earth; the earth and the moon; or the earth and a falling apple—is equal to the product of the masses of the two bodies divided by the square of the distance between them, all multiplied by a "universal gravitational constant" that was the same for all matter everywhere. This was the only way the force of gravity could obey Newton's third law.

## HOOKE IS SILENCED

It would be another two years before Newton would publish his calculations in *De motu* ("On Motion"). Predictably, Hooke claimed he had come up with the law of gravity before Newton, though he could never explain why he could not collect Wren's reward. When, in 1687, Newton published his masterwork, *Philosophiae naturalis principia mathematica* ("Mathematical Principles of Natural Philosophy," known simply as the *Principia*), there could be little doubt that Newton had gone further than anyone in explaining and calculating the motions of the celestial bodies. And Hooke was silenced, ironically never appreciating the fact that he had given Newton the key to unlocking the secrets of the heavens.

THIS PORTRAIT OF SIR ISAAC NEWTON (1642–1727), BY GODFREY KNELLER, WAS PROBABLY PAINTED FROM LIFE. NEWTON WAS A RECLUSIVE ECCENTRIC WHO DEVOTED MUCH OF HIS LIFE AND HIS GENIUS TO NUMERICAL ANALYSIS OF THE BIBLE AND THE STUDY OF MYSTICAL TEXTS.

# Was Captain Kidd a Scapegoat?

**The question remains whether the pirate William Kidd, tried for murder and hanged in Britain, got a fair trial.**

THIS 19TH-CENTURY PORTRAYAL OF CAPTAIN KIDD ON THE DECK OF HIS SHIP SHOWS HIM AS ANYTHING BUT A RESPECTABLE BRITISH SEA CAPTAIN.

ONE OF THE MOST FAMOUS PIRATES IN HISTORY may not have been much of a pirate after all. Captain William Kidd, hanged in Britain on May 23, 1701, has been celebrated in Western literature as a wild, swashbuckling outlaw. But does he really rate such a reputation?

Born in Scotland in 1645 to a family of modest means, Kidd had by 1690 settled in New York, where he was employed by the local government to keep the coast free of enemy privateers. Kidd was a respectable sea captain and citizen. He married a rich widow, owned a luxurious mansion and a pew at Trinity Church, and participated in local political and commercial life. He was even cited on one occasion for being a gentlemanly, clever man by the New York Assembly.

In 1695, in London on business, Kidd received a commission from the British government to keep pirates from seizing ships in the Indian Ocean and the Red Sea. But Kidd had little success: Pirates consistently eluded him, his ship became overrun with worms and weeds, and many crewmen died of cholera.

## A PIRATE IS BORN

In 1697, Kidd traveled to the Comoro Islands off East Africa. There, bowing to the pressures he was facing—including hunger and an ailing ship—he apparently gave up the task of preventing piracy and got into the game himself.

One early attack, on ships sailing with coffee from Yemen, was unsuccessful, but Kidd did manage to seize smaller boats. His boldest act came in 1698, when he replaced his own leaky *Adventure Galley* with a grand Armenian ship. During his travels Kidd also amassed a fortune in gold, silk, and jewels.

Upon discovering that he had been labeled a pirate back home, Kidd abandoned the Armenian ship in the West Indies in 1699. He bought a new ship and sailed back to New York to try to clear his name. Kidd held he had been forced into stealing by a rowdy crew who wanted gold at any cost—not a far-fetched claim, given that an attempted mutiny had taken place on his ship, in which he had killed a crew member. But acting on orders from London, authorities in Boston seized Kidd's papers and threw him into a damp, cold prison. Within months, he was sent to England to be tried.

## A QUESTIONABLE TRIAL

Kidd was found guilty on May 9, 1701, of piracy and of the murder of the mutinous man. He was hanged two weeks later, his body displayed as a warning to other potential pirates. But did Kidd get a fair trial? He wasn't allowed to consult his lawyers until the morning of the trial. Key evidence was suppressed by British officials, and many later questioned whether there was enough evidence to warrant the verdict.

At the trial Kidd claimed he possessed a permit that legalized piracy in the case of raiding French ships. Although the ships Kidd attacked were not French, he claimed that they were traveling under French safe-conduct passes. Kidd was ordered to present the passes, but he could not locate them, and his claim did little to bolster his case. Only later was it discovered that the passes in question had been seized in Boston; they later turned up in the prosecutor's office, and the prosecutor denied having known anything about them.

One theory about the botched trial is that the British made Kidd into a scapegoat, to send a message to would-be pirates and to pacify the Mogul empire in India and the East India Company. Another is that Kidd was the victim of partisan wrangling. The Tories may have been intent on finding Kidd guilty, since his pirate-hunting expedition had been sponsored

## KIDD'S SUNKEN TREASURE

After Kidd was executed in 1701, the authorities recovered much of his treasure, some of it from Gardiners Island, off Long Island, New York. But stories persisted in popular folklore about Kidd's lost treasure. Legend has it that the booty may be hidden off the coast of Connecticut or near the island of Hispaniola.

But fortune seekers have had no luck. Now, three centuries after Kidd's ship, the *Adventure Galley*, was abandoned off the coast of Madagascar, explorers think they have located the sunken wreckage. While scholars believe the wreckage proba-

**PIECES OF THE PUZZLE**

bly does not contain the lost treasure, explorers do hope to find artifacts such as guns, tools, china, and glassware. There is also the possibility of discovering silver, used in ships of Kidd's time to help keep boats steady.

A STONE TABLET MARKS THE SPOT ON GARDINERS ISLAND WHERE KIDD'S (KNOWN) TREASURE WAS FOUND.

by the rival Whigs. Had Kidd repudiated the Whigs and expressed support for the Tories, some say, his life might have been spared.

Kidd may have been guilty of the charges of piracy and murder, but there is little doubt that his trial was tainted by politics and corruption, and that he does not deserve the reputation born of his fictional characterizations.

SOME PORTRAYALS OF CAPTAIN KIDD ARE OF A COURTLY, GENTLEMANLY PIRATE (FAR LEFT). BUT THE ONLY CONTEMPORANEOUS IMAGE OF KIDD SHOWS HIM CHAINED, HANGED, AND DISPLAYED ON LONDON'S EXECUTION DOCK (LEFT).

# Casanova's Conquests

**Literary titan or lascivious philanderer? In his memoirs, did Casanova, a figure of vanity and decadence, embellish the tales of his countless conquests?**

ACCORDING TO HIS ADMITTEDLY SELF-SERVing and gratuitous memoirs, *The History of My Life*, Giovanni Giacomo Casanova frequently ate 50 oysters for breakfast, bedded the most beautiful women of the day, and charmed many rulers of 18th century Europe. These memoirs run to 12 volumes and some 1,500,000 words, but take us only to Casanova's 49th year. Casanova justified his exploits with the handy maxim, "man doubles his existence when he has the talent of multiplying his pleasures, no matter of what nature they may be." With this in mind, scholars have wondered whether Casanova's memoirs may have been a literary multiplication themselves, an expansion of pleasures through imaginative fabrications.

## GENIUS OR LIBERTINE?

In fact, there have been two distinct trends in the recent scholarly interest paid to Casanova. One attempts to demonize him, and the other tries to elevate him from the treacherous mire of his sexual braggadocio. The latter group views the famous paramour less as a lover than as a great thinker and a virtuosic writer. "Has any novelist or poet," wondered the literary critic Edmund Wilson, "ever rendered better than Casanova the passing glory of the personal life?" They consider the record of his sexual accomplishments something of a red herring; all those descriptions of clever seductions and skillful assignations have distracted posterity's attention from Casanova's role as a religious thinker, philosopher, and diplomat. One scholar went so far as to calculate the number of sexual encounters described in the memoirs. Arriving at the figure 132, he then concluded that it "doesn't add up to being a great lover." They remind us that Casanova wrote works of

philosophy, and translated the *Iliad* into Venetian. This man of many talents was a friend of Voltaire and of Catherine the Great. He was a European celebrity after his spectacular escape from prison in 1756 (he was jailed the year before because of his suspected dealings with the occult), and the inventor of the national lottery (Paris was the lucky city).

Unimpressed, Casanova's detractors call attention to his dark side, arguing that though he might not be as reprehensible as the notorious Marquis de Sade, he is admirable by no stretch of the imagination. They point out that this great lover was also guilty of pedophilia—and thought little or nothing of it. In one case Casanova turned his attention first to a mother and then to her daughter; in another, he seduced an eleven-year-old girl, then abandoned her at an English school. Although his flattery often worked, when he did not have his way Casanova could be abusive; he was not above taking women by force. On one occasion, he trained a parrot to call a woman who rebutted his advances, "more of a whore than her mother" and placed it in a cage in one of London's most crowded thoroughfares.

These historians have labeled the lascivious Casanova an exploiter of women and an inveterate misogynist, and they trace this characteristic back to his traumatic childhood. Casanova was the eldest child of Venetian comedy actors, and was left at an early age in the care of strangers. His mother, in fact, was one of the leading ladies of a successful Italian acting troupe, but had little time for her son. According to one historian, Casanova suffered all his life from the "double stigma of low birth and neglect," and his fascination with women was nothing more than a desperate attempt to compensate for his mother's abandonment.

## A QUIETER LIFE

More than his literary talents or his over-sized vices, perhaps what is most surprising about Casanova's life is the sedate and—dare it be said—respectable manner in which it ended. At the age of 60, penniless and probably impotent, Casanova took up the offer from a friend, the Count von Waldstein, to become his librarian in the Bavarian city of Duchcov.

It was in that castle library, pent up with some 12,000 books, that Casanova spent 12 hours a day penning his autobiography—staid environs indeed in which to write of such shocking activities. And there is even some evidence that while at Duchcov, Casanova might have repented a bit from his lecherous ways.

Enfeebled by what some claim was cancer and what others, in a stab at poetic justice, call the effects of venereal disease, Casanova finally passed away in 1798 at the age of 73. According to one witness, his final words were, "I have lived as a philosopher, and die as a Christian."

But that is probably not how Casanova wanted to be remembered. Two years before his death, he was accused of impregnating the daughter of a local gatekeeper. Although from the very start the girl admitted the identity of the real father, the legendary lover did little to squelch the rumor. Those who knew him in his final years suggested that the unrepentant Casanova was proud of the little *scandale.*

# Paul Revere's
## Midnight Ride

**JOHN SINGLETON COPLEY PAINTED THIS PORTRAIT OF REVERE AROUND 1770. AS WELL AS RUNNING A THRIVING BUSINESS AS A METALWORKER, REVERE FASHIONED BRACES AND DENTURES (BUT NOT, AS LEGEND HAS IT, FOR GEORGE WASHINGTON). IN 1776, REVERE MADE AN ELEGANT SILVER BOWL (BOTTOM) FOR THE SONS OF LIBERTY.**

**Though Paul Revere had an important career, the silversmith's famous ride was given more than a bit of polish.**

IF IT WASN'T FOR THE ATTENTION OF A CERTAIN distinguished American poet, Paul Revere would have been another obscure Revolutionary hero, and not the great icon of patriotic vigilance that he is today. In fact, William Allen's comprehensive bibliographical dictionary of Americans (1832) did not mention him at all, though it featured over 7,000 entries. It was only at the end of the 19th century that the Daughters of the American Revolution honored Revere's home in Boston with a plaque.

The key date in the history of Revere's renown is 1863, when Henry Wadsworth Longfellow penned "The Midnight Ride of Paul Revere"; the following year, it was published in the *Atlantic Monthly*, one of the nation's most prominent literary journals. Its famous opening lines ("Listen, my children and you shall hear/ Of the midnight ride of Paul Revere"), its portentous tone, and its solemn linkage of Revere's heroism with the cause of American freedom made the silversmith a national icon practically overnight.

Revere certainly did assist the cause of freedom in his ride, but Longfellow was more attentive to his poetic muse than to the historical record. Most significantly, Longfellow made no mention of the two other messengers who joined Revere for much of his famous ride; their names are now forgotten, just as Revere's might have been. On the evening of April 18, 1775, the three men set out from Boston to Lexington, anxious to warn Samuel Adams and John Hancock that British troops were on their way to arrest them. Revere had been recruited for the task by Dr. Joseph Warren—a prominent physician and one of Samuel Adams's most devoted protégés—for several reasons. First, he was a trustworthy devotee of the colonial cause. He also knew several of the more famous Boston patriots from his membership in that city's Masonic Lodge, including Warren, and had supported the colonists previously by gathering intelligence of British troop movements. Besides, Paul Revere was a tested messenger, employed for the previous year as an express rider by various committees of the Massachusetts government.

### THREE ON HORSEBACK

On that fateful night, Revere left Boston at about 10 P.M., and then crossed the Charles River to enter Charlestown. While there, he quickly stopped to check that the "Sons of Liberty" had seen the signals he had hung the previous weekend in the bell tower of Christ Church (the two lanterns signaling that the British would come "by sea," or across the Charles into Cambridge). Then, around an hour later, he made his way to Lexington. On the road, Revere was joined by William Dawes, another express rider sent on a different route for the same task. After rousing the citizens of Lexington, the two men decided to travel on to Concord, where much of the min-

That was as much military glory as Revere would ever see. After that one dramatic night his career as a soldier was unimpressive and marred by at least one failure: the 1779 Penobscot Expedition, which was one of the most overwhelming naval defeats in American history. (The losses were not surpassed until the attack on Pearl Harbor, in 1941.) In the expedition, 41 American ships launched an attack on a British fort off the coast of Maine, but the invasion was so poorly planned that the British had time to call in a fleet. The British chased the Americans up the Penobscot River, destroying nearly all the American boats.

Almost 500 men were killed or captured, and 1,500 men fled into the Maine woods. Revere, the artillery commander and one of the deserters, was charged with both disobedience and incompetence, ending his military career.

But if Revere wasn't the nation's greatest soldier, his service to the young country as a manufacturer and craftsman was indeed considerable, worthy of posterity's respect. By the age of 19, Revere had taken over his father's silversmith's shop: He would become one of the nation's preeminent metalworkers, famous for his elegant engraving and fine silverware.

utemen's weaponry was hidden. They were joined on the way by a third rider, Dr. Samuel Prescott. Soon after this group left, however, all three men were arrested by a British patrol. Prescott and Dawes quickly escaped and rode on, whereas Revere was unable to make it to Concord to warn the colonial militia there. Revere was, however, released in time to catch the end of the battle on Lexington Green.

# The Real George Washington

## Was George Washington as perfect as history made him out to be?

THE EARLIEST KNOWN PORTRAIT OF WASHINGTON, PAINTED BY CHARLES WILLSON PEALE IN 1772, IS MORE HUMAN THAN MOST RENDERINGS OF OUR FIRST PRESIDENT, LIKE THE TRIBUTE OF AN UNKNOWN EARLY 19TH-CENTURY ARTIST (OPPOSITE). WASHINGTON'S WIFE, MARTHA (INSET), IS SHOWN WITHOUT THE CAPS SHE AFFECTED IN LATER YEARS. THIS IS THE LIKENESS THAT HER HUSBAND CARRIED WITH HIM, IN A GOLD LOCKET WORN AROUND HIS NECK, DURING THE REVOLUTION.

THE FAMOUS PORTRAIT ARTIST GILBERT Stuart, who is responsible for some of the best-known likenesses of George Washington (including the one reproduced on the dollar bill), once declared that conveying Washington's essence on canvas was practically impossible. Two centuries later, historians can only concur. Though the first American president has been the subject of countless biographies and museum exhibitions, he is considered by many essentially unknowable—a venerated, inscrutable icon smiling rigidly from his confinement on our most frequently used piece of currency.

Washington is himself responsible for some of this mystery, carefully cultivating his public persona and letting few know the real man. "Be courteous to all, intimate with few," Washington once counseled his young nephew. Self-conscious about his own lack of formal education, the new president unearthed the letters and schoolbooks of his youth and corrected his spelling mistakes, lest they be reviewed and cast him in an unfavorable light.

### PARSON WEEMS'S EMBROIDERY

Much of the difficulty in studying Washington's life is that it was so instantly mythologized. Soon after he died, Parson Weems was crafting a biography which, in humanizing Washington, strayed wildly from the rather meager historical record. We know that young George never chopped down the cherry tree. But neither did he kneel in the snow to pray before the Battle of Valley Forge.

That, too, was one of Weems's fictions: Washington was a typical 18th-century deist, like Benjamin Franklin and Thomas Jefferson, who believed in a "Supreme Architect of the Universe," a god who did not interfere in the daily workings of the world. Nor was Washington especially pious; when he attended Philadelphia's Christ Church during his presidency, he chose not to take communion; eventually he stopped going altogether when he realized he was setting a bad example.

Indeed, though his countrymen looked to him as an American saint, Washington was very much a man. He had a temper, he made mistakes, he even became enamored of a married woman—Sally Fairfax, the wife of his best friend. Some of his contemporaries managed to see through the gauze of myth and celebrity (Jefferson, though holding Washington in the utmost respect, privately suggested that his mind was not "of the very first order"). And some of Washington's generals even conspired to remove him as commander-in-chief, believing him incapable of leading an army. In part,

WASHINGTON EMBRACES HIS ARTILLERY COMMANDER, MAJOR GENERAL HENRY KNOX, AT HIS FAREWELL DINNER WITH HIS OFFICERS AT NEW YORK'S FRAUNCES TAVERN. MAJOR BENJAMIN TALLMADGE SAID HE HAD NEVER WITNESSED "SUCH A SCENE OF SORROW AND WEEPING. THE SIMPLE THOUGHT THAT WE SHOULD SEE HIS FACE NO MORE IN THIS WORLD SEEMED TO BE UTTERLY INSUPPORTABLE." BELOW, A WARM FAMILY PORTRAIT OF THE WASHINGTONS BY EDWARD SAVAGE.

he was selected by the Continental Congress for that position because of his military record: At 21, he first served as a messenger for the governor of Virginia, then as a colonel in the French and Indian War, and finally, in 1775, as a military advisor for New York, responsible for defending it against British attack. But the

## FATHER WASHINGTON?

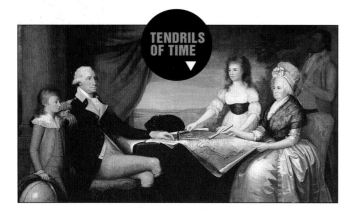

TENDRILS OF TIME
▼

Inspired by the attempts of those to prove that Thomas Jefferson fathered a child by his slave Sally Hemmings, the descendants of West Ford (a slave owned by one of Washington's younger brothers) have claimed that Ford was actually fathered by Washington. Unlike in the Jefferson case, this assertion seems unlikely. There is no evidence that Washington ever met Ford's mother (a slave named Venus), nor is there evidence that Washington was near his brother's farm during the time Ford was conceived. Most convincingly, it seems "the Father of our Country" fathered no one at all: His wife Martha had given birth to four children in a previous marriage, but she was unable to conceive with George. So many historians now believe he was probably sterile.

Continental Congress also desperately needed a leader from Virginia to ensure the support of the southern colonies. Washington himself claimed that he did not have enough experience, and even today some military historians question Washington's tactical genius, claiming that he was a novice whose victory over the British forces was due to the British general's even greater incompetence.

What no one doubts is Washington's skill at rallying his troops after demoralizing defeats: his ability to marshal all the forces of propaganda and persuasion to get his men to fight. Some of this has to do with his commanding presence—he was almost 6' 3" (nearly as tall as Lincoln) and wore a size 13 boot. But it also can be attributed to Washington's keen understanding of human nature and his refusal to depend too heavily on the nobler instincts of his men. As he observed in 1778, in the heat of battle: "We must take the passions of Men as Nature has given them...I do not mean to exclude altogether the Idea of Patriotism. I know it exists, and I know it has done much in the present Contest. But I venture to assert, that a great and lasting War can never be supported on this principle alone." His own youth bore testimony to this conviction. Despite his virtuous demeanor and his reputation as a "simple farmer," when Washington was a Virginia surveyor he quietly obtained land west of the Alleghenies that was decreed off-limits to settlers, enriching himself considerably.

### ABOUT THOSE WOODEN TEETH…

It is somewhat ironic, then, that Washington has been painted as such a prudish, wooden figure. In a way, the popular conception of Washington having wooden dentures confirms the misreading of the man. For the false teeth were in fact not wooden; they were made by a New York City dentist out of hippopotamus ivory and attached to a solitary tooth in Washington's mouth. But they never satisfied Washington, causing him to press his lips together tightly. The resulting unnatural set to his jaw gave him such deeply sunken cheeks that Gilbert Stuart had to stuff them with cotton before painting his portraits. Thus the image we know of our first president—that severe, noble visage—is something of a fiction. It could be said that the real Washington was the one with the rather gaunt face and the jaw ache.

# The Cherry Tree Legend

Before press secretaries and rabid reportorial scrutiny of every president's past, there was Parson Weems. And few writers on presidents have been more influential—or more historically inaccurate.

### MINISTER OF CONFABULATION

Mason Locke ("Parson") Weems, born in 1759, was an Episcopalian minister, a brilliant sermonizer, and a gifted storyteller. Dissatisfied with the ministry, he turned to selling Bibles door-to-door for a Philadelphia publisher. Children would rush to his carriage crammed with books to sit enraptured as he spun elaborate tales and played his fiddle. Soon, Weems began writing his own books catering to the religious sentimentality of the colonial citizenry. His "catchy" titles sound quaint to us now—among the most imaginative were *The Philanthropist: A Good Twenty-Five Cents Worth of Political Love-Powder* and *God's Revenge on Gambling*—yet according to Parson Weems, the books "sold like hotcakes."

But Weems's most famous work was "The Life of George Washington; With Curious Anecdotes, Equally Honourable to Himself, and Exemplary to His Young Countrymen," a 12-page pamphlet published in 1800. The pamphlet went through some 70 editions, growing in

**"PARSON WEEMS'S FABLE," BY GRANT WOOD, SATIRIZED THE TALE OF THE CHERRY TREE.**

length as the nation sought desperately to understand its enigmatic first hero. Weems indulged his readers with a largely invented portrayal of Washington's youth, painting the young president as a paragon of honesty and virtue —a sort of updated and secularized biblical hero.

Weems's most famous and oft-repeated fib is the cherry-tree story, though it did not appear until the book's seventh edition; what's more, in the earliest versions George barked the tree instead of chopping it down. "'George,' said his father, 'do you know

who killed that beautiful little cherry-tree yonder in the garden?' That was a tough question; and George staggered under it for a moment; but quickly recovered himself. Looking at his father, with the sweet face of youth, he cried out, 'I can't tell a lie, Pa; you know I can't tell a lie. I did cut it with my hatchet.'"

### A FIB WITH LEGS

There is no evidence that this incident is based on historical fact. Parson Weems attributed it to someone he knew from his time spent near Mt. Vernon, "an aged lady, who was a distant relative [of Washington's], and when a girl spent much of

her time in the family." But the lack of evidence hasn't prevented the fable from spreading and becoming a presidential "fact." It is too enticing to resist, and it speaks to Weems's talent for giving us what we want: a hero. And so the legend's roots have grown deep in the American soil. On Washington's boyhood farm, across the Rappahannock River, a bronze tablet now lies next to a sturdy tree: "Beside this stone stood the cherry tree, which, according to tradition, George Washington, when a boy, cut down. The present tree was planted by the Fredericksburg Chamber of Commerce Feb. 22, 1935."

# Was Mozart Murdered?

### At the pinnacle of his career, Mozart died after suffering an illness. Or did he perish at the hand of an envious arch rival?

**MOZART BELIEVED, AS SAYS THE POPULAR LEGEND, THAT HIS FINAL COMPOSITION, *A REQUIEM MASS FOR THE DEAD*, WAS BEING WRITTEN FOR HIS OWN FUNERAL. AN EXCERPT FROM THE UNFINISHED PIECE (ABOVE) FEATURES THE VOCAL CHORUS *REQUIEM AETERNAM DONA EIS, DOMINE*, MEANING "GIVE THEM ETERNAL PEACE, OH LORD."**

THE SUBLIME AND RAVISHING MUSIC OF WOLFGANG Amadeus Mozart will live on and be played forever, but Mozart himself was not even given the length of a normal lifetime. When he died on December 5, 1791, after a short battle with inflammation and fever, he was 35 years old.

As a child, Mozart had been famous throughout Europe as one of the most astonishing child prodigies in the history of music. He possessed virtuoso talent on multiple instruments before he was ten years old, and began composing minuets when he was only five. While still a child he had written accomplished operas and symphonies, and had been feted in the royal courts from Vienna to London. But Mozart's adult life was marked by financial struggle and professional conflict.

Though he was composing perhaps the best music of any living composer, as an adult Mozart failed to find swift success with the Viennese of his native Austria. His triumphs were often overshadowed by frustrations and failures. Worse still, he had to maneuver through the political intrigues of popular composers who resented his talent, dodge the caprices of the ruling Hapsburgs, and literally finish commissions at fever pitch simply in order to pay his bills. When he passed away, the official death register in Vienna listed Mozart's cause of death as "acute military fever," but it would not be long before another diagnosis was proposed: murder.

## AN ODOR OF FOUL PLAY

The enduring legend that Mozart was murdered began only a few weeks after his death, when a Berlin newspaper ran an article claiming that "because his body swelled up after death, people even thought he had been poisoned." Normally, a dead body quickly becomes cold and stiff, but, as Mozart's son Carl later recalled, the composer's body swelled and remained soft—traits common to the bodies of poison victims. Because of the stench emitted by the corpse, the body was

**ANTONIO SALIERI, MOZART'S MUSICAL RIVAL, TOLD BEETHOVEN'S STUDENT IGNAZ MOSCHELES TO ASSURE THE WORLD THAT "THERE IS NO TRUTH IN THAT ABSURD RUMOR; YOU KNOW THAT I AM SUPPOSED TO HAVE POISONED MOZART."**

buried hastily, and was not subjected to an autopsy. And, most intriguing of all, Mozart himself is reported to have believed that he was poisoned by a rival. A few weeks before his death, he purportedly told his wife Constanze that "Someone has given me acqua toffana and has calculated the precise time of my death." (Acqua toffana was the name of a slow-acting arsenic poison frequently invoked in 17th- and 18th-century murder cases.)

The composer certainly had enough enemies to warrant suspicion of foul play. Most prominent among his rivals was the jealous, ambitious court composer to Emperor Joseph II, Antonio Salieri. At the time, the middle-aged composer was the most prominent musician in Vienna, his music held in high regard and in great demand by the city's aristocracy. But Salieri was convinced—rightly, as it turns out—that the less fashionable Mozart possessed a far superior musical gift. And though he attended a performance of *The Magic Flute* and may have been one of the few mourners at Mozart's memorial service, Salieri was consumed by envy for Mozart's creative power.

More than 30 years after Mozart's death, Salieri unexpectedly fanned the flames of suspicion that it was he who had murdered Mozart. As he approached his own death, Salieri became increasingly preoccupied with the idea that he was responsible for Mozart's death. He not only attempted suicide but tried to confess what he believed to be his sin. His once-fashionable music now silent throughout Vienna, the court composer died a delusional and broken old man in 1824.

### A MORE PROSAIC END?

Another man with a motive to murder Mozart may have been Franz Hofdemel, whose beautiful wife, Magdalena, studied piano with Mozart, stirring up speculation that she and the composer were involved in an affair. Only a few days after Mozart died, Franz Hofdemel attacked his wife—then pregnant—with a razor, slashing her face and throat and then killing himself. Magdalena and her unborn child both survived. Years later, Beethoven refused to play in her presence because of her intimacy with his great predecessor.

Despite these intriguing coincidences, historians and biographers have given very little credence to the legend of Mozart's murder. Most

believe, based on physicians' later reconstructions of the event, that he died of rheumatic fever, kidney failure, or pneumonia. Mozart's own paranoid belief that he had been poisoned may have stemmed from the delusions that often accompany kidney failure. Salieri's fantasy that he was responsible for Mozart's death may have been related to illness as well. As for Franz Hofdemel, no evidence has shown that he murdered Mozart, and contemporary sources do not indicate that the composer ever strayed in his marriage to Constanze.

Because Mozart was buried in an unmarked public grave, the precise location unknown, we will never know for sure what caused the great composer's death. We do know of his life, however, as his sublime music lives on.

**THE EASE WITH WHICH MOZART COMPOSED LED SOME TO THINK OF HIM AS A LAZY, FUN-LOVING RASCAL WHO GAVE LITTLE THOUGHT TO HIS WORK. BUT WHEN HE DIED IN 1791, MANY OF MOZART'S CLOSEST FRIENDS AND FAMILY MEMBERS BELIEVED HE HAD WORKED HIMSELF TO DEATH.**

# Napoleon's Rise and Fall

NAPOLEON I STRUCK A TRADEMARK POSE: ONE HAND TUCKED INTO VEST (ABOVE). ANOTHER IMAGE WAS THAT OF TRIUMPHANT LEADER. IN A PORTRAIT BY JACQUES LOUIS DAVID, THE MAN WHO WOULD BE EMPEROR LEADS HIS ARMY INTO BATTLE (OPPOSITE).

NAPOLEON BONAPARTE I'S RISE AND fall left a mark on France in innumerable ways. Exalted by many, he is cloaked in legendary splendor, with the glorious Arc de Triomphe in Paris (a monument to his numerous military victories) bearing witness to his influence. The laurels notwithstanding, during his reign the megalomaniacal Bonaparte was very much his own publicist, promoting his own triumphs. As both first consul and emperor, he engaged the best writers and artists of France and Europe to magnify his deeds. He also staged elaborate ceremonies to celebrate his own rule, envisioning himself as the architect of France's greatest glory.

Napoleon maintained that he had preserved the achievements of the French Revolution and offered their benefits to Europe. His goal, he said, was to found a European State—a "federation of free peoples." Whatever truth there was in this, he did become France's arch-hero and a martyr to the world. This sense of self-importance, however, became one of the primary reasons for Napoleon's demise.

Even today the French revel in his glory days—and most remember his idiosyncrasies. Popular opinion came to believe that Napoleon's short height accounted for his desire to rule the world, so much so that the term "Napoleonic complex" has entered the language. Yet by the standards of his time, Napoleon was not that short. After his autopsy, it was reported that he measured 5' 2" in height, a figure based on an old French system of measurement known as *pieds de roi*. Using our modern system of measurement, he was actually a little over 5' 6". As well, the emperor's characteristic pose—with one hand placed smartly in his vest—has intrigued history buffs

**Was it the brutally cold Russian winter—or his miscalculation of British military tactics—that led to the shattering of Napoleon's empire?**

for generations. People have concocted psychological theories about its significance. But, interestingly enough, the reason behind this pose is physical, not psychological. For his entire adult life Napoleon suffered from acute stomach pains, and holding his hand on his abdomen helped ease his suffering.

## THE EMPEROR'S RISE

Napoleon's ascent to power and two-decade dominance of Europe was a rapid one. His military career began in 1785 when, at age 16, he received a commission as second lieutenant in the French artillery. (He had received an education at Brienne and at the Ecole Militaire in Paris, at the expense of King Louis XVI.) Little did Europe know what was coming.

In 1791, after the Revolution began, Napoleon became a lieutenant colonel in the Corsican National Guard. In 1793, Corsica declared independence and Bonaparte, a French patriot and a Republican, fled to France with his family. Taking on the role of captain, he was assigned to an army besieging Toulon, a naval base that, aided by a British fleet, was in revolt against the republic. Having replaced a wounded artillery general, he seized ground, driving the British fleet from the harbor and triumphing over Toulon. Because of this victory, Bonaparte was promoted to brigadier general at the age of 24.

In 1795, he saved the revolutionary government by dispersing an insurgent mob in Paris. One year later Napoleon married Josephine de Beauharnais, the widow of an aristocrat guillotined in the Revolution—a pairing that has been called one of the world's greatest love stories. Although Napoleon did grow to love her, he supposedly married her for her connections.

BONAPARTE

In 1796, Napoleon was also made commander of the French army in Italy. He defeated
four Austrian generals in succession (each having more troops) and forced Austria and its
allies to make peace. Napoleon then led an
expedition to Turkish-ruled Egypt in 1798, to
strike at British trade with the East. He
emerged victorious—but having lost his fleet at
the hands of a British admiral, he was left
stranded. Never shy about expressing himself,
Napoleon reformed the Egyptian government
and law, abolishing serfdom and feudalism and
guaranteeing basic rights, while the French
scholars he had brought with him began the
study of ancient Egyptian history.

In 1799, he tried but failed to capture Syria,
but won a smashing victory over the Turks at
Abukir. Meanwhile, France faced a new coalition as Austria, Russia, and lesser powers allied
themselves with Britain. No modest soul,
Napoleon decided to leave his army and return

to save France. The intrepid soldier joined a
conspiracy against the government, and in
November 1799, he and his colleagues seized
power and established a new regime—the
Consulate. Under its constitution, Napoleon,
as first consul, had almost dictatorial powers.
The constitution was revised in 1802 to make
Napoleon consul for life—and in 1804 to make
him an emperor. Each change received the
overwhelming assent of the electorate.

The British, however, were not to be won
over. In April of 1803, Britain resumed the
naval war with France; two years later Russia
and Austria joined the British in a new coalition. Napoleon then abandoned his plans to
invade England and turned his armies against
the Austro-Russian forces, defeating them at
the Battle of Austerlitz on December 2, 1805.

The following year Napoleon seized the
kingdom of Naples and began to build a
dynasty of sorts, installing his elder brother,

Joseph, as king. He then converted the Dutch republic into the kingdom of Holland, and this time it was his brother Louis who became king. He established the Confederation of the Rhine (most of the German states), of which he was protector. Prussia then allied itself with Russia and attacked the confederation. Napoleon destroyed the Prussian army at Jena and Auerstadt (1806) and the Russian army at Friedland.

At Tilsit (July 1807), he made an ally of Czar Alexander I and greatly reduced the size of Prussia. Unstoppable, Napoleon added even more new states to the empire, including the kingdom of Westphalia (ruled by his brother Jérome) and the Grand Duchy of Warsaw.

### THE SEEDS OF HIS UNDOING

Meanwhile, in 1806 Napoleon had established the Continental system, which ultimately led to his failure. It was a strategic measure in his economic war against Britain, its purpose being to destroy Britain's commerce and credit—to starve it economically into surrender. But it failed for several reasons. Foremost was that Britain retained control of the seas throughout the war. The British naval blockade of the Continent, implemented in 1807, therefore served as an effective counter to Napoleon's system. While the empire labored to transport goods and raw materials overland to avoid the British blockade, the British worked successfully to develop a lively trade with South America.

Internal tariffs were a second reason for the failure of his system. Europe's divided and isolated economic units were fortified against each other by tariffs and were at odds as they tried to live on nothing more than what the Continent could produce. Basically, the Continent had more to lose than Britain. As unemployment rose, trade-stagnated ports and manufacturing centers were not as productive.

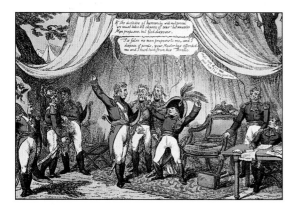

In one personal account—as historian A.J.P. Taylor has noted—Napoleon, in a delusional state, persuaded himself that he had won the battle of Waterloo. In his memoir, which he spent his final days scribing on the

**VIEW FROM THE FRINGE**

bleak island of St. Helena in the South Atlantic, his confused synopsis of the battle ends with an expression of sympathy for the people of London—"where they learnt of the catastrophe which had befallen their army."

NAPOLEON, EXILED BY THE BRITISH TO THE ISLAND OF ST. HELENA, LIVED ON THE ESTATE LONGWOOD (ABOVE). HE DIED ON MAY 5, 1821, AFTER WHICH NAPOLEON'S IMAGE WAS TURNED TO THAT OF A MARTYR TO REACTIONARY MONARCHS. DURING THIS PERIOD OF ROMANTICISM, NAPOLEON BECAME A LARGER-THAN-LIFE FIGURE, ALONG WITH DON JUAN, FAUST, AND PROMETHEUS.

In 1809, Napoleon beat the Austrians again, at Wagram. He divorced Josephine in 1810—mainly because she hadn't provided an heir—and married Marie-Louise, the daughter of the Austrian emperor. By 1810, the empire had also reached its widest extension with the annexation of Bremen, Lubeck, and other parts of northern Germany, together with the entire kingdom of Holland following the forced abdication of Louis Bonaparte.

While Napoleon reigned over the new kingdoms, the "Code Napoleon" was established as law. Feudalism and serfdom were abolished and, with the exception of Spain, freedom of religion legalized. Each state was granted its own constitution, providing for universal male suffrage and a parliament containing a bill of rights. French-style administrative and judicial systems were required, and schools were placed under a centralized administration. Free public schools were envisioned, and higher education was open to all who qualified, regardless of class or religion. Every state had an academy or institute for the promotion of the arts and sciences. Constitutional govern-

NAPOLEON'S HUBRIS WAS CARICATURED BY ARTISTS OF THE TIME, AS IN THE WORK AT LEFT: "NAPOLEON OMNIPOTENT, OR THE ACME OF ARROGANCE AND PRESUMPTION."

ment remained only a promise, but progress and increased efficiency were widely realized. Not until after Napoleon's fall did the people of Europe—alienated from his governments by war taxes and military conscription—fully appreciate the benefits he had given them.

## NAPOLEON'S DECLINE

In 1812, Napoleon, whose alliance with Alexander I had dissolved, launched an invasion of Russia that ended in a disastrous retreat from Moscow. His famous defeat in Moscow seemed likely because of the harshness of the Russian winters. Most wonder not why he was beaten but why he ever attempted an invasion in the first place, and, having undertaken it, why he left so belatedly that his army inevitably had to fight through such a bitter winter.

In reality, the winter of 1812 in Russia was unusually temperate. Napoleon's army left Moscow on October 19, and the first severe frost didn't occur until October 30. The temperature did not fall into the teens until November 12, and then only briefly. A thaw came in late November. The real reason the illustrious November 26 crossing of the Beresina was so lethal was that the stream had melted, holding French troops on one side until Napoleon could build a makeshift bridge for their escape. The winter temperatures there didn't drop below zero until December 4.

Some historians tend to blame Napoleon's downfall on the Russian winter because Napoleon himself did, to decrease his own responsibility for the failure. But his army was dismantled long before the winter cold arrived. Napoleon had left Moscow with nearly 100,000 troops, but by November 12—the first day the temperature dropped into the teens—only 41,000 were left. The brutal cold had not killed the army—they were done away with by disease. The winter weather had weakened Napoleon's men, but the temperature was hardly chilly enough to have led to their deaths.

If Napoleon had departed Moscow, he would have fared better if he had left before the onset of the cold weather. His real mistake, according to biographer Vincent Cronin, was deciding to leave at all. He probably could have stayed, given that most of the Russians had evacuated and Moscow was fairly safe.

**The Little Emperor's gigantic army may have been too big for its own good.**

The quality that made Napoleon a great leader—impatience in getting things done—seemingly contributed to his error in judgement in Russia. The strangest findings of historians is that his army possibly suffered as much from the heat as from the cold—the Russian summer of 1812 was so hot that tens of thousands of his soldiers died from heat exhaustion.

However, the historian David Chandler has another theory. The Grand Army's demise was done in by its size. The army, 655,000 soldiers strong, was simply too large to lead through a hostile land, making it impossible for Napoleon to supervise and protect them properly. Again, Napoleon's ego had outdone him.

## DEFEAT AT WATERLOO

Most agree that the battle at Waterloo was the decisive defeat of Napoleon's career. But there is disagreement over who won. The English and the Americans believe the Duke of Wellington won. The Germans think that General G. von Blucher (the commander of the Prussian army, who came to Wellington's rescue) won. The Belgians reason that it was only because one of their own generals ignored Wellington's order to retreat that the English won; thus, in their texts, Belgium triumphed over Napoleon's army. In his memoirs, Napoleon was convinced that he won the final battle.

But why did Napoleon ultimately lose? Some have said, controversially, that he was distracted by painful hemorrhoids. Others claim he suffered from sleeplessness because of (his own) loud snoring. But he was probably in good health. Vincent Cronin has remarked, "the one surviving order in his own hand is neatly and clearly written: always, with Napoleon, a sign of physical and moral being."

Biographer Cronin wrote that Napoleon had lost the battle of Waterloo because he had spent the critical morning of the battle inspecting the wounded, when his army should have been fighting; that he had underestimated the English, who had analyzed his traditional tactics and figured out how to neutralize them; and that he had been overconfident, pursuing war on the naive assumption that the worst wouldn't happen. But it did. The Prussians, whom he believed he had defeated for the last time, charged to Wellington's rescue.

THE BATTLE AT WATERLOO ULTIMATELY LED TO NAPOLEON'S DEMISE. HIS FALLEN STATE IS DEPICTED IN ARTIST PAUL DELAROCHE'S PORTRAIT OF THE GREAT EMPEROR AFTER HIS ABDICATION (OPPOSITE). WHO DID TRIUMPH IN THE FINAL BATTLE? THE ENGLISH AND THE AMERICANS BELIEVE THAT IT WAS THE DUKE OF WELLINGTON, SHOWN IN THE PORTRAIT ABOVE.

# Louis Pasteur
## and His Accusers

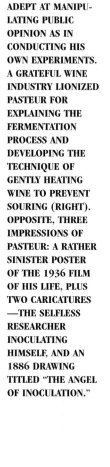

### Was it scientific integrity or sour grapes that caused rivals of Louis Pasteur to accuse him of unethical practices?

THE ORIGINATOR OF THE pasteurization process, developer of vaccines for three deadly diseases (rabies, anthrax, and chicken cholera), and celebrated patriot, French chemist and microbiologist Louis Pasteur is also recognized for his work in stereochemistry, the complex spatial arrangement of atoms and groups in molecules.

Born in 1822 in Dole, France, Pasteur has been described as a scientist who focused his talents on solving his country's problems. Pasteur developed the method to keep France's wine and beer from souring, and went on to study the bacterium that caused diseases threatening France's silkworm industry. Horrified at the rate at which French women were dying from puerperal fever during childbirth, Pasteur discovered the connection between puerperal fever and the lack of sanitary conditions which were prevalent at that time. Until then, unaware of the importance of hygiene in eliminating germs passed between doctor and patient, doctors were not in the habit of washing their hands before delivering babies.

### PASTEUR'S DETRACTORS

Yet the man proclaimed a national hero by the French government—and considered globally one of the greatest scientists of all time—was accused of both faking his own findings and committing unethical acts. Were these mere rumors spread by Pasteur's disgruntled rivals, or was Pasteur something of a fraud?

Even during his lifetime, Louis Pasteur was accused of obtaining scientific data in unethical ways and of claiming sole origination of scientific methods. These included methods that

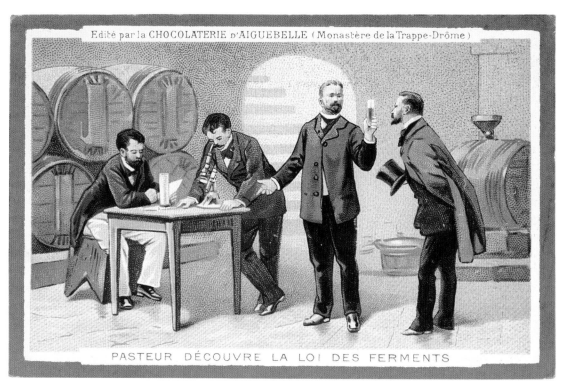

Edité par la CHOCOLATERIE D'AIGUEBELLE (Monastère de la Trappe-Drôme)

PASTEUR DÉCOUVRE LA LOI DES FERMENTS

other scientists either had come up with before or were in the process of developing.

Records of the French Academy of Science show that certain colleagues of French biologist Antoine Bechamp argued vociferously that Bechamp had published a germ theory well before Pasteur, in works that Pasteur surely read. And the legendary English nurse Florence Nightingale had made similar observations well before Pasteur published his papers on germ theory. Yet the French Academy hailed Pasteur as the theory's originator.

Pasteur was also given distinct credit for his work on puerperal fever, even though German scientist Robert Koch had done some of the most advanced work in that area. Even so, Pasteur was praised by the French press for the patriotic act of single-handedly saving the lives of countless French women.

After studying Pasteur's notebooks—which had only recently become accessible to scientists upon the death of Pasteur's last remaining male descendant—Princeton historian Gerald Geison published *The Private Science of Louis Pasteur* (1995). Geison discovered serious discrepancies between Pasteur's published accounts and entries in the notebooks, noting at least three incidents that suggest fraud. Pasteur also has been found to have been guilty of self-promotion, pushing aside a rival and getting the government license to produce the successful rabies vaccine once he realized that there was "big money to be made."

## UNETHICAL TESTS?
Most damning, it was found that Pasteur subjected two children to being repeatedly bitten by rabid dogs as test cases. He then pretended to cure them by methods he claimed had already been proven through animal testing. Fortunately for Pasteur's reputation, both boys recovered, but it appears from Pasteur's notebooks, says Geison, that there was no real proof that the boys even had rabies.

In an earlier case, Pasteur treated two patients, both of whom claimed to be in advanced stages of the disease, with his untested rabies vaccine. One patient recovered, but the other died. Again, it appears that the patient who recovered may not have had rabies in the first place, according to reports of the time. Given that Pasteur strongly advocated the use of animal trials before human trials, this

would have been a violation of his own standards. Pasteur's own assistant, Emile Roux, refused to have anything to do with Pasteur's experiments on anthrax, chicken cholera, and rabies, claiming the trials to be unethical.

It can be argued that the undeniably great Louis Pasteur broke the rules in order to rid his countrymen of some of the most feared and deadly diseases of his time. Historian Geison claims, however, that the risks Pasteur took were not with his own life but with the lives of others. If true, Pasteur's pattern of self-promotion led to unprofessional conduct.

LOUIS PASTEUR'S LABORATORY WAS ADJACENT TO HIS HOME. ELSEWHERE IN PARIS, THE PASTEUR INSTITUTE, WHICH PASTEUR DIRECTED, SERVED AS A MODEL FOR RESEARCH LABS ALL OVER THE WORLD.

# The Siege of the Alamo

**The siege at the Alamo is steeped in legend—the tales of Bowie and Crockett will always endure—but what did happen on that fateful day?**

THE PAINTER H.A. MCCARDLE'S "DAWN AT THE ALAMO" DEPICTS THE SIEGE IN SAN ANTONIO, A FEROCIOUS BATTLE BETWEEN THE 187 TEXANS COMMANDED BY WILLIAM B. TRAVIS AND THE MUCH LARGER MEXICAN ARMY LED BY SANTA ANNA. THE SIEGE BEGAN ON FEBRUARY 23, AND THE FINAL BATTLE WAS FOUGHT ON MARCH 6, 1836.

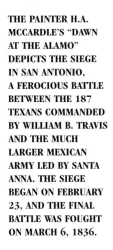

GENERAL ANTONIO LÓPEZ DE SANTA ANNA

THE DEFENSE OF THE ALAMO IS ONE OF THE classic battles in the story of American freedom, its legend embellished, embroidered, and devoured by generations of schoolchildren. But there are many ways to "remember" an event: For historians, the task is accomplished by uncovering the details of the occurrence, while to those who cherish the myth, it is remembrance that gains more importance. The challenge is to honor the myth and the facts at the same time.

## A SETTLERS' REBELLION

The story of the Alamo begins in the 1820s, when Mexico, faced with lands populated by unruly Indians, opened her northern territories to American pioneers, a potentially stabilizing force. Though abiding by Mexico's laws was a condition of settlement, once Americans flocked to the territories they soon rankled under Mexico's levying of taxes, trials without juries, and abolition of slavery. In 1835, the settlers finally rebelled against the Mexican gov-

ernment, and Mexico's dictator, General Antonio López de Santa Anna, quickly moved troops into the region, determined to quell the insurgency by any means necessary.

After conducting a string of battles against the insurgents, Santa Anna focused on a group of Texans who since December had occupied a mission-fortress in San Antonio—the Alamo. Sam Houston, the commander of Texas's army, had ordered the fort abandoned; but the men, under the leadership of James Bowie and William Travis, had decided to defend it.

Santa Anna determined that the area was essential to his conquest of the region. By January of the next year, he arrived at the fort with a sizable army. Santa Anna's official siege began on February 23, 1836, with 2,400 well-trained men, though the troops also included boys aged 13 to 14 from a nearby military academy. At first, only 145 settlers guarded the Alamo; that number was increased to 187 when reinforcements arrived eight days later.

WILLIAM B. TRAVIS

JAMES BOWIE

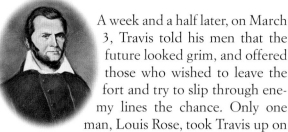

A week and a half later, on March 3, Travis told his men that the future looked grim, and offered those who wished to leave the fort and try to slip through enemy lines the chance. Only one man, Louis Rose, took Travis up on his offer—and he was the only man to survive. Legend has it that Travis drew a line in the sand and asked that everyone willing to die with him step across it. But the anecdote comes from an account of the siege some 40 years after it occurred, by a man who heard it from his parents, who in turn had heard it from Louis Rose. Though Travis has been lauded for his decision to stay, his refusal to retreat might have been a tactical one; the Americans' inferior cavalry doomed them in open space, and Travis probably considered them to be safer behind the walls of the fort.

## THE FATAL THIRD ASSAULT

**DAVY CROCKETT**

But even Travis knew there was little hope. There is an unverified legend of a woman messenger sent to Santa Anna by Travis, stating that the Americans would surrender if they were guaranteed that their lives would be spared. If the story is true, Santa Anna rebuked the offer, because on the night of March 5 the historic attack began.

Initially the Americans were able to turn back the Mexicans but, exhausted by the siege, they were unable to hold out. While the next morning brought another failed assault, the third assault by the Mexicans proved successful. By nine o'clock that night the fighting was over; some 200 Mexicans were dead and another 400 wounded. It is impossible, however, to arrive at accurate casualty figures, since Santa Anna gave faulty reports to mask the damage done to his force; some historians have put the number as high as 1,600.

Santa Anna did not leave a single American prisoner alive, though recent evidence suggests that several Texans, including David (Davy) Crockett and others, survived the initial attack and were executed afterwards. The bodies of all the men were stripped, thrown into a pile, and then burned. One local Indian who had been staying at the fort convinced the Mexicans he was a prisoner and was spared, as were the women, children, and Travis's black slave.

# REMEMBERING THE ALAMO

We know the details of the battle over the Alamo from the survivors' recollections—either from civilians spared by Santa Anna or from the Mexican troops themselves. The Mexicans' account of the battle was, understandably, less charitable toward the Texans' heroism, claiming that they were mostly drunk at the time of the attack.

Of the civilian accounts, the most reliable are those by Colonel Travis's black slave, Joe, and by the 8-year-old son of a Texan soldier.

**HOW DO WE REALLY KNOW?**

Then there were the women, many of whom were hiding in various rooms and did not see all of the battle—like Susanna Dickinson, the wife of the fort's artillery officer, who is often named as a primary source. But she was interviewed about the battle three decades after it occurred.

Of course, for weeks after the fight, men wandered around San Antonio claiming to be the sole survivor. Their tale-telling is responsible for many of the spurious legends surrounding the Alamo.

"You are two bloody villains, and to treat you as you deserve, I ought to have you shot as an example... Remember the Alamo an Fannin.!!"

"I consent to remain your prisoner, most excellent Sir.!! / Me no Alamo.!!"

"So de I most valiant Americano.!! / Me no Alamo.!!"

IN AN 1836 CARTOON (ABOVE), SANTA ANNA AND AN OFFICER HUMBLE THEMSELVES BEFORE SAM HOUSTON AFTER TEXAS INDEPENDENCE IS WON. JIM BOWIE AND DAVY CROCKETT (ABOVE LEFT) WERE MORE GLORIOUS IN DEATH THAN LIFE. BOWIE HAD BEEN DENIED OFFICER RANK AND CROCKETT HAD JUST LOST HIS BID TO BECOME A SENATOR IN TENNESSEE.

Though military historians now consider the decisions of the Texans to defend the fort somewhat foolhardy, the personalities of those involved—Davy Crockett, James Bowie, and William Travis—were so oversized that their deaths necessarily became legendary.

The valor of their final days provided the ammunition, six weeks later, for troops led by Sam Houston—who would become president of the Republic of Texas—to overwhelm a Mexican force at San Jacinto, securing Texas's independence and its most enduring legend.

# Custer's Last Stand

## Was George Armstrong Custer a martyr in the face of battle, or a reckless man consumed with greed?

THE MASSACRE AT THE BATTLE OF LITTLE BIGHORN WAS A FAVORITE SUBJECT OF ARTISTS IN THE LATE 19TH CENTURY (ABOVE). GENERAL GEORGE ARMSTRONG CUSTER (OPPOSITE) WAS KNOWN AS "LONG HAIR" TO HIS INDIAN ADVERSARIES.

THE DIFFERENCE BETWEEN A MARTYR AND A FAILure is sometimes a matter of just how the story is told. George Armstrong Custer—dashing, flamboyant, and foolhardy—is one of the more prominent of America's martyrs, and his Last Stand against Sioux and Cheyenne Indian warriors has been portrayed as a model of gallantry in the face of overwhelming odds. But when looked at from a century's distance, given time to examine all of the details, Custer's Last Stand seems more a reckless gamble.

Custer had been a Civil War hero—the youngest general in the Union Army, in fact—and was first called out to the Black Hills of South Dakota in 1874. His ostensible purpose was to establish a new military post to protect Indians from trespassing white settlers. But Custer's real mission was to verify the claims that the Dakota lands were rich with gold. And, according to Custer, they were indeed; he sent back word that there was "gold among the roots of grass." Soon the region flooded with more settlers, and by 1876, they had overrun the sacred hunting grounds of the Sioux, dis-

regarding the Fort Laramie Treaty, which had granted the Dakota lands to the Indians.

The Indians tried reasoning with the government, but to no avail. They then left their reservation for the hills of southeastern Montana, but the government responded by issuing an ultimatum declaring that any Indian found in "unceded territory" would be treated as an enemy, shot on sight, or taken prisoner. Having little choice but to resort to violence, the Sioux, led by chiefs Crazy Horse and Sitting Bull, joined forces with their Cheyenne allies and resolved to encamp together in a valley along the Little Bighorn River. There, the 1,500 warriors would fight to the death, if necessary.

## THE BATTLE BEGINS

At the beginning of 1876, the U.S. Army responded by sending three army columns to surround the Indian encampment and return them to the reservation. Custer led the 600 men of the Seventh Cavalry, part of General Alfred H. Terry's column. On June 22, they were told to proceed ahead and scout the position of the Indians, and then to wait for the other columns, which would arrive on June 27.

Some historians have argued that Terry actually gave Custer a free hand in the situation, leaving the time of attack to Custer's discretion. Regardless, Custer did not heed the counsel of a fellow officer who told him before he left camp: "Don't be greedy. There are Indians enough for all." Vanity seemed to get the better of Custer; it appears he wanted all of the Indians for himself. As soon as he left Terry, he led his troops on an exhausting three-day march to the Little Bighorn valley, to within a few miles of the Indian encampment.

Historians are still puzzled about what happened next. Custer knew the approximate size of the Indian force; his favorite scout warned

A SIOUX DRAWING OF THE BATTLE OF LITTLE BIGHORN DEPICTS INDIANS DEFENDING THEIR ENCAMPMENT, SHOWN IN THE LOWER RIGHT-HAND CORNER. THE JULY 6, 1876 EDITION OF THE *NEW YORK HERALD* (BELOW) REPORTED ON THE BATTLE THAT HAD TAKEN PLACE ON JUNE 26.

A BLOODY BATTLE.

An Attack on Sitting Bull on the Little Horn River.

GENERAL CUSTER KILLED.

The Entire Detachment Under His Command Slaughtered.

SEVENTEEN OFFICERS SLAIN.

Narrow Escape of Colonel Reno's Command.

A HORRIBLE SLAUGHTER PEN.

Over Three Hundred of the Troops Killed.

him that there were more warriors than bullets in the belts of his men. But Custer apparently feared that he had been spotted by the Sioux, and considered immediate action necessary.

Custer sent 125 troops on a scouting mission to ascertain the exact position of the Indians, and then sent another 140 men, led by Major Marcus Reno, to approach the camp from its southern end. He himself took command of a frontal-assault force of some 210 men that would then take the enemy head on.

Raising his sword and striking a gallant pose, Custer led his men westward to the camp, splitting them into two wings. The right wing waited on a nearby ridge while he took the left wing down the river. But Indians soon infiltrated the positions. Cut off from his two flanking columns, outnumbered and surrounded, Custer's men panicked. Some managed to escape, although about 20 from the right wing joined Custer's 85 men on a nearby hill.

## A MARTYRED HERO?

The archeological remains and accounts by Indian warriors paint a rather unheroic picture of the Last Stand. It lasted only a few minutes as Custer and his men, crouching behind the carcasses of their dead horses, were picked off one by one. Reno and the other officers heard the shots, but it was not until a day and a half later that they were able to extricate themselves from battle and see the carnage for themselves.

Several factors have conspired to protect Custer's reputation. He was able to win the respect of people in power, who throughout his life protected him from his indiscretions: Once, for instance, he went AWOL to visit his wife, but was never severely disciplined. Even today, some military historians have claimed that given the situation that Custer found himself in (though it was entirely of his own making), Custer's decision was the only one that could be made. Experience had taught Custer that American troops could defeat Indians despite being outnumbered—and since he believed he had been spotted, it was imperative to attack before the Indians regrouped.

After the debacle at Little Bighorn, the army was reluctant to assign blame on Custer. Instead, a court of inquiry, which was directed by people friendly to Custer, sought to mark one of the officers as the scapegoat—Major Reno. Their efforts were thwarted, however, and Reno was ultimately exonerated.

The varnishing of George Armstrong Custer's reputation continued for years afterward. Until her death in 1933, Custer's devoted wife, Elizabeth Bacon Custer, traveled around the country, stoking the fires of his legend. Also crucial to Custer's valorization, according to some scholars, was the timing of the Last Stand. The year of the battle, 1876, was the nation's centennial, a time of unrestrained patriotism. The higher-ups would not have wanted to dull those sentiments by maligning a national martyr.

## THE INDIANS' LOSS

In fact, the army acted swiftly after Custer's defeat, realizing that their reputation was at stake. By refusing to let the Indians exult in victory, the army won the nation's sympathy for their military valor. Within two years, most of the Indians involved in the battle had been rounded up or killed. Sitting Bull led his followers to Canada. And even though Crazy Horse finally agreed to move his Oglala Sioux tribe into a reservation in 1877, he was charged with instigating a revolt, and was shot—reportedly while resisting imprisonment.

IN THE EARLY 1870S GENERAL CUSTER (SEATED) GUARDED CREWS BUILDING THE NORTHERN PACIFIC RAILROAD IN MONTANA TERRITORY (NOTE THE INITIALS N.P.R.R. ON THE TENT). STANDING BEHIND CUSTER IS BELIEVED TO BE CURLY, CUSTER'S TRUSTED SCOUT AND THE SOLE SURVIVOR OF THE BATTLE OF LITTLE BIGHORN. A PORTRAIT OF SITTING BULL (BELOW) WAS TAKEN AFTER HIS SURRENDER IN 1881, FIVE YEARS AFTER THE BATTLE.

# Gunfight at the OK Corral

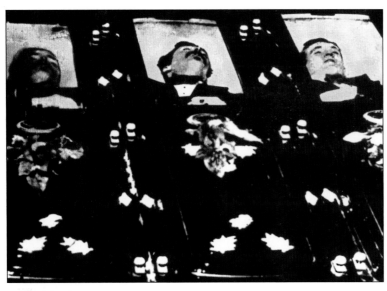

ON SHOW AFTER THE SHOWDOWN ARE THE EARPS' THREE COFFINED VICTIMS—FROM LEFT, BILLY CLANTON AND THE BROTHERS FRANK AND TOM MCLAURY. THE BODIES WERE DISPLAYED IN THE WINDOW OF A TOMBSTONE HARDWARE STORE.

**What really happened on that fateful day in Tombstone, when bad blood among three sets of brothers ended in violence still remembered?**

TOMBSTONE, ARIZONA, WAS ONE OF THE MORE notorious towns in the American West, a rough-and-ready place where the line between law and outlawry was as insubstantial as gunsmoke, and murders not infrequent. Today the 4-square-mile town is remembered for a gun battle that occurred on Wednesday, October 26, 1881. It pitted two pairs of brothers against each other: the Clantons and their allies the McLaury brothers versus the Earp brothers (Wyatt, Virgil, and Morgan) and the consumptive John H. (Doc) Holliday, who earned his nickname from his profession as a dentist.

Despite the name, the gunfight at the OK Corral did not occur at the corral but in a nearby alley. Far from being a balletic display of marksmanship, it was a brief and brutal burst of gunfire, lasting no more than half a minute. And, when the smoke cleared away, Billy Clanton and the two McLaurys lay dead in the dust.

### A DEAL GONE WRONG

What happened? The events leading up to the gunfight are sketchy. Afterwards, the participants told different stories, to vindicate the killings or to present themselves in an heroic light. By all accounts, most townspeople saw the fight coming; there had been plenty of warnings. For several days, the Clanton clan, a particularly violent, foul-mouthed bunch led by brother Ike, had gone around town making provocative threats against the Earp brothers and Doc Holliday.

The Earp-Clanton hostility had been brewing since the previous March, when a stagecoach was held up and suspicion fell on the Earps. Wyatt, who was running for mayor, had to clear up the matter quickly. When he found out that the robbers were hiding on Clanton land, he made a $1,000 deal with Ike to set up an ambush for their capture. The deal fell through, however, and the robbers were shot dead before they could be captured. Many Tombstone residents believed the Earps had done the killings to silence any witnesses.

In any case, the plot was about to thicken. Wyatt was forced to reveal his deal with Ike, earning him the hatred of the entire Clanton clan. Tempers flared even more wildly when Old Man Clanton was shot while rustling cattle in Mexico. (Many also blamed the Earps for the murder, although there was no evidence to support this view.) When the Clantons rode into town on October 26 to pick up some supplies and started issuing their menacing taunts, the Earps and Holliday, who had been drawn into the feud through his friendship with the Earps, had reason to take them seriously.

When approached by the town sheriff, the Clantons claimed that they weren't looking for a fight—yet they refused to give up their guns.

Virgil, who was then a town marshal, was determined to not take any chances. Quickly deputizing Wyatt and Doc, he set out to arrest the Clantons—even though after the battle the Earps couldn't say for what crime.

The Clantons had left their horses at the OK Corral, but some say that they were waiting to ambush Doc Holliday, who usually walked by that corner at the same time each day. On this day, however, Doc had gone to intercept the Earps to offer his assistance—a little piece of luck that stunned the Clantons when the two sides met in the alley, 90 yards from the corral.

The shoot-out was quick, and some say its brevity was due to the fact that the Earps did most of the shooting. There were even reports that some of the Clantons threw up their hands in surrender and protested that they were unarmed. But when the firing was over, Billy Clanton and both the McLaury brothers lay dead. The other Clanton allies either fled or were wounded. On the other side, Virgil and Morgan Earp and Doc Holliday were wounded, with Wyatt the only one left unhurt.

### THE LEGEND OF WYATT EARP

Wyatt wasn't particularly lionized in his own day, as some gunfighters were. But by the 1920s, he was embraced as an American hero, the paragon of Western machismo. To a considerable extent, Wyatt's popularity was due to his own talent for self-promotion—in particular, the peddling of his story to several pulp novelists. But when examined more closely, Wyatt's life before and after the famous gunfight becomes somewhat less heroic.

Wyatt Earp was one of seven children in a family that was constantly on the move, roving from California to Illinois to Missouri. Wyatt would inherit this restlessness. He became a constable in Lamar, Missouri, in 1870, but—inconsolable after his wife died—he wandered throughout Indian territory, finally settling in Wichita, Kansas, where his brother James ran a saloon and brothel. There, Wyatt had several run-ins with the law, and

was arrested at one point for horse stealing. But in best Western-movie fashion, he escaped before the trial. Wyatt next moved on to Dodge City, where he befriended John Henry "Doc" Holliday, who was known as much for his tippling as his dentistry.

Together, Wyatt and Doc Holliday moved to Tombstone. Wyatt's dedication to the town's stability was based largely on his business interests. Along with his brothers, he purchased one of the town's largest saloons, and made much of his money from gambling there.

After the infamous gunfight, Wyatt—restless as ever—left for Nome, Alaska, to cash in on the Klondike gold rush. He later moved to San Francisco, marrying a vaudevillian actress he had met in Tombstone. True to form, he refereed a boxing match, and was responsible for throwing the fight in a fix.

Wyatt Earp spent the final years of his life in Los Angeles, polishing his legend as a lawman might his badge. In 1929, he died quietly in his sleep at the age of 80. Sadly for Earp, death came before the OK Corral gunfight took its place in the American frontier mythology.

BURT LANCASTER AND KIRK DOUGLAS PLAYED WYATT EARP (BELOW LEFT) AND DOC HOLLIDAY IN THE 1957 *GUNFIGHT AT THE OK CORRAL* (ABOVE). WHY THE GUNFIGHT SHOULD HAVE BECOME SO MUCH A PART OF THE LORE OF THE OLD WEST MAY BE SIMPLY A MATTER OF CHANCE. THEN AGAIN, IT COULD HAVE BEEN BECAUSE THE INCIDENT WAS AN AFFIRMATION THAT THE WILD WEST WAS GOING TO SUBMIT TO THE RULE OF LAW.

# The Case of Lizzie Borden

## "Lizzie Borden took an axe..." or did she?

EVERY SCHOOLCHILD USED TO KNOW THE RHYME: "Lizzie Borden took an axe, and gave her mother forty whacks/And when she saw what she had done, she gave her father forty-one." But did she really do it?

In the summer of 1892, Andrew Borden, age 70, lived with his second wife Abby and his two daughters from his first marriage, Lizzie and Emma, in a cramped three-story house in Fall River, Massachusetts. There was no love lost between the daughters and their stepmother—indeed, the relationship was acrimonious.

On August 4th, Emma Borden was out of the house, visiting friends in Fairhaven. The girls' uncle, John Vinnicum Morse, of nearby Dartmouth, had dropped in unannounced the evening before and stayed the night. Also at home was the Borden's maid, Bridget Sullivan. Mr. Morse had left the house first that morn-ing, to visit his niece and nephew; Andrew Borden left shortly thereafter to go downtown; Bridget was busy washing windows outside.

By all accounts, Mrs. Borden went back upstairs after breakfast to straighten the guest room. With Emma away, Lizzie was left to her own devices. At about quarter of ten in the morning, Mr. Borden returned home and Lizzie informed him that Mrs. Borden had gone out to visit a sick friend. (This visit is a matter of contention—no sick friend ever came forward later, and so it is highly possible that Abby Borden was already dead when her husband returned to the house.)

At one point Mr. Borden had gone upstairs to his bedroom, and then went back down-stairs in the main room to take a nap. Bridget, too, came back indoors and retired to her room in the attic for a nap soon thereafter. Then, at 11:10 A.M., Lizzie woke Bridget with a cry up the stairs: "Come down quick! Father is dead. Somebody came in and killed him!"

### THE EVIDENCE DESTROYED

Lizzie immediately sent Bridget out to fetch a doctor. By the time Bridget returned, neighbors had started to gather. Lizzie told the crowd that her father had been murdered while she was in the barn looking for sinkers to fashion a fishing lure—although she had never before shown an interest in fishing. In the midst of this confusion, someone thought to ask where Abby Borden was. Lizzie replied that she did not know. Alarmed, Bridget and a neighbor ventured upstairs and discovered Abby Borden's body in the guest room.

The police still had not arrived at the scene of the murder. Unfortunately for the cause of justice, August 4th was the day of the Fall River police picnic, and there were very few officers on duty. The original policeman sent to investigate ran back to the station house in search of more help, leaving neighbors, doctors, and the surviving family to willfully or inadvertently destroy the crime scene, helping to ensure that a murderer was never caught.

## DID EMMA DO IT?

Uncle John was under suspicion briefly, but his alibi proved airtight. Bridget was also investigated, but she had even less of a motive than Lizzie, who inherited half of her father's estate. The other half of the estate went to Emma, who claimed to have been visiting friends out of town. But another eyewitness claimed to have seen Emma speaking with Lizzie outside of the house on the morning of the murders. It has been speculated that Emma could well have sneaked back into town in enough time to attack her parents, and then fled back to Fairhaven to establish her alibi.

However, when it was discovered that Lizzie had purchased a small ax a few days before the murder, she was detained in the city jail and then tried for murder. During the trial, one of the factors that weighed heavily in Lizzie's favor was the absence of blood on her person. Such a spotless appearance would have been impossible with only 20 minutes to clean up and hide the murder weapon after bludgeon-

ing her father. Moreover, Abby's murder occurred almost certainly an hour or two prior to Andrew's—surely Bridget would have noticed were Lizzie covered in blood. In addition, another neighbor testified to having seen Lizzie emerge from the barn, thus seemingly backing up her alibi. As most of the evidence seemed to be in her favor, Lizzie was acquitted.

To this day, the crime has never been truly solved. The destruction of evidence and Bridget and Lizzie's silence only add to the aura of mystery that has surrounded Andrew and Abby Borden's deaths for more than a century.

**ABBY BORDEN, KNOWN AS A KIND AND GENEROUS WOMAN (ABOVE), WAS THE SECOND WIFE OF ANDREW J. BORDEN. A LARGE SHAREHOLDER IN MANY MILLS, MR. BORDEN WAS CONSIDERED ONE OF THE LEADING CITIZENS OF FALL RIVER. AT THE TIME OF HIS MURDER, HE WAS FOUND LYING IN A POOL OF BLOOD ON THE BLACK OVERSTUFFED HORSEHAIR SOFA IN HIS PARLOR (LEFT). MRS. BORDEN'S BODY WAS FOUND LATER IN A SPARE BEDROOM OF THEIR HOME (TOP).**

# Misquoted American History

American history is steeped in famous quotations, with certain noted phrases inspiring great pride in many a patriot's heart whenever they are read or uttered. Everyone recalls the words of John F. Kennedy when he proclaimed, "Ask not what your country can do for you—ask what you can do for your country." However, many historical quotations are not so much remembered as mangled, misquoted, or misremembered. What is more, the more famous the quote, the more likely it was said by someone else.

PATRICK HENRY

## "GIVE ME LIBERTY OR GIVE ME DEATH."

Patrick Henry's famous line is often quoted, but there's no definitive proof that these were his words. The quote was attributed to Henry by William Wirt, his first biographer, who created so many factoids in his book that historians constantly ask the question "Is it fact or is it Wirt?" We do know, however, that in 1765, when Henry was accused of treason, he uttered the words "If this be treason, make the most of it." His reply, more courageous than any other speech given that year in response to the reviled Stamp Act, caused a sensation. If the quote didn't find a place in history, it is probably because Henry apologized for his strong words.

## "I ONLY REGRET THAT I HAVE BUT ONE LIFE TO LOSE FOR MY COUNTRY."

Nathan Hale is attributed with saying "I only regret that I have but one life to lose for my country" just before he was hanged by the British at the young age of 21. But according to the journal of Captain Frederick Mackenzie, a British officer who was with Hale at his death, Hale's last words actually were: "It is the duty of every good officer to obey any orders given him by his commander-in-chief."

NATHAN HALE

## "THE MASS OF MANKIND HAS NOT BEEN BORN WITH SADDLES ON THEIR BACKS..."

Thomas Jefferson is purported to have originated this metaphorical paean to the democratic spirit: "The mass of mankind has not been born with saddles on their backs, nor a favored few booted and spurred, ready to ride them legitimately by the grace of God." In fact, Jefferson must have based the remark on a speech made by 17th-century English politician Richard Rumbold. In a famous speech delivered on the scaffold in 1685, just before he was hanged, Rumbold told the assembled that he did not "believe that Providence had sent a few men into the world, ready booted and spurred to ride, and millions ready saddled and bridled to be ridden."

**THOMAS JEFFERSON**

**ABRAHAM LINCOLN**

## "YOU CAN FOOL ALL THE PEOPLE..."

"You can fool all the people some of the time and some of the people all the time, but you cannot fool all the people all of the time" may ring true, but it's doubtful that Lincoln said it. He is supposed to have made the remark in September, 1858, in Clinton, Illinois. Lincoln was running for the Senate against Stephen Douglas, but no mention of the quote appeared in the local newspapers. A few individuals who alleged they heard the speech said they had heard him say something similar in response to a survey by the *Chicago Tribune* and the *Brooklyn Eagle*, but this was 50 years after the speech was given.

## "...OF THE PEOPLE, BY THE PEOPLE..."

"Government of the People, by the People, for the People shall not perish from the Earth," said Lincoln in the Gettysburg Address. But this thought was expressed in at least two prior speeches. Unitarian minister and abolitionist Theodore Parker said: "[Government] becomes more and more of all, by all, and for all." In Daniel Webster's words, it went this way: "The people's government, made for the people, made by the people, and answerable to the people."

**DANIEL WEBSTER**

**FRANKLIN D. ROOSEVELT**

## "THE ONLY THING WE HAVE TO FEAR..."

In the throes of the Great Depression, Franklin Delano Roosevelt told the American people, "The only thing we have to fear is fear itself." But similar statements have been attributed to other equally distinguished people and sources. A similar quote is found in the Bible, which says "Be not afraid of sudden fear." Closer to FDR's idea is Montaigne's "The thing I fear most is fear." Francis Bacon's "Nothing is terrible except fear itself" is also a noteworthy precedent, as is the Duke of Wellington's "The only thing I am afraid of is fear" and Henry David Thoreau's "Nothing is so much to be feared as fear."

# Robert E. Lee and the Battle of Gettysburg

## Is this heroic figure's unequivocal praise deserved, or is his canonized reputation a historical misconception?

HISTORY, THEY SAY, IS WRITTEN BY THE WINNERS. Had the outcomes of some of history's wars been different, a very different group of heroes would be celebrated today: Pompey, not Julius Caesar; King George III, not George Washington. This trend toward a glorification of the victors has been prevalent throughout recorded history; but it does have some exceptions. Among these is the case of Robert E. Lee.

Although Lee commanded the losing side during the bloodiest military conflict America has ever seen, he has been lionized by the passage of time. Today he is remembered, perhaps just behind Abraham Lincoln, as the most beloved and admired figure to emerge from the Civil War, a mild-mannered man, kindly but full of patriotic intensity, opposed to the war but deeply loyal to his native Virginia and by extension to the Confederacy.

Lee was certainly beloved by his own men; he was an astonishingly potent leader, and inspired a loyalty in his Army of Northern Virginia that far exceeded anything mustered by the generals fighting for the Union. Before the devastating defeat at Gettysburg, Lee led his badly outnumbered army to victory after victory. But his status as national hero was cemented by a vigorous public relations campaign following his death in 1870, five years after the end of the war. To the lead-

ers of the defeated South, establishing Robert E. Lee as a hero was a sensible priority—it gave some much-needed historical legitimacy to their lost cause.

### SEARCH FOR SCAPEGOATS

In the late 1860s and early 1870s, as it became clear to history that the tide of the Civil War was turned at Gettysburg (between 20,000 and 28,000 Confederate soldiers were killed in the three days of fighting), it became increasingly vital to those concerned with elevating Lee's reputation to assert that he was not responsible for the Confederate defeat. Instead, they blamed a number of other generals, including J.E.B. Stuart, who made a mess of the cavalry reconnaissance in the days before the battle, and Lieutenant James Longstreet, Lee's right-hand man. In a speech delivered at Washington College (now Washington & Lee University), former Confederate General Jubal Early laid the blame for the mishandling of the battle squarely at the feet of Longstreet. It was Longstreet, he said, who insisted on the misguided assault that culminated in the bloody charge of General Pickett's division, and it was Longstreet who botched Lee's orders in carrying out his own assault. (Perhaps not coincidentally, the irascible Longstreet had accused Lee of poor decision making at Gettysburg in an interview some months before.) After Early's speech, a wave of print criticism engulfed Longstreet; he, and not Lee, was held to blame for losing the Gettysburg campaign, and hence the Civil War. This belief has persisted, especially in the South, for generations.

## LONGSTREET'S VINDICATION?

But is it fair? There were certainly other motivating factors in the collective decision to blame Longstreet for the loss. For one, he had become a Republican in the years following the war, a move that amounted to suicide in the fervidly Democratic South. On Lee's side is his record of improbable victories preceding Gettysburg; and it is difficult to deny the simple nobility that biographers have long perceived in his character. But at Gettysburg, as historians have begun to acknowledge, Lee may well have been guilty of the poor decision making of which Longstreet accused him.

The charges against Longstreet simply do not hold up. One of Early's claims—that Longstreet was responsible for the decision to attack the larger Union force, which held a superior position atop the Round Top hills—is false. All records indicate that Longstreet advocated a more prudent defensive posture that would have enabled the Confederate army to cut off the Union forces in the Pennsylvania battlefield and get between them and Washington, D.C. Longstreet's theories of defensive warfare were well ahead of their time, and there is no telling what might have happened had his approach been implemented.

The other charge—that Longstreet handled his own assault poorly, beginning too late—is also dubious. Longstreet was not able to begin his attack until late afternoon on the pivotal second day of the battle, but this did not cause the assault to fail. In fact, Longstreet was forced to wait due to the late arrival of one of his brigades. Had he attacked earlier, he would have done so with a substantially smaller force.

It was Lee who insisted on pressing the attack even when a defensive stance made more sense. Lee had gambled often in the Civil War, and almost always won—but at Gettysburg, his luck finally abandoned him. It is telling that, after the battle, Lee blamed himself for the loss. "It is all my fault," he told Longstreet. "I thought my men were invincible."

WHILE ROBERT E. LEE (OPPOSITE) WAS INDEED A GREAT GENERAL, THE GETTYSBURG DEFEAT MAY HAVE TO BE LAID AT HIS FEET—MEANING JAMES LONGSTREET (ABOVE) WAS NOT TO BLAME. BELOW, A CASUALTY OF THE FIERCE BATTLE THAT COST MANY THOUSANDS OF LIVES.

# Who Was Jack the Ripper?

**SEVERAL YEARS AFTER THE HORRIFIC** events that had taken place in London, Sir Melville MacNaghten, head of the city's Criminal Investigation Department, wrote "Even now I can recall the foggy evenings, and hear again the raucous cries of the newspaper boys: 'Another horrible murder. . . mutilation, Whitechapel.' Such was the burden of their ghastly song; and, when the double murder of 30 September took place, no servant-maid deemed her life safe if she ventured out to post a letter after ten o'clock at night." The subject of his reminiscence, dubbed Jack the Ripper, was a serial murderer who in 1888 terrorized Whitechapel, a poor district of London's East End.

## MURDERS MOST FOUL

The first serial killer to strike a bustling metropolis, Jack the Ripper reveled in the city's fear. His very name conjures up the eerie gloom of Victorian streets, the stuff of which legends are made—and real legends have long lives. And so it is with Jack the Ripper. The mystery has become the source of diversions of all kinds, from Sherlock Holmes adventures to off-Broadway musicals. The term "Ripperologist" has needled its way into the dictionary, describing any student of the case. An international club called Cloak and Dagger and a quarterly journal, *Ripperana*, publish essays galore on the killer. To say that the Jack the Ripper murders have been escalated into cult lore is an understatement. But the case, more than a century old, has become so diluted with unsubstantiated "facts" that the real truth has possibly become harder to find.

> **The first serial murderer to become famous brought new meaning to the word "gruesome."**

Between August and November of 1888, Jack gruesomely eviscerated his victims, and then disappeared without a trace. The slayings were brutal. The first attributed to Jack was of Mary Ann (Polly) Nichols on the last day of August; her throat was slashed, her abdomen ripped open "like a pig in the market."

Annie Chapman was found a week later on the cold street, gutted in much the same manner, having had large pieces of flesh stolen from her body. After these deaths sparked a frenzied hunt for the murderer, another woman was added to the list of victims: Her name was Martha Tabram, and her body was discovered in early August.

The Ripper lay low for a couple of weeks until September 30th, when his "double event" raised a public panic. In one part of Whitechapel, Elizabeth Stride lay on the street, her throat cut, but with no signs of mutilation (the prevailing theory is that Jack was interrupted before he could begin his trademark handiwork). His thirst not sated, he fled to another part of Whitechapel and attacked his second victim of the night, Catherine Eddowes. After ferociously disemboweling her, he absconded with one of her kidneys.

The final killing blamed on Jack came more than a month later, on November 10, and was perhaps the most gruesome of them all. Jane "Black Mary" Kelly was found in her room, severely mutilated, and pieces of flesh were arranged around the room. Her heart had been removed from her body.

While the Ripper may have disappeared into thin air, the heated speculation about his

**IN AN UNDATED DRAWING FROM THE POLICE GAZETTE (RIGHT), JACK THE RIPPER DOES HIS EVIL WORK. FOG VEILED VICTORIAN LONDON'S STREETS, CREATING AN EERIE ATMOSPHERE WHERE EVEN A POSTMAN ON HIS ROUNDS COULD TAKE ON AN OMINOUS AIR (OPPOSITE).**

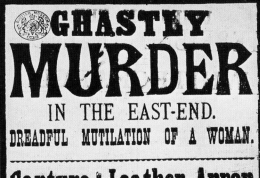

**GHASTLY MURDER IN THE EAST-END. DREADFUL MUTILATION OF A WOMAN. Capture : Leather Apron**

Another murder of a character even more diabolical than that perpetrated in Buck's Row, on Friday week, was discovered in the same neighbourhood, on Saturday morning. At about six o'clock a woman was found lying in a back yard at the foot of a passage leading to a lodging-house in a Old Brown's Lane, Spitalfields. The house is occupied by a Mrs. Richardson, who lets it out to lodgers, and the door which admits to this passage, at the foot of which lies the yard where the body was found, is always open for the convenience of lodgers. A lodger named Davis was going down to work at the time mentioned and found the woman lying on her back close to the flight of steps leading into the yard. Her throat was cut in a fearful manner. The woman's body had been completely ripped open, and the heart and other organs laying about the place, and portions of the entrails round the victim's neck. An excited crowd gathered in front of Mrs. Richardson's house and also round the mortuary in old Montague Street, whither the body was quickly conveyed. As the body lies in the rough coffin in which it has been placed in the mortuary —the same coffin in which the unfortunate Mrs. Nicholls was first placed—it presents a fearful sight. The body is that of a woman about 45 years of age. The height is exactly five feet. The complexion is fair, with wavy dark brown hair; the eyes are blue, and two lower teeth have been knocked out. The nose is rather large and prominent.

identity did not. The police were never able to learn his real name, but they used the chilling alias taken from one of the many letters the murderer supposedly wrote:

*Dear Boss,*
*I keep on hearing the police have caught me but they won't fix me just yet. I have laughed when they look so clever and talk about being on the right track...I am down on whores and I shant quit ripping them till I do get buckled...My knife's so nice and sharp I want to get to work right away if I get a chance. Good Luck.*

*Yours truly,*
*Jack the Ripper*
*Don't mind me giving the trade name*

This letter was later deemed a hoax, written by a newspaperman in an attempt to generate more stories. In fact, almost all of Jack's letters were considered to be fakes.

### THE PRESS IN FULL CRY

One of the reasons the legend has lived so long, and continues to garner attention, is the exhaustive job the press did of reporting it. In a way, these murders (disregarding their brutal nature) weren't even so special. We may think of the slayings as having occurred in the proper top-

hatted London of the stuffy Victorian era, but in actuality, Whitechapel was a slum.

The Ripper murders snatched the public's attention for two reasons—the ghastly nature of the deaths and the press's sensationalism. These two factors fed into one another perfectly: At a time when the press was beginning to become a vehicle for social change, the murders directed attention to the injustice of London's attitudes toward the lower classes.

In fact, in London during the Victorian era, it is believed that one in 16 women were whores. When the Whitechapel prostitute murders were made so very public, a light was drawn to the social ills the darker areas of London were facing. In an attack against city officials, the press sensationalized the horrific slaughters to highlight the incompetence of the Metropolitan Police. When the Commissioner, Sir Charles Warren, resigned on the day of the last murder, it was largely considered that the onslaught of verbal assaults in the tabloid press was a primary reason.

### MAN OF MYSTERY

Who was this elusive Jack? One of the prime suspects at the time was a con-man, Michael Ostrog, who was using multiple aliases. But he was never charged. As Jack's legacy lives on in fiction, film, and our imagination, so does the search for his true identity, perhaps with more vigor now than a century ago. Ripperologists have designated Jack the Ripper as everything from a cannibal to a mad social reformer.

In 1970, Dr. T.E.A. Stowell claimed that the cold-blooded killer had been Edward, Duke of Clarence, grandson of Queen Victoria. But in *Clarence—Was He Jack the Ripper?*, author Michael Harrison emphatically refutes claims that Edward was the Ripper, and thoroughly examines the theory that the murderer was the Duke's tutor: a Cambridge man named J.K. Stephan, a poet and blatant misogynist. But the evidence against Stephan is little more than supposition, and much of that is fairly slim.

The truth of Jack the Ripper's identity must lie somewhere, amidst pilfered documents and hidden diaries. But for more than a hundred years, the famous killer has kept his secret.

## NOT YOUR USUAL SUSPECTS

Jack the Ripper's identity has been the obsession of many amateur detectives and professional sleuths, yet we still don't know who he was.

For unknown reasons, the police declared the case closed three weeks after the murder of Jane Kelly in November, 1888. According to some reports, the White-chapel Vigilance Committee

received notice that soon after the Kelly slaying Jack drowned in the Thames. A body, washed up on the riverbank in early December, was identified as Montague John Druitt, who had been named as a prime suspect. But police information on who they supposed to be Druitt was erroneous, listing the

**WE MAY NEVER KNOW** ▼

wrong age and occupation. Other suspects included a butcher, a midwife, and an insane professor. Another was Aaron Kosminski, a Jewish barber-surgeon who ate food from the gutter and was eventually institutionalized in 1890. Still another was Francis Tumblety, an American quack doctor living in London at the time

of the murders. (After the police arrested Tumblety for homosexual activity, he jumped bail and fled back to the U.S., where he actually kept a collection of female body parts.)

Despite the intriguing aspects of these men as suspects, there is not enough hard evidence to consider any of them very likely.

# PART 5

# THE LATE MODERN AGE

THE YEARS BETWEEN THE MID-19TH AND MID-20TH CENTURIES WERE marked by vast improvements in transportation. By 1900, large and powerful boats roamed the oceans, motor cars were hitting the roads, and railways crisscrossed Europe and North America. Communication had also improved astonishingly, with the telegraph and telephones making it possible to transmit information at a great distance in seconds.

While these developments made the world in many ways easier to navigate and comprehend, they also created a new set of questions to ponder. We begin to wonder, for instance, just how the Wright brothers figured out how to fly? How did a grand and powerful ship like the *Titanic* sink in the Atlantic? Who brought us photography, and how? And for that matter, who really invented baseball, America's pastime? These questions capture our imagination not only because they involve curious or legendary personalities but because they feel so close.

# The Invention of Photography

**The birth of photography in the early 19th century was a groundbreaking step toward further technological innovation.**

LEFT, THE FIRST OUTDOOR PHOTOGRAPH, BY NIÉPCE IN 1826. ABOVE, A DAGUERRE CAMERA. BELOW, TALBOT'S EARLIEST PAPER PHOTOGRAPH (1835) SHOWS A WINDOW IN LACOCK ABBEY.

WHEN TRACING THE HISTORY OF AN INVENTION, it is difficult to pinpoint a single instance as the moment of discovery. Discovery usually follows a long and winding path, and new inventions are seldom the work of one individual.

The invention of photography is no different. Its development was largely the result of experimental work by four men—Thomas Wedgwood and William Henry Fox Talbot in England, and Joseph Nicéphore Niépce and Louis Jacques Mandé Daguerre in France. Daguerre and Talbot would gradually perfect photographic techniques during the first 50 years of the 19th century.

Photography's first stirrings go back a long way, possibly to antiquity. The camera's forerunner was the camera obscura (literally "dark room"), which first appeared in the Middle Ages. The device consisted of a darkened room with a small opening, later replaced by a lens.

Through the opening an inverted image of an outdoor daylight scene formed on the opposite wall. Eventually, smaller, portable devices were used by artists who sought to obtain realistic perspectives in landscape paintings and to create truthful human likenesses in portraits.

The development of the chemical processes essential for photography began in 1727, when the German physicist Johann Heinrich Schulze demonstrated that silver salts turned dark when they were exposed to light. In 1777, the Swedish chemist Carl Scheele demonstrated that ammonia retarded the effects of light on these salts after they had been altered by light. Scheele's discovery indicated how the photochemical process might be stabilized.

## WEDGWOOD'S IMAGE

The first known attempt to produce a photographic image was made by the porcelain manufacturer Thomas Wedgwood, who thought light-sensitive materials might be used to produce painted designs on chinaware. In 1802, he had some success recording images on paper and leather sensitized by silver nitrate. But the best he could do was hold an object or cutout against a sensitized surface and wait for the sun to produce a silhouette, which quickly vanished. Despite this flaw, Wedgwood's experiment was noted in a London journal. The stage was set for the development of a new art.

About 1815, the Frenchman Joseph Nicéphore Niépce conducted experiments that combined light-sensitive materials with lithography. His son Isidore was a talented draftsman who drew images on lithographic stone, but Niépce himself had little skill in this direction. When Isidore entered military service, his father set out to devise a method by which the

A MAN HAVING HIS SHOES SHINED—THE FIRST PHOTOGRAPHED PERSON—APPEARS IN THIS 1839 DAGUERREOTYPE OF A PARIS BOULEVARD. THE STREET TRAFFIC MOVED TOO FAST TO REGISTER IN THE IMAGE.

light itself would do the drawing for him. His technique involved spreading a light-sensitive solution on a pewter plate. Then, he oiled a printed engraving to make it translucent, placed it on the plate, and exposed both to light. Later, he immersed the plate in a solvent that brought out the image. The result was a permanent copy of the engraving.

In 1826, Niépce produced a portrait from an engraving of Cardinal d'Amboise. Later that

year, he fitted a pewter plate to a primitive camera and took a view of the courtyard at his country estate. It was the first successful experiment to get an image from nature, although the exposure time was eight hours.

## DAGUERREOTYPES VS. TALBOTYPES

In 1829, Niépce teamed up with Louis Jacques Mandé Daguerre, a painter who specialized in creating settings for the Paris theaters and whose work with theatrical lighting had interested him in photographic experiments. But Niépce would die four years later, before the two had made any real progress on their work.

In 1835, however, Daguerre discovered the principles of photographic development, using mercury vapor to draw out the latent image formed on a metal plate of iodized silver. This reduced exposure time to a half hour. Unfortunately, the image produced was impermanent. But two years later Daguerre found that a solution of table salt would fix the image. Daguerre named the process after himself. In 1839, he sold the rights to his process to the French government for a pension of 6,000 francs a year, while Isidore Niépce received 4,000 francs.

During the 1830s, the English scientist, mathematician, and linguist William Henry Fox Talbot used a camera obscura to record the images he could not capture by drawing. By 1835, he had achieved some success. He soaked paper in two solutions of table salt and silver nitrate, producing silver chloride in the fibers of the paper. Exposing the paper to the light darkened the silver chloride, and this became a negative. Talbot found that he could make any number of prints by placing a freshly sensitized piece of paper against the negative and holding it to the light. For a fixative, Talbot used sodium hyposulphite (sodium thiosulfate), usually referred to as "hypo," which was developed by his friend, the astronomer and scientist Sir John Herschel.

Sharper lenses and faster exposures appeared in the 1840s. As photography became cheaper, public demand for portraits grew. Despite its lovely silvery images, the daguerreotype was doomed, because it could not be easily duplicated, but it co-existed for a while with paper photographs, called briefly "talbotypes" after their inventor. Despite their limitations, both inventions gave photographers the power to fix transient images from the world of light.

## TRAVELING DAGUERREOTYPISTS

**THE STUFF OF LEGEND**

Improvements in the daguerreotype process—most notably those of József Petzval and Friedrich Voigtländer in the 1840s—reduced the exposure time to less than 30 seconds. Such advances made daguerreotyping an extremely popular industry. By 1850, nearly every city had at least one "daguerrean artist" (in New York City there were 77 parlors). Traveling daguerreotypists outfitted wagons with darkroom materials and began carting their product to villages and towns all over the world.

The services of these roving photographers were in great demand. They would pull into town to find great numbers of townsfolk waiting for them, dressed in their best clothes and practicing the poses that would soon be recorded for all eternity.

# Creative Cinematography

**IN A 1912 PHOTO, EDISON EXAMINES A REEL OF FILM IN HIS WEST ORANGE, NEW JERSEY, STUDIO.**

In 1899, when war broke out between the British and Dutch settlers in South Africa, Americans had an insatiable appetite for news of the conflict. Crowds jammed into theaters like Koster and Bial's Music Hall on West 34th Street in New York City to watch images of the battles of the Boer War, made possible by the new inventions produced by the factory Thomas A. Edison: the Kinetograph, which recorded moving images, and the Vitascope (far right), the first projector. The film industry was only a few years old when the Boer War began, but already "flickers" were in great demand.

But how was Edison's motion picture team able to obtain such close-up shots of combat and return the images so quickly to the U.S.? And didn't the vista surrounding the soldiers, supposedly views of South Africa, look an awful lot like rural New Jersey?

### THE BLACK MARIA
Edison's desire to create moving pictures intensified about a decade before the start of the Boer War. He was becoming interested in creating a machine that would make pictures of objects in motion, which he could then synchronize with the sounds and voices of the phono-graph (also his own invention). Only with the advent of celluloid film did the idea become feasible.

Edison was anxious to try the Kinetograph's applications. On the grounds of his studio in West Orange, New Jersey, his team of inventors assembled the world's first motion picture studio, the Black Maria, a shed covered with black tar paper. Most of the earliest films shot there recorded popular subjects: Buffalo Bill, ballet girls, boxing matches, a dental patient reacting to laughing gas.

While it was easy to bring acts to the Black Maria, how was Edison's team going to satisfy the public's desire to see scenes of war? Edison's trick was to stage large-scale reenactments in the back yard of his studio, using troops from the New Jersey National Guard. In a matter of a few days, Edison staged some of the Boer War's most bloody battles—and with artistic flair to boot.

Though Edison's films never owed up to the fakery explicitly, it is probable that much of the public knew they were watching reenactments, while others were clearly fooled. More talented upstarts would eventually run Edison's film company out of business. But these early examples of "special effects" reveal that Thomas Edison, among his numerous other accomplishments, was the George Lucas of 1900.

### SHAKY GROUND
Six years later, the Biograph Company put Edison's celluloid confabulation to shame when, after the San Francisco earthquake of 1906, they contrived a cardboard and clay model of the city so they could produce the first newsreel of the earthquake and fire. Other films of the quake's devastation were real, but didn't hesitate to sensationalize: One scene, showing a family picnicking among the debris, was certainly staged for the camera.

Another fraudulent film scenario: At the height of the Cold War in 1965, the competition between the U.S. and the Soviet Union over who would be the first to travel in space led the Soviets to film a spacewalk—but they shot it underwater. The film, they believed, would support their claim that the first human to walk in space was a cosmonaut.

If these cinematic relics seem quaint, they stand in history's corner as an eerie premonition. What they foreshadowed was a phenomenon born of the Entertainment Age: that the movie version of an event is often perceived as being as real as the event itself.

# How Did We Learn to Fly?

**Two brothers from America's heartland barely won the race to be the first to fly.**

IT IS OFTEN ERRONEOUSLY SAID THAT THE PREVAILING opinion at the dawn of the 20th century, even among scientists, was that humankind would never fly. While there were certainly those who scoffed at the idea, others thought it was only a matter of time before all the technical problems would be solved and people would take to the air. The technology of lighter-than-air dirigibles was well along on both sides of the Atlantic, and newspapers would periodically report on the exploits of glider pilots in Europe and the United States.

It was, in fact, one such spate of stories that captured the imagination of two young brothers running a small printing shop and newspaper in Dayton, Ohio. Wilbur and Orville Wright, sons of the local bishop of an evangelical Protestant church, had tried their hand at many things. Though neither had finished high school, they were voracious readers and talented tinkerers. In their newspaper, they featured stories of the exploits of Otto Lilienthal, a German engineer who had taken glider design to the limit. It was rumored that Lilienthal was about to attach a motor to his gliders when he died during a test flight in August, 1896. It was during this period that interest in the possibility of flight was kindled in the Wrights.

## BICYCLE RICHES

Orville and Wilbur were considered a remarkable pair since childhood. It seemed to most people that there was an eerie bond between them; they were constantly in each other's company, finished each other's sentences, and seemed to read each other's thoughts. They also shared characteristics they inherited from their father and their Yankee forebears: a steely determination and a clear-eyed, skeptical approach to life. In their quest for flight, they would draw on these qualities heavily.

By the late 1890s, the Wright boys had become financially independent by inventing and manufacturing a wildly successful bicycle, called the "Flyer." Their newfound wealth gave them the opportunity to pursue first their studies, and then their experiments, in flight.

To say their approach was thorough and methodical would be an understatement: they read and mastered absolutely everything pub-

OTTO LILIENTHAL GETS AIRBORNE IN GERMANY IN 1896 (LEFT). LILIENTHAL AND HIS BROTHER CONDUCTED THE MOST EXTENSIVE GLIDER TESTS UP TO THAT TIME, AND WERE ABOUT TO ATTACH A MOTOR TO THEIR DESIGN WHEN OTTO WAS KILLED.

WILBUR MANS THE WRIGHTS' 1902 GLIDER (RIGHT), A SOPHISTICATED MACHINE IN WHICH THE BROTHERS FLEW SOME 1,000 TEST FLIGHTS.

AT LEFT, A.M. HERRING FLIES A GLIDER IN TEST FLIGHTS ON THE WINDY SHORE OF LAKE MICHIGAN IN 1896. THE DESIGN WAS BY OCTAVE CHANUTE, THEN AGE 64. CHANUTE DREW ON HIS EXPERIENCE AS A RAILROAD ENGINEER TO BUILD STRONG YET LIGHTWEIGHT GLIDER FRAMES.

the Wrights would spend the summer testing the gliders they built in their machine shop back in Dayton during the winter.

Using wing designs they had developed from the work of fellow researchers like Octave Chanute and Samuel Langley, the Wright gliders performed well, and to the casual observer the Wrights seemed to be making great progress. But the brothers were sorely disappointed in their test flights of the summer of 1902. Having spent the winter carefully calculating the lift their particular glider wing design would experience in a given wind, they were disappointed to discover that their design produced 30 percent less lift than expected.

lished on the subject, corresponded and visited with every known researcher, and even asked the U.S. Weather Bureau where the best winds could be found for their experiments. On the basis of the Bureau's answer, they chose the Kill Devil Hills sand dunes near Kitty Hawk, North Carolina, a desolate area on the Outer Banks of the Atlantic shore.

The trips there were major undertakings—much equipment had to be moved by train and by mule over land. The brothers lived an isolated and spartan existence on the windy dunes during the summers of 1901, 1902, and 1903. Working alone and virtually around the clock,

## PERSISTENCE PAYS OFF

Others would have shrugged their shoulders and made seat-of-the-pants adjustments to the gliders until they obtained the lift they needed. But not the Wrights. They returned to Dayton and built a small wind tunnel in the back of their shop. They reviewed the entire literature, testing every assumption and subjecting every claim and number to careful experimentation.

The brothers tested more than 200 different designs in their six-foot wind tunnel that winter, amassing a massive body of experimental data. It came as no surprise to them that many of the figures they had been using were

wrong—the product of hasty or shoddy experimentation, or possibly just guesswork.

The Wrights redesigned their glider (like the famous bicycle, named the *Flyer*) and took it to Kitty Hawk for testing. This time the glider performed as predicted, and the brothers were ready for the next phase: attaching a motor and propellers to the glider for propulsion.

Ordinarily, the Wrights would have returned to Dayton and spent the winter testing their engine; they had already conducted exhaustive tests on the propeller design, an area of aeronautical research in which the Wrights were in a class by themselves. But the race to be the first to fly had heated up. The rival who concerned them most was Samuel Langley, secretary of the Smithsonian Institution. Langley had tested scale models of an aircraft powered by a gasoline engine and had constructed a full-size version by the fall of 1903; it was to be launched from a houseboat on the Potomac River.

Langley's machine failed spectacularly on October 7, 1903, and again on December 8. While the press heaped ridicule on Langley's attempts, the Wrights were afraid he would try again soon—and that he just might succeed. That year, they had not arrived at Kitty Hawk until late September. By December, winter had set in and living conditions on the wind-swept sand dunes were nearly intolerable. Still the brothers persevered. On December 17, 1903, using a small makeshift internal combustion engine constructed by their machinist, Charles Taylor, the Wrights conducted the first controlled flight of a heavier-than-air aircraft.

While the Wrights' achievement at Kill Devil Hills was heroic and groundbreaking, it was really in the back room of a bicycle shop in Dayton—during the laborious hours testing and recording the performance of wing after wing, comparing calculated lift against what they observed through their wind tunnel's small glass window—that the Wright brothers, and the rest of us, learned to fly.

AT LEFT, LANGLEY'S MACHINE IS POISED ATOP A HOUSEBOAT ON THE POTOMAC. SUBSEQUENT ANALYSIS SHOWED THE AIRCRAFT COULD HAVE FLOWN BUT WAS FAILED BY A POORLY DESIGNED LAUNCH MECHANISM. BELOW IS WHAT MAY BE THE MOST FAMOUS PHOTOGRAPH IN THE HISTORY OF TECHNOLOGY, TAKEN BY JOHN T. DANIELS: WILBUR WRIGHT RUNNING ALONGSIDE THE *FLYER* (HAVING KEPT THE WING CLEAR OF THE SAND) JUST AS HIS BROTHER ORVILLE LIFTS OFF ON THE FIRST SUCCESSFUL FLIGHT, IN 1903.

# What Struck Siberia in 1908?

## Did the mysterious explosion that flattened a vast area in Siberia come from outer space? Or was it a premature nuclear blast?

**NEAR WINSLOW, ARIZONA, THE GREAT BARRINGER METEOR CRATER MAKES OBVIOUS ITS ORIGIN. THE FORCE THAT DESTROYED THE SIBERIAN FOREST LEFT NO CRATER, BUT CAME WITH A BLAST THAT WAS HEARD SOME 500 MILES AWAY.**

TOWARD THE MIDDLE OF THE NIGHT ON JUNE 30, 1908, the most powerful explosion in recorded history rocked the Tunguska region in the heart of Russia's remote Siberian wilderness. It felled virtually every tree within a radius of 20 miles. Considering the immensity of the blast and the scale of the area it affected, it is miraculous that not even one person was killed.

It is equally surprising that an explosion of such magnitude hardly got a mention in the international press. Residents of the region reported that just beforehand they spotted a fireball crossing the sky, and from Kirensk, 250 miles away, a "pillar of fire" was seen.

Imperial Russian officials ignored the event. But in the 1920s, after the Russian Revolution, the new Soviet government appointed the scientist Leonid Kulik to investigate the explosion. His investigation was just the beginning of a search for answers to an event that still remains unexplained. The impact site has offered several clues, although much of the evidence is confusing, even contradictory.

Kulik set off on the first of several expeditions to the site of the explosion in early 1927, fully convinced that the blast had been caused by a meteor that had crashed into the earth. On his arrival near the site, Kulik noticed that as far as the eye could see there were thousands upon thousands of uprooted pine trees. As he continued walking around the perimeter of the devastated area, he noticed that the tree tops invariably pointed in one direction—away from a specific site, which, he concluded, had to be the blast's ground zero.

Investigating further, Kulik noticed dozens of large holes in the area. He was convinced the holes contained fragments of the meteor that had smashed into the earth. Kulik was so sure of his theory that the expedition's photographer withheld contrary evidence to avoid arousing the scientist's displeasure. (The photographer had discovered, and recorded on film, a tree stump standing at the bottom of one of the holes; this suggested that a meteor that had crashed into the earth would leave the stump untouched—implausible, to say the least.) What Kulik never learned before his death in the 1940s was that such holes were common throughout Siberia, and resulted from a perfectly normal change in weather patterns.

### SIMILARITIES TO HIROSHIMA

With the dropping of the atomic bomb on Hiroshima in August 1945, several similarities between the Siberian explosion and a nuclear blast became apparent. At the point of detonation in Hiroshima, there was surprisingly little damage done to the surrounding area. Likewise, many trees remained standing in the very center of the Siberian blast.

Furthermore, plants and trees at both sites regenerated at an extraordinary rate after each explosion, far faster than normal. In addition, eyewitnesses reported the appearance of a huge cloud of smoke after the explosion, eerily reminiscent of the mushroom cloud that follows nuclear blasts. Finally, there was nothing to suggest that anything like a meteor had hit the earth at the Siberian site. Instead, whatever exploded had blown above ground level and left an impact site that was similar to that created by an atom detonation over a target.

Could some sort of nuclear explosion have occurred in Siberia some 40 years prior to the creation of atomic weapons? Probably not. Atomic detonation leaves high levels of radioactivity at the site of the explosion and surrounding areas, and no such radiation was ever discovered at the blast site in Siberia.

Instead, minuscule pieces of silicate and magnetite were found lodged in nearby trees. Upon further examination, it became clear that these particles had the attributes of something from out of this world. Did whatever exploded over Siberia in 1908 come from outer space?

## SPACECRAFT OR COMET?

It appears the largest known natural explosion in modern times was not caused by a meteorite; nor was it caused by some precursor to the atomic bomb. If it did come from outer space, what could it be? A spaceship, perhaps? Several Russian scientists have speculated that the silicate and magnetite particles located near the blast site were remnants of an alien spaceship that was smashed to smithereens when it slammed into earth. According to some students of the blast, this theory is supported by the accounts of eyewitnesses to the explosion. The witnesses reported having seen a cylindrical object in the sky, which was descending slowly toward earth but then suddenly changed direction in midflight. These accounts seem to indicate that the "spaceship" was controlled by some force other than gravity.

Despite such intriguing theories, some experts say the explosion may have been caused by a small comet colliding with an air pocket equal to its mass several miles above the earth. Fortunately, the region directly below was virtually unpopulated; if it had been built up, the death toll would have been enormous.

Most comets, however, are seen before they come anywhere near earth. Why wasn't this one? Science fiction writer Arthur C. Clarke suggests that, because some comets approach the earth only during the day, they are not visible. Interestingly, one of these comets nears earth at the same time every year: June 30, the same day the explosion shook Siberia.

LEONID KULIK (ABOVE) HEADED A 1927 SOVIET EXPEDITION INVESTIGATING THE TUNGUSKA REGION, WHERE THE 1908 BLAST OCCURRED. THE SIBERIAN FOREST (BELOW) WAS UTTERLY DEVASTATED BY THE ABOVEGROUND EXPLOSION.

# Who Invented Baseball?

"I CLAIM THAT BASE BALL OWES ITS PRESTIGE AS OUR National Game to the fact that as no other form of sport it is the exponent of American Courage, Confidence, Combativeness...The founder of our National Game became a Major General in the United States Army!" So wrote Albert G. Spalding in 1911, in *America's National Game*. But did the officer really deserve the credit?

By about 1910, it was common knowledge that Abner Doubleday, the Civil War army general, was the inventor of baseball. The legend of Doubleday's creation was steeped in the history of the country and entrenched in the fields of the frontier and the forts of the Civil War, with players young and old employing physical and mental agility and American know-how. Yet had Doubleday been around to hear such praise (he died in 1893), he would have been a bit confused to find himself a legend—most likely because he did not invent the game.

### A SPORT FOR THE TIMES
By the turn of the century, baseball had become the national pastime; it had skyrocketed in popularity for its—believe it or not—quick pace, as opposed to three-day-long British cricket matches. It was also considered more refined than the gambling sports, boxing and horse

CIVIL WAR GENERAL ABNER DOUBLEDAY (LEFT), FROM COOPERSTOWN, N.Y., IS WIDELY BELIEVED TO HAVE INVENTED BASEBALL. BUT THE FIRST GAME (DEPICTED ABOVE IN AN 1866 PRINT) WAS PLAYED IN HOBOKEN, N.J., AND DOUBLEDAY'S INVOLVEMENT IS QUESTIONABLE.

racing. Alongside this rising interest in baseball an idealistic national identity had begun to form, including a belief in a strong work ethic, the rural roots of society, and the importance of a healthy mind and body.

In 1905, to connect the American spirit and its national game, Spalding, a baseball executive and sporting goods manufacturer, sought to discover the "true" story of baseball's creation. After he and his handpicked committee of learned men (which included several senators) launched a nationwide search for tales of the origin of the sport, letters started rolling in, suggesting different theories. One letter, from an 84-year-old Colorado mining engineer named Abner Graves, particularly pleased the committee. It talked of the spring of 1839, when Abner Doubleday, then Graves's boyhood friend, divided up some boys in a park in Cooperstown, New York, for a new game. The game was like Town Ball (which had been played in America since the 18th century), only it used four bases and two even sides, with modern baseball rules. In 1907, without checking the veracity of the letter, Spalding and his group accepted the letter's account and proclaimed Doubleday the inventor of the game.

## A VARIANT OF ROUNDERS

An Army general directing boys to play a new sport in an upstate village: It had the makings of poetic majesty. But it was false. The legend was released to the public, even though enough people knew the true story of baseball's creation. America's game, in fact, was derived from a British ball game called rounders. In 1842, Manhattan's upper-middle class men slightly altered that game's rules to fit the American environment, and began to play this new "Base Ball" for entertainment and relaxation.

Enter Alexander Cartwright, who suggested that social clubs, each composed of men from certain jobs or neighborhoods, form in the cities. His club, the New York Knickerbockers, elected its members not because of their baseball skills, which were secondary, but for their manners and refinement. When other clubs started popping up, challenges became common. Contests between two clubs would end when one team scored 23 (later, 21) "aces," or runs, whereupon all the players would go out for a banquet and engage in friendly revelry.

On June 19, 1846, in Hoboken, New Jersey, Cartwright's Knickerbockers played the first known recorded baseball game, getting massacred 23–1 by the New York Nine. Baseball was purely an urban game; in fact, rural society regarded the sport as a game for young

ALEXANDER CARTWRIGHT, THOUGHT BY MANY TO BE THE TRUE FATHER OF BASEBALL, ORGANIZED THE NEW YORK KNICKERBOCKERS IN 1845 AND DEVISED RULES FOR THE YOUNG SPORT.

children. So, it seems, baseball's origins lie in the pursuits of well-to-do men of good upbringing. It was not until 1869, when the professional movement of baseball began and athletes started to play for money, that the idea of sporting fraternities fell by the way.

When the true foundation of the sport was brought to the attention of baseball officials in the 1930s, it was a little too late to change the path of the sport's starry-eyed history. Plans for the National Baseball Hall of Fame, established in 1935 in Doubleday's hometown of Cooperstown, were already in the works. Later, in 1939, a United States postage stamp commemorating the 100th birthday of Doubleday's invention was introduced. Even though Alexander Cartwright is accepted as the first statistician of the game, if not the founder, it is Doubleday whose name will live on in baseball history.

As for Spalding, a little research would have proved that Doubleday wasn't even in Cooperstown when Abner Graves said he was, and that he wasn't known by any of his friends to play baseball. (These facts could have been found in his exhaustive diaries, in which the word "baseball" never appeared.) Spalding could also have checked up on Graves, who, a few years after writing the letter that would change the way baseball history is remembered, was checked into a mental asylum.

A BASEBALL CLUB POSES IN 1858. THE FIRST PROFESSIONAL TEAM, THE CINCINNATI RED STOCKINGS, WAS FORMED IN 1869.

# Who Reached the Poles First?

**There is much controversy surrounding who first reached two of the most distant regions of the world—the North and South Poles.**

THEY ARE LITERALLY THE ENDS OF THE EARTH, THE points where maps begin and end. Among the most inaccessible places in the world and surrounded by seas of drifting ice, frost-bound mountains, and volcanoes, they are steeped in bone-numbing cold, with average daily temperatures of 20 to 80 degrees below zero. They may not sound like promising places to visit—but for years, the quest to reach the poles was an international preoccupation, generating intense competition among nations and claiming the lives of several explorers.

The polar expeditions mounted between the years of 1901 and 1912 were testaments to human ingenuity, courage, and endurance. What is more, they were highly controversial. In the howling wind and desolate isolation of the polar ice caps, the truths of history can be very hard to ascertain. But though questions remain, we know more about the race for the South Pole than about the race for the North.

## AMUNDSEN GOES SOUTH

The South Pole was almost certainly first visited by Roald Amundsen and his team of Norwegian explorers, who reached the bottom of the world on December 14, 1911, after a trek that lasted almost two months. The Norwegians' success was due to their extraordinary foresight and preparation. They had mastered the techniques of dog-sledding, and devised in advance a scheme to overcome every obstacle—in particular the ring of volcanic mountains surrounding the site of the pole.

Not so lucky was the British team led by the heroic but ill-fated Captain Robert Falcon Scott. Although they left earlier than Amundsen's team, they arrived at the South Pole more than a month late, discovering Amundsen's camp on the site they believed they would discover first. The British team was far less prepared and far less lucky than the Norwegians. They attempted the trek with cumbersome Mongolian ponies rather than using only dogs, and ended by shooting the ponies for food and pulling their own supplies on skis—200 pounds per man, in some cases. Scott and his men showed almost unfathomable endurance, trekking through the frozen wastes for nearly

ROALD AMUNDSEN, THE DISCOVERER OF THE SOUTH POLE. AMUNDSEN REACHED THE BOTTOM OF THE WORLD WITH A TEAM OF NORWEGIAN EXPLORERS IN DECEMBER, 1911.

# A RACE TO THE DEATH

**EYE-WITNESS** ▼

The horrible tragedy that befell Robert Scott's British team on its journey to the South Pole was meticulously recorded in Scott's diary, discovered in his camp along with his frozen corpse nearly eight months after his death. On his first trip to the Antarctic in 1902, Scott had written boldly: "We cannot stop, we cannot go back, and there is no alternative but to harden our hearts and drive." But as his second expedition wore on, as obstacles mounted and time was lost, a note of trepidation began to creep into his words. "It is always rather dismal," he wrote shortly after his departure, "walking over the great snow plain when sky and surface merge in one pall of whiteness." After the ponies had been killed, Scott complained in his stoic way about the burden of pulling his own supplies: "I never had such pulling." At last, the captain and his four companions neared the pole, only to discover Amundsen's tent waiting for them. "All the daydreams must go," Scott wrote. "It will be a wearisome return." The next day, he was even more despondent: "Great God! This is an awful place, and terrible enough for us to have laboured to it without the reward of priority." By the 14th of February, the party's quest to return to their ship across the fields of ice was flagging. Scott wrote that "There is no getting away from the fact that we are not going strong." One of Scott's companions died; another, realizing he was done for, forced the others to abandon him. Trapped by a howling blizzard in tent, his foot so badly frostbitten he could no longer walk, Scott saw his death approaching. "The end cannot be far," he wrote. "It seems a pity, but I do not think I can write more." Mere hours after those words were written, Scott and his two surviving companions had frozen to death.

**BRITISH EXPLORER ROBERT FALCON SCOTT FROZE TO DEATH WITH HIS TEAM. IT WAS THEIR SECOND EXPEDITION TO THE SOUTH POLE.**

**AT FAR LEFT, SCOTT AND CREW POSE AT THE SOUTH POLE BEFORE THEIR FATAL TREK. ABOVE, THE GROUP HEADS FOR THE POLE. AT LEFT, SCOTT'S GRAVESITE.**

ROBERT PEARY (TOP) IS GENERALLY CREDITED WITH DISCOVERING THE NORTH POLE ON APRIL 6, 1909, ALTHOUGH MANY QUESTIONS ABOUT PEARY'S ACCOUNT REMAIN. PEARY'S CREW INCLUDED MATTHEW HENSON, SHOWN ABOVE.

five months before eventually freezing to death on the way back to their ship. It happened less than ten miles from a cache of supplies they had planted on the first leg of their journey.

## THE RACE TO THE NORTH

A deeper mystery involves the North Pole, which two Americans claim to have discovered first. Robert Peary, a former U.S. Navy surveyor in Greenland, is generally credited with the discovery of the North Pole on April 6, 1909. But his former associate and rival Dr. Frederick Cook claimed to have discovered the pole nearly a year earlier, on April 21, 1908. For years, Cook's claims were dismissed by the National Geographic Society and other important organizations—each of which had provided financial backing for Peary's expedition.

Peary's account of his journey to the heart of the Arctic with only a team of Eskimos and his black assistant, Matthew Henson, is deeply problematic. Peary claimed to have consistently achieved speeds of travel more than twice

what might have been believable, and his diary, which supposedly survived months of hard conditions, returned in immaculate shape— even though the dietary staple of his trip was an extremely greasy mixture of fat and berries, and Peary would have had no way to wash his hands before writing in the book. None of the landmarks Peary described actually exist, and his charts were discarded as worthless several years later by the Navy. Frederick Cook's claim is in many ways more believable, but lacks documentary confirmation (he supposedly lost his records on the voyage home).

In the heat of the controversy, Cook quickly developed a tainted reputation. In 1908, he had published a book in which he claimed to have scaled Mount McKinley. In 1909, as the polar argument raged, his companion on the McKinley trip, Edward Barrill, signed an affidavit swearing that they had not made it to the top of the mountain. Barrill later confessed that he had been paid by Cook's enemies to draw up the affidavit—but he continued to claim it was true that the ambitious Cook had never made it to the peak.

So who walked on the North Pole first? Both Peary and Cook had titanic egos (Cook took great pride in having been knighted by the king of Belgium for an Antarctic voyage, while Peary was a known philanderer with many Eskimo "wives"). Each man's claim is easily viewed with suspicion. During a Congressional inquiry into his story, Peary provided only vague and unconvincing testimony, even contradicting his earlier version of events. Cook—when asked to explain what had happened to his evidence—explained lamely that he had left his records in a trunk in Greenland.

It is possible that neither man made it to the pole, and that each tried to swindle the public. If that is the case, Peary, with his powerful backers at the National Geographic Society and in the United States government, was the more successful swindler. The real discoverer of the North Pole, however, may well have been Richard Byrd, who claimed to have flown over the site in his airplane in 1926.

A TICKER TAPE PARADE IN 1930 IN NEW YORK CITY HONORED ADMIRAL RICHARD E. BYRD, WHO FLEW HIS AIRPLANE OVER THE NORTH POLE IN 1926.

Actually, the first expedition to reach the North Pole on land beyond the shadow of a doubt didn't take place until 1968, when American Ralph Plaisted led a snowmobile expedition that reached the site. Plaisted's claim, unlike virtually all the others, is indisputable.

FREDERICK COOK CLAIMED TO HAVE DISCOVERED THE NORTH POLE ON APRIL 21, 1908—ALMOST A YEAR BEFORE ROBERT PEARY'S ARRIVAL.

# The Sinking
# of the
# Titanic

**The Titanic came face to face with its icy adversary, and went down—
both in the bitterly cold water and the annals of history.**

**"GOD HIMSELF COULD NOT SINK THIS SHIP" BOASTED A CREW MEMBER ABOARD THE WHITE STAR LINE'S 46,000-TON *TITANIC*. ON APRIL 10, 1912, THE GIGANTIC LUXURY LINER SET SAIL TOWARD NEW YORK FROM SOUTHHAMPTON, ENGLAND.**

NO OTHER SHIP OR MARITIME DISASTER CONJURES up as many immortal images as the "unsinkable" *Titanic*. The ship has been the recurring subject of documentaries, books, and movies, while explorations continue to probe around its corpse on the Atlantic's floor. Although its fate on April 14, 1912, may be universally known, the causes of its doom may not be.

How did it really go down? Was it humanity's hubris that forced this floating monument to high living into an icy crag? The reason the disaster occurred, as some 1,500 people died on that grim evening, was multifold. A number of factors came into play at the right time in the right order, and led the ship to its doom.

## THE KINGDOM ON THE OCEAN

The *Titanic* was an embarrassment of riches. It was an island of wealth, and its sheer length (880 feet) and weight (46,000 tons) overpowered any other liner on the sea. Its extravagance was unsurpassed, with everything lavish and nothing mediocre (save the lower class rooms). One of the main intrigues of the calamity was not only the loss of such luxury but of such eclectic guests, from millionaires and socialites to steerage class immigrants. Moreover, the disaster was a gigantic blow in terms of human accomplishment and ego. Days after captain E.J. Smith proudly announced its infallibility, the unsinkable liner lay at the bottom of the Atlantic, a hollowed husk of splendor that used to be.

The details of the night were so cemented in the memories of the survivors that conversations from that fateful eve were later transcribed verbatim—stories of heroism and cowardice were the only possessions brought back to land: how Ida Strauss, the wife of millionaire Isidor Strauss, although offered a spot on a lifeboat, refused to leave her husband (the pair went down to their bedroom to meet their fate together); how Ben Guggenheim, another millionaire, took his place on deck and declared "We've dressed in our best and are prepared to go down like gentlemen"; how J. Bruce Ismay, the ship's managing director, sneaked on board one of the lifeboats and later endured vilification from newspapers all over the world.

## A Survivor's Recollection

STRIKES STARBOARD BOW - 11¹ P.M.    11 25 P.M.

SETTLES BY HEAD - BOATS LOWERED OUT    12 05 A.M.

SETTLES TO FORWARD STACK BREAKS BETWEEN STACKS    1.40 P.M.

WHEN THE *TITANIC* BEGAN TO SINK, CAPTAIN E.J. SMITH BATTLED TO KEEP THE PASSENGER LINER AFLOAT. IN THE END, HE ABIDED BY THE CAPTAIN'S CODE OF HONOR AND WENT DOWN WITH HIS SHIP. AS THE LINER SAILED ON ITS MAIDEN VOYAGE, SMITH GOT REPEATED WARNINGS THAT ICEBERGS WERE AHEAD—BUT HE DECIDED TO RELY ON A SHARP LOOKOUT RATHER THAN REDUCING THE SHIP'S SPEED. IN DEATH, THE CAPTAIN WOULD BE HARSHLY CRITICIZED BY A LONDON COURT OF INQUIRY.

WITH THE AID OF AN ARTIST, A SURVIVOR NAMED JOHN B. THAYER TRACED THE LINER'S BREAK-UP JUST AFTER HIS RESCUE (BELOW). THE THIRD STAGE OF THE DRAWING SHOWS THE SHIP'S STERN HEAVING INTO THE AIR, BUT COMPUTER MODELING INDICATED THAT THE BOW OF THE *TITANIC* ROSE FIRST AS IT SPLIT IN TWO.

FORWARD END FLOATS, THEN SINKS.  1.50 A.M.

STERN SECTION PIVOTS AMIDSHIPS AND SWINGS OVER SPOT WHERE FORWARD SECTION SANK.  2.00 A.M.

LAST POSITION IN WHICH "TITANIC" STAYED 5 MINUTES BEFORE THE FINAL PLUNGE.  S.S. "CARPATHIA" APR. 15TH 1912.

The image has lived in infamy: the ship standing straight up in the water, then a ferocious split of wood and metal as it slams into frigid water. But it was an unfortunate combination of events that led to the tragedy—design flaws in the ship, human error, and weather conditions that paved the way to the initial collision with the iceberg.

The ship contained 16 compartments in its base; even if four of them were flooded, the ship could still float to safety. That night, five filled up with water; if the liner's watertight bulkheads were built one deck higher, as they should have been, the water would not have flooded the ship. But the biggest blunder was the failure of the Board of Trade to update their lifeboat capacity requirements. The last requirements were specified in 1894, but they didn't even consider ships over 10,000 tons—and the *Titanic* was four times that size. In the later court hearings, it was revealed that plans were made to include 32 more lifeboats, but whether out of confidence or foolhardy space-saving they were cut from the final design.

Human error, of course, was the biggest factor in both the collision and the loss of so many lives. Throughout the day on April 14, warnings came in over the transmitter about ice fields and ice patches. From 9 A.M. to 11 P.M., six warnings came from five different ships, and none of them were heeded. One was posted on the bridge five hours later; one of them was never delivered to the captain; and the most important one, the last—received from the nearby *Californian* about 40 minutes before the fateful crash—was never heard; this was because the Titanic's wireless operator cut off the sender of the message before he could find out that the ice field described lay directly ahead of them. With none of the cautions properly noted, the ship sped at the dangerous speed of 22 knots toward danger.

Later, once the danger was fully realized, lifeboats were lowered into the water. Yet, with room for over 1,000 passengers on the 16 lifeboats and four collapsibles, only four of the boats left the sinking ship with full capacity. And only two collapsibles made it to safety.

## JACK PHILLIPS, WIRELESS OPERATOR

Jack Phillips, a wireless operator on board the *Titanic,* has been called a hero by many for remaining at the radio to broadcast distress signals until the very end. (The only operator to survive was Harold Bride, shown below.) Others, however, have blamed him as one of the causes of the collision with the iceberg. Phillips was not a member of the White Star crew but an employee of the British Marconi Company, the telegraph corporation. Though the sole radio operator that fateful day, Phillips was hired only to operate the radio and receive messages for the important passengers on board. After fielding five warnings from the *Californian* about ice, Phillips balked when he was sent one last warning at 11 P.M. He snapped at the wireless operator of the *Californian*, telling him to stay off the line and quit carping about ice. But when the SOS went out an hour later, the *Californian*, which was at anchor only 10 miles away, was unable to receive the signal. Why? Because the radio operator, perhaps angry at Phillips, had shut off the radio and gone to sleep. Although the *Californian* crew saw the distress flares in the distance, they thought nothing of it. Had the radio operator stayed on the job, they might have been able to make it to the foundering *Titanic* in time to save scores of people.

**THAT NAME AGAIN?** ▼

The final nail in the *Titanic*'s coffin was the unlucky weather conditions that evening. The calmness of the sea and the absence of the moon provided the perfect camouflage for the iceberg. Moreover, the berg that would go down in history had recently flipped over in the ocean, leaving its hard-to-detect watery portion pointing out. When the lookout finally shrieked the warning and the ship frantically swerved to the left, the iceberg scraped along the right side of the hull. Some people felt a slight tremor, some felt less. It was "as though someone had drawn a giant finger all along the side of the boat," Lady Lucile Duff-Gordon later remarked. Only 12 square feet of the ship was opened by the ice, but they were drawn out over 300 feet in length: enough to flood five compartments, enough to flood the decks, and enough to drag a 46,000-ton behemoth and more than 1,500 people into 32-degree water.

The fascination over the tragedy remains even today. For all the ship's glory, the *Titanic* reminds us of Icarus, the youth whose cocksureness led him to fly too close to the sun.

# The Attack on the Lusitania

**While the 32,000-ton Lusitania rests in shallow water off the coast of Ireland, controversy surrounds the cause of her destruction.**

S.S LUSITANIA

A POSTCARD SHOWS THE *LUSITANIA* SETTING SAIL FROM NEW YORK. THE IMPACT OF THE LUXURIOUS SHIP'S SINKING WAS GREAT AND IMMEDIATE, AS REFLECTED IN THE FRONT PAGE OF *THE NEW YORK TIMES* (BELOW RIGHT) ON MAY 8, 1915.

SHE WAS MORE OPULENT THAN THE *TITANIC*, widely touted to be unsinkable, and the nautical wonder of the Edwardian era. Equipped with electrical elevators between decks, private showers and tubs in first-class cabins, a double-bottomed hull, and watertight compartments, the British Cunard passenger liner *Lusitania* was as familiar to Europeans and Americans in the early 20th century as British Airways' supersonic Concorde is to us today.

The British had even reserved the right to retrofit the *Lusitania* as an auxiliary cruiser for the war that had begun with Germany and its allies in 1914; if the need arose, they were confident of her ability to withstand whatever came her way. Most passengers and crew members had little reason to believe that the ship's 202nd transatlantic voyage, carrying civilian passengers on a routine trip from New York to Liverpool, would be more eventful than any other.

Yet on May 7, 1915, just 12 miles off the coast of Kinsale, Ireland, the *Lusitania* sank in a mere 18 minutes after being struck by a torpedo from a German U-20 submarine. Shockingly, the disaster claimed 1,195 lives of the 1,998 people on board; 128 of the casualties were American. The sinking would not only stun the world but would indirectly precipitate America's entry into World War I.

## NAGGING QUESTIONS

More than 80 years after the disaster, questions remain about the catastrophe. How could a ship that was much more durable than the *Titanic* sink in less than 20 minutes, while the larger ship took two hours to submerge after its impact with an iceberg? And could the British government have orchestrated such a tragedy to bring America into the war?

Engineers agree that a ship of the *Lusitania*'s design should have been able to make it to shore even after being hit by a large torpedo. Many witnesses who were on board the luxury liner claim that it was not the torpedo's impact that created the biggest noise but a second explosion, the cause of which remains a topic of heated controversy. Some speculated that the U-20 submarine captained by Walther Schweiger had fired two torpedoes (later proven untrue). Even more provocative, German privy councilor Oswald Flamm was convinced that the English had persuaded someone to set off a bomb moments after the torpedo, to make sure that the ship would sink rapidly. United States Congressman Richmond Hobson claimed that the British had arranged

to have the *Lusitania* sunk to try to pull the isolationist Americans into the war.

These sparks of conspiracy have been fanned over the years by the record of the behavior of the *Lusitania's* captain, William Turner, who failed to take simple actions to ensure the safety of his ship even though he had received several radio warnings that submarines were in the passenger liner's vicinity. As he sailed into Irish waters, Turner slowed the *Lusitania* from 21 to 18 knots, despite previous directions from the British Admiralty that ships should proceed at full speed in war zones to make them harder for submarines to track. Turner also ignored (or misunderstood) an admiralty directive to zigzag, which would foil an approaching submarine. Turner later said that he slowed to 18 knots so that he could bring the ship into Liverpool with the tide, but this could have been accomplished by zigzagging at 21 knots.

## SPECULATIONS ON THE CAPTAIN

Some students of the tragedy speculate that Turner, under secret direction from the British Admiralty or the German government, drove the *Lusitania* slowly in a straight line so that it would be an easy target for the U-20 submarine. A year after the incident, the German kaiser reportedly told U.S. ambassador James W. Gerard that the British government had given the order for the ship to move at low speed.

In his 1972 book *The Lusitania*, Colin Simpson tried to clear Captain Turner of any blame, but claimed that the British Admiralty, to an extent, created the situation in which the ship could be sunk—thereby leading America into the war. Simpson made much of an Admiralty conference held on May 5, 1915. The Admiralty War Diary of this session stops short after describing a conversation between Vice Admiral Henry Oliver and Winston Churchill about military escorts. No escort was provided to the *Lusitania,* despite the obvious danger.

Simpson speculates that it was at this conference that Churchill chose to place the liner in peril, though solid evidence for this theory has yet to be provided. The underwater explorer Robert Ballard visited the ship in 1995 and thought the second explosion was caused by coal dust that caught fire when ignited by the flame of the torpedo. Today, the 32,000-ton *Lusitania* lies still as a corpse in shallow water off the coast of Ireland, still holding its secrets.

AN ADVERTISEMENT ANNOUNCING WHAT WOULD BE THE FINAL VOYAGE OF THE *LUSITANIA* APPEARED IN THE *NEW YORK HERALD* (LEFT). BENEATH IT IS A NOTICE PLACED BY THE GERMAN EMBASSY, WARNING PROSPECTIVE PASSENGERS OF THE PERILS OF TRAVELING IN THE WAR ZONE. WOODROW WILSON (ABOVE) CAMPAIGNED IN 1916 ON THE SLOGAN "HE KEPT US OUT OF THE WAR." BY 1917, HOWEVER, PRESIDENT WILSON WOULD COMMIT FORCES TO THE CONFLICT.

# Who Were the Harlem Hellfighters?

**The heroism of the African-American 369th Infantry was embodied in the person of Sergeant Henry Johnson.**

HENRY JOHNSON (ABOVE), A RAILROAD PORTER FROM ALBANY, N.Y. WON FRANCE'S HIGHEST MILITARY HONOR FOR SAVING THE LIFE OF A FELLOW AMERICAN SOLDIER IN A SKIRMISH WITH GERMAN TROOPS ON MAY 14, 1918. JOHNSON STOOD OUT IN THE 369TH INFANTRY.

IN WORLD WAR I, ONE UNIT OF THE AMERICAN military served in combat longer and received more decorations than any other: the 369th Infantry. The 369th was entirely made up of American men, but it did not fight with fellow nationals for one reason: they were black. Only the French army would accept them, and they stormed to the front under the French banner. The men of the 369th were so tough that they were labeled "Hellfighters" by the Germans on the other side of the line.

The regiment was formed in 1913 by New York Governor Charles Whitman. Initially, the men who would become Hellfighters trained on the streets of Harlem and in an empty dance hall. But in 1916, the unit was designated the 15th Infantry Regiment of the New York National Guard, and by 1917, it had grown large enough and strong enough to fight.

## A TIME OF EXCLUSION

African-Americans had served in the Spanish-American War and in skirmishes along the frontier. They also fought for the Union in the Civil War, but they had never been allowed to serve in state militias. At the time of the First World War, blacks were barred from the Marines and the Coast Guard, and were allowed in the navy only as messmen. The army accepted black volunteers for certain regiments, but quotas for blacks filled within a week of the United States entering the war.

As American involvement in World War I became increasingly likely, the 15th asked to be assigned to a newly formed "Rainbow" Division, but was denied. Nonetheless, in 1917, the unit headed overseas. Rejected by the U.S. high command, the troops served labor duties until allowed into combat—assigned to the French Army. Now called the 369th U.S. Infantry Regiment, the unit was welcomed by the French, who needed their help.

The members of the 369th didn't let their commanders down. The Hellfighters became the first Allied unit to reach the Rhine River, and served for 191 continuous days on the front—the longest of any American unit in the war. Most impressive, the 369th never lost a man by capture or a single foot of ground.

## THE BATTLE OF HENRY JOHNSON

One of the Hellfighters stood out. His name was Henry Lincoln Johnson, and he was a black railroad porter from Albany, New York. Sergeant Johnson was the first American soldier in World War I to receive France's highest military honor, the croix de guerre with star and palm. He earned his accolades on May 14, 1918, in what would become known as "the battle of Henry Johnson."

Johnson and Needham Roberts, a soldier from Trenton, New Jersey, were manning an observation post one night when they heard suspicious noises. Suddenly, they were attacked by a raiding party of German soldiers. Both men were wounded, but they beat back the German troops and may have killed as many as four and wounded 32 between them. But Roberts had been seriously injured early in the battle. It was Johnson who, singlehandedly, not only thwarted the enemy but saved the life of

# JAMES REESE EUROPE, BANDLEADER

During and after the war, James Reese Europe, a lieutenant with the 369th, led what may have been the greatest military band in history. The band was received with enthusiasm in every city they visited, entertaining troops and citizens and even giving one performance to Supreme Allied Commander Marshal Foch. Most significantly, the band is credited with spreading the "jazz germ" and introducing the distinctly American music to France.

The band was conducted by Europe, the most respected black bandleader of the 1910s. Europe had enlisted with the Hellfighters in 1916, apparently to set a good example for other men in

**THAT NAME AGAIN?** ▼

Harlem. He was trained to fire French machine guns, but he was soon designated to lead a band to increase troop morale.

While with the Hellfighters Band, Europe wrote compositions inspired by the wartime experiences of the musicians. When the band returned to the U.S. in 1919, there were large crowds waiting to hear the songs.

Europe's music was rich with syncopation and other jazz effects. Although he was stabbed to death after a concert in Boston in 1919, his legacy lived on—not only in American music, but in France, where his band had introduced the art of jazz to a whole new audience.

NINE U.S. SOLDIERS RETURNING HOME FROM EUROPE AFTER WORLD WAR I PROUDLY DISPLAY THE CROIX DE GUERRE, FRANCE'S HIGHEST MILITARY HONOR. THE AWARD WAS RECEIVED BY 171 OFFICERS AND ENLISTED MEN OF THE 369TH REGIMENT, WHICH WAS ALSO KNOWN AS THE HARLEM HELLFIGHTERS.

his fellow American. But Johnson was only the first in a line of heroes: By the end of the war, 171 officers and enlisted men from the 369th were awarded the croix de guerre. The unit as a whole was cited 11 times for its bravery.

## THE INFANTRY EXCELS

The Hellfighters returned to a victory parade on Fifth Avenue. In the years between the World Wars, the 369th settled into new quarters in Harlem and produced the nation's first African-American general, Benjamin O. Davis. In 1940, the unit was again called to active duty, and part of the 369th was sent to the Pacific theater, where they were decorated for their help repulsing the Japanese at Okinawa. In the Korean War, the 369th Infantry again was decorated for its service.

In 1997, 80 years after they first established their reputation as "Hellfighters," members of the 369th were honored by the French government with a monument. The unit is still working to erect a similar monument on American soil, in Harlem itself, and to at last bestow the Congressional Medal of Honor on the hero Henry Lincoln Johnson.

# Was Mata Hari a Spy?

## She was beautiful and glamorous, and led an unconventional life. But was Mata Hari really a spy?

IN HER ALTER EGO AS MATA HARI, MARGARETHA ZELLE ADDED A HINDU DANCE TO HER SEDUCTIVE REPERTOIRE. WHEN SHE WAS TRIED FOR ESPIONAGE, HER ACCUSERS CLAIMED THAT THEY HAD DECIPHERED A CODE BASED ON MUSICAL NOTES, WHICH SHE USED TO CONVEY SECRETS TO THE ENEMY.

BORN INTO A WEALTHY DUTCH home on August 7, 1876, Margaretha Geertruida Zelle seemed an unlikely basis for several Hollywood movies and a humorous cartoon strip. And yet, nearly 125 years after her birth, young Margaretha has come to symbolize mystery, espionage, erotic beauty, and intrigue. For this Dutch girl became Mata Hari, an exotic dancer, a prostitute, and the best known female spy in history.

That Mata Hari was indeed a German spy during World War I is generally accepted as fact. Debate persists, however, as to her capabilities and accomplishments in this regard. To the French, who claim to have suffered thousands of war dead as a result of Mata Hari's treachery, she was a master spy, well practiced in the art of utilizing her sexual allure to extract information from eager military men. To others, most notably the British, Mata Hari was simply a bumbling, wannabe spy with delusions of grandeur and venereal disease. Whichever of these two poles more accurately describes Mata Hari's espionage skills, her pleas for mercy and contentions of innocence fell on deaf ears when, on October 15, 1917, she was shot to death by a French military court-ordered firing squad.

### SEDUCTRESS TO DANCER TO…

Mata Hari learned the art of seduction in the late 19th century at the urging of her first husband Rudolph MacLeod, a Dutch military officer of Scottish extraction. At his behest, Margaretha would seduce important men, bring them back to her quarters, and initiate lovemaking. As they carried on, MacLeod would barge into the room with a camera, photograph the compromising scene, and proceed to blackmail the unlucky man for all he was worth.

After separating from her husband, the lovely Margaretha moved to Paris in late 1903, determined to make a career for herself as a dancer. After an initial period of failure, during which she earned her keep as a busy harlot, the well-born Dutch woman decided an image change was in order. Thus was born Mata Hari, exotic foreign dancer, and a blossoming international dancing career was underway.

It was in this phase of her career that Mata Hari first met Trauffaut von Jagow, chief of the Berlin police. He fell in love with her, and the two began a lengthy, amorous relationship. Jagow's attentions notwithstanding, Mata Hari kept busy in the bedroom. Though Jagow was upset by his lover's dalliances, he saw a way to use her fame to his—and Germany's—advantage.

Jagow suggested to Mata Hari that she continue her lucrative business as a call girl. But instead of just any clients, he explained, she would cater to important military, political, and diplomatic personnel and, in the process, pry from them important state and military secrets. She agreed, and so began the espionage career of German agent H-21.

Mata Hari traveled far and wide in her new capacity, attending the most exclusive parties and initiating amours with rich and powerful men. In the course of the affair, she would coyly draw sensitive information from them, passing it along to Jagow and the Germans.

Her seductive prowess is said to have been most devastating during World War I. As she tended to injured French officers near the village of Vittel, Mata Hari elicited from them details of a planned French offensive later in the year. She dutifully passed this information along to the proper German authorities, who moved into action. The eventual French onslaught was greeted by an overpowering German presence, which wiped out well over 100,000 French soldiers. This defeat, say the French, can be traced directly to the information Mata Hari gleaned as a nurse in France.

## GUILTY AS CHARGED

But Mata Hari's luck soon ran out. In early 1917, she was arrested by French police and imprisoned in a padded cell at Faubourg Saint-Denis prison. When confronted with proof of her high-level sexual liaisons, she confirmed having had such encounters. At the same time, she refused to admit that she had extracted secret information from any of her clients. She claimed that although a prostitute, she was no spy, and maintained her innocence until the day she died, several months later.

The French military court, convinced of Mata Hari's guilt, did not deliberate long before issuing the guilty sentence and handing down the death penalty. On the morning of her execution, Mata Hari maintained a remarkably peaceful countenance, remarking that she would have preferred to die in the afternoon. She even performed one of her trademark dances for those who were guarding her.

After being led to the firing post, Mata Hari was offered a blindfold by the presiding officer.

She refused. He attempted to tie her to the post and, again, she demurred. The firing squad then raised its weapons toward the condemned spy, focused the crosshairs on her delicate body, and squeezed the triggers. Several shots rang out, and this once world-renowned woman lay in an inelegant heap on the ground.

Mata Hari may have been the most beautiful spy the world has ever seen. Her glamorous life, prodigious talents, and violent death have locked her into the public psyche. Perhaps that is what Margaretha would have most desired—international fame. Sadly for her, such ambitions have proved to lead even the most skillful spies to an inglorious end.

THE ALLURE OF MATA HARI IS EVIDENT IN PICTURES, WITH HER ELEGANCE CAPTURED IN A PHOTO TAKEN IN PARIS (LEFT). NEEDLESS TO SAY, HER GRACEFULNESS AS A DANCER WAS AN UNUSUAL TALENT FOR A SPY (BELOW).

# Did a Romanov Survive the Massacre?

**In 1917, Czar Nicholas II and his family were taken prisoner, then brutally murdered. Or did a family member escape?**

TO CLOSE PROPERLY, A HISTORICAL chapter must end with verifiable death. Without this final image, date, or word, the rigor of fact gives way all too easily to conjecture, hope, and in some cases, fraud. An example: Historians believe that Adolf Hitler committed suicide in his Berlin bunker in April 1945; but as there was no one to verify this, theories of his escape persist.

Among the most famous of such cases is the uncorroborated death by execution of Anastasia Nikolaievna Romanova (in Russian, adjectives and last names take a feminine ending), the third daughter of Nicholas II, the last czar of Russia. After Nicholas abdicated the throne on March 15, 1917, yielding to the furious tide of revolution, the Romanovs were taken prisoner and moved to Siberia. Nicholas had been a less than stellar figure in the line of czars—indeed, when he inherited the job at 27 he ominously declared, "I am not prepared to be a czar, nor did I ever want to become one."

During Nicholas's reign, the lower classes of Russian society became increasingly dissatisfied with their lot, and with good reason. Food shortages were not uncommon, humiliation at the hands of their harsh workplace superiors was routine, and worst of all, their distant czar seemed to have no sympathy for their suffering. Nicholas repeatedly ignored the mounting tide of rage and revolt that churned through the working class, observing simply that there had been a growth among Russian peasants of "senseless dreams of participation in matters of internal administration."

## THE NIGHT OF JULY 16

Because of both Nicholas's disregard, which bordered on parental condescension, and his family's magnificent standard of living (the opulence of their palaces belongs to a lost age of wealth), the revolutionaries were none too kind to the Romanovs. The family members were held captive at a house in Siberia for 78 days until the night of July 16, when they were taken to the cellar, lined up in a row, and shot.

Nicholas, his wife Alexandra, and their son Alexei died at once, as did their doctor and three servants. The three daughters were harder to bring down. According to one story, the girls had sewn diamonds into their clothing to hide them from palace looters, and the executioners' bullets ricocheted harmlessly off the

inadvertently armored fabric. This gave the guards some pause, but they quickly recovered and bayoneted the girls to death.

There was, however, a great deal of confusion surrounding Anastasia's death. Apparently she had crawled into a corner of the smoke-filled cellar to hide; there, a guard may have bayoneted her. In any case, the location of the imperial family's bodies was kept secret for years, and in the air of uncertainty this created numerous Anastasias were to arise.

## ANNA ANDERSON APPEARS

By far the most famous—and most credible—of these claimants was a woman named Anna Anderson. Her claim surfaced in Berlin, just three years after the executions. Following an attempt to kill herself by jumping from a bridge, Anderson (she began using the name in the mid-1920s) was taken to an asylum. After spending a year in the asylum, she announced that she was the Grand Duchess Anastasia. It is perhaps a testament to the power of unre-

**IN THIS FAMILY PORTRAIT, CZAR NICHOLAS II AND THE CZARINA ALEXANDRA ARE SURROUNDED BY THEIR FOUR DAUGHTERS, WITH ANASTASIA AT HER FATHER'S ELBOW AND PRINCE ALEXEI SITTING AT HIS PARENTS' KNEES.**

solved historical chapters that her claim was taken seriously in some circles. One of Alexandra's ladies-in-waiting came to visit her immediately, but Anderson hid beneath the covers. The woman pronounced her an impostor. Nevertheless, when she was released from the asylum in 1922, she had a fair number of supporters—enough, at least, to provide her with the modest stipend she lived on.

According to Anderson's version of the events, she had survived the bayoneting because of a dull sword blade and had then been rescued by a chivalrous soldier named Tschaikovsky, who took her to Romania,

impregnated her, and later died in a street fight. Bereft, she gave up their son for adoption and went to find her aunt, Princess Irene, in Berlin. Worried that she wouldn't be recognized, she chose to jump off a Berlin bridge.

Despite her fantastical story—or perhaps because of it—Anderson attracted much interest, and some very serious defenders. When Princess Irene did finally see her, she at first denied a resemblance, but later broke down in tears, crying, "She is similar, she is similar." A former mistress of the czar contended that Anderson had his eyes. Anderson also knew a great many details of Anastasia's life. Princess

Irene's son, a childhood friend of Anastasia's, sent Anderson a list of questions. Convinced by her answers, he announced that she was indeed the lost grand duchess. Then Anastasia's childhood tutor met with her and arrived at the same opinion (though later he recanted, calling her a "first-rate actress").

Gleb Botkin, the son of the imperial family doctor, reported that upon meeting Anderson, she asked him about the "funny animals" that he used to draw for her as a child. Indeed, Botkin had once entertained Anastasia with drawings of animals dressed in courtly attire. He, too, became convinced.

In 1938, Anderson brought before a German court an official suit to have her battered identity restored, not to mention her healthy inheritance. The case dragged on for 32 years.

## THE STORY'S END

In 1968, Anna Anderson married a wealthy American history professor, John Manahan, and moved to Virginia. Her suit was finally thrown out of court in 1970, on the grounds that she had not offered sufficient proof.

Many followers of the case had come to believe that, in truth, she was one Franziska Schanzkowska, a Polish factory worker who disappeared around the time that Anderson jumped from the bridge in Berlin. Anderson died of pneumonia in 1984 and was cremated.

In the early 1990s, DNA analysis of the exhumed remains of the imperial family, plus samples of Anderson's hair and tissue, finally closed the chapter. As expected, Anna Anderson was not the Grand Duchess Anastasia Nikolaievna, but the simple Polish factory worker named Franziska Schanzkowska.

ANNA ANDERSON (LEFT, IN 1955) FOUGHT FOR OVER 40 YEARS TO PROVE SHE WAS ANASTASIA. FURTHER DNA ANALYSIS CONDUCTED WITH TISSUE SAMPLES FROM PRINCE EDWARD OF ENGLAND, WHO WAS RELATED TO THE ROMANOVS, PROVED CONCLUSIVELY THAT ANDERSON'S CLAIM WAS SPURIOUS.

---

## ANASTASIA ON THE SILVER SCREEN

The belief that Anastasia could have escaped death at the hands of the revolutionaries has inspired a number of books and movies. In fact, a whole generation put the face of Ingrid Bergman on the adult princess. Bergman won the Oscar for her portrayal in *Anastasia* (1956), a highly fictionalized account of Anna Anderson's pretense to princesshood. In the movie, set in 1928 Paris, exiled White Russians claim to have found the missing daughter; but Anna is exposed as a fake, tutored by the Russian general she loves. A truer version of the Anderson story is told in a 1986 TV film based on Peter Kurth's book *Anastasia: The Riddle of Anna Anderson,* with Amy Irving playing the title role.

Not surprisingly, the film that takes the most liberties with the Anastasia/Anna Anderson connection is the 1997 animated musical version produced by 20th Century-Fox. To set the stage, this *Anastasia* skims over the entire Russian Revolution, focusing on mad monks, stormy seas, green goblins, and young romance. Anastasia's childhood comes to an abrupt end when the evil magician Rasputin places a curse on the czar's family, thus inciting the Russian Revolution. Thrown off of her pedestal, the newly orphaned girl grows up into "Anya" (played by Meg Ryan), a perky 18-year-old vagrant with only a dim recollection of her royal roots. She then runs into the character Dimitri, a former palace servant turned dashing con man; he is looking for someone to pretend to be the princess so that he can return her to her exiled grandmother in Paris and collect his riches.

So it is that Anastasia joins, with Pocahontas, the pantheon of princesses whose stories have been spun into the realm of fantasy, enchantresses from the Hollywood dream factory.

A MUSIC BOX ROMANTICIZES THE STORY OF ANASTASIA, A BEAUTIFUL PRINCESS WHO SOUGHT TO RETURN TO HER ROYAL BIRTHRIGHT.

# Warren G. Harding

IN JUNE OF 1923, WARREN G. HARDING, THE 29TH PRESIDENT of the United States, was touring the nation on an exhausting good will tour, a "Voyage of Understanding." Harding was indeed in desperate need of some understanding, as his administration had been riddled with scandals. His secretary of the interior, Albert Fall, was convicted of bribery, becoming the first cabinet officer to go to jail. But it seems that Harding was also in need of some rest. Returning from a stop in Alaska, the president complained of severe stomach cramps and indigestion.

On doctor's orders, Harding cut his traveling short and stopped in San Francisco to recover. Holed up on the eighth floor of the Palace Hotel, Harding grew worse. On July 30th, his temperature soared to 102°F and he developed pneumonia in his right lung. But on the next day he began to improve, and by August 1 his temperature had returned to normal. His doctors then declared to Harding and his wife that the danger had passed.

The following day, Harding was sitting up in bed, chatting cheerfully about a fishing trip he planned to take. According to his wife, Florence Kling DeWolfe Harding, that night she had read him a flattering profile in the *Saturday Evening Post* before leaving for her own room. A nurse then entered the room, and found President Harding's face set in an agonized expression. She alerted Mrs. Harding, who called for a doctor. But it was too late: The president was pronounced dead at 7:35 P.M.

## FIRST LADY AS SUSPECT

Initially, it was assumed that Harding died from a stroke; five doctors who had examined him in the days prior to his death signed a document stating that it was caused by "some brain evolvement, probably an apoplexy." Many scholars have theorized that his distress and guilt over his corrupt administration might have exacerbated his already high blood pressure. Others have pointed to the grueling, relentless pace of his cross-country tour, which required giving some 85 speeches over a six-week period and often forced the president to stand out in the bright sunlight or pouring rain. In a recently discovered copy of Mrs. Harding's journal, it was revealed that doctors had actually counseled Harding against making the trip, because of his weak heart. But Mrs. Harding insisted, believing it a necessary public relations stunt.

WARREN G. HARDING CUT A HANDSOME FIGURE THAT INSPIRED TRUST AND CONFIDENCE, BUT HIS SEXUAL INDISCRETIONS AND HIS CORRUPT ADMINISTRATION MOVED THE NATION EVER CLOSER TO THE BRINK OF THE GREAT DEPRESSION. ALTHOUGH HIS POOR HEALTH AND TAXING SCHEDULE MAY HAVE BEEN LARGELY RESPONSIBLE FOR HIS SUDDEN DEATH, HE MAY HAVE BEEN GIVEN A SHOVE BY A DISREPUTABLE PHYSICIAN AND AN AMBITIOUS WIFE WHO WAS HOPING TO AVOID SHAME.

THE FLAG-DRAPED COFFIN BEARING THE PRESIDENT IS CARRIED FROM THE PALACE HOTEL IN SAN FRANCISCO TO A SPECIAL FUNERAL TRAIN BOUND FOR HIS OHIO HOME. FLORENCE DEWOLFE HARDING (BELOW) WAS A FIRST LADY WHO MADE THE MOST OF HER PRIVILEGED POSITION.

Posterity will never know the exact cause of Warren G. Harding's death because his wife, for some mysterious reason, refused to allow an autopsy on the body; it was embalmed while it was still in the hotel. In the months following the president's death, Mrs. Harding's suspicious behavior came under scrutiny. Rumors quickly circulated that somehow she was either actually responsible for her husband's death or was covering up someone else's involvement. Harding had, in fact, been an infamous philanderer, and there was little love lost between the First Couple.

Harding had married Florence DeWolfe, a domineering and rather homely divorcée five years his senior (and the daughter of his hometown's richest banker), when he was 25; many speculated that he did so only out of social ambition. Florence took an active interest in Harding's political career, planning his ascent through the ranks of the Ohio Republican Party.

While Warren G. Harding was president, Florence sat in on many of his staff meetings, vetted some of his appointments, and even rewrote part of his inaugural address. Her solicitude earned her the nickname "the Duchess" from Harding, but there was little tenderness in that sobriquet; the couple's vicious fights rattled the White House walls and mortified the servants. And they were not only arguing policy issues.

An especially touchy subject was Harding's many mistresses. While still a newspaper editor in Marion, Ohio, he had begun a relationship with one of Mrs. Harding's best childhood friends, fathering a daughter. His second affair was with his wife's best friend, lasting some 15 years. His final affair—with several in between—was with a 22-year-old campaign volunteer, whom the secret service ferried in and out of the White House.

## A CHARLATAN CASHES IN

Did Mrs. Harding murder her husband in a jealous fit? She never spoke about the subject, and died a year after her husband. It was not until 1930, with the publication of a book by Gaston Means, *The Strange Death of President Harding*, that the murder theory took off. Means, a former FBI agent and personal investigator, claimed he had been hired by Mrs. Harding to follow the president and report on his infidelities. He suggested that Mrs. Harding poisoned her husband for two reasons: because of his affairs and (more charitably) because she wished to spare him embarrassment, not to mention possible impeachment when the corruption of his administration was revealed.

But Means was a shadowy underworld figure who might not hesitate to capitalize on the country's fascination with the private lives of its public figures. A telling bit of Harding's personal history is that despite his calm demeanor, he suffered from nervous breakdowns, the first at the age of 22. This fact, plus Harding's weakened physical condition at the conclusion of the tour, may have more to do with Harding's death than the unverifiable musings of a charlatan like Means.

Within the last several years, a convincing picture of President Harding's final days has emerged. Mrs. Harding's favorite doctor—Charles Sawyer, a Rasputin-like figure who had cured her of a kidney ailment—had originally diagnosed the president's stomach problems as food poisoning, and had given him an especially strong dose of purgatives to flush out the toxins. With the president's regular doctor out of the room, Sawyer may have given Harding one pill too many, causing his death. Mrs. Harding's suspicious behavior afterward may thus have been an attempt to protect her favorite doctor.

# Who Conquered Everest First?

**Sir Edmund Hillary gets the credit, but could a Cambridge professor have been first to reach the Himalayan summit?**

CLIMBING MT. EVEREST (BELOW, AT AN ALTITUDE OF 25,600 FEET) WAS A POPULAR BRITISH ADVENTURE OF THE TWENTIES. A PHOTOGRAPH OF THE 1921 EXPEDITION (ABOVE) SHOWS GEORGE MALLORY SEATED AT LEFT.

GEOLOGIST NOEL ODELL LOOKED UP NEAR THE summit of Mount Everest at about 1 P.M. on June 8, 1924, and saw two distant figures he knew: the 38-year-old Welshman George Leigh Mallory and his 23-year-old assistant, Sandy Irvine. Mallory, a Cambridge professor and a veteran of two other attempts at the summit, was a man of remarkable courage and daring; it was he who replied famously to the question of why he kept trying to climb Everest: "Because it is there." Irvine, who had no pre-vious experience climbing at high altitudes, was a strong, handsome Oxford student and an expert in the operation of oxygen tanks. When Odell spied the men at 1 P.M. working their way up a section of the mountain's diffi-cult north slope, higher than anyone had ever gone before, he thought they would reach the summit, making them the first men ever to ascend the 29,000-foot peak. Not long after this sighting, however, clouds concealed the men. They were never seen alive again.

More than three-quarters of a century after the 1924 expedition, the question still remains: Did Mallory and Irvine manage to conquer the world's highest mountain, 29 years before the first acknowledged ascent of the summit by Edmund Hillary and Sherpa Tenzing Norgay?

### CHALLENGE OF THE SECOND STEP

When Odell last spotted Mallory and Irvine, they were trying to climb an area that has since become known as the Second Step—a diffi-cult, 30-foot-high wall of rock at about 28,000 feet (1,000 feet shy of the summit). For a climber scaling Everest on the north side, as Mallory and Irvine were, there is no feasible way to reach the summit without surmounting this difficult rock outcrop. In addition, the men were burdened with oxygen tanks that weighed about 30 pounds. And the layers of wool clothing that Mallory and Irvine wore to keep warm (and alive) were considerably heavier than the garb available to later climbers.

Several experts have contended that it would have been impossible for Mallory and Irvine to ascend the outcrop by virtue of their own strength alone. The first group to complete Mallory's route up the mountain—a Chinese expeditionary force in 1960—was able to mount the Second Step only by taking their boots off and standing on each other's shoulders—an effort that resulted in severe frostbite for a number of the climbers.

### THE MYSTERY DEEPENS

In the 1960s, climbers were able to assemble a permanent ladder into the rock of the Second Step. But the notion that Mallory and Irvine couldn't have mounted the Step has been disproved: It has since been scaled by human power alone—once when the ladder was broken, and another time in 1999 by a climber investigating Mallory's climb. So the door stays open to speculation that extraordinary will might have carried the men to the top.

In 1975, a Chinese climber kindled hopes that the mystery might be solved. He reported in broken English that at 27,000 feet he had found an "English dead," whose clothing disintegrated when touched. About 750 feet above the body, another climber had found Irvine's ice-ax, and several mountain climbers speculated that the corpse might be Irvine's body. The climber who claimed to have found the body could not pinpoint its location—an expedition would be needed to relocate it.

In late April of 1999, a crew called the Mallory and Irvine Research Expedition began their climb up the north side of Everest with two objectives: to try to locate the body seen by the Chinese climber and to reach the mountain's summit. On May 2, climber Conrad Acker set off from the approximate point of the 1975 Chinese campsite, at 25,700 feet.

He found several bodies in his search that morning, but their clothing and equipment indicated they were from recent times (146 lives have been claimed by Everest). But after climbing a section of rock near Everest's Camp VI, Acker looked to the west and "saw a patch of white. . . and went there. And within a few minutes. . . I realized that this wasn't a body from recent times; it was something that had been there quite a while." At first the members of the expedition thought Acker had found Irvine, but then the monogrammed handkerchief of George Leigh Mallory was discovered in the man's pocket.

The legend had been found, and Irvine has yet to show up. Nothing in Mallory's possession revealed whether he had made it to the summit. Notes found in his pockets were illegible, and it could not be determined whether the fall he appears to have suffered came while going up to the summit—or on his way down.

**EDMUND HILLARY IS SHOWN WITH HIS GUIDE, TENZING NORGAY, AT THE SUMMIT ON MAY 29, 1953. BUT IS THIS REALLY THE FIRST PHOTOGRAPH TAKEN ATOP MT. EVEREST?**

## Mallory's Personal Effects Found on Everest

CLIMBERS SEARCH-
ING FOR MALLORY
AND IRVINE IN 1999
FOUND MALLORY'S
BODY—BUT NOT
IRVINE'S. THESE
ARTIFACTS OF THEIR
EXPEDITION OF
1924—AN OXYGEN
TANK; CLOTHING;
ROPE; A WATCH;
GOGGLES; A BOOT;
AND "SAVOURY MEAT
LOZENGES"—WERE
FOUND SCATTERED
AROUND MALLORY'S
FROZEN BODY.

WHAT WAS NOT
DISCOVERED WAS
MALLORY'S KODAK
VEST POCKET MOD-
EL B CAMERA, BUT
NEW EXPEDITIONS
ARE PLANNED TO
FIND IT; IT MAY
WELL BE IN IRVINE'S
POCKET. IF THE
PAIR MADE IT TO
THE SUMMIT, THEY
MUST HAVE PHO-
TOGRAPHED IT—
AND NEW TECHNOL-
OGY CAN DEVELOP
THE IMAGE.

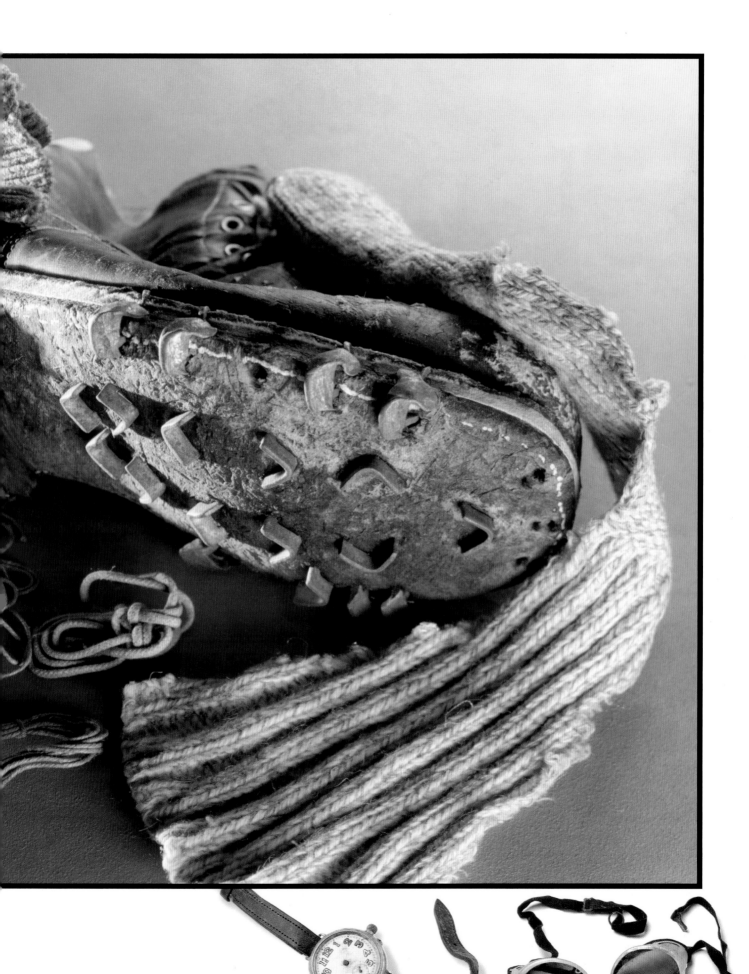

# The Lindbergh Kidnapping

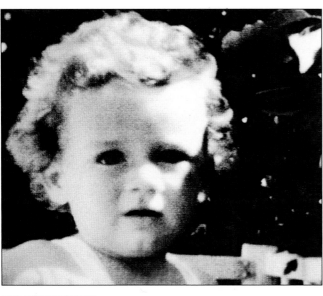

**THE ANGELIC "MOST FAMOUS BABY IN THE WORLD" WAS NONETHELESS CALLED "BUSTER" BY HIS PARENTS. CHARLES JR. (ABOVE) WAS PHOTOGRAPHED IN 1932, WHEN HE WAS NEARLY 20 MONTHS OLD. CHARLES SR. AND WIFE ANNE (OPPOSITE) POSED IN 1929, THE YEAR OF THEIR MARRIAGE.**

**An American hero's baby son is kidnapped and murdered, and forensic evidence leads investigators to a handsome German carpenter named Bruno Hauptmann.**

ON MAY 21, 1927, WHEN CHARLES LINDBERGH stepped out of the tiny *Spirit of St. Louis* and placed his feet on a Paris runway after 33 hours aloft, he instantly became one of the most celebrated men on the planet. Yet Lindbergh, for all his audacity and bravado, was a man who valued privacy as much as celebrity. It isn't surprising that he soon grew to resent the public's fascination with the details of his private life.

Lindbergh made elaborate plans to escape the press when, two years after his historic flight, he was married to Anne Morrow, the daughter of the ambassador to Mexico. And once Lindbergh learned that Anne was pregnant, he excitedly began planning the construction of an isolated, palatial summer home in Hopewell, New Jersey. It was named High

Fields, and it was accessible by only one winding and lonely dirt road.

### THE FATEFUL DAY

The months rolled by and High Fields neared completion. Only a few details needed attention—a warped shutter, for instance, prevented a second-story window from closing properly—and so the Lindberghs began to retreat there on weekends. But on March 1, 1932, a blustery Tuesday, the Lindberghs had decided to stay past Sunday. Charles Jr., their 20-month old son, had a bit of a cold, and they didn't want to risk making the boy feel worse by traveling in the inclement weather.

At 10 P.M. that night, Charles Jr.'s nursemaid went upstairs to the second-story nursery—the room with the faulty window—to check on the baby. Entering, she was surprised to find his crib empty. She quickly alerted Anne, and they went to see if Lindbergh had taken "Buster." He had not. The three raced back upstairs, where they noticed footprints near the empty crib. The window was wide open. The Lindbergh baby had been kidnapped.

Lindbergh immediately contacted the New Jersey state police, who began a thorough search of the area. A rickety, home-built ladder with one rung snapped off was discovered 75 yards away from the house; a carpenter's chisel was found underneath the window. In the

AN INVESTIGATOR
STUDIES THE
WINDOW IN THE
NURSERY OF THE
LINDBERGHS' HOME,
ONE OF THE MANY
DETECTIVES WHO
COMBED THE SCENE
OF THE CRIME.

baby's room, a ransom note was placed on the windowsill. In broken English, it demanded $50,000 for Charles Jr.'s return. And the note was signed with a curious insignia—two interlocking circles, colored blue and red.

### DEMANDS FOR RANSOM

The Lindbergh house soon pulsated with police activity, as 20 phone lines were installed in the garage and detectives combed the house for clues. To their dismay, they had to contend with the curiosity seekers and reporters who swarmed to the scene; much important evidence was undoubtedly destroyed in the process. The Lindberghs themselves were flooded with thousands of letters offering help. Even the notorious Al Capone got involved, promising from prison to track down the kidnapper with his underworld connections—in exchange, of course, for a full pardon.

Within a week, two more letters from the kidnapper arrived, each with the telltale signature. The ransom demand increased to $70,000, but no mention was made of the baby's condition. A new wrinkle to the case emerged on March 8, when John Condon, a public-spirited retired principal, placed an ad in a local Bronx newspaper offering an extra $1,000 to the kidnapper and his services as a go-between. The next day, the kidnapper con-

tacted Condon, and three nights later Condon met a man with a thick foreign accent in a nearby cemetery. The man called himself John.

On April 2, Condon brought Lindbergh along to the next meeting, where he listened from an automobile nearby as Condon gave "Graveyard John" $50,000 in exchange for Charles Jr.'s sleeping suit. He also gave him an envelope supposedly containing the baby's location—"on a small boat" off the coast of Martha's Vineyard. Lindbergh was euphoric as he took off in a seaplane to search the area, but his hopes quickly vanished. The famous aviator circled and circled the coast, but no boat could be found. Lindbergh had been duped.

A WOODEN PLANK WITH FOUR HOLES WAS DISCOVERED IN BRUNO HAUPTMANN'S GARAGE IN NEW JERSEY. A TOTAL OF $860 IN RANSOM MONEY WAS FOUND IN THREE OF THE HOLES; IN THE LEFT HOLE WAS A LOADED GUN.

On May 12, the sad truth was revealed when two truckers discovered the body of a small baby on a road within sight of High Fields. Lindbergh was called to identify the body, and it was indeed the body of his son.

As news of the murder spread, the investigation grew ever more fervent. The police first considered the kidnapping an inside job; how else to explain the fact that the baby was taken on the first weekday night the Lindberghs had chosen to stay over? The nurse's boyfriend was suspected, but was soon exonerated. Worse, one of the housemaids was actually driven to suicide by relentless police questioning.

The bills from the ransom had been marked; some were appearing in the Bronx, and FBI quickly assigned agents to the area. But none of the leads produced a suspect. And then came a lucky break. On September 15, 1934, a man paid for gas with a $10 gold certificate—a form of currency made illegal when the country went off the gold standard—and the suspicious attendant had taken down the license plate number. The certificate was traced to the ransom money. Five days later, the police tracked down the vehicle and arrested a 36-year-old German carpenter with a criminal record. The suspect's name: Bruno Richard Hauptmann.

## "THE TRIAL OF THE CENTURY"

The first "trial of the century" began in the sleepy town of Flemington, New Jersey on January 2, 1935. The population of the town was barely more than 2,000, but 60,000 spectators showed up for the opening session. Hucksters were out in force, selling miniature ladders and faux locks of Baby Lindbergh's hair. The prosecution's team was led by David Wilentz, a cocky young lawyer with political ambitions. The defense lawyer was an over-the-hill alcoholic whose retainer was provided by the Hearst company, who hoped a dramatic trial would help boost newspaper sales.

The evidence against Hauptmann was overwhelming. Three witnesses (Lindbergh included) identified Hauptmann's voice as Graveyard John's. Tests matched Hauptmann's handwriting to that of the ransom notes. Condon's number was found written on the wall of Hauptmann's closet. The wood of the ladder found near the crime scene matched that of Hauptmann's attic floor. And $14,000 of the ransom money was found in his garage. His carpentry tool kit was also missing a chisel.

And yet a few still proclaimed his innocence. Some crowd members became enamored with Hauptmann's strong, Germanic good looks

**"The Trial of the Century" began in the sleepy town of Flemington, New Jersey, on January 2, 1935—and the evidence against accused kidnapper Bruno Hauptmann seemed overwhelming.**

and were convinced by his unwavering avowals of innocence. Hauptmann insisted that he received the money from a friend, and claimed the police had planted all the other evidence in his house. And how could Hauptmann have known that the Lindberghs would be at the house on a weekday, some wondered?

While the jury deliberated, a large crowd formed outside the courthouse and chanted, "Kill the German!" Swayed by both the mob and the rock-solid nature of the evidence, the jury pronounced Hauptmann guilty. On April 3, 1936, still proclaiming his innocence, Hauptmann was executed in the electric chair. A reporter sneaked a camera into the room, and a picture of Hauptmann moments before his death was emblazoned across the front page of newspapers the next morning.

## LINGERING DOUBTS

But did they get the right man? To this day there are some who believe that Hauptmann was wrongly accused. Hauptmann had no greater defender than his wife, Anna, who until her death in 1994 insisted that she was with Hauptmann on the night of the kidnapping. Some consider problematic the rivalry between prosecutor Wilentz and the governor of New

Jersey, Harold Hoffman, which could have meant the prosecution withheld evidence that might be beneficial to Hauptmann. Others point to Paul Wendel, a discredited lawyer who at one point admitted to the kidnapping; Wendel also knew the man Hauptmann claimed had given him the ransom money. (Wendel was actually kidnapped himself, probably by the agents of Governor Hoffman, and the confession was likely forcibly extracted.)

The Lindbergh baby kidnapping still remains a mystery in the minds of some. Most investigators reviewing the case conclude that Hauptmann was indeed the culprit, and that his trial was mangled by the influence of Lindbergh's celebrity. Hauptmann probably did not get a fair trial by today's standards, but his claims of innocence—now only faintly audible after more than half a century—are further muted by the preponderance of fact.

A WELL-DRESSED BRUNO HAUPTMANN HARDLY LOOKED THE PART OF KIDNAPPER, MUCH LESS MURDERER. HERE THE DEFENDANT CONFERS WITH AN UNIDENTIFIED MAN AT THE 1935 TRIAL.

# What Caused the Great Depression?

**Was it the wild ride on Wall Street or the skewed distribution of wealth that plunged the country into years of economic hardship?**

Winston Churchill, working in New York as a correspondent for the British newspaper *The Daily Telegraph,* took a walk down the narrow lane of Wall Street at the worst moments of the stock market panic in October 1929. A stranger approached and offered to accompany him to the gallery of the New York Stock Exchange. "I expected to see pandemonium," wrote Churchill, "but the spectacle that met my eyes was one of surprising calm and orderliness. These gentlemen are precluded by the strictest rules from running or raising their voices unduly. So there they were, walking to and fro like a slow-motion picture of a disturbed ant heap, offering each other enormous blocks of securities at a third of their old prices and half their present value."

The eerily becalmed Stock Exchange on "Black Thursday," October 24, 1929, was the eye of a storm that soon plunged the United States—and the world—into economic misery. In the following weeks, there were many crash-related suicides. Under Churchill's window in New York, a man who had lost everything threw himself from the 15th floor.

In the early 1930s, the effects of the crash spread through virtually every sector of the economy. By 1932, a quarter of all American

workers were unemployed, and in the "Dust Bowl" of the Midwest, thousands abandoned their farms and headed for California in search of work. The Great Depression came to threaten the stability of the United States like no other event since the Civil War. But what had caused an economic crisis of this magnitude? And how was it brought to an end?

## ROAR HEARD 'ROUND THE WORLD

It is commonly believed the Crash of 1929 was the main cause of the Great Depression. But the seeds of economic disaster had been quietly sown in the reckless, irresponsible speculation of the Roaring Twenties—roughly, the years between 1924 and 1929. Although many think of the 1920s as an era of prosperity matched by few others in the country's history, the wealth was more unevenly distributed than at any other time. Calvin Coolidge, American president from 1923 to early 1929, said that "the business of America is business" and

AFTER THE CRASH, A SPECULATOR FROM WALL STREET TRIES TO FIND A BUYER FOR HIS CAR (LEFT). PANICKY INVESTORS CONGREGATE OUTSIDE THE NEW YORK EXCHANGE (ABOVE) ON "BLACK THURSDAY," OCTOBER 24, 1929—THE CRASH'S DARKEST DAY.

SOUP LINES WERE THE ORDER OF THE DAY FOR MANY IN THE 1930S, AS IN THIS NEW YORK CITY SOUP KITCHEN (ABOVE). AT RIGHT, THE POOR WAIT FOR SHELTER AT THE CITY'S MUNICIPAL LODGING HOUSE.

advocated a *laissez faire* approach to the economy. The Coolidge administration introduced incredible tax breaks for the rich. In 1925, the top tax rate for the rich was lowered 25 percent. As a result, the richest 0.1 percent of the population in 1929 had a total income equal to the bottom 42 percent. Meanwhile, the lower 93 percent of the non-farm population, rather than enjoying the economic boom, experienced a 4 percent drop in disposable per capita income from 1923 to 1929.

What America had in the 1920s was the mere illusion of great wealth, created by a speculative frenzy and a growing reliance on personal credit. "The key to economic prosperity," proclaimed a General Motors executive in 1929, "is the organized creation of dissatisfaction." In the United States, manufacturers encouraged people to save less and to buy products they did not really need.

There were some weak spots, such as mining, farming, and textiles, in the American economy. But the buoyancy of other business sectors sent the stock market soaring. Wall Street's Dow Jones Industrial Averages grew from 88 in 1924 to 381 in September, 1929. In a heady, optimistic atmosphere, even the less well-off borrowed money from banks to buy stocks,

laying bets that they could eventually sell their stock to pay off the loan and make a tidy bundle to boot. This was an extremely dangerous proposition, because there was often no real money to back the rampant speculation.

Still, many investors thought all would be well. "Everyone dabbles in stocks," Winston Churchill observed in *The Daily Telegraph.* "Millions of men and women are in the market, all eager to supplement the rewards of energetic toil by 'easy money.'" America's edifice of speculation was built on a flimsy foundation, and the 1929 crash brought it toppling down.

## HAPLESS HOOVER

Herbert Hoover won the presidency in 1928 by one of the largest landslides in electoral history. Four years later, he lost by a similarly large margin to Franklin D. Roosevelt. He was defeated because he was widely perceived as having exacerbated the economic crisis that followed in the wake of the stock market crash.

Hoover was a decent man who became president at the wrong moment. Before the 1928 election, he had been much admired as someone who had risen to prominence by dint of his own hard work and his humanitarian activities. But the stock market crashed only eight

months after Hoover had assumed office. Like so many others at that time, he did not fully comprehend what was happening. "We have gone through a crisis in the stock market," he said at a news conference in November 1929, "but for the first time in history the crisis has been isolated to the stock market itself."

As a self-made man, Hoover was reluctant to give handouts to the growing number of unemployed. He thought that cutting federal spending and raising taxes would put the economy in

LIFE IN THE "DUST BOWL" WAS ONE OF HARDSHIP TO MANY, AS SEEN IN THIS 1935 PHOTOGRAPH TAKEN AT SPRINGFIELD, COLORADO. THE DUST CLOUDS BLOT OUT THE SKY IN THE TOWN OF LAMAR, COLORADO, IN 1932 (TOP).

SHOWN FROM LEFT
ARE PRESIDENTS
CALVIN COOLIDGE
(IN OFFICE, 1923–
1929); HERBERT
HOOVER (1929–
1933); AND
THE FATHER OF
THE NEW DEAL,
FRANKLIN DELANO
ROOSEVELT
(1933–1945).

order, but these policies backfired and led to more misery. In Seattle, like many other cities across the U.S., unemployed, destitute people built temporary dwellings from crates and leftover bits of metal. These shantytowns were derisively nicknamed "Hoovervilles." Hoover's reputation was seriously damaged when, in May 1932, he called in the National Guard to disperse some 25,000 poverty-stricken World War I veterans who had descended on Washington demanding government bonuses.

### THE ROOSEVELT RECOVERY

At the end of his term, Hoover tried some government relief programs, but it was too late. He had lost touch with the public. What Roosevelt brought to the presidency was "the importance

of psychology," says Pulitzer Prize-winning historian Garry Wills. "[He understood that] people have to have the courage to keep seeking a cure, no matter what the cure is."

In his March 1933 inaugural address, Roosevelt acknowledged openly that "values have shrunken to fantastic levels; taxes have risen; our ability to pay has fallen; the withered leaves of industrial enterprise lie on every side; farmers find no market for their produce; the savings of many years in thousands are gone." But he also had the audacity to say that "the only thing we have to fear is fear itself."

Immediately upon assuming office, Roosevelt called an emergency session of Congress—FDR's famous "100 Days." By late spring, it passed the most remarkable and far-reaching legislation the U.S. had ever seen. The most memorable program of FDR's "New Deal" was the Works Progress Administration (WPA), which, by the time it closed in 1943, had put nine million people to work. The enduring legacy of WPA schools, hospitals, and roads built still remain throughout the U.S.

During FDR's first term, the economy of the U.S. slowly recovered. By 1939, it was back to where it had been in the late 1920s, although unemployment was still at 15 percent. However, America's entry into the Second World War led to a boom that created huge numbers of jobs and propelled the nation into prosperity.

Whether the New Deal—without the war effort—could have revived the economy is a question still debated by historians and economists alike. What is indisputable is that, under Franklin Delano Roosevelt, Americans showed a remarkable resiliency and mutual sympathy for hardship, which affirmed American poet William Cullen Bryant's claim that difficulty can be "the nurse of greatness."

THE WPA PUT MANY
ARTISTS TO WORK
THROUGH ITS
FEDERAL WRITERS,
ARTISTS, AND
THEATER PROJECTS.
THIS INSPIRATIONAL
POSTER WAS THE
FRUIT OF ONE
OF THE GRAPHIC
ARTIST'S LABORS.

# "DEAR MRS. ROOSEVELT"

Few personal accounts of the miseries of the nation's economic woes are as vivid as those written by children to the First Lady. Eleanor Roosevelt received such letters every day during the height of the Depression. The children often made personal appeals for leftover clothes, radios, or food on behalf of their parents. In return, the children received a letter from Mrs. Roosevelt's secretary, Malvina T. Scheider. The letter assured the sender of Mrs. Roosevelt's sympathy and expressed regret that "because of the great number of similar requests, she has found it impossible to comply with them, much as she would like to assist all those who appeal to her."

Here is a portion of a typical letter (its spelling intact), sent from a child in Alabama on New Year's Day, 1936.

*Dear Mrs. Roosevelt,*
*For some time I have wished to aqainted with you. Or maybe to receive a letter from you. I haved wish much to see you, but as I am a poor girl and have never been out of our state that will be impossible I guess.*

*Mrs Roosevelt, don't think I am just begging, but that is all you can call it I guess. There is no harm in asking I guess eather. Do you have any old clothes you have throwed back. You don't realize how honored I would feel to be wearing your clothes. I don't have a coat at all to wear.*

*The clothes may be too large but I can cut them down so I can wear them.*

*Not only clothes but old shoes, hats, hose, and under wear would be appreciated so much. I have three brothers that would appreciate any old clothes of your boys or husband.*

*I will close now as it is about mail time. I hope to hear from you soon.*
*Your friend,*
*M.I.*

THE FIRST LADY IS SHOWN AT AN NBC BROADCAST IN 1934. FDR WAS KNOWN TO RELY ON HER ASSESSMENTS OF SOCIAL ISSUES IN THE 1930S.

# The Hindenburg Disaster

**Was the explosion and crash of the world's
first transatlantic commercial aircraft a result
of faulty workmanship—or foul play?**

THE FAMOUS PHOTO OF THE EXPLODING *HINDENBURG* MAKES IT APPEAR TO BE JUST NEXT TO THE MOORING; THE AIRSHIP WAS IN FACT ABOUT 100 YARDS AWAY FROM THE TOWER. A POPULAR MISCONCEPTION IS THAT THE ZEPPELIN BLEW UP ON ITS MAIDEN VOYAGE. ACTUALLY, IT HAD CROSSED THE ATLANTIC 20 TIMES BEFORE MEETING ITS FIERY END IN NEW JERSEY.

IN 1937 THE LUXURY ZEPPELIN *HINDENBURG* departed Frankfurt, Germany, bound for Lakehurst, New Jersey. Ninety-seven passengers were on board. The airship, 804 feet long and 135 feet wide at its largest diameter, was the world's first transatlantic commercial aircraft. The mammoth craft was kept airborne by 7,200,000 cubic feet of hydrogen, and powered by four diesel engines. The engines could propel the *Hindenburg* at a top speed of only 80 knots per hour, but during the three-day crossing the passengers had plenty of ways to pass the time. They could browse the shelves of the library, dine with elegance in the ship's dining room, or relax in the magnificent lounge.

The flight went smoothly until the zeppelin reached New Jersey, where stormy weather prevented an immediate landing. After the airship had cruised the area for several hours, the weather abated enough to permit a landing. With the craft finally situated above the landing spot, crew members dropped the mooring lines that would be used to bring the *Hinden-*

*burg* down from its altitude of 200 feet. The passengers collected their belongings and prepared to disembark. Suddenly, a small puff of smoke appeared at the zeppelin's stern, followed by a larger one. Almost immediately the zeppelin was in flames. Some passengers were able to jump safely to the ground, others were burned alive inside the flaming blimp, and still others perished in the craft's plummet to the ground. Radio correspondent Herb Morrison, who was covering the landing for his station, broadcast a description of the disaster and uttered his now-famous words, "Oh, the humanity!" All told, 36 people lost their lives.

At first it was reported that St. Elmo's fire, a flaming phenomenon seen in stormy weather, had been the cause. But this phenomenon had never caused a fire before, and the report was quickly revised after officials deduced that the fire had been caused by the ignition of the ship's hydrogen, an extremely flammable gas.

At the time, neither German nor American officials were willing to investigate the possibility of sabotage for fear of the international incident that would result. Yet in later years, Germany began to suspect that sabotage had indeed played a role, citing the United States's desire to tarnish the image of the then-nascent Nazi party on the world stage. But no conclusive proof of foul play ever arose.

## A FLOATING POWDER KEG

In 1997, hydrogen specialist (and advocate) Addison Bain and a team of NASA researchers claimed that hydrogen was not to blame. To begin with, the *Hindenburg* flames were a colorful red, but hydrogen makes no visible flame. Furthermore, accounts of passengers and crew members never mentioned any overpowering scent of garlic, the odor that had been added to the hydrogen to help detect a leak.

The weather conditions at Lakehurst might have had something to do with the fire; the storm that raged as the craft tried to land was full of electrical currents, and lightning split the sky throughout the landing. When the mooring lines were dropped and winched to the ground, a grounding for the electricity around the ship could have been created .

Bain suspected that something in the fabric of the aircraft had been the cause of the fire, and he obtained two 60-year-old fabric sam-

ples like those used in the construction of the *Hindenburg*. Tests proved that the fabric had been coated with a strengthening compound composed of nitrate, a component of gunpowder. Over this explosive coating another equally ill-advised coat had been applied, this time of aluminum powder, which is used to make rocket fuel. The ship was then held together with wood spacers coated with a flammable lacquer. The *Hindenburg* was a floating powder keg, just waiting for a spark.

Bain's researchers subjected the scraps to atmospheric conditions similar to those faced by the zeppelin on that May night. The fabric ignited, and then quickly vanished in a puff of smoke. Significantly, Bain later found that in 1935 a helium-filled ship painted with acetate-aluminum had exploded in flames much in the same manner as the *Hindenburg.* "I guess the moral of the story," commented Bain, "is don't paint your airship with rocket fuel."

THE SPEED WITH WHICH THE SKIN OF THE *HINDENBURG* BURNED OFF (EVEN BEFORE THE HYDROGEN INSIDE WAS CONSUMED) IS EVIDENT IN THIS PHOTO OF THE EXPLOSION. A GERMAN ENGINEER, OTTO BEYERSDORF, CAME TO THE SAME CONCLUSION AS ADDISON BAIN— AND JUST SIX WEEKS AFTER THE DISAS-TER. HIS REPORT WAS BURIED BY GERMAN DIPLOMATS WHO WERE MORE INTERESTED IN BLAMING THE U.S. FOR NOT SUPPLYING HELIUM TO THE HUGE AIRSHIP.

# What Happened to Amelia Earhart?

### Soaring through life, the famed aviatrix slipped the bonds of gravity and gender when she vanished in 1937.

AMELIA EARHART AND HER HUSBAND GEORGE PUTNAM (ABOVE) PORE OVER MAPS IN PREPARATION FOR HER 1937 ATTEMPT TO CIRCLE THE GLOBE. HER DISAPPEARANCE SPAWNED A STORM OF NEWS COVERAGE, MUCH OF IT ACCOMPANIED BY MAPS OF THE SOUTH PACIFIC (OPPOSITE). ON THE DAY AFTER SHE COMPLETED HER LANDMARK SOLO FLIGHT ACROSS THE ATLANTIC IN MAY 1932, THE INTREPID EARHART (RIGHT) CLIMBED ABOARD HER LOCKHEED ELECTRA SURROUNDED BY A CHEERING CROWD AT THE LONDONDERRY AIRFIELD.

ANTOINE DE SAINTE-EXUPÉRY, WHO gained fame through his writing as well as through his explorations as an aviator, once wrote, "One of the miracles of the airplane is that it plunges a man directly into the heart of mystery." Earhart's Lockheed twin-engine Electra did just that, when in the final stage of her historic 1937 around-the-world flight it disappeared, along with her navigator Fred Noonan.

Earhart's trip had generated considerable attention. By 1937, she was easily the foremost woman pilot in the world. Her husband, publisher George Palmer Putnam, shares some responsibility for her fame. Following their marriage in 1931, he began promoting her with businesslike energy, having her launch a line of clothing and luggage and give lecture tours and press conferences. Earhart became a much-sought-after name on the guest lists of the nation's most exclusive dinner parties.

## THE FLIGHT TO HOWLAND ISLAND

On July 2, 1937, Earhart and Noonan left Lae, New Guinea, for the most difficult segment of their round-the-world flight—the 2,556 miles of open ocean to tiny Howland Island. The U.S. Coast Guard cutter *Itasca* had been stationed at Howland to aid in navigation. Yet neither Noonan nor Earhart was proficient in radio homing or Morse code, the two methods the *Itasca's* crew planned to use. Earhart, who disdained electronic gadgetry, mixed up the units of radio frequency measurement and repeatedly asked the *Itasca* to transmit on a frequency well above the tuning range of the Electra's radio. Communication with the cutter was

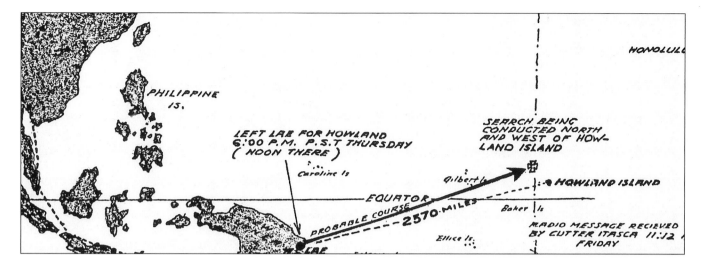

LEFT LAE FOR HOWLAND 6:00 P.M. P.S.T THURSDAY (NOON THERE)

SEARCH BEING CONDUCTED NORTH AND WEST OF HOWLAND ISLAND

PHILIPPINE IS.

HONOLULU

Caroline Is

EQUATOR

Gilbert Is

HOWLAND ISLAND

PROBABLE COURSE — 2570 MILES

Baker Is

RADIO MESSAGE RECIEVED BY CUTTER ITASCA 11:12 FRIDAY

Ellice Is.

confused, and the crew determined that Earhart was lost. For several months the Coast Guard and Navy searched the Pacific for the Electra, but found nothing. In 1939, Earhart was officially declared dead.

Soon, theories of her whereabouts and demise began to appear. In the 1943 film *Flight for Freedom,* a heroine based on Earhart flies a spy mission to fictional Gull Island. She then purposely dives her plane into the ocean to grant the Navy an excuse to search an area thought to be heavily fortified by the Japanese.

Rumors that Earhart had flown with ulterior motives abounded. In 1948, her mother, Amy Earhart, claimed that her daughter had been flying a secret mission for FDR.

### A SEA OF SPECULATIONS

The first serious attempts to explain Earhart's disappearance were published in the 1960s. In 1966, radio journalist Fred Goerner wrote *The Search for Amelia Earhart,* in which he concluded that the Electra had landed on the island of Saipan, where Earhart and Noonan were taken prisoner by the Japanese and later died. Goerner's book was based on the testimony of Saipanese who recalled a white man and woman who came from the sky and were captured by Japanese forces on the island.

In 1985, Vincent Loomis's *Amelia Earhart: The Final Story* says that the plane landed on an island in the South Pacific, where Earhart and Noonan were seized by Japanese officers and taken to Saipan. Basing his account on interviews with eyewitnesses, Loomis concludes that Noonan was beheaded for disobedience and Earhart died in a cell after months of gruesome dysentery.

## OFF-THE-WALL THEORIES

**VIEW FROM THE FRINGE ▼**

Like any unsolved mystery, Earhart's disappearance brought dubious theorizers out of the woodwork. Vincent Loomis's book claims that an ex-marine named Thom Thomas reported seeing Earhart in Japan after the war, working as a prostitute for a Japanese fisherman who rescued her from death. After having sex with the famed aviatrix, Thomas decided that she was "suffering from amnesia."

Another theory arose in 1970, when two men named Joe Klass and Joe Gervais penned a book claiming that Earhart was alive and living in New Jersey—as one Irene Bolam. Their book bore striking similarities to the plot of the movie *Flight for Freedom*: Klass and Gervais believed that Earhart had purposely gotten lost and landed on "Hull [not Gull] Island," giving the U.S. Navy the chance to investigate the area. According to the book, Earhart was captured and imprisoned at the Imperial Palace in Japan until the war ended, whereupon she was released.

The authors' theory was dubious at best: In the book they sinisterly note that if put together and lightly edited, the names of the eight Phoenix Islands—an archipelago southeast of Howland—would spell out Irene Bolam's husband's name.

But such conjecture is still theory. It is now largely believed that the Electra simply ran out of fuel, forcing Earhart and Noonan to crash on an uninhabitable island with no source of fresh water, where they slowly died of thirst. Yet theories continue to abound, and though it seems unlikely that any will provide a complete explanation, the sea of speculations might be thought of as Earhart's final resting place.

# The Allies Victory in World War II

**Was it their own trenchant power or Hitler's hubris that led the Allies to win the war?**

IT GOES WITHOUT SAYING THAT THE VICTORY OF the Allies in World War II was a feat for the ages. The sheer manpower unleashed on the Axis forces of Germany, Italy, and their satellites by the U.S., Great Britain, France, Canada, the ANZACs, and others was staggering. Just as inspiring, the logistics of an operation this enormous were executed with great aplomb, and the sacrifices made by those involved were nothing short of heroic. We have all heard of the Normandy invasions of June, 1944; the name Enola Gay is forever etched in our collective memory; and films like *Schindler's List* and *Saving Private Ryan* have

made real to a younger generation the importance of this war—and the price of victory.

Yet, despite the Allies' sophisticated weaponry and inspired leadership, they might have emerged from WW II as subjugated losers were it not for Adolf Hitler's military shortsightedness and hubris. Despite what some have called Hitler's expert political timing, his military foresight was proved inferior.

## HITLER'S BLUNDERS

Ever the opportunist, Hitler was unable to gauge the consequences of his actions. To Hitler, the future—militarily speaking—was a

THE ALLIES LAND ON OMAHA BEACH ON D-DAY—JUNE 6, 1944. THEY HAD CONVINCED HITLER THE ATTACK ON EUROPE WOULD BE LAUNCHED AT CALAIS, WHICH WAS WHERE THE FÜHRER DEPLOYED THE GERMAN FIFTEENTH ARMY.

hazy abstraction, a period during which vague, undefined goals would sort themselves out as he approached them. He rarely tried to stay one step ahead, never considered contingencies. Instead, as Hitler scholar Ronald Lewin has said, he would rely on "The swift and unexpected blow—and then, see what happens!"

Hitler's first blunder, one that would assure his ultimate defeat, was initiating war at all. Militarily, the German army was completely unprepared for a large-scale conflict. The German air force, the Luftwaffe, had fuel stores sufficient for only six months when the war began. It was also lacking in trained personnel,

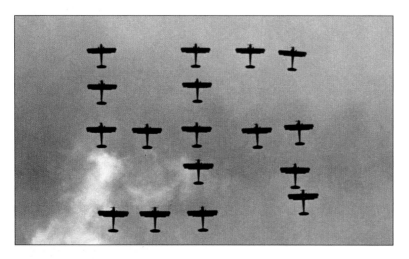

HITLER'S INTEREST IN THE MENTAL ASPECTS OF WAR-FARE—HE DEEMED IT IMPORTANT TO STRIKE TERROR IN THE HEARTS OF THE ENEMY—LED TO THE DEVELOPMENT OF NOISY ATTACK AIRCRAFT, LIKE THE STUKA CABOSVE (TOP, FLYING IN SWASTIKA FORMA-TION AT A 1937 RALLY), AND THE FEARSOME PANZER TANKS (BOTTOM), TERRIFYING AT THE EXPENSE OF TACTI-CAL ADVANTAGE. THE STUKA PROVED TOO SLOW, AND APPROACHING PANZERS GAVE GROUND TROOPS AMPLE WARNING IN CLOSE-QUARTER COMBAT.

## THE ALLIED ATTACK

The Allied invasion of Europe commenced on June 6, 1944. Although the fighting persisted throughout Europe until May of the following year, the outcome could be foreseen within several days of the Allied landings. German intelligence had failed in predicting both the time and place of the invasion, allowing the Allies the element of surprise on two levels. The Germans would never recover.

In order to repel the Allied attack, the German Army needed desperately to unleash the power of its panzer tank divisions against the invaders. Hitler, however, had issued an order forbidding the use of this equipment without his express permission. When contacted by the generals in charge of the areas of attack, Hitler denied their initial requests to employ the panzer divisions, choosing instead to wait and see how the situation unfolded. While the Allied forces advanced as far as six miles inland from the beaches, Hitler napped, awakening several hours later to give the belated—and ill-fated—order to deploy the tanks.

As the situation deteriorated even further for the Germans, two of Hitler's top generals, Gerd von Rundstedt and Erwin Rommel, confronted the Führer with the seriousness of the situation. Rommel pointed out that the Allies had achieved land, sea, and air superiority, and that unless the German army retreated and regrouped, all would soon be lost.

Rommel suggested that German forces pull back, retool, and launch an attack out of the line of fire of the Allied navy's powerful weaponry. Hitler, too proud and deluded to consider any sort of retreat, ignored the generals' advice, choosing instead to continue what was quickly becoming a hopeless defense.

## A FAILED COUP

Rommel and Rundstedt made further attempts to change Hitler's mind, all to no avail. Concerned that the Führer's misguided strategy would prove fatal to the Fatherland, the two generals and several other individuals hatched a plan to oust Hitler from power. Rommel opposed assassinating Hitler, but after Rommel himself was critically wounded in an Allied attack on his staff car, more assassination-minded conspirators were left at the coup's helm. Chief among them was the one-armed Lt. Colonel Klaus Philip von Stauffenberg.

particularly at the commander level. Furthermore, the Luftwaffe's bomb supply was adequate only for a three-week engagement with a weak enemy—not a lengthy, international conflict with militarily powerful nations.

But Hitler was not deterred; he clearly believed the conflict would remain regional in nature. When the Germans launched provocative raids against Poland in 1939, he was convinced that British Prime Minister Neville Chamberlain's guarantee had been a bluff. Chamberlain, reacting to the German destruction of Czechoslovakia two weeks before, had given a speech in the House of Commons on March 31, 1939, during which he pledged British intervention should Germany threaten the independence of Poland. Hitler, believing Chamberlain's promise a ruse, invaded Poland, convinced the British would not react. He was, of course, wrong. On September 3, 1939, Britain and France plunged into conflict with Germany. This error in judgment threw Germany's under-equipped, unprepared forces into a war that soon became global.

THE HISTORIAN'S VIEW OF HITLER HAS ALTERNATED BETWEEN SEEING HIM AS A MADMAN (DRIVEN BY A PSYCHOTIC VISION HE HAD WHILE BEING TREATED FOR TEMPORARY BLINDNESS CAUSED BY MUSTARD GAS DURING WORLD WAR I) AND AS A COLD, CALCULATING OPPORTUNIST WITH THE CHARISMA TO DRIVE AN AUDIENCE TO A FRENZY WITH INFLAMMATORY RACIST RHETORIC. THE FORMER VIEW SEEMS TO ABSOLVE THE NAZIS OF RESPONSIBILITY; THE LATTER PAINTS A PICTURE OF EVIL THAT STAGGERS THE IMAGINATION.

Along with his co-conspirators, von Stauffenberg was convinced that, even though a revolt could not save Germany from being overrun by an occupying army, it would at least put an end to the war, saving many lives and showing the world that the Nazi way was not the only way in Germany.

After several abortive attempts, von Stauffenberg finally set off a bomb in Hitler's headquarters on July 20, 1944, killing several people in the room. But to the colonel's frustration, his target—the Führer himself—survived.

Despite brilliant political intuition, Hitler displayed one quality that proved fatal in the military sphere: pride. While his pride may have at first inspired many Germans, it eventually brought upon them inglorious defeat and led some to wish Hitler dead. Although the Allied victory was convincing, it was made possible in part by Hitler's prideful arrogance.

# Were the Rosenbergs Atomic Spies?

## The Communist couple were executed for revealing secrets about the atomic bomb to the Soviets. But was the wife unfairly condemned?

ETHEL AND JULIUS ROSENBERG ARE SHOWN AFTER BEING TAKEN INTO CUSTODY. SEVERAL ATTEMPTS WERE MADE TO ALLOW JULIUS TO PLEAD GUILTY IN RETURN FOR SPARING HIS WIFE. ETHEL WOULD HEAR NONE OF IT.

IN THE SUMMER OF 1950, JULIUS AND ETHEL Rosenberg, both committed Communists, were arrested for selling atomic secrets to the Soviet Union. Julius had become a Soviet spy while working as a civilian employee with the U.S. Signal Corps during World War II. He persuaded his brother-in-law David Greenglass, a machinist at the atom bomb project at Los Alamos, New Mexico, to collect bomb data.

Greenglass was given half a Jell-O box top and told to give the data to a courier who had the other half. That courier, Harry Gold, met Greenglass at Albuquerque in June 1945. Gold took the data back to the man who had given him his half of the box top—Alexander Feklisov, a Soviet official in New York City. This box top became evidence used to convict the Rosenbergs for what FBI director J. Edgar Hoover called the "crime of the century."

During the late 1940s, the FBI learned through intercepted secret Soviet cables that a spy ring was operating in the United States. In the spring of 1950, FBI investigators caught up with Gold and Greenglass. In his confession, Greenglass admitted that he had been recruited by the Rosenbergs. Julius was arrested on July 17, and his wife Ethel, a month later. At the beginning of the following year, a grand jury indicted Gold, Greenglass, the Rosenbergs, and other conspirators. The Rosenberg trial began on March 6, 1951, and ended on March 29 when the jury returned a guilty verdict. Judge Irving R. Kaufman imposed the death sentence on April 5. Greenglass, the chief witness against the Rosenbergs, drew a term of 15 years but served only half of it. Gold was sentenced for 30 years.

## TWENTY-THREE APPEALS

Throughout their trial, the Rosenbergs steadfastly maintained their innocence. Their case passed through 23 appeals—7 at the Supreme Court. At a special session on June 19, 1953, the Supreme Court denied a stay of execution. On the same day, the Rosenbergs were executed at Sing-Sing Prison in New York State. They were the first civilians to be executed for espionage in U.S. history.

Abroad, many condemned the execution. The left-wing French philosopher Jean-Paul Sartre labeled it a "legal lynching." The Soviets denied the Rosenbergs had ever spied for them. In the U.S., the case set off a controversy that continues to the present day. For the American left, the innocence of the Rosenbergs became an article of faith. For the right, the couple's guilt was a certainty that confirmed the seriousness of the Communist threat.

Neither side found much support for its position in the information about the Rosenbergs that was released in the late 1990s. The Venona documents—the U.S. intercepts of Soviet intelligence dating from the 1940s—

THE ROSENBERGS WERE ARRESTED IN 1950, AFTER THE BRITISH LEARNED ATOMIC SCIENTIST KLAUS FUCHS WAS TURNING OVER ATOMIC SECRETS TO THE SOVIETS. FUCHS'S DESIGN FOR THE ATOM BOMB DATES FROM HIS STAY AT LOS ALAMOS IN THE MID-1940S.

were released in 1995. They mention Julius's industrial espionage but suggest his atomic spying was considered only peripheral.

On a visit to the United States in 1997, an aging Feklisov disclosed that Julius had spied for the Soviets. He admitted to more than 50 meetings at which Julius had passed on U.S. military electronics secrets. At their last meeting in August 1946, Feklisov urged Julius to flee the country, giving him $1,000 to cover any expenses. Feklisov also said he had never met Ethel,

nor had she passed on information, although she probably knew about her husband's activities.

The atomic secrets supplied under Julius's aegis were tidbits. The Soviets had truly knowledgeable agents at their command, notably the German-born physicist Klaus Fuchs, one of the architects of the atomic bomb. It was his arrest in February 1950 that also helped to alert U.S. officials to the activities of Gold, Greenglass, and Julius and Ethel Rosenberg.

# The Holocaust

**The Nazi war machine was responsible for one of the darkest chapters in human history.**

THE HOLOCAUST REFERS TO NAZI PERSECUTION OF European Jews and other minorities that began in Germany in February 1933 and was expanded throughout Europe until the Allied liberation in May 1945. During this period, an estimated six million Jews and six million other "undesirables" were systematically murdered at the hands of the Nazi war machine and its police arm, the SS *(Schutzstaffel)*. Victims of the exterminations included Jews, Gypsies, homosexuals, POWs, the handicapped, the mentally infirm, and others regarded by the Nazi regime as unsuitable human material for the establishment of a racially pure continent inhabited by a "master race."

Sadly, there have arisen fringe groups that preach that the horrors of the Holocaust are a fabrication. Attempts to deny the Holocaust ever happened—the pseudohistory of men and women whose writings are routinely embraced and promoted by the most rabidly anti-Semitic quarters of society—speak more to the guilt of the perpetrators and the hatred that festers in some modern hearts. A look at the documented and undeniable acts of the Nazi war machine shows the Holocaust deniers as not only sorely misguided but blind.

## THE TRUTH OF THE TERRORS

The Holocaust's initial phase was marked by Adolf Hitler's campaign against German Jewry, which began gradually but was stepped up with increasing ferocity. Jews were expelled from public posts and driven from professional life. Jewish-owned businesses were boycotted and vandalized. In 1935, the Nuremberg Laws deprived Jews of German citizenship and forbade their marriage with other Germans. Jews lost property and wealth through confiscation and punitive fines. Then, on November 9–10, 1938, the Nazi-incited riots of *Kristallnacht* ("the night of broken glass") destroyed German synagogues and Jewish institutions.

When the Germans invaded the Soviet Union on June 22, 1941, they launched a new policy toward the Jews—the systematic destruction of Jewish communities. Under the

**"LIVING CORPSES" GREETED THE ALLIED LIBERATORS OF THE EVENSEE CONCENTRATION CAMP, LOCATED IN THE AUSTRIAN ALPS, IN 1945.**

cover of war conditions, the Nazis began deporting Jews to the death camps. Until that time, the Jews in German-occupied lands had been deprived of their human rights and herded into ghettoes. (In Poland, the Germans confined more than half a million people in the Warsaw ghetto, where thousands perished from starvation and disease.)

Five days after the Germans entered the USSR, they besieged the city of Bialystok, Poland, home to about 56,000 Jews. Early that morning the Germans surrounded the town square by the Great Synagogue and forced residents from their homes into the street. Some were shoved up against building walls and shot dead. Others—some 800 men, women, and children—were locked in the synagogue, which was subsequently set on fire and where they burned to death. The German onslaught continued with the grenading of numerous homes and further shootings. As the flames from the synagogue spread and merged with the grenade fires, the entire square was engulfed. On that day—June 27, 1941—some 2,000 Jews lost their lives at Bialystok. The next day, many more of the city's Jews were murdered.

About 1,600 Jews lived in the Polish village of Jedwabne. On July 10, some three weeks after the German invasion, many were burned alive in a barn. A week later 10,000 Jews were liquidated in Kishinev over a two-week period. In fact, according to eminent Holocaust scholar Martin Gilbert, during the first five weeks of the German invasion of the USSR, more Jews were killed than during the eight years since the Nazis had come to power.

Despite the enormous number of Jews the Germans were able to eliminate during this short period, Heinrich Himmler and other

**ONE OF THE MOST FEARED AND HATED MEN OF THE NAZI REGIME WAS REINHARD HEYDRICH, WHO BECAME KNOWN AS THE "HANGMAN OF EUROPE." HE ORCHESTRATED ANTI-JEWISH RIOTS BEFORE THE WAR, THEN SUPERVISED THE NAZI'S GENOCIDAL POLICIES.**

gas chambers. The rest were put to work, frequently in the harshest conditions imaginable. The work often included the burial of victims in massive, unidentified pits.

At arrival and departure points, or wherever the trains passed through towns, local populations were made aware of the fate that awaited the miserable passengers. The Nazis pursued the policy of extermination so diligently that troops and arms were sometimes forced to wait while the "relocation" transports passed through. Children who saw the trains watched with fascinated horror, and, sometimes at the instigation of their parents (or at least with their tacit approval) taunted the condemned by shouting their fate at them as they passed.

Nazi leaders were dissatisfied, and so began to search for a less clumsy method for solving the "Jewish problem." (Himmler headed the secret police, or Gestapo, and in the last years of World War II was the virtual dictator of German domestic affairs.) The first step toward streamlining the genocide was the use of trains to transport Jews from central Germany to ghettos being set up in the east. These trains, which became emblematic of Nazi atrocities, were first used on October 16, 1941.

## PASSAGEWAYS TO DEATH

The trains heralded the beginning of the end for European Jewry. What had been a frenetic campaign of decentralized violence became a highly efficient killing apparatus aimed at nothing less than the destruction of Europe's non-Aryan population. And while the legacy the trains left in their tracks is partly symbolic—as a passageway to death—they are equally notorious for their inhuman conditions. Large cattle cars, packed well beyond capacity with human cargo, were so insufferably hot, so devoid of sufficient oxygen, and so intensely unclean that they became caskets for thousands of Jews who did not live long enough to die by the Nazi's appointed method: gas.

The trains were only the first step in the Nazi selection process: Those who did not survive the trains were clearly unfit for labor and would have been executed in any case. Once detrained, the remaining passengers were split into two groups. The old, the young, the sick, and the infirm were sent immediately to be killed, initially in gassing vans and later in the

## THE WANNSEE PROTOCOL

So thorough was the Nazi program of extermination that a special conference of top Nazi officials was called by Reinhard Heydrich to sort out the logistical problems involved in carrying out the Final Solution to the Jewish Question. The conference was held at Grossen-Wannsee, a suburb of Berlin, on January 20, 1942; its subject was how to handle the great number of Jews that had suddenly come under German control with the invasion of Poland and Russia. The Wannsee Protocol that was issued from that conference (authored by its secretary, Adolf Eichmann) was nothing less than a blueprint for the systematic genocide of all of Europe's Jews.

More than 50 years after this dark chapter, the Holocaust continues to haunt and disquiet the collective consciousness of the Western world. International efforts to end racial killing in Yugoslavia, to stem the development of weapons of mass destruction in Iraq and Iran, and to prevent a xenophobic politician from attaining power in Austria are all manifestations of the hard-learned lessons of the Holocaust.

Despite the propaganda of the Holocaust deniers, the odor that filled the air for miles around the concentration camps where the crematoria incinerated the victims was unmistakable. There was no doubt in any of those many cities and towns, or in the farmhouses that dotted the countryside, what that stench was and what was happening in the camps. The Holocaust will eternally serve as a reminder of what people are capable of doing, and the consequences of waiting too long to intercede.

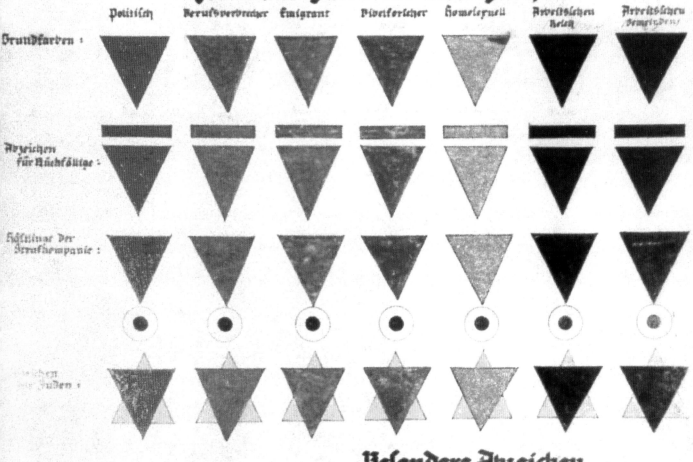

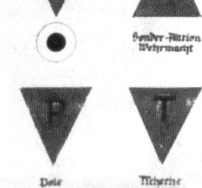

# Hitler's Diaries

HITLER'S TAGEBÜCHER ENTDECKT, shouted the magazine cover: "Hitler's Diaries Discovered." On April 25, 1983, the German weekly newsmagazine *Stern* shocked the world when it announced the discovery of 62 notebooks containing the secret journals of Adolf Hitler, in which he had chronicled his thoughts, feelings, and experiences during his reign atop the Nazi hierarchy from 1932 until his suicide in 1945. The story was an international sensation. Obtained for the magazine by a reporter named Gerd Heidemann, the diaries were the subject of a 13-page cover story in *Newsweek*, and the *London Sunday Times* paid $400,000 for the right to publish excerpts of the earthshaking find in England.

**A GERMAN CARTOON FROM APRIL 1983 WAS TITLED "MY STRUGGLE [MEIN KAMPF] WITH EVERYDAY LIFE."**

Historians were dumbfounded: Hitler had never been known to keep a diary. In fact, he had always hated writing, and dictated even his personal letters to a secretary. Nevertheless, the notebooks seemed authentic. *Newsweek* wrote that the discovery "reeks of history," and historians who had examined the diaries—including Britain's Hugh Trevor-Roper and America's Gerhard Weinberg—believed them to be genuine. It was the historical discovery of the century, the chance to read the private thoughts and feelings of the most hated villain of the bloodiest war in the history of the world.

## THE STORY'S QUICK DEATH

Virtually overnight, the discovery fell to pieces. At the April 25 press conference in Hamburg, the historian David Irving asked a very basic question: Had the ink in the diaries been tested to determine its age? The representatives from *Stern* were forced to answer, "No."

Gradually, it emerged that the diaries had undergone almost no historical verification at all, from handwriting

analysis to an examination of the chronicled events' continuity with real history. No one could explain how no one among Hitler's retinue had known about the diaries. And no one could authenticate Heidemann's story—that the notebooks had been unearthed by a local farmer in the Swiss Alps following the crash of the cargo plane onto which the diaries had been loaded in great haste in 1945, as the Russians marched into Berlin. (This, Heidemann had heard only from Konrad Kujau, the man who sold him the diaries.) All that was for certain was that the two had pocketed nearly $4 million of the magazine's money for their "discovery," and that *Stern* had raised its cover price in anticipation of the big story.

When the diaries were analyzed, they were revealed to be fakes—and poorly executed fakes, at that. *Newsweek*'s handwriting expert declared that they were "not only forgeries, but bad forgeries."

They also contained historical inaccuracies. For one, "Hitler's" handwriting was consistent throughout the 12 years chronicled in the books, but Hitler had suffered from palsy after 1943 and was unable to control the shaking of his hand. More damning, German scientists determined that everything about the notebooks—from the red ribbons on their cover to the glue used in the binding—dated from the postwar period.

**THIS *STERN* COVER STORY SHOCKED THE WORLD IN APRIL 1983—BUT IT SOON TURNED OUT TO BE A HOAX.**

In the end, the editor in chief of *Stern* was forced to resign, and Kujau and Heidemann were sent to jail. Under pressure, Kujau confessed to forging the diaries—in fact, he had spent 10 years prior to his transaction with *Stern* selling fake merchandise from the Third Reich; the Hitler diaries were only his most outlandish, daring, and dishonest scheme. What is remarkable is not that Kujau was caught, but rather that his swindle lasted as long as it did. The willingness of so many people to believe in the forgeries stands out as a telling example of the hypnotic power the past wields over the present— a power that can, at least sometimes, distract those in pursuit of history from also pursuing the truth.

# The Bombing of Japan

**Truman's decision to drop the atomic bomb on Hiroshima was one of the most controversial decisions in military history.**

ON THE MORNING OF August 6, 1945, Hiroshima was a bustling city, Japan's seventh largest, with a population of over 250,000. By the end of the day it was a graveyard. That morning, a B-29 Superfortress from the 509th Composite Group of the 20th Air Force, named the *Enola Gay* after the mother of the pilot, took off from the small Pacific atoll of Tinian. In its belly was the 9,000-pound, 10-foot-long "Little Boy," the first uranium bomb. The bomb utilized the process known as fission, in which the atomic nucleus was bombarded with neutrons and split, setting off a chain reaction that releases massive amounts of energy—the equivalent of approximately 20,000 tons of TNT.

The *Enola Gay*'s target was the Aioi Bridge in downtown Hiroshima. Ironically, since the city was largely unscathed in the many Allied air raids that had devastated urban centers like Tokyo and Osaka, the Japanese believed that the Americans were planning to preserve Hiroshima as a residential area in the case of a successful invasion. Citizens were unimpressed by the torrent of leaflets, rained down upon the city by passing bombers just two days before, which read, "Your city will be obliterated unless your Government surrenders."

THE GROUND CREW OF THE B-29 *ENOLA GAY* POSES BY THE PLANE THAT DROPPED THE ATOMIC BOMB ON HIROSHIMA. ABOVE, A WATCH STOPPED AT 8:16—THE EXACT MOMENT WHEN THE BOMB FELL ON THE CITY, DESTROYING NEARLY EVERYTHING BELOW AND LEAVING THOUSANDS DEAD.

A PICTURE OF A STREET SCENE IN HIROSHIMA WAS TAKEN TWO HOURS AFTER THE BLAST (TOP), TWO MILES FROM THE POINT OF IMPACT; THE PHOTOGRAPHER DIED OF INJURIES SUSTAINED IN THE BOMBING. THE BOMBING LED TO JAPAN'S SURRENDER, WHICH TOOK PLACE AT A CEREMONY ABOARD THE *USS MISSOURI* IN YOKO-HAMA HARBOR (ABOVE RIGHT).

At precisely 8:16 A.M., the bomber dropped its cargo, which exploded 580 yards above ground and only 300 yards from its target. There was a blinding flash of light—called a pika—produced by a fireball 180 feet in diameter but brighter than 1,000 suns. Buildings melted instantly, the sky turned a dark yellow, and a huge mushroom cloud rose to the heavens. On the ground, the survivors (mostly naked, since the heat of the blast melted their clothes) walked around as ghosts, dazed and searching for landmarks or loved ones. Three days later, after an equally devastating attack upon Nagasaki, Japan surrendered.

## A TRAGIC NECESSITY?

Dropping the bomb was the decision of one man: President Harry Truman. After the Japanese released a statement that described their plans to "ignore" the threats, the president's mind was set. Said Truman, "If they do not now accept our terms, they may expect a rain of ruin from the air the like of which has never been seen on this earth." In the years that

followed, Truman would be severely criticized, but he never doubted his decision.

To be fair, both before and after the bombing, the nature of the devastation was greatly underestimated. Military leaders and scientists, even those who worked on the bomb's creation, did not think it would cause radiation deaths. According to one scientist, Dr. Norman Ramsey, his peers were convinced that "any person with radiation damage would have been killed with a brick first." When the Japanese began reporting radiation casualties, the Americans assumed they were lying.

But did the bombing even make sense strategically? The defense by scholars after the war was that the atomic bomb was a tragic necessity; without it, America would have had to invade Japan, which might have resulted in over a million American casualties and as many as ten times as many Japanese deaths. In light of these harrowing projections, the death figures from Hiroshima and Nagasaki (less than half a million dead) seem justified.

Apologists also point to Japan's fierce tenacity, demonstrated by the discovery of secret documents approved by the Japanese Supreme Council on June 6, 1945, which revealed the government's resolve to "prosecute the war to the bitter end." Japan also intended to dispatch tens of thousands of suicide planes, and even to rouse a civilian militia of 30 million soldiers.

## A COMMISSION OPINES

In 1946, a U.S. government commission was charged with surveying the effectiveness of the bombing campaigns in the Atlantic and Pacific theaters of operation. This they did, but they also overstepped their bounds and surmised that Japan was actually prepared to surrender when the bombs were dropped: "It is the Survey's opinion that certainly prior to 31 December 1945, and in all probability prior to 1 November 1945, Japan would have surrendered even if the atomic bombs had not been dropped." It was later revealed that as early as June 20, 1945, Emperor Hirohito (who was relatively powerless) had met with members of his Supreme War Direction Council and decided on surrender. Survey member John Kenneth Galbraith suggested that the "usual bureaucratic lags" slowed the emperor's announcement. True? If so, bureaucracy has never been responsible for so much pain.

# The Attack on Pearl Harbor

On December 7, 1941, Japanese forces crippled America's Pacific fleet in a sneak attack on the Pearl Harbor base in Hawaii, bringing the nation into World War II. But did America ignore warnings about the strike in order to inspire American outrage against Japan as the aggressor?

The damage to American forces was so severe that the Japanese military temporarily took control of the Pacific. Some 2,403 American troops were killed and another 1,178 were wounded.

Tension between the U.S. and Japan had been building steadily since 1931, when Japan invaded Manchuria. By 1937, Japanese forces had invaded China proper, and from there they hungrily eyed the Asian territories of Britain, France, Holland, and the U.S. When Germany subjugated France in 1940,

Japan saw an opportunity. On July 24, 1941, it invaded French Indochina (now Vietnam). In retaliation, FDR placed embargoes on all Japanese exports, except oil.

Japanese ambassador Nomura offered an oil-for-peace deal that seemed to interest Roosevelt, but Winston Churchill and Chiang Kai-shek objected. Meanwhile, Admiral Isoroku Yamamoto, commander of Japan's fleet, secretly planned an attack that would incapacitate his new enemy "on the very first day."

The American ambassador to Japan, Joseph C. Grew, got wind of the plan and warned Washington. Secretary of the Navy Frank Knox and Secretary of War Henry Stimson were alarmed, but President Roosevelt insisted that the countries could work out a deal. When Japan refused to budge, the U.S.

added oil to the embargo, which would have soon crippled Japanese industry.

Having cracked the Japanese naval code (code named "Purple"), the U.S knew Japan had been tracking the U.S. Pacific fleet. On November 25, 1941, Stimson warned FDR that a Japanese attack was imminent. On December 6, the night before

the attack, American intelligence had intercepted a Purple message indicating Japan was going to declare war the next day. A warning was sent to Pearl Harbor base commander General Short—by telegraph, because telephone lines were too easy to tap—but, tragically, the message did not arrive until after the attack had begun.

ADMIRAL ISOROKU YAMAMOTO (AT LEFT), COMMANDER OF JAPAN'S FLEET, SAW WAR WITH THE UNITED STATES AS INEVITABLE, AND PLANNED A SECRET ATTACK AT THE OUTSET OF THE CONFLICT. JAPAN CARRIED OUT JUST SUCH AN ATTACK ON PEARL HARBOR, HAWAII, ON DECEMBER 7, 1941 (ABOVE).

# PART 6

# THE AGE OF CONSPIRACIES

CONSPIRACIES HAVE BEEN AROUND AS LONG AS HUMAN BEINGS HAVE: people creating and carrying out secret plots against one another. But only one period could be called the Age of Conspiracies—and we're living in it. In part due to the legacy of the Cold War and Watergate, many remain cynical about government and suspicious of their leaders' motives. In this climate everybody and everything is often second-guessed, with the Internet's rapid-fire spread of information adding fuel to the flames.

If a rancher reported finding a UFO in the New Mexico desert and the government denied it, who is to be believed? If President Kennedy was killed and his assassin killed two days later, couldn't the Communists or Mafia have been behind it? Then again, as Henry Kissinger put it, "Even a paranoid can have enemies." Just because a theory seems paranoid or far-fetched does not mean it is necessarily wrong. For true believers, the case may never be closed, and the conspiracy theories will live on.

# The Death of Marilyn Monroe

## The death of America's most enduring sex symbol was listed as a "probable suicide." But what really happened on that sultry evening in August?

**THE SAD END OF AMERICA'S NUMBER ONE BLOND BOMBSHELL CAME IN A BEDROOM THAT BORE NO TRACES OF GLITTER OR FAME.**

ON THE EVENING OF AUGUST 4, 1962, MARILYN Monroe telephoned Peter Lawford, the British actor who was also the husband of President John F. Kennedy's sister, Pat. Monroe's voice was strangely slurred, and she ended their conversation ominously. "Say goodbye to Pat," Monroe told Lawford drowsily. "Say goodbye to the president, and say goodbye to yourself, because you're a nice guy." Hours later, the most enduring sex symbol ever to grace the American screen was found dead in her Los Angeles mansion, her graceful body lying face down and naked on her bed.

Eunice Murray, Monroe's housekeeper, claimed that she noticed a light on in the bedroom around 3:30 A.M.; troubled, she called Monroe's psychologist, Dr. Ralph Greenson, and her personal physician, Dr. Hyman Engelberg. Greenson arrived around 3:40 and found Monroe's body; when Engelberg arrived a few minutes later, he pronounced her dead. The coroner's report subsequently listed the cause of her death as "acute barbiturate poisoning, ingestion of overdose," and "probable suicide."

There is no doubt that Monroe had been depressed. She had always struggled against the demands of her stardom and she relied on a regimen of psychiatric treatment and drugs to help her cope. She had recently been fired for constant lateness from her latest film for 20th Century Fox, and her many marriages—her high-profile husbands included baseball legend Joe DiMaggio and playwright Arthur Miller—had all ended in divorce. Lonely, distraught, and under pressure, Monroe felt her life had become unmanageable, and then killed herself. This, at least, is the official version.

### A KENNEDY CONNECTION?

But the official version of Monroe's death fails to account for the discrepancies that might indicate murder. Many of the most prominent witnesses involved with the case later cast doubt on their original reports. Some alleged that they were forced to participate in a cover-up, and have implied that the cover-up was designed to protect President Kennedy and his brother, Attorney General Robert Kennedy.

Speculation that Monroe had had an affair with the president had been rampant since May 1962, when Monroe performed a seductive "Happy Birthday" number for him, singing to the president in front of a crowd of 20,000 people at Madison Square Garden. It is now known that Monroe and the president were among overnight guests at Bing Crosby's house in Palm Springs on the same evening, and met on several other occasions. It is also speculated that Monroe was involved in an even longer-term affair with Robert Kennedy, the president's brother, who may have been trying to distract Monroe from a mutually damaging relationship with the president.

Conspiracy theories abound about the Kennedy connection and Monroe's death. Could she have been killed to prevent her from going public with her relationships with the two leading members of the most prominent political family in America? Was Robert trying to end his affair with Marilyn at the time of her death? A few days before her death, Monroe purportedly told the writer Robert Slatzer that if "Bobby" continued to avoid her, "I might just call a press conference and tell them about it." In his biography of the deceased star, Slatzer alleged that Bobby had actually visited Monroe on the day she died, and spent the night at the home of his brother-in-law Peter Lawford. But who really knows the truth? Seymour Hersh, while writing the biography *The Dark Side of Camelot,* uncovered documents proposing that Bobby had set up a trust fund for Monroe's mother, supposedly to buy Monroe's silence—but after further investigation, the documents were found to be false.

## YET TO REST IN PEACE

Monroe's death has also been tied to the Mafia, who had a long and adversarial relationship with the Kennedys; they may have struck out at her to get back at John and Bobby. There exists evidence that in the months before her death, Monroe's phone was tapped by both the Justice Department of Robert Kennedy and the agents of Teamsters boss Jimmy Hoffa.

Was Monroe really a pawn caught between the country's most powerful politicians and criminals? No one knows, but the medical explanation for her death is full of holes. The suicide investigation team reported that Monroe swallowed "one gulp" of around 47 Nembutal pills; but her prescription, given to her by Dr. Engelberg, was for only 25 of the pills.

If Monroe had killed herself by swallowing pills, the residue from their digestion should have been found in her stomach; they were not. It has been speculated that Monroe died of an injected overdose of drugs, but she had no access to injection barbituates—the injection would have had to come from another source. The coroner's report stated that there were no punctures on Monroe's body—but Dr. Engelberg's bill to her estate showed he had given her an injection the day before her death; that mark should have been clearly visible.

Was Marilyn Monroe administered a homicidal lethal injection, which the coroner's report covered up? The answer may never be known. But given Marilyn's complicated connections to so many men in positions of power, a cloud of suspicion may always hang over the events of that August night.

**MARILYN MONROE CAUSED NO SMALL STIR WITH HER INTIMATE "HAPPY BIRTHDAY" SONG TO PRESIDENT JOHN F. KENNEDY; SHE SANG AT A BIRTHDAY PARTY AT NEW YORK'S MADISON SQUARE GARDEN (ABOVE). AT HER LOS ANGELES HOME (LEFT), THE FILM LEGEND'S BODY IS REMOVED BY THE CORONER'S OFFICE.**

# The Assassination of John F. Kennedy

**JFK's assassin was apprehended but killed on television two days later. Forty years later, conspiracy theories still abound.**

WHEN ASKED IN AN INTERVIEW BY BIOGRAPHERS Peter Collier and David Horowitz how he would choose to die, if he had the luxury of a choice, President John F. Kennedy said "a gunshot is the perfect way—You never know what's hit you." And so it would come to pass, in a story branded into American memory, that on November 22, 1963, the young president was assassinated by gunfire in Dallas, Texas, while riding with his wife, Jacqueline, and the governor of Texas in an open motorcade. The site of the shootings was Dealey Plaza.

Eighty minutes after the fatal shots rang out, police arrested a wiry 24-year-old ex-Marine and pro-Cuban activist, Lee Harvey Oswald, in a movie theater in Dallas. Two days later, in a turn of events more bizarre than fiction, a Dallas nightclub owner named Jack Ruby shot Oswald dead in front of millions watching on

**THE 1964 WARREN COMMISSION PRODUCED A 26-VOLUME REPORT ON JFK'S MURDER. AT LEFT, A RANGE OF ITS EVIDENCE.**

**Did Lee Harvey Oswald act alone in committing the murder that shocked the nation? To this day, many insist that others were involved.**

THE KENNEDYS AND CONNALLYS WERE ALL SMILES IN SAN ANTONIO, ONE DAY BEFORE JFK IS ASSASSINATED IN DALLAS. AT LEFT, THE MOTORCADE ARRIVES IN NEIGHBORING FORT WORTH ON THE FATEFUL DAY OF NOVEMBER 22.

live television as the police were moving their prime suspect from the city to the county jail.

Perhaps there has been no other week in American history so emotionally fraught as the last in November of 1963, and no other wound in the American psyche that has festered so long. Ruby's murder of Oswald sealed the mouth of the accused without him confessing to the crime. As there were no criminal proceedings to pursue, the new president, Lyndon B. Johnson, decided to appoint a commission to investigate the assassination and determine if there was a conspiracy involved.

### THE "MAGIC BULLET"

The commission, headed by Supreme Court Chief Justice Earl Warren, heard from 552 witnesses and combed through thousands of pages of evidence; their report of 26 volumes, issued in 1964, said that the evidence could only lead them to believe that Lee Harvey Oswald acted alone in the killing. Over the ensuing decades, however, hundreds of books

PRESIDENT JOHN F. KENNEDY SLUMPED INTO THE ARMS OF HIS WIFE, JACKIE, IMMEDIATELY AFTER BEING SHOT BY A SNIPER'S BULLET WHILE RIDING PAST DALLAS'S DEALEY PLAZA. AT THE BOTTOM, A SECRET SERVICE AGENT STANDS ON THE BUMPER OF THE PRESIDENT'S CAR TO OFFER ASSISTANCE.

and thousands of articles would appear to dispute or question the findings of the Warren Commission. Forty years later, we still find ourselves asking: Who killed JFK?

To many conspiracy theorists, the soft underbelly of the Warren Report is in its claim that Oswald only could have fired three bullets, one of which missed the motorcade altogether. The report found that the second bullet then struck the president behind the neck, passed through his body, pierced Texas Governor John Connally's shoulder, and then fractured his wrist. This shot often has been called, incredulously, "the magic bullet." The third and final shot was the one that killed Kennedy. Dozens of books have claimed that the second bullet could not have inflicted all of the damage that the Warren Commission suggested. A fourth bullet at least would be needed, the authors contend, and that means a second gunman.

## THEORY UPON THEORY

Books such as *High Treason*, by Robert J. Gordon and Harrison Edward Livingstone, have presented diagrams suggesting that the trajectory of the Warren Commission's "magic bullet" would also have required that the projectile do a mid-air swerve after it exited the president in order to strike Governor Connally—a physically impossible maneuver by any stretch of the imagination. Suspicions of a second gunman have been aided over the years by the witnesses who told the Warren Commission that they saw some sort of smoke coming from behind the fence on the grassy knoll of Dealey Plaza, an incline that leads up to railroad tracks. (Many of those witnesses said that they thought it resembled "exhaust" and not gunfire, however.) Witness Julia Ann Mercer even said that she saw Jack Ruby behind the wheel of a pickup truck a couple of hours before the assassination, and that she saw another man take a gun case from the truck and walk up the grassy knoll.

But if Oswald didn't act alone, if he was framed, or if he was part of some larger conspiracy, who else was involved? There are enough theories to fill a whole library.

A book titled *The Texas Connection* (1991), by Craig I. Zirbel, suggested that Lyndon Johnson, bitter over his defeat by Kennedy for the 1960 Democratic nomination and fearing that he would be dumped as vice president on the

FROM THE BACK,
JACK RUBY IS
CAPTURED BY A
CAMERA AS HE
SHOOTS LEE
HARVEY OSWALD,
WHO IS BEING
ESCORTED BY
GUARDS TO THE
COUNTY JAIL. CLAY
SHAW (BELOW
RIGHT) WENT TO
TRIAL AS PART OF
A CONSPIRACY TO
ASSASSINATE THE
PRESIDENT, BUT
THE CASE AGAINST
HIM WAS PHONY.

1964 ticket, helped orchestrate the killing. The book also hints that a close inspection of photographs might show Johnson, who was also in the motorcade, starting to duck before the first shots were fired. More books have described the "three hoboes"—caught in reporters' photos—who were arrested in a rail car on the grassy knoll directly after the shooting; their identities prompted wide speculation (some argued that two of the men were E. Howard Hunt and Frank Sturgis of Watergate fame). Other theories centered upon the strange sight of a man captured in a Dealey Plaza photo on the day of the shooting; he was holding an umbrella on a perfectly sunny day.

### A CASE IN NEW ORLEANS

Another theory, supported by the director Oliver Stone in his 1991 movie *JFK*, is that New Orleans businessman Clay Shaw was involved in a conspiracy to kill Kennedy. Witnesses said they had seen Shaw with Oswald and another alleged conspirator, David Ferrie, in the town of Clinton, Louisiana, and one witness claimed to have overheard the trio discussing plans to kill Kennedy. In March 1967, controversial New Orleans District Attorney Jim Garrison had Shaw arrested; he was tried

in 1969. But the evidence tying Shaw to the murder was weak, and he was acquitted by a jury after just 54 minutes of deliberation. In fact, in *False Witness*, a 1999 book examining the claims against Shaw, writer Patricia Lambert contends that a key witness for the prosecution made his allegations while under hypnosis, and that Garrison tried to bribe another potential witness to give false testimony.

Despite the talk of conspiracy, it is likely that Oswald acted alone. (Marina, Oswald's wife, thought all along that only her husband was to blame.) One of the more compelling points

made by those who argue that there were shooters on the grassy knoll regards the motion of the president's head, recorded in the famous movie by Abraham Zapruder. Kennedy's head moves suddenly back and to the left, seemingly an illogical movement if the bullet came from behind. In tests with melons, however, ballistics experts found that very often only a small hole opened on the side of the marksman but that the bullet created such internal pressure in the melon that the backside blew out and caused the melon to jump toward, and not away from, the shooter. The same model might be applied to human skulls, the experts argued. Closer investigation of the position of Kennedy's seat and Governor Connally's seat also reveals that the path of the "magic bullet" needn't have been so complex as conspiracy theorists make it out to be.

But why do so many still seek an organized cause behind the murder, rather than ascribing it to one deranged individual? "The search for conspiracy," suggests *New York Times* columnist Anthony Lewis, "[temporarily] obscures our necessary understanding, all of us, that in this life there is often tragedy without reason."

MEMBERS OF THE WARREN COMMISSION VISIT THE SCENE OF THE CRIME (ABOVE). THE TEXAS SCHOOL BOOK DEPOSITORY IS IN THE REAR. IN NEW ORLEANS IN 1968, DISTRICT ATTORNEY JIM GARRISON DISCUSSES THE UPCOMING TRIAL OF CLAY SHAW FOR CONSPIRACY IN JFK'S MURDER (BELOW).

# How Movies "Make" History

"History," wrote the novelist and poet Michael Ondaatje in his memoir *Running in the Family*, "is an agreed-upon fiction." If we can accept Ondaatje's definition as true, motion pictures may be considered one of the great definers of history in the 20th century. From *The Great Train Robbery* in 1903 to *Saving Private Ryan* 95 years later, movies have taken such a large slice of the public imagination that sometimes they seem to supplant the historical events they represent. The American perception of the antebellum South has been forever romanticized by the 1939 film *Gone With the Wind*. And William Randolph Hearst is perhaps remembered today mainly because Orson Welles used him as his inspiration for Charles Foster Kane in his film *Citizen Kane.*

But if movies "make" history, sometimes they have also taken liberties with the real record. By age 25, Welles had become Hollywood's enfant terrible with his 1941 masterpiece, *Citizen Kane*. Welles had sprung to national prominence only a few years earlier with his radio broadcast of "The War of the Worlds," which had convinced thousands of listeners that the world was being attacked by aliens. His historical sleight of hand would be more subtle in *Citizen Kane*. The picture examines through a series of flashbacks the psychological state of a penniless boy turned newspaper tycoon.

## CITIZEN HEARST

Though the film entrances audiences today for its brilliance, viewers in 1941 had a context in which to place the story. The parallels between Charles Foster Kane and William Randolph Hearst could hardly be missed.

Hearst had started his yellow-journalism newspaper enterprise by owning a small paper in San Francisco, but he soon spread out to own papers in most of America's major cities. Hearst amassed, like Kane, a great fortune; he had a predilection for purchasing expensive works of art; and, perhaps in the most striking parallel, Hearst had built a castle in California on a property half the size of Rhode Island. He named it San Simeon, which would serve as the prototype for the film's Xanadu.

Hearst and his Hollywood friends tried to buy the original negative and destroy the film, but when that proved impossible Hearst did his best to make sure it didn't get a wide viewing—mainly because of the portrayal of Susan Alexander, the simple and rather dim girl who becomes Kane's wife and whom he tries to force into the opera world. Hearst himself had married a showgirl, Marion Davies, whose career he attempted to advance in movies. It has been said that Hearst tried to suppress the film to preserve Davies's honor.

William Randolph Hearst's money and clout meant that much of the Hollywood establishment of the time publicly reviled the film, to the point that it was kept from most theaters. But now, more than half a century later, the film is often cited as one of the great movies of all time; it may well survive as the record by which both Hearst and his wife will be remembered.

## LASTING IMPRESSIONS

One of the strange advantages films have over real history is that they outlast (or are produced long after) the times they depict; an audience member rarely has enough understanding of the era or the events to be able to question the authenticity of their portrayal. *Gone With the Wind* shows slavery as a benevolent institution corrupted by the arrival of the Northern army and carpetbaggers—a message that also marks D.W. Griffith's 1915 film *The Birth of a Nation*, which glorifies the Old South and blames the rise of the Ku Klux Klan on carpetbaggers and congressional efforts to raise the station of African-Americans after the Civil War.

The release of *The Birth of a Nation* sparked rioting, lawsuits, and protests across the country, but the movie remains largely unseen today except by film students. *Gone With the Wind*, however, continues to be thought of in much of the world as a largely accurate representation of the life of the Old South.

## JFK: THE MOVIE

Then there is the assassination of John F. Kennedy, one of the most controversial events of the century. In his 1991 Academy Award-winning film and tour de force of paranoia, *JFK*, director Oliver Stone presents such a nefarious and complicated countermyth to the single-assassin theory that it prompted *Time* magazine to ask, "So, you want to know who killed the President and connived in the cover-up? Everybody! High officials in the CIA, the FBI, the Dallas constabulary, all three armed services, Big Business, and the White House." Stone particularly suggests a link to the assassination with the military-industrial complex; Kennedy intended to get America out of the war in Vietnam, his movie argues, and the powers that profit from the war industry were less than happy.

Stone's movie is an extreme case, but most people—even participants in a historical event—seem quite willing to forgive slight manipulations of the historical record for the sake of dramatic effect. The main plot and climactic battle in *Saving Private Ryan* are entirely fictitious creations. Nevertheless, veterans of the war have praised the accuracy of the Normandy landing sequence, and seem inclined to forgive the rest.

As historical movies outlive the history they describe, however, to what extent can they replace—and not merely represent—history? Perhaps in an era like ours, when people live a large part of their existence secondhand, a film called *Titanic* can become as almost historic as the sinking itself. "The movies make emotions look so strong and real," said pop artist Andy Warhol, "whereas when things really do happen to you, it's like watching television—you don't feel anything."

A SURVEY TAKEN AFTER THE MOVIE *JFK* HAD BECOME CONTROVERSIAL FOUND THAT MORE THAN HALF OF AMERICANS BELOW AGE 30 BELIEVED STONE'S VERSION OF EVENTS—ONE OF THE MOST WORRISOME EXAMPLES SO FAR OF A FILM BENDING HISTORY TO ITS OWN PURPOSES.

# The Murder
## of
# Bobby Kennedy

ROBERT F. KENNEDY SPEAKS TO HIS SUPPORTERS AT THE AMBASSADOR HOTEL IN LOS ANGELES ON JUNE 5, 1968, JUST MINUTES BEFORE HE IS FATALLY SHOT. OPPOSITE, THE DYING KENNEDY IS HELD BY A BUSBOY.

ON MAY 18, 1968, SEVENTEEN DAYS before Democratic presidential candidate Robert F. Kennedy would be murdered in the kitchen pantry of the Ambassador Hotel in Los Angeles, the young Palestinian immigrant Sirhan B. Sirhan scribbled in his journal that "my determination to eliminate R.F.K. is becoming more and more of an unshakable obsession." Sirhan, once an avid supporter of Robert Kennedy, felt betrayed by the candidate's comments in favor of providing military planes to Israel. The rest of Sirhan's journal page that day is a long string of repetitive statements: "R.F.K. must die. . . R.F.K. must be killed."

When Kennedy was fatally shot on June 5— shortly after he celebrated his victory in the California Democratic primary with supporters—Sirhan was seen a short distance from Kennedy, firing a gun. From all indications, the case against Sirhan seemed remarkably cut-and-dried, even to those who had doubts about

**The case against Sirhan Sirhan seemed closed, but skeptics are busy prying it open.**

a lone gunman in the assassination of Kennedy's brother John. At the trial Sirhan even confessed to the crime, though he said he had drunk too much alcohol that evening and remembered nothing.

More than 30 years later, however, several people have cast some doubt on the official verdict. At his most recent parole hearing in 1997, Sirhan made for the first time an assertion of his innocence. And notable figures such as presidential historian Arthur M. Schlesinger, Jr. and writer Norman Mailer have signed a petition asking for a Los Angeles grand jury to review the case.

The comments of witnesses in the hotel pantry that evening who said they thought they saw other guns—as well as the 1987 release of the Los Angeles Police Department's and the FBI's record of the case—have led several independent investigators to examine the events in the pantry more closely. There is the question of the number of bullets, for example:

Sirhan's .22 caliber gun only held eight, and some independent investigators argue that pictures of the crime scene reveal there were more than eight bullets fired—some lodged in a door frame and stuck in ceiling tiles. (Several ceiling tiles, scores of photographs, and this door frame were later destroyed by the LAPD.) Second, there is the autopsy report of coroner Thomas Noguchi, which found that the bullet that killed Kennedy was fired less than three inches from the back of his head, while most witnesses place Sirhan one to six feet away from Kennedy, firing at him from the front.

### MANCHURIAN CANDIDATE REDUX?

None of the skeptics of the official verdict question that Sirhan was firing a gun that evening, but whether it was Sirhan's bullets that killed Kennedy and if there could have been other gunmen. Some even speculate that Sirhan might have been lured into a *Manchurian Candidate*-style setup. (In that 1962 film, a former war prisoner was hypnotized and sent on a mission to assassinate the president.)

The theory that Sirhan could have been mesmerized into committing the murder was given wide currency by a radio documentary called *The RFK Tapes*, by Bill Klaber. In the 1993 broadcast, Klaber uncovered slight discrepancies in the case and suggested that the LAPD was careless in its failure to follow other leads. He also exposed Sirhan's casual link with the late California therapist Dr. William Joseph Bryan Jr., who was experienced in hypnosis and might have had CIA connections. Bryan told acquaintances after Kennedy's murder that he had once hypnotized Sirhan when he came to his office, launching a sea of speculation on the Internet and among conspiracy theorists about the possibility that Sirhan might have been used.

Sirhan testified in his trial that the last thing he remembered before being hit by someone and forced against a table in the pantry was sitting at a bar next to an attractive woman who said: "Pour me a cup of coffee with plenty of milk and sugar." He then said he saw a shiny coffee urn, but then remembered nothing until after the shots were fired.

## THE POLKA-DOT DRESS THEORY

This testimony has been used as corroboration for the "polka-dot dress theory," which places others behind a scheme that led a hypnotized Sirhan to try to murder Kennedy.

A policeman who arrived on the scene after the shots were fired said a couple told him they had seen another man and woman coming out of the hotel, saying, "We shot him! We shot him!" An all-points bulletin was put out for the couple, but was soon canceled when Sirhan became the suspect. The Los Angeles Police Department later suggested that the couple was saying "They shot him" and had been misheard. But some suggest that this woman coming down the stairs in a polka-dot dress—who is also considered by some to be the girl who asked Sirhan for coffee—could have also served as a "baby-sitter" for a hypnotism scheme. Why she would be so blatant as to say "We shot him"—loudly and in public—after being clever enough to help mesmerize Sirhan is highly problematic for the skeptics.

Many who are not willing to go so far as to suggest that Sirhan was hypnotized still are bothered by the autopsy findings that show the bullet was shot at close range from the rear—as well as the indication that there were more than eight bullets fired at the scene. Pinpointing other suspects in the pantry has been almost entirely speculative, however, and evidence is scant. Writer Dan Moldea, who was once inclined to entertain suggestions that security guard Thane Cesar was a second gunmen, eventually changed his mind after issuing Cesar a lie-detector test. Moldea now believes Sirhan acted alone.

Despite the ostensible lack of other leads, the LAPD's handling of the investigation has come under litigious criticism from several quarters: Jamie Scott Enyart, a photographer who claims to have been in the pantry that night and to have taken a photograph just as Kennedy fell, was awarded $450,600 in 1996 because the department lost his confiscated negatives. No photo is known to exist of the moment of the shooting, and the LAPD has admitted to destroying scores of photos that they said were "duplicates." This has led skeptics to believe that crucial pictures may have been suppressed to ensure an airtight case against Sirhan.

## A QUESTION OF MOTIVE

But if there were other gunmen, what would have been their motive? Several historians note that Kennedy, with his considerable warmth, intelligence, and genuine concern for people suffering under conditions of social injustice, also had strong enemies due to his tough stance on organized crime. He was also campaigning against America's involvement in the Vietnam War, a point of view that did not win him friends in the military-industrial complex and in the intelligence community.

Two days after his death, Kennedy's body was carried by train from St. Patrick's Cathedral in New York to Washington, D.C., and Americans of every race lined the railroad tracks, weeping. Richard Nixon would win the presidency in 1968 and America's involvement in Vietnam would continue. A certain kind of American idealism and innocence—embodied in RFK, who fought against social injustice wherever it persisted—perhaps was lost with his murder.

THE LOS ANGELES POLICE RELEASED THIS MUG SHOT OF SIRHAN B. SIRHAN, THE 24-YEAR-OLD PALESTINIAN IMMIGRANT WHO WAS CONVICTED OF THE MURDER OF SENATOR KENNEDY. SOME STILL BELIEVE HE WAS NOT THE ONLY GUNMAN.

# The Assassination of
# Martin Luther King, Jr.

**In a controversial case, the life of one of the nation's most revered leaders was cut short in 1968.**

THE 1960S IN THE UNITED STATES WERE A PERIOD of great tumult and violence. In this ragged topography of unrest, the deaths of two men, John F. Kennedy and Martin Luther King, Jr., stand out as twin summits of tragedy and chaos. Questions surrounding both killings have gone unanswered for years, with JFK's giving rise to more conspiracy theories than any event in recent American history. And with good reason: His alleged shooter, Lee Harvey Oswald, was shot before he could present his case. Into this dearth of hard evidence have

stepped numerous hypotheses. And so it has become with the death of Martin Luther King.

Almost from the moment he was imprisoned, King's alleged shooter, a petty thief by the name of James Earl Ray, claimed he was innocent. Ray died in prison in 1998, after failing to persuade the state to grant him a retrial. Yet questions about his guilt and the true identity of King's killer, or killers, persist.

King was shot and killed on April 4, 1968, on a balcony of the Lorraine Motel in Memphis, Tennessee, as he was preparing for a rally.

Shortly thereafter, Ray was arrested and charged with the killing. Police claimed that Ray had acted as a lone gunman. According to their report, he had checked into the boarding house across from the motel where King was staying. He crouched in the bathroom with a rifle and waited for King to walk out on his balcony, and then fired the fatal shot.

## RAY'S TURNABOUT

Ray refused to plead guilty, insisting on a trial, but he was eventually convinced by his attorney that a guilty plea was his best chance to avoid the death penalty. Indeed it was, and Ray was sentenced to 99 years in prison. Only three days after his conviction, however, Ray recanted his plea and filed for a retrial. He would never be granted a retrial, although until his dying day he remained firm in his claim that he was not guilty of the assassination.

THE REV. KING STOOD WITH OTHER CIVIL RIGHTS LEADERS, INCLUDING THE REV. JESSE JACKSON, ON THE BALCONY OF THE LORRAINE MOTEL ON APRIL 3, 1968—ONE DAY BEFORE HE WAS KILLED AT THE SAME LOCATION. PROTESTERS, LIKE THESE SANITATION WORKERS (TOP), WERE OUT IN FORCE IN MEMPHIS BEFORE DR. KING'S VISIT.

Several problems still persist in the case against Ray. It is clear now that his initial confession, while not overtly coerced, was certainly encouraged to a degree that is questionable in such a high-profile capital murder case. Ray's confession came after he had been held for eight months in a special jail cell, under bright lights 24 hours a day, and under constant pressure from his attorney to save his own life by pleading guilty.

Furthermore, the bullet removed from King's body was never conclusively matched to Ray's rifle, despite a 1997 reexamination of the ballistic evidence. And, as in the case of Kennedy's assassination, the shot that killed King was a tremendously difficult piece of sharp shooting, which Ray, who had little serious experience with firearms, seems unlikely to have been capable of doing.

### HOLES IN THE CASE

In addition to these problems with the allegations made against Ray, details of the prosecution's case are unsettling. The prosecution's prime eyewitness, Charles Stephens, an alcoholic who was in the boarding house with his wife at the time of the shooting, at first gave highly inconclusive testimony, saying that he saw a very short man (Ray was 5'10") but only from the back. After his $30,000 bar tab was

cleared up, Stephens' memory improved and he positively identified Ray. (He later repudiated the identification on television.) Stephens' wife disputed her husband's identification, and soon after was sedated and placed in a mental institution—this, even though she had had no prior history of mental illness.

Also troubling is the fact that many eyewitnesses who were at the scene of the crime recalled seeing movement from shrubbery facing the balcony. A young reporter for the *New York Times*, Earl Caldwell, who was staying at the Lorraine Motel, claimed he saw a puff of smoke come from the bushes. To complicate matters further, the angle of the shot points to these bushes. In Caldwell's *Times* story the next day, he quoted several witnesses who mention them. That evening, under the dark of night, the bushes were cut and cleared away. What's more, Caldwell, who firmly believes that he saw another shooter in the bushes, was never contacted for questioning by authorities investigating the case.

Various other questions lead one to wonder whether Ray really acted alone in the murder. The day before the shooting, an unidentified man arrived at the Lorraine Motel and, claiming he was part of King's security team, changed King's room from the first to the second floor—where he would have a balcony.

And the next day, King's police security detail was reduced from eight officers to two.

In 1976, the House of Representatives appointed a committee to look into the case. The committee upheld Ray's guilt but concluded that he may not have acted alone. Before wrapping up the matter, the committee ordered that all records pertaining to the case be locked up for 50 years, until 2029.

## MORE TWISTS AND TURNS

But the committee's findings were no match for the force of conspiracy theories. Before Ray died, his attorney, William Pepper, published *Orders to Kill: The Truth Behind the Murder of Martin Luther King* (1995), in which he argues for Ray's innocence and pins the blame on the FBI. But can we trust Pepper's account?

On the one hand, Pepper bases his accusations—including that a team of FBI snipers shot King from the roof of a nearby building, with perhaps some help from a team on the ground—on interviews with unidentified sources. On the other hand, King's wife and children have all supported Pepper's efforts to clear Ray from the murder. To the consternation of many objective observers, the Kings believe, along with Pepper, that agents of the government were behind the assassination.

The case took an even more controversial turn in December, 1999, when the jury of a civil suit brought by the King family concluded that Loyd Jowers, owner of a restaurant opposite the motel where King was shot, was part of the conspiracy. Jowers had stated in a 1993 television interview that he had hired a Memphis police officer to kill King from the bushes behind his restaurant, and said he had been

Photographs taken 1960
Photograph taken 1968 (eyes drawn by artist)

Aliases: Eric Starvo Galt, W. C. Herron, Harvey Lowmyer, James McBride, James O'Conner, James

paid to do so by a Memphis grocery store owner with Mafia connections. Despite the fact that authorities never really took Jowers's confession seriously (he was desperate to pitch a book deal), the jury found that he—as well as "others, including governmental agencies"—had been a part of the conspiracy.

The verdict was greeted by many historians with more than a little skepticism. To other observers, the outcome of the trial cleared up some of the murkiness surrounding King's assassination. But then came another twist: In June, 2000, it was announced that a government investigation conducted over the previous months had found no evidence whatsoever of a conspiracy, and that Ray had acted alone.

The split in opinion points up something undeniable: that the circumstances surrounding King's death are so convoluted that the truth about who killed Martin Luther King, Jr. may remain a mystery for years to come.

THE FBI ISSUED THIS FLYER AFTER PLACING JAMES EARL RAY ON ITS "TEN MOST WANTED" LIST IN APRIL, 1968. RAY WAS SOON CAPTURED AND SENTENCED TO 99 YEARS IN PRISON.

## J. EDGAR HOOVER VS. MLK

King's trip to Memphis was his last excursion before he was to mount his "poor people's march" on Washington, D.C. The proposed march had the FBI deeply worried about the potential for riot. J. Edgar Hoover, then director of the FBI, was suspicious of King, whom he had nicknamed "Zorro" and whom he also thought a Communist. The FBI had already made several attempts to sabotage the movement by disrupting King's life. King was under constant FBI surveillance wherever he went, and his phone lines were always tapped.

Perhaps most alarming was a letter sent to King shortly before his trip to Sweden to accept the Nobel Peace Prize. With the letter was an audio tape, doctored to make it seem as if King had been recorded engaging in sexual activity with a woman other than his wife. Unless King revealed the affair before going to Sweden, the letter said, the tape would be released to the media.

**PIECES OF THE PUZZLE** ▼

# The Tet Offensive

## In 1968, the Lunar New Year ushered in an unexpected attack by the enemy in the Vietnamese War.

**BLACK SMOKE COVERS THE STREETS OF SAIGON, THE SOUTH VIETNAMESE CAPITAL, AFTER SURPRISE ATTACKS BY THE VIETCONG DURING THE TET HOLIDAY IN LATE JANUARY, 1968. THE TET OFFENSIVE ERODED POPULAR SUPPORT FOR THE WAR AMONG THE AMERICAN PUBLIC.**

As AMERICANS ENTERED THE ELECTION YEAR OF 1968, it looked like the situation in Vietnam might at last be under control, seven years after President John F. Kennedy had sent in the first sizable number of American military advisers. Throughout 1967, military and civilian targets in North Vietnam were regularly bombed, and the number of American troops in Vietnam had risen to 389,000. Although protests against America's involvement in the war were frequent, a majority seemed to support President Lyndon B. Johnson's commitment to fight until the Communist threat in Southeast Asia had been pushed back. Many believed General William Westmoreland when he asserted that America "had reached an important point where the end begins to come into view."

### A HOLIDAY SURPRISE

As the Lunar New Year (Tet) festival approached in January 1968, both sides agreed to a truce to mark the Vietnamese holiday, when Vietnamese traditionally visit family, prepare special foods, and adorn their homes with flowers. But rather than a peaceful break from the fighting, Tet would prove to be a bloody turning point that would signal the end of American involvement in Vietnam.

On January 30, the second day of the holiday, Communist General Vo Nguyen Giap launched simultaneous surprise attacks throughout South Vietnam. Enjoying their holiday, a full half of the South Vietnamese army was off duty. In the city of Hue, North Vietnamese units initiated a reign of terror marked by assassination squads armed with death lists. In Saigon, the capital of South Vietnam, a suicide squad of 19 Vietcong in civilian clothing occupied part of the grounds of the American Embassy for six hours before being fought back by Marines. On the lawns of the presidential palace nearby, South Vietnamese and Communist troops squared off.

By February 24, the Americans and the South Vietnamese were successful in forcing the Vietcong back out of Hue, Saigon, and the other cities they had invaded. Members of the Vietcong had hoped that the masses in South Vietnam would rise up and support them, but the cities' residents failed to mobilize.

On the one hand, the Tet Offensive was a failure for the Communists: The Vietcong gained little ground and lost thousands of soldiers. The U.S. Army proclaimed victory, estimating that between 45,000 and 60,000 North

Vietnamese and Vietcong had been killed, compared to just 2,600 Americans and South Vietnamese. President Johnson told reporters as early as February 2 that the offensive had been a "complete failure" for the Vietcong.

But in political terms, the Tet Offensive proved to be the biggest defeat of all for the United States. Many at home were stunned by the success of the Vietcong's stealth missions. Critics pointed to the symbolic attack on the American Embassy and the temporary loss of control of so many cities as evidence that the Americans were not winning after all. To an increasing segment of the public, America had been embarrassed by the continued strength of the Communists, after all the years spent and lives lost attempting to weaken their position.

### JOHNSON'S DEFEAT

In fact, the U.S. military may not have been so unprepared for the Tet Offensive. Just before the attacks began, the United States and South Vietnam, concerned about a Communist buildup, had themselves canceled the Tet truce for five northern provinces. According to later comments by President Johnson, the U.S. had urged South Vietnam to take the threat of an invasion more seriously, but soldiers were permitted to go on holiday leave nonetheless.

But that did not matter after Tet; it was now too late to regain popular support for the war. One month after the offensive, President Johnson halted most of the bombing in North Vietnam and called for peace negotiations. Stunning the nation, he also said he would not run for reelection. The Tet Offensive had turned the public inexorably against the war, with Johnson's political career among its victims.

LYNDON JOHNSON CONSULTS WITH ADVISERS (LEFT) ON FEBRUARY 9, 1968, AS THE TET OFFENSIVE CONTINUES. IN SAIGON (BELOW), SOUTH VIETNAMESE SOLDIERS DRAG THE BODY OF A VIETCONG GUERILLA ON JANUARY 31, 1968.

## POWS IN SOUTHEAST ASIA

According to the Defense Department, as of 1996 there were 2,153 Americans unaccounted for in the Vietnam War—giving loved ones, friends, and independent observers sufficient reason to believe that there are American POWs still alive. More surprisingly, some reports from North Korea have claimed that Americans are living in group compounds in Pyongyang, working as servants or teaching English in local colleges. One estimate among POW advocates is that there may be between 10 and 15 American POWs living in the two countries today.

Since 1973, however, the U.S. government has official-

**PIECES OF THE PUZZLE** ▼

ly claimed that there is no evidence of POWs living anywhere in Southeast Asia. In the mid-1990s, the Vietnamese government searched for evidence of American captives and turned over the results of their search, including dog tags and other remnants of deceased servicemen, to the United States. But they found no evidence of American POWs living in Vietnam.

But what about Korean POWs? No similar investigative effort has been made by the North Korean government, leaving room for continued speculation—even though American POWs from the Korean War would now be well into their seventies.

# What Happened to Jimmy Hoffa?

## Was the famous union leader murdered by the Mafia, or did he engineer his own disappearance?

AT 12:30 P.M. ON JULY 30, 1975, FORMER TEAM-sters leader Jimmy Hoffa kissed his wife good-bye and climbed into a bullet-proof limousine waiting outside his Michigan home. The former president of the International Brotherhood of Teamsters—a union of drivers, store clerks, and department store workers more than 1.7 million strong—was on his way to a lunch meeting in a Detroit suburb.

Hoffa had told friends he was planning to meet Detroit mobster Anthony Giacalone and Tony Provenzano, a New Jersey Teamsters official with reputed mob ties. Provenzano had held a grudge against Hoffa ever since their days together in prison in the late 1960s, but he seemed ready to bury the hatchet.

A few hours later, around 2:30 P.M., an aide received a call from an irate Hoffa. "Where the hell is Tony Giacalone?" Hoffa screamed. "I'm being stood up?" Later, Giacalone claimed he had spent the day at a nearby gym, and Provenzano said he was playing cards at his local union hall in Hoboken, New Jersey, at the time they were to meet with Hoffa.

## THE TEAMSTERS' BOSS

Ever since Hoffa's 1957 appointment as President of the Teamsters' Union, his tenure had been marked by corruption and violence. He was accused of stealing almost $2 million from the organization, and of employing mob-style tactics to stay in power. Not surprisingly, Hoffa became a target of Attorney General Robert F. Kennedy, who called his leadership a "conspiracy of evil." Kennedy had 30 FBI agents and 13 grand juries investigate the union boss.

Kennedy's persistence paid off when Hoffa was convicted of jury-fixing and defrauding the union's pension fund. In 1967, Hoffa began serving a 13-year sentence at a Pennsylvania prison. Richard Nixon, whose presidential campaigns were generously funded by the union, commuted Hoffa's sentence to four years on the condition that he not hold a union office of any sort until 1980.

But when Hoffa was released in 1971, he immediately embarked on a campaign to get the ban lifted. He also began maneuvering against a one-time colleague, Frank Fitzsimmons, who had replaced him as the Teamsters' leader in 1967. Challenging Fitzsimmons was risky, but Hoffa knew he had the support of the rank and file; indeed, a 1974 poll showed that 83 percent of union members supported him.

### SECRET FILES

Were rivals behind Hoffa's disappearance? Some think so, while others believe Hoffa was murdered by the Mafia to prevent him from exposing links between the union and organized crime. And there is a third possibility: sensing his life was in danger, Hoffa might have engineered his own disappearance.

Police found no clues in Hoffa's car, located with the help of an anonymous caller. Inside lay a pair of white gloves, neatly folded on the back seat. In the months that followed, police and private citizens searched woods and landfills in the hope of turning up Hoffa's corpse, but turned up nothing.

Twenty-two years afterward, in 1997, a cache of secret FBI files was found in a filing cabinet in the basement of a Detroit recreational facility. The 1,500 pages of documents represented the work of the FBI in the first five months of the investigation of Hoffa's disappearance. Government investigators had conducted hundreds of interviews, grilling top union officials and members, petty criminals and mob bosses, as well as reputable politicians and influential businessmen who had dealt with Hoffa.

## WHERE IS HOFFA BURIED?

If Jimmy Hoffa was murdered in 1975, what happened to his body? According to one police theory, he was strangled and his body was disposed of in a mob-owned fat purification plant.

**WE MAY NEVER KNOW** ▼

But another theory, widely popular in American folklore, says Hoffa is buried in a very public place: under the west end zone in Giants Stadium, the football arena in East Rutherford, New Jersey. Another version suggests a specific burial spot in front of Section 107. Others say his body may lie beneath the stands or under nearby highways. The rumors probably started because of mobster Tony Provenzano's New Jersey ties—and because Giants Stadium was under construction at the time of Hoffa's disappearance.

The FBI investigation centered on one man: Chuckie O'Brien, whose father was close to Hoffa. Chuckie became like a son to the union chief, even living for a time in his house. But in 1974, relations between the two became strained when O'Brien asked to be made president of Hoffa's old local in Detroit, one of the union's most coveted positions. Hoffa refused to support him, and O'Brien moved to Fitzsimmons's camp.

### THE SUSPECT PROTESTS

But O'Brien denied any involvement in Hoffa's disappearance, claiming that he "loved the old man." He went on television in 1993 to proclaim his innocence, passing a lie detector test on *The Maury Povich Show.*

The FBI still lists the case as "open." But as key witnesses grow older—both Provenzano and Fitzsimmons died in the 1980s—the mystery will not grow any easier to solve.

**FOR ALL THE POLICE KNOW, ANY NEW JERSEY LANDFILL COULD BE HOFFA'S FINAL RESTING PLACE. THE FBI TRACED THE CAR CHUCKIE O'BRIEN WAS DRIVING ON THE DAY OF HOFFA'S DISAPPEARANCE; IT CONTAINED TRACES OF HOFFA'S HAIR, BLOOD, AND SKIN—AND POLICE DOGS DETECTED HOFFA'S SCENT IN THE BACK SEAT.**

# The Watergate Scandal

**In 1974, for the first time in American history a president was forced to resign. What events led to the fall of president Richard Nixon?**

BOB WOODWARD (LEFT) AND CARL BERNSTEIN WERE IN THE FOREFRONT OF INVESTIGATIVE JOURNALISM. THE TOLL WATERGATE TOOK ON RICHARD NIXON (OPPOSITE) WAS EVIDENT, BUT THE SCANDAL WAS NOT THE SUM OF HIS LEGACY. NIXON NOT ONLY OPENED RELATIONS WITH CHINA, BUT ALSO NEGOTIATED THE FIRST ARMS TREATY WITH RUSSIA.

SHORTLY AFTER 1:30 AM ON JUNE 17, 1972, A security guard on a routine check of the Watergate hotel and apartment complex in Washington, D.C., found duct tape holding open a door lock in a stairwell. He had little reason to suspect that his discovery would lead to the most famous political scandal in American history. The guard notified the police, who found five prowlers in the headquarters of the Democratic National Committee, which had set up temporary shop in the building to guide the campaign of Richard Nixon's Democratic challenger in the 1972 election, George McGovern.

Only a few months later, in November of 1972, Nixon would win a second term by one of the largest electoral landslides in the nation's history. But a small part of an intricate web of political sabotage and corruption had been exposed by the break-in; and due to the grit of two young *Washington Post* reporters, Bob

Woodward and Carl Bernstein, this web of deceit and misconduct would soon begin to unravel, culminating in the resignation of President Nixon on August 9, 1974. The Watergate scandal and its attempted cover-up would cloud the American public's trust of its government, indict more than 30 people associated with Nixon's administration, and expose the mysterious ways power can be used—and misused—in Washington. And some of the episode's mysteries still remain today.

### THE PLUMBERS' DIRTY WORK

Bernstein and Woodward—with the help of a secret source called "Deep Throat" and several other confidential sources (including a bookkeeper at the Committee to Re-Elect the President [CRP] and Hugh Sloan, the former treasurer of the CRP)—were slowly able to piece E. Howard Hunt, Donald Segret-

been perpetrated by a group organized by Hunt—called the White House "Plumbers"—that forged letters leading to the undoing of certain Democratic political candidates who were opposed to the Nixon administration.

## CONTINUING MYSTERIES

Two great mysteries about the Watergate scandal remain today. One may be solved in the near future, and one may remain unknown forever. The first is the identity of Deep Throat, who served as the most vital source for Bob Woodward throughout the newspaper's investigation. Nicknamed by the *Post* managing editor after the title of a famous pornographic movie of the same name, Deep Throat had a position "in the Executive Branch [and] had access to information at CRP as well as at the White House," Woodward writes in *All the President's Men.* "He was, incongruously, an incurable gossip, careful to label rumor for what it was, but fascinated by it. . . . He could be rowdy, drink too much, overreach. He was not good at concealing his feelings, hardly ideal for a man in his position." Woodward agreed never to quote the man, even as an anonymous source. Deep Throat would only confirm information gleaned elsewhere and suggest whether Bernstein and Woodward were heading in the right direction.

As the atmosphere surrounding Watergate became more intense, Woodward would

**THE WATERGATE OFFICE AND HOTEL COMPLEX (ABOVE) WAS THE SITE OF THE "THIRD RATE BURGLARY" THAT TOPPLED THE PRESIDENT. BELOW, ROBERT REDFORD, AS BOB WOODWARD IN THE FILM *ALL THE PRESIDENT'S MEN,* MEETS IN A GARAGE WITH THE INFORMANT KNOWN AS DEEP THROAT.**

ti, G. Gordon Liddy, and many others together in a network that ruthlessly tried to trip up opponents of the Nixon administration, often with the President's knowledge. "Watergate" became the catch phrase for a host of offenses.

The two reporters linked John Mitchell, Nixon's former law partner and attorney general before he chose to head the CRP, to an office safe where cash donations to the Nixon candidacy were kept: Mitchell was discovered to have approved $250,000 for the Watergate break-in. Other mischief was found to have

arrange to meet Deep Throat by moving a little pot with a red flag on it to the back of his balcony. If Deep Throat saw the pot in this position, he would know to meet Woodward at 2:00 A.M. in a prearranged spot in a parking garage. If Deep Throat wanted to meet Woodward, he would put a circle around the page number on page 20 of Woodward's morning *New York Times,* and draw clock hands indicating when he wanted to meet.

Conjectures about the identity of Deep Throat have ranged from people inside the White House at the time—Alexander Haig and Henry Kissinger, for two—to people at the CIA and elsewhere. Yet to this day, only four people—Woodward, Bernstein, Ben Bradlee (the editor of the *Post* at the time), and Deep Throat himself—are known definitively to have the identity of the informant.

## THE 18-MINUTE GAP

The second large mystery is the strange 18½-minute gap in one of Nixon's Oval Office tape recordings, subpoenaed by Special Watergate prosecutor Archibald Cox as part of the investigation. A conversation about the Watergate scandal between Nixon and White House Chief of Staff H.R. Haldeman is covered by a long, two-toned humming noise that makes it impossible to hear the dialogue.

Nixon's personal secretary, Rose Mary Woods, said that she might have caused a 4- or 5-minute interruption in the tape when she accidentally pushed a wrong button while receiving a telephone call, but claimed that she could not have erased a segment so long.

She noted that while she was at Camp David reviewing the tapes, the President dropped by briefly and monitored a few excerpts, "pushing the buttons back and forth." Some have wondered if Nixon himself could have created the gap in the tape; Nixon's White House Chief of Staff Alexander Haig conjectured during his appearance before the federal court that "perhaps some sinister force had come in and applied the other energy source and taken care of the information on that tape."

Richard Nixon may have been the only man who knew if the two-toned hum was the result of some "sinister force" or the purposeful action of a man fighting for personal vindication and his own political survival. He carried the secret with him when he died in 1994.

## THE REAL DEEP THROAT?

**PIECES OF THE PUZZLE ▼**

Some of the legions of journalists and Beltway observers who've speculated on the identity of Deep Throat have noted that the *Washington Post's* investigation of the Watergate misdeeds had much in common with the course of the investigation by the FBI. One of the more credible guesses about Deep Throat's identity is L. Patrick Gray III, who took over as acting director of the FBI in 1972 after J. Edgar Hoover's death, just a month before the Watergate break-in. Gray had much in common with Woodward's description of Deep Throat's temperament and lifestyle; he also lived only four blocks from Woodward, so he could have swung by easily to look for the flower-pot signal.

Was L. Patrick Gray III Deep Throat? Woodward has said that he will most likely disclose the identity of the informant upon his death, meaning that this long-standing secret probably won't last for another generation.

**A PROTEST POSTER SHOWS THE COST OF WATERGATE TO MANY CAREERS.**

# The CIA and the KGB

**Some of these two agencies' activities have seemed not so much real as the stuff of spy movies.**

THE CIA BEGAN IN 1947 AS THE POSTWAR equivalent of the first U.S. intelligence agency, the Office of Strategic Services. In the Soviet Union, czars had long used secret police to keep the populace in line, a practice that was eagerly adopted by the Communist government. The KGB was officially disbanded in 1991, with the collapse of the Soviet Union. The CIA is still active today.

The Soviet secret police began its life as Vecheka, known colloquially as the Cheka, in December 1917, just after the 1917 Bolshevik Revolution. Thereafter, it went through a series of shake-ups, as Soviet leadership and political winds changed its name, its loyalties, and some of its staff. It was known by a number of acronyms, finally becoming the KGB following Joseph Stalin's death in 1953, and remaining so until its dissolution. The Soviet secret police combined the duties of the FBI and the CIA in the United States, working as the Soviet Union's internal law-enforcement agency as well as its foreign intelligence gatherer. The Soviet policing system was also intended to prevent internal dissent and to spread propaganda both internally and in foreign countries.

It was as the NKVD that the agency first became notorious for its savagery. Under the guiding hands of Nikolay I. Yezkov and Lavrenty P. Beria, Stalin's brutal and bloody purges were carried out, in which hundreds of thousands of Soviet citizens were imprisoned, executed, or assassinated. The NKVD's most notorious murder was that of Bolshevik leader and Stalin rival Leon Trotsky, whose skull was crushed by an ice pick outside of the Mexico City home of his friends, the artists Frida Kahlo and Diego Rivera.

Beria quickly rose through the Soviet bureaucracy, becoming known for his cruelty and his loyalty to Stalin. He is widely credited with developing the USSR's network of forced-labor camps, and became known for his skill in torturing enemies of the state and in falsifying evidence. By 1946, he had become a member of the Politburo, the ruling body of the USSR and second in power only to Stalin. Upon Stalin's death in 1953, Beria assumed a position of still greater power as first deputy premier, but was himself purged. By the end of the year he was convicted of treason and executed.

### BERIA'S EXIT

After Beria's death, the agency moved in a new direction. Although it sought to soften its violent methods, it continued to grow, developing a large network of informers and agents both inside and outside the Soviet Union. Under KGB Director (later General Secretary) Yuri Andropov, the agency sought to promote itself as legitimate while still expanding its influence to unprecedented levels.

At the height of its power in the 1970s and 1980s, the KGB was the largest organization of its kind in history. This changed when Mikhail Gorbachev came to power in the 1980s, promoting a new openness in Soviet society. After the collapse of the Soviet Union and the subsequent release of secret documents, it was found that the KGB had aided and funded rev-

AN INTELLIGENCE SPECIALIST LEANS THROUGH THE DOORWAY OF THE OPERATIONS CENTER AT CIA HEADQUARTERS IN LANGLEY, VIRGINIA. THE CIA WAS THE AMERICAN COUNTERPART TO THE SOVIET UNION'S KGB, WHOSE EMBLEM WAS THE SHIELD AND SWORD (ABOVE).

olutionary movements around the world, the United States Communist Party included.

## THE CIA STORY

While the various incarnations of the KGB played a part in perpetuating war and undermining democracy around the world, many feel that the agency's counterpart in America, the CIA, had almost as much to answer for. Created by Congress with the passage of the National Security Act, the CIA was intended to be America's peacetime intelligence-gathering agency. The CIA kept the U.S. out of harm's way in numerous cases, and it quickly grew to become a major Cold War player. While such an agency is essential to national interest and most citizens enthusiastically support it, others came to believe that the CIA was a tool of powerful American industrial interests who wanted access to Third World resources.

FORMER CIA OFFI-CER ALDRICH AMES (RIGHT) IS SHOWN AFTER RECEIVING A SENTENCE OF LIFE IN PRISON IN 1994. HIS CRIME? SELLING SECRETS TO THE SOVIET UNION IN EXCHANGE FOR AN ESTIMATED $1.5 MILLION.

In 1953, the agency successfully over-threw the government of Iran, which had nationalized that country's oil industry. The following year, a CIA-backed coup toppled Guatemala's presi-dent, who had just annexed 234,000 acres of land from the United Fruit Company.

The agency received major scrutiny in 1961, after the disastrous Bay of Pigs invasion. In March 1960, President Eisenhower approved a CIA plan to train and arm 1,400 anti-Castro Cuban exiles, with the intention of invading Cuba. President Kennedy continued that plan, and the exiles invaded on April 17, 1961. With-in three days, the invasion was crushed.

The CIA also had a major role in two events that divided the nation like none had since the Civil War: Vietnam and Watergate. During the Eisenhower administration, the CIA had sent agents to train and arm the South Vietnamese. By 1972, with the unpopular Vietnam War winding down, Washington, D.C., police caught five burglars breaking into the Democ-ratic National Committee's offices in the Watergate apartment complex. Three of the burglars were veterans of the Bay of Pigs inva-sion, and one, James McCord, carried a phone book with information for E. Howard Hunt, the CIA agent who had led the invasion.

### A STRING OF SCANDALS

In the ensuing scandal, corruption within the Nixon administration was exposed, including, among many other things, collusion between the FBI and CIA to suppress evidence; secret bombings of Cambodia; and the revelation that International Telegraph and Telephone had offered the CIA $1 million to aid in the over-throw of Chilean President Salvador Allende. In 1975, Congress bent to public demand and investigated the CIA, revealing that they had dosed test subjects with LSD throughout the 1950s, and that they had used biological war-fare against Cuba in the early 1970s.

But there were more scandals to come. In 1984, it was revealed that the CIA had deliber-ately exaggerated Soviet military expenditures since 1975. And in 1986, the famous Iran-Con-tra scandal broke. CIA director William J. Casey and other U.S. intelligence officials appointed by President Ronald Reagan were found to be selling arms to Iran in order to ille-gally fund the Nicaraguan Contras.

It was after the Cold War, however, that the agency received one of its greatest embarrass-ments: the highly-publicized Aldrich Ames spy scandal. Ames is reported to have compro-mised American intelligence security more than any other spy in history. From 1986 to the early 1990s, Ames sold secrets to the Soviets for an estimated $1.5 million; what's more, he flashed his money around conspicuously, buy-ing a $540,000 home and a $65,000 Jaguar—both in cash—while claiming a government salary of $69,843. CIA director James Woolsey was forced to resign when it was revealed that he had not substantially punished the agents who had let Ames go unobserved.

# Operation Mongoose

**FIDEL CASTRO
LIGHTS A CIGAR IN
1959. AFTER ASSUM-
ING POWER IN CUBA,
HE PROMISED MOD-
ERATE REFORMS.**

Among the covert operations that the CIA arranged during the 20th century, Operation Mongoose must take the prize for peculiarity. Begun by an administration in the grip of cold war paranoia, the aim of the operation was to disrupt, defame, and to ultimately depose Fidel Castro's regime in Cuba.

Castro came to power in 1959 with the promise that he would reform the 1940 constitution and undertake moderate reforms. But he had grander plans. He nationalized Cuba's private commerce and industry, instituted massive land reforms, and took over American agricultural estates. American officials were deeply disturbed. Enlivened by Cold War rhetoric and ideology, they had come to see the insidious spread of Communism as their main postwar concern. Castro's Cuba was the first Communist regime in the Western Hemisphere, and it was feared that he might wield influence over other Latin American countries. In 1960, Castro signed a trade agreement with the Soviet Union, confirming all the worst American fears. In January 1961, the United States broke diplomatic ties with Cuba.

## THE BAY OF PIGS AFTERMATH

The controversy that ensued after the 1961 Bay of Pigs invasion convinced the Kennedy administration that covert acts were a far more manageable means of eroding Castro's power than invasion, and Operation Mongoose was inaugurated. The operation was headed up by Brigadier General Edward G. Lansdale, who was famous for his propaganda warfare tactics in the Philippines. A firm believer in psychological operations (what the CIA termed PSYOP), his initial contributions to the cause were inspired. The proposed operations included such schemes as convincing the Cuban people that Castro was the anti-Christ, and equally bizarre activities.

During the Cuban Missile Crisis of October 1962 Operation Mongoose was dismantled, but it put no end to the group's shenanigans. The CIA continued their PSYOP planning, and in 1963, Lt.

Colonel James Patchell conceived of a new plan to topple Castro—the invention of a mythical anti-Castro rebel, whom Patchell decided to call "The Fighting Friend." Patchell believed that as the imaginary friend's fame grew, other anti-Castro rebels would be drawn to his cause, and eventually, when victory was certain, one of them would claim his identity.

None of these ideas were ever enacted. Anti-Castro radio was the main form of covert action practiced by the United States. But these broadcasts failed to foment anything close to an uprising, perhaps because of their cryptic messages. During the Bay of Pigs invasion, the American-based Radio Free Cuba repeatedly issued this rousing call to arms: "The fish will rise very soon."

**FIDEL CASTRO
AND NIKITA
KHRUSHCHEV
EMBRACE IN 1960.
THEIR ALLIANCE
SCARED THE U.S.**

# The Fall of the Soviet Empire

### The collapse of the USSR left Eastern Europe and Russia in complete and utter disarray. What contributed to the downfall?

JOSEPH STALIN (ABOVE) HELD THE USSR TOGETHER WITH HIS BRUTAL TACTICS. BY 1991, THE UNION HAD COME APART AS THE REPUBLICS DECLARED INDEPENDENCE. AT LEFT, CITIZENS OF RIGA, LATVIA, TOPPLE A STATUE OF LENIN.

AMERICANS HAVE BECOME inured to the instability of empires. When William Jefferson Clinton, the 42nd president, said in his final State of the Union address that the sun of America was still rising, Americans nodded their heads. Yet throughout the world, the 20th century told a different story. Nations fell apart, empires crumbled, new nations were born. The flux so unknown to our citizenry was the rule of life across much of the globe. Certainly the most affecting of these collapses was the fall of the Soviet Empire.

In 1917, Vladimir I. Lenin's Bolshevik party (Bolshevik means "majority") overthrew the czarist regime and took control of Russia, believing themselves to be the vanguard of a world revolution that would take power from the hands of the wealthy elite and scatter it among the working class, thereby doing away with the great social evil of class struggle. Seventy-four years later, on December 8, 1991, Russian President Boris Yeltsin declared that the Union of Soviet Socialist Republics no longer existed, bringing an end to decades of

**AT A 1988 MOSCOW SUMMIT, MIKHAIL GORBACHEV AND RONALD REAGAN INTRODUCED REFORMS THAT PAVED THE WAY FOR THE END OF THE USSR (ABOVE). GORBACHEV WOULD RESIGN AS THE LAST GENERAL SECRETARY OF THE SOVIET UNION IN DECEMBER, 1991. THE BERLIN WALL (BELOW) HAD BEGUN TO COME DOWN IN 1989.**

repression, fear, violence, and turmoil. Just what happened to the great Lenin's vision?

### REPRESSION UNDER STALIN

The collapse of the USSR had its roots in an insensitive, confused, and often cruel foreign policy. For one thing, the Bolsheviks had been wrong about the inevitability of the world revolution. The transition to a socialist state was not easy, and in many cases was an act of pure force. Yet Lenin firmly believed that the ultimate aim of socialism could not be achieved in a single country, and his policy of expansionism was dutifully picked up by Joseph Stalin following Lenin's death in 1924.

Stalin's rule did more to doom the Soviet empire than any other Russian leader's. He was callously brutal. Under his guidance the USSR became a place of fear and repression, where any dissent from the party line was met with arrest, exile, or execution. In the 1930s, while attempting to enforce collectivism in Ukraine, Stalin created a famine that wiped out millions of peasants who had refused to give up their small land holdings to the Soviet state.

Following World War II, the Soviet empire expanded into what became known as the Second Empire. The countries of Poland, Hungary, Czechoslovakia, Romania, and Bulgaria were all brought under Soviet control, as well as East Germany. It was the difficulty of maintaining socialism in these states that would eventually lead to the collapse of the Soviet Union.

## THE FALL'S AFTERMATH

The breakup of the Soviet Union left the entire region of Eastern Europe and Russia in disarray. Attempting to ensure the interdependence, and thus unity, of its many republics, the USSR had seen to it that no one republic was self-sufficient. Thus, in the whole country, the only plant that manufactured light meters was located in Lithuania; the only one that made condoms was in Azerbaijan. Furthermore, the divvying up of military equipment caused

a tremendous headache, as the military districts drawn up by the Kremlin did not corre-

**TENDRILS OF TIME** ▼

spond to republic boundaries.

Far more difficult, however, was the large-scale

attempt to revamp governments that for more than 40 years had been mere rubber stamps for centralized Soviet policy. Spreading nationalism complicated matters further. During Stalin's rule, millions of ethnic minorities had been deported all over the country. As the republics became independent, the question of who comprised a nation and where the lines were to be drawn flared up into numerous civil wars, conflicts that continue to this day.

After Stalin's death in 1953, East Berliners, angered by a new Soviet work quota, revolted. Their uprising was squashed by Russian tanks, and 25 people died. Such violent, repressive events were soon to become the norm.

The Second Empire did not necessarily want to live under socialism; it was imposed from outside. In 1956, former Hungarian Prime Minister Irme Nagy's independence movement was crushed by Soviet military force. Nagy was executed. By 1959 more than two million people had fled the Soviet Union through Berlin. Fearing that the exodus would continue, the USSR erected the Berlin Wall, citing protection from a possible Western attack as their motive. Few believed this excuse, of course, and many inside and outside the country began to see the Soviet Union as a foolish tyrant: What kind of country, they asked, needs to build a wall to keep its citizens from leaving?

## GORBACHEV AND GLASNOST

By 1979, Russia was constantly quelling uprisings throughout its empire. Though it was none too popular with the nations of the Second Empire, Soviet policy was still largely unquestioned by Russian citizens themselves, and the climate of fear created by Stalin's regime permeated Russian society. But all of that would change as a result of the 1979 war in Afghanistan. By the time the war had ended, 15,000 Russians had died. It was both a domestic and international disaster for the USSR.

In 1985, Mikhail Gorbachev took over a country that was obviously falling apart; throughout Russian society, dissatisfaction and apathy were spreading like a virus. In all of the republics, years of outrage and resistance were nearing a climax. Gorbachev attempted to ease some of these tensions by implementing his policy of glasnost, or openness, which cleared the way for some dissent to be expressed throughout the republics. Without the element of fear controlling these nations, there was little to keep them from expressing their long-standing dissatisfaction.

In the Baltic states of Estonia, Latvia, and Lithuania, anti-Soviet popular fronts formed. Similar movements took hold in Poland and Hungary, where proponents of independence were most outspoken. In the dramatic events of 1989, East and West Berliners alike began physically tearing down the hated wall. In

Prague, demonstrators flooded the streets, and by the year's end, Vaclav Havel, a writer imprisoned as a dissident at the beginning of the year, was president of a new, democratic Czechoslovakia. Bulgaria and Romania followed suit.

All that was left was for Communism to fall in Russia herself. Throughout 1989 and 1990, strikes and demonstrations were waged all across the country. Gorbachev made some modest attempts at reform that appeased no one. In August 1991, led by the State Committee for the State of Emergency, a coup was staged in Moscow. But after three days, it was clear that the coup had no popular support.

The coup's leaders backed down, but the damage had been done. Several days later, Gorbachev resigned as general secretary. In December, Yeltsin declared that the Soviet Union was no more—and over the Kremlin, the Soviet flag was replaced with the three-stripe white, blue, and red of the Russian flag.

AFTER AN ATTEMPTED COUP IN AUGUST 1991, RUSSIAN PRESIDENT BORIS YELTSIN HELD A VICTORY RALLY IN MOSCOW. THAT DECEMBER, YELTSIN DECLARED THAT THE SOVIET UNION WAS NO MORE.

# What Brought Down
# TWA
# Flight 800
# ?

U.S. COAST GUARD MON 1

**After this airplane blew apart over the sea, the universal horror escalated as a lingering question remained unanswered: Why?**

THE SEARCH FOR WRECKAGE OF TWA 800 IN THE DEPTHS OF THE ATLANTIC OFF LONG ISLAND WAS DIFFICULT AND DRAMATIC—AND CONDUCTED UNDER THE EYE OF ANXIOUSLY WATCHFUL MEDIA. ABOVE, A COAST GUARD LIFE RAFT USED TO GATHER DEBRIS. THE LARGER PIECES (OPPOSITE) WERE RAISED THROUGH THE COMBINED USE OF SURFACE AND SUBMARINE EQUIPMENT.

ON JULY 17, 1996, AS TWA 800 ASCENDED FROM New York's John F. Kennedy Airport—in a flight bound for Paris—the flight captain remarked off-handedly how the plane was climbing up to its coasting altitude like "a homesick angel." Only a few minutes later, at 8:31 P.M., just southeast of Long Island, the Boeing 747 exploded, killing all 230 on board.

There had been no sign of difficulty before the explosion. The tape of the voice recorder at its end captures only a brief burst of sound before disconnecting. After 17 months of deliberation—the country's longest and most expensive probe into an aviation disaster—the National Transportation Safety Board (NTSB) and the FBI offered an explanation that left more than a few lingering questions.

### A STORM OF SPECULATION

TWA 800 has become the most mysterious and contentious air disaster in America's history. Though early speculation suggested the catastrophe could be the result of a bomb or a missile, the U.S. government's official investigation soon abandoned these theories, citing a lack of evidence. Public hearings held by the National Transportation Safety Board in Baltimore in December, 1997, argued instead that the explosion was a rare mechanical failure that could be attributed to a build-up in the plane's center gas tank of dangerous vapors being ignited by an errant spark.

Records reveal that when the aircraft arrived at JFK from Athens, Greece, the center tank was drained of fuel. For the trip to Paris, the plane was to rely solely on the gas tanks in the wings. Investigators noted that the plane had been idling, with its air-conditioning on, for nearly two hours above a hot tarmac. The air-conditioning system on the Boeing 747 sits directly below the middle gas tank, and investigators suggested that the heat produced from this system could have vaporized the small amount of gas above, leading to a combustible mixture in the tank. The only thing needed to turn these vapors into flame, the NTSB argued, would be an electrical impulse. A panel of aviation experts was not able to provide any definitive source for that spark, but conjectured that faulty wiring or even static electricity could have done the work.

Among the strongest critics of the government's conclusions were several people who witnessed TWA 800's explosion from the Long Island coast, the water, or the air. The NTSB had noted in its Witness Group Factual Report that 183 witnesses had observed a streak of light that evening before the explosion. Of these 183, "102 gave information about the origin of the streak. Six said the streak originated from the air, and 96 said that it originated from the surface." James Kallstrom, the FBI's assistant director in charge of the TWA

THE DEBRIS FROM TWA 800 WAS PAINSTAKINGLY LAID OUT, AND THEN THE PLANE WAS RECONSTRUCTED IN AN OLD GRUMMAN HANGAR IN THE NEW YORK TOWN OF CALVERTON. MORE THAN 90 PERCENT OF THE AIRCRAFT WAS RECOVERED—BUT NOT ENOUGH TO INDICATE DEFINITIVELY THE CAUSE OF THE DISASTER.

investigation, also conceded early in his investigation that there was a good number of "highly credible witnesses" who observed something resembling a missile. "We do have information that there was something in the sky," Kallstrom said. "A number of people have seen it. A number of people have described it similarly. It was ascending."

Lou Desyron, who was on the Long Island coast on the night of the crash, told *ABC World News Sunday* on July 21, 1996: "We saw what appeared to be a flare going straight up. As a matter of fact, we thought it was from a boat. It was a bright reddish-orange color . . . once it went into flames, I knew it wasn't a flare." Accounts like that challenged the government's position in interviews.

### SUSPICION OF FRIENDLY FIRE

Though some had conjectured that a missile could have been fired by a terrorist with a handheld launcher, Pierre Salinger, former press secretary under President John F. Kennedy and an ex-ABC News correspondent, claimed to have obtained evidence that the United States Navy was responsible for a "friendly-fire" accident. Department of Defense spokesman Kenneth Bacon originally denied reports that there were military exercises on July 17 in restricted zone W-105, located just a few miles south of the TWA 800 flight path. But in November 1997, the Navy conceded that there had been a military exercise on July 17 in W-106; officials would not, however, disclose the exercise's nature.

Several blurry photos seem to support the "friendly-fire" theory. Foremost among these is a snapshot taken by a Long Island secretary, Linda Kabot, at a Republican fund raising event held at an oyster bar in East Quogue, Long Island, near the time of the disaster. In the background of one picture, which takes in the sky above Shinnecock Bay, there is a dimly-seen, elongated flying object with a tail of light behind it. Though some have suggested that this is a picture of the missile that downed TWA 800, more have remarked that the object resembles a Navy drone—a fake target with a taillight—which is towed far behind a ship and is often used in missile tests. Could this have been the intended target of the errant missile? The FBI said that the image in the Kabot photo was only "an unknown type of aircraft."

The FBI has also been unable to account for one ship on the water that was about 2.9 nautical miles from the position of Flight 800 when it exploded. The boat has been called the "thirty-knot track" because it continued to travel at approximately 30 knots in a south-southwesterly direction, away from the accident, until it was out of radar range.

### MISSILE, OR FUSELAGE?

The official video animation of the disaster, sponsored by the NTSB and the CIA, suggests that the "missile" that so many saw was actually the rear part of the fuselage, which they claim rose a couple of thousand feet after separation from the plane's nose before descending and exploding. Several eyewitnesses contended that the video animation did not resemble what they saw, and Boeing quickly issued a press release disassociating themselves from the animated reenactment. Others have expressed wonder that an open fuselage, which would have all the poor aerodynamic qualities of an open cup, could climb as high as the official account maintains.

Many of the mysteries of the TWA 800 tragedy may never be resolved. With the lack of conclusive evidence, there have been many theories, some far more unlikely than the specter of a bomb or missile fire. No matter what the cause, there is the haunting incongruity of the scene in Linda Kabot's photo, with a carefree party in the foreground and a strange object, possibly connected to the TWA 800 disaster, crossing the night sky in the background.

# The Captain's Last Words

While most experts heard nothing unusual in the cockpit voice recording of TWA 800's short flight, Harvard humanities professor Elaine Scarry, in her article "The Fall of TWA 800: The Possibility of Electromagnetic Interference," suggests that the cabin crew's words may have had hints of what was to come. The author speculates that TWA 800 might have been a victim of a

one day comes to be held responsible, we may listen again to that voice recording and hear in the pilots' words the first tremors of the event. Registered there may be the two problems Colonel Charles Quisenberry identified as the classic signature of electromagnetic interference: sudden interruption in fuel flow and false instruction to the control surfaces on the wing flaps or rudder.

called trimming: "Somewhere in here I better trim this thing (in/up)." His co-pilot does not understand or hear (he says "Huh?") and the pilot repeats: "Some place in here I better find out where this thing's trimmed."

Trimming is a routine process, but the captain's words—"Somewhere in here . . . some place in here. . . I better trim this thing. . . I better find out where this thing's trimmed"—suggest that the plane was not handling with the split-second responsiveness the pilot was seeking. The time interval in each of these interactions is small—only seconds. But just as one would be alarmed if when turning the steering wheel of a car there were a three-second pause before the car began to turn, so the pilot's sentences suggest the expectation of greater agility from the plane.

THE "BLACK BOX" VOICE AND FLIGHT RECORDERS OF FLIGHT TWA 800 HELD FEW CLUES.

triangulation of what are called High Intensity Radio Fields, which were produced by the ten military transports in the area, which jammed the 747's electrical equipment and could have led to an electrical incident and the explosion.

The cockpit voice recording on Flight 800 contains, as has been widely observed, no indication of the disaster awaiting the plane's passengers and crew. But if electromagnetic interference

One minute and fifty seconds before all electricity ceases on TWA 800, the captain comments on the fuel flow: "Look at that crazy fuel flow indicator there on number four." Eight seconds later he continues to look at the indicator, directing the first officer's attention to it: "See that?" Twelve seconds later he expresses the sense that the wing flaps are not in the right position, and he now works to adjust them, an action

## "POWER'S SET"

The same is true of the conversation that begins 30 seconds later, less than a minute before the recordings stop. Boston Control Center tells the pilots to climb from 13,000 to 15,000 feet: "TWA 800, climb and maintain one five thousand." The captain issues an instruction to the second officer to adjust the plane's power level, "Climb thrust," and the first officer recites back to Boston the words they have received: "TWA 800 heavy climb and maintain one five thousand leaving one three thousand."

Now the captain speaks as though the second officer has not yet responded (that is, the plane feels to the captain as if it has not yet received an increase in power): "Ollie. . . Climb thrust." And three seconds later "Climb to one five thousand." The second officer assures him that the command has already been carried out: "Power's set." Here the voices cease.

# The
## Death of
# Princess Diana

**What exactly happened on the eve of this beloved figure's tragic accident. . . and who is to blame?**

**PRINCESS DIANA IS PHOTOGRAPHED IN LONDON IN AUGUST 1996, ONE YEAR BEFORE THE CRASH THAT TOOK HER LIFE. FOR YEARS, PAPARAZZI FOLLOWED DIANA'S EVERY MOVE.**

IT WAS JUST AFTER MIDNIGHT ON AUGUST 31, 1997, when Diana, Princess of Wales, and her companion Dodi Fayed left the Ritz Hotel in Paris, en route to Fayed's house in the city's 16th district. At about 12:15 A.M., the couple left the hotel in their black Mercedes limousine. At roughly the same time, a Range Rover departed from the front entrance in an attempt to decoy the waiting pack of nearly 40 paparazzi. According to one observer, the Range Rover was trailed by the photographers, but the paparazzi were soon tipped off that the couple was not inside. Half of the group, some on motorcycle, split off to follow the Mercedes.

Diana's limousine was driven by Henri Paul, assistant security chief at the Ritz, which was owned by Fayed's father. Trying to evade the paparazzi, the limousine reached speeds of 90 mph as it came down the Place de la Concorde, police later estimated. Paul had left most of the photographers in the dust, but a few cars and motorcycles kept up as he entered a bend at the entrance to an underpass under the Alma bridge—a spot that had already seen two fatal car accidents in recent years.

At this point Paul lost control of the Mercedes, police later concluded, possibly just seconds after striking a white Fiat Uno thought to have been carrying several paparazzi. The limousine smashed head-on into a concrete post in the center divider, and then slammed into the right wall of the underpass. It took 90 minutes to cut through the roof of the limousine and free the occupants. Fayed and the car's driver, Henri Paul, had been killed instantly. Diana had suffered head injuries and was bleeding from the chest, but ambulance workers were able to revive her at the scene.

### A DEADLY CONVERGENCE

The Princess was rushed to the intensive care unit at a nearby hospital. By the time Diana arrived, her heart had stopped beating. French surgeons quickly opened her chest and closed a wound in the left ventricle of her heart, then massaged her heart for two hours. But Diana had suffered massive internal bleeding, and at 4 A.M., the Princess was pronounced dead.

Blame for the crash immediately focused on the paparazzi, with seven photographers detained by police at the site of the incident. One photographer was attacked by onlookers at the crash site as he tried to take pictures of the wrecked vehicle, and a public outcry rose up against the paparazzi. Witnesses told investigators that they had seen two cars pass the limousine just before the crash. Brian Anderson, a California businessman who was riding in a taxi just in front of Diana's car, told CBS News that the Mercedes was being closely followed by two motorcycles, one of which "was driving aggressively and dangerously."

But when tests revealed that Paul, the limousine driver, had had a blood alcohol level three times the legal limit at the time of the crash, the investigation shifted away from the paparazzi. Tests also showed that Paul had Prozac, the antidepressant, and tiapride, a prescription drug used to treat alcoholism and prevent aggression, in his blood. Both medications can cause drowsiness, impaired judgment, and loss of concentration when used with alcohol. Paul was seen by witnesses drinking a couple of glasses of French liqueur at the Ritz Hotel, and then consuming whiskey at a nearby bar.

Others defended the driver. The bodyguard who survived the crash with a smashed jaw, Trevor Rees-Jones, told investigators that he did not remember the crash itself, but that when he got in the Mercedes, driver Paul "seemed fine." Several of Paul's friends and associates spoke out on his behalf, calling him "very serious" and "calm and very competent."

During the course of a two-year probe into the cause of the accident, other possibilities arose. A chauffeur who regularly drove the limousine reported having had persistent problems with the brakes. "You had to know it well to drive it safely," the chauffeur said of the car; Paul had never driven it before. Clouding matters further, a former French marine came for-

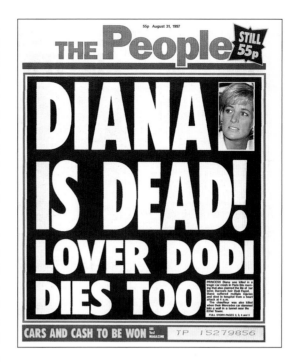

DIANA'S TRAGIC CAR CRASH SHOCKED MILLIONS THE WORLD OVER. THE PRINCESS'S FAMILY (BOTTOM LEFT) WALKS OUTSIDE WESTMINSTER ABBEY DURING THE FUNERAL PROCESSION ON SEPTEMBER 6, 1997.

ward and claimed he was speeding in a gray Ford just a few feet behind the limousine when the crash occurred, and that his own erratic driving may have contributed to the accident.

But officials concluded that just one man was to blame: Henri Paul. Announcing his decision in 1999, a French judge dismissed the charges against the paparazzi and declared that "The driver of the car was inebriated . . . and not in a position to maintain control of the vehicle." But not everyone was satisfied with the ruling, and it may never be possible to know what role, if any, overzealous photographers played in the crash that took the life of a princess.

## A FATHER'S THEORY

At least one man publicly challenged the judge's ruling. Mohamed Al Fayed, Dodi's father and owner of the upscale London department store Harrods, maintained through a spokesperson that Paul was not at fault. More than a year earlier, Al Fayed had told British media that he was "99.9 percent certain" the fatal crash was not accidental, but was part of a conspiracy to prevent his son

**VIEW FROM THE FRINGE** ▼

from marrying Diana. Al Fayed claimed that Diana and Dodi were engaged, and that while he didn't know who had engineered the crash, some people—including many in the "British establishment"— were happy the couple died. Buckingham Palace expressed dismay at Al Fayed's theory, saying it was "causing a lot of stress to the family," and rejecting the claim that the couple was engaged.

# UFOs
# & Alien Abductions

## How real are the encounters people swear they have had with extraterrestrial beings?

UFOs AND ALLEGED ALIEN ABDUCTIONS HAVE spawned a virtual mythology. It all began in 1947, when the public was gripped by stories of UFO sightings in the Cascade Mountains of Washington State and, then, at Roswell, New Mexico. Could they mean, people wondered, that aliens were in contact with the earth?

Reports of alien abductions began with the story of Barney and Betty Hill, a couple from New Hampshire. On September 19, 1961, according to the Hills, a group of humanlike figures with gray skin and slanted eyes abducted them from their car, taking them aboard a wingless aircraft. The strange beings placed the Hills on an examination table and told the two not to worry—they were just running a few tests. Betty later claimed a long needle was inserted into her navel; Barney claimed a sample of his sperm was taken. Long after the incident, a circle of warts appeared on Barney's thigh in a place where he said an alien instrument had probed him.

When the Hills were returned to their car, they remembered nothing of their abduction. It was only a few years later that they pieced together their story, after undergoing months of hypnosis to recover their memory.

### OF THE MEDIA BORN?

This kind of story has since been repeated several times, although with variations. The alleged victims often report scars from wounds they do not remember, and most report a feeling of "lost time," which they believe coincides with their abductions.

Believers in alien abduction argue that so many people reporting so many similar experiences cannot be explained by mere chance. Indeed, a coincidence of this magnitude seems highly improbable. But the phenomenon can be explained without a theory as grand as covert extraterrestrial kidnapping: The Hills' story was widely publicized. Books were written about the couple's adventure, and the Hills even worked with an artist to create a composite sketch of the alien species they saw. As the number of abduction stories multiplied, media attention increased, circulating an alien visage and an abduction scenario that soon became widespread. Given the lack of physical evidence suggesting alien contact, media bombardment seems a more likely source for this suspiciously formulaic scenario.

### A PROFESSOR'S VIEWS

Despite the shaky origins of alien abduction stories, there arose a small industry of abductee therapists who claim they can help their clients uncover repressed memories of alien abductions. And while most people remain doubtful, their skepticism may have been shaken when Dr. John Mack—a psychiatrist on the faculty at Harvard Medical School—professed belief in his patients' abductions in the book *Abductions* (1995) and in numerous television interviews.

Mack proposed a doctrine that "the power or intensity with which something is felt" is a guide to whether it is true. Any credence given Mack was compromised, however, when Boston writer and researcher Donna Bassett debunked the doctor's practices by going undercover as one of his hypnotherapy clients. According to Bassett, Mack gave her a brochure about alien abduction to read

THE U.S. AIR FORCE HOLDS THAT TEST DUMMIES (ABOVE), DROPPED FROM HIGH-ALTITUDE BALLOONS, HAVE BEEN MISTAKEN AS ALIENS. IN THE MEANTIME, A FILM STILL BEING SHOWN IN ROSWELL, N.M., CLAIMS THE DEAD EXTRATERRESTRIAL EXHIBITED IS REAL (BELOW). ABOVE RIGHT: BELIEVERS IN UFOS CLAIM THIS PHOTOGRAPH SHOWS AN OBJECT FROM OUTER SPACE OVER ZANESVILLE, OHIO, IN 1967.

before their sessions even began, and later asked leading questions during her "hypnosis," encouraging her to remember alien abduction experiences she had never had.

## SPATES OF SIGHTINGS

As for UFOs, an extraterrestrial hypothesis hardly seems the most likely explanation for this phenomenon. Roughly 90 percent of UFOs are immediately identifiable by scientists. Most people honestly report what they see, but what they see typically turns out to be heavenly bodies, atmospheric phenomena such as UFO-shaped clouds or ball lightning, man-made objects (including space equipment reentering the atmosphere and high-altitude balloons), or even birds reflecting weather

**IS THIS AN ALIEN?**

**Riddle of bodies filmed after 'spacecraft' crash 50 years ago**

searchlights. The remaining ten percent could be the result of some unrecognized combination of those things, bad reporting, optical illusions, or hoaxes—all of which are more plausible than alien spacecraft defying the laws of physics as we now understand them.

Then there is what could be called the mother of all UFO legends: the Roswell Incident. According to one source, that story began in June 14, 1947, when New Mexico ranch foreman W.W. Brazel found some debris—heavily waxed paper, metal-foil strips, and tape bearing a floral pattern—strewn across a remote corner of the ranch. Ten days later the UFO craze began—not because of Brazel, but because of a civilian airplane pilot named Kenneth Arnold, who told reporters he had seen nine strange objects flying at 1,200 miles per hour over the Cascade Mountains.

Arnold's story soon led to hundreds of "flying saucer" sightings across the United States. As soon as Brazel heard of the sightings, he turned his discovery over to an Air Force official, who immediately issued a press release stating that a flying saucer had been captured near the town of Roswell. A higher ranking officer soon issued a second statement apologizing for the first release. The case was closed on the Roswell Incident until 1978.

It was in that year that UFO researcher Stanton Friedman proclaimed the incident a "cosmic Watergate." Friedman, who had a physics background, was the first of many reporters to interview New Mexico residents who told similar stories of finding tiny corpses buried in the wreckage of what they believed was a spacecraft. After this, questions about what happened in 1947 refused to be put to rest.

## LAST WORD ON ROSWELL?

In the 1990s, multiple investigations were carried out by the federal government. One report stated that in 1947 the Air Force was working on a classified project known as "Mogul," in which it launched acoustical equipment in balloons, hoping to monitor Soviet nuclear tests. The vessels were made from materials that matched the debris found by Brazel—including a tape with "flower-like designs."

Another report found that, in the early 1950s, the Air Force had conducted impact tests using dummies that matched eyewitness accounts of small corpses. Since these witnesses made no mention of alien bodies until 1978, it is quite possible they no longer remembered the precise year in which they viewed the "corpses." It could be that UFOlogists like Friedman were responsible for connecting their stories with the "crash landing" of 1947.

Although some people wrote off the government's findings as an attempt at a cover-up, the U.S. government's explanation does have some hard evidence to back it up. That is something believers in alien abduction and UFOs have yet to present to a skeptical world.

NEW MEXICO MIGHT BE SAID TO BE THE PLACE WHERE THE UFO CRAZE GOT ITS START, WITH THE TOWN OF ROSWELL THE MOST FAMOUS UFO SITE IN THE U.S. NEARBY, LIGHT-HEARTED ROAD SIGNS WARN OF EXTRATERRESTRIAL CROSSINGS AND STRANGE AIRCRAFT.

## MODERN DAY DEMONS?

In his 1997 book *The Demon-Haunted World,* Carl Sagan sees in the UFO phenomenon a link to the demons, witches, fairies, and ghosts of the ancient world. In the Middle Ages, many people believed in demonic seducers who came from the skies (an incubus was a demon who seduced women, and a succubus, men). "There is no spaceship in these [incubus and succubus] stories," says Sagan. "But most of the central ele-

**TENDRILS OF TIME** ▼

ments of the alien abductions account are present, including sexually obsessive non-humans who live in the sky, walk through walls, communicate telepathically, and perform breeding experiments on the human species."

Sagan also quotes the folklorist Thomas E. Bullard, who wrote in 1989 that "abduction reports sound like rewrites of older supernatural encounter traditions, with aliens serving the functional

roles of divine beings." Bullard concludes: "Science may have evicted ghosts and witches from our beliefs, but it just as quickly filled the vacancy with aliens having the same functions. Only the extraterrestrial outer trappings are new. All the fear and the psychological dramas for dealing with it seem simply to have found their way home again, where it is business as usual in the legendary realm where things go bump in the night."

# PART 7

# MYSTERIES FOR THE MILLENNIUM

Looking forward to 3000 and beyond, we wonder what the future holds. Will the world change more or less than it has since the Dark Ages? Some may say the world has already changed so much and advanced so far that we will begin to slow down in the next millennium. But others see it differently, saying that the pace of change seems to be accelerating. In truth, we cannot reasonably predict where technology will take us in 10 years, let alone 100 or 1,000. Will print become an artifact of the 20th century, replaced entirely by electronic media? Will natural cycles continue to sustain human life, or will humanity's presence doom life on the planet? Will we find that we are not alone in the universe, and will we ever travel to other planets? Only time will tell.

What is certain is that new mysteries await us in the next 1,000 years. In fact, daily life in the year 3000 will probably be different beyond recognition. The only things that may stay the same are the questions that still can't be answered—some we ask today and many yet to be asked.

# Is There Intelligent
# Life Out There?

**Speculation about the existence of extraterrestrial intelligence
dates back as far as human thought.**

LIGHTS ILLUMINATE
THE PLATFORM
ABOVE THE 1,000-
FOOT RADIO TELE-
SCOPE DISH IN
ARECIBO, PUERTO
RICO, THE LARGEST
RADIO DISH IN
THE WORLD. IN THE
EARLY 1990S, THE
TELESCOPE WAS
AN ESSENTIAL PART
OF THE SETI
PROGRAM, WHICH
TURNED OUT TO BE
SHORT-LIVED.

MANY SCIENTISTS HAVE CONCLUDED THAT HUMANS are not alone in the universe, imagining thousands of complete civilizations dotting the heavens above—as many as one million in the Milky Way galaxy alone. Supporting their belief is the fact that the chemical elements that led to the formation of life on earth are known to be present elsewhere in the universe. Organic compounds have been discovered in asteroids, comets, meteorites, and other interstellar matter, and the existence of molecules of a certain complexity may be all that is required for the development of life. Moreover, high-tech observation of the heavens has detected matter in distant space that does not emit stellar radiation, indicating the possible presence of planetary systems like our own. Other scientists, of course, beg to differ.

## THE DRAKE EQUATION

The actual search for signs of extraterrestrial intelligence began with the invention of radio telescopes in the 1940s. Radio waves are thought to be the best means of communication over interstellar distances. The first major radio search was carried out in 1960 by Frank Drake, who searched for signals from two stars that resemble the Sun. But more significant than his search was an equation Drake devised to estimate the likelihood of intelligent life existing elsewhere in the cosmos.

The so-called Drake Equation factors in estimates about the rate at which stars are born; the probability that the conditions would be met in a given solar system for life to arise; and the average lifetimes of civilizations. Based on these criteria, the equation concludes that there are now about 10,000 observable civilizations in the Milky Way, with the closest civilization to earth just 300 light years away. Drake's estimate was later revised by astronomer Carl Sagan, who estimated that the number was closer to one million alien civilizations in our galaxy. By that estimate, with the hundreds of millions of galaxies, there could be as many as 10 trillion other civilizations in all.

But some scientists have long questioned Drake's equation. One problem is that it assumes each technological civilization keeps to itself. But as humanity has shown, travel in space is a reality for advanced civilizations. Over the course of time, it seems likely that growing civilizations capable of galactic colonization would spread. So, if another advanced civilization exists in the Milky Way, it is probably not confined to its own planet.

On the other hand, if the galaxy seems largely empty of intelligent life—as it does—it would suggest that few civilizations exist, and, possibly, just our own. It has also been suggested that other advanced civilizations know humans exist, but choose not to communicate with us. Or, more likely, other civilizations may have come and gone, dying out before intergalactic colonization became possible.

## CONDITIONS SO RARE

Recent work has also raised questions about Drake's assumptions about the conditions needed for civilizations to exist. One factor is the frequency with which planets containing the seeds of life are bombarded with large rocks. In our solar system, Jupiter absorbs many such "killer rocks" and sends others into space, helping make civilization possible on earth. Although some giant, Jupiter-like planets have been discovered elsewhere in the galaxy, their orbits are thought to be erratic, and they may only increase the chaos on smaller planets nearby.

On the galactic edges, meanwhile, supernovas are rare and elements such as iron, magnesium, and silicon may be in short supply. Lacking these elements, the formation of planets with the water and atmosphere required for life is unlikely. And only spiral galaxies—one of several possible forms—appear rich enough in metals to sustain life as we know it.

Some scientists believe that the conditions allowing life on earth are incredibly rare and unlikely to be found elsewhere in the same combination. They note that a planet must be sufficiently far from its star to keep water in liquid form; a moon must be at just the right distance to ensure climatic stability; there must be just enough carbon to allow life but not to have it overheat. Even if primitive microbes exist somewhere in the heavens, they say, it is highly unlikely that other advanced civilizations have formed.

But Drake—who as of 2000 was involved in searching faint radio signals from space for signs of life—maintains that life is hardier than some believe, and can survive under a variety of conditions. Who is right? New advances in astronomy provide more information daily, but it is possible that we will never know.

**FRANK DRAKE CARRIED OUT THE FIRST MAJOR RADIO SEARCH FOR SIGNALS FROM DISTANT STARS IN 1960. ACCORDING TO THE EQUATION HE DEVISED, WHICH REMAINS CONTROVERSIAL, ANOTHER CIVILIZATION IS JUST 300 LIGHT YEARS FROM EARTH.**

# THE FATE OF SETI

In October, 1992, a promising search for extraterrestrial intelligence was initiated—the SETI program. Organized and operated by NASA at the behest of scientists, it had a unique mission: to examine the entire sky over a 10-year period, employing receivers of unprecedented sensitivity and frequency range. If anyone on any of the 100 billion stars that make up the Milky Way had been sending a radio message, SETI could receive it. Receiving stations were used in the Mojave Desert and Puerto Rico, but Congress stopped funding for the program after only one year. SETI was deemed too expensive and of little importance. Since 1994, however, the privately-funded Project Phoenix has been trying to fill the void by observing 1,000 sunlike stars within 200 light years of Earth.

**WE MAY NEVER KNOW** ▼

# The Coming of
# Computers

**The final story of the computer's effect on society has yet to be told, but it has wrought a revolution unlike any ever seen.**

THE FIRST LARGE-SCALE AUTOMATIC digital computer was developed during World War II by a Harvard graduate student, Howard H. Aiken. Named the Mark I, the machine weighed 5 tons and contained 500 miles of wires and 3,304 electromechanical relay switches. It could perform 23-digit additions and subtractions in three-tenths of a second. Amazing, yes, for its time. But on Valentine's Day 1946 came a breakthrough in computer technology: Engineers at the University of Pennsylvania unveiled ENIAC, a computer that used electronic pulses instead of mechanical switches for calculations.

This hulking giant used 18,000 vacuum tubes, 1,800 square feet of floor space, and 180,000 watts of electrical power—enough to dim the lights in West Philadelphia homes. In response to increased need for computer capacity during World War II, ENIAC was built specifically to calculate trajectory tables and other such military data. Only a few decades later a desktop version of the computer would become a fixture in the workplace and in millions of households worldwide.

ENIAC and similar early computers are called first-generation computers. The next major step in the history of computing was the invention of the transistor in 1947; these second-generation computers dominated the late 1950s and early 1960s. But the true explosion began with so-called third-generation computers, which relied on the integrated circuit, or microchip. The first integrated circuit was produced in September 1958, though computers using them didn't

begin to appear until 1963. While large "mainframes" such as the IBM 360 increased storage and processing capabilities further, the integrated circuit allowed many smaller businesses to use computers. The microprocessor also was the force behind a giant step for the ages: the development of microcomputers—personal computers (PCs) that were small and cheap enough to be available to ordinary people.

## DAWN OF THE NET

Though the invention of the microprocessor made the PC possible, manufacturers at first failed to see its potential. It wasn't until 1977 that Americans Steve Jobs and Steve Wozniak launched the Apple II, the first mass-market microcomputer available already assembled. In the decades since, computers have become more and more user-friendly and powerful, and have changed lives in unimaginable ways.

The Internet, for example, has become commonplace in the American home, with the World Wide Web its most familiar feature. The Web is a collection of hyperlinked pages distributed over the Internet via a network protocol called HTTP (hyper-text-transfer-protocol). The Web was started in the late 1980s by scientists wanting to share information on their projects, although at that time it was text-only. In a landmark development that came later, graphics were made possible with a browser called NCSA Mosaic.

The graphical interface opened up the Internet to novice users, and in 1993 its use exploded as ordinary people began to dial in to the Internet using their computer at home and a modem to get their connection. Before this, the only net-linked computers were at universities and other large organizations—but now anyone could use the Internet, and the medium quickly evolved into the worldwide Information Superhighway we know today.

**THE MARK I WAS THE FIRST LARGE-SCALE AUTOMATIC DIGITAL COMPUTER (ABOVE). IT WEIGHED 5 TONS AND CONTAINED 500 MILES OF WIRES. TODAY ITS DESCENDANTS ARE SMALL ENOUGH TO FIT ON A CLASSROOM DESK (BELOW).**

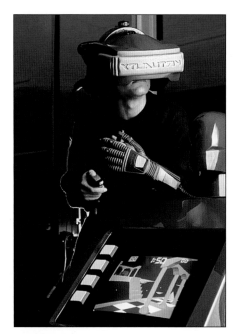

VIRTUAL REALITY HEADSETS AND DATA GLOVES ARE AMONG THE MANY ADVANCES COMPUTERS HAVE BROUGHT TO THE FIELD OF PERSONAL HOME ENTERTAINMENT. FOR MILLIONS OF CHILDREN (AND ADULTS) AROUND THE WORLD, LIFE WITHOUT COMPUTER GAMES IS NOW ALMOST UNIMAGINABLE.

## AGENTS OF CHANGE

A world of literature has been devoted to the effect computers have had on our lives in the past few decades. But much what has been written is either overly enthusiastic about the benefits or overly skeptical about the imposition of computers. However, with the changes resulting from the widespread use of PCs and computer networks, it is no longer possible to say that computers have not had a profound effect in one way or another on the lives of nearly everyone.

Arguably the most noticeable effect computers have had on modern life is in their ability to store vast quantities of information. Since the invention of Gutenberg's press, humans have had efficient means of sharing information, but computers have exponentially increased the speed with which that information flows, as well as the quantity of data stored. In fact, the coming of computers has given rise to a kind of information overload, in that computers can store data in ways that exceed human capacity to absorb it. In this vein, computers have changed education; no longer is memorization as critical a skill, for example, when that same information can be easily referenced at any time by means of a simple keystroke.

Another effect computers have had on daily life is that of time compression. The ability of computers to transfer data instantly has revolutionized industry, especially in the financial world. Instead of checks that take up to a week to cash, cash is now readily available to the consumer because the bank's computers share balance and account information with other banks. The modern stock market could not exist without computers. And sometimes, money itself seems to threaten to become obsolete—even groceries can now be bought with a PIN number and a computer.

Hand-in-hand with time compression comes the change in the job market. Computers have influenced the profound shift away from performance tasks toward the service-oriented jobs that have arisen. No longer is it necessary for a worker to sit next to a conveyor belt when a computer can perform the same task.

## A TOOL FOR SIMULATIONS

Computer simulations are another valuable contribution of the computer. Modeling and simulation allow researchers to study the effects of experiments without having to conduct trials that may be both risky and expensive. The simulation power of computers has been exploited extensively in the realm of aeronautics, such as those used for trajectory analysis in the Mercury and Apollo space programs, which sent astronauts to the moon.

Simulations can also help solve history's mysteries. For one, a computer simulation commissioned by the National Geographic Society revealed that the destruction of the Battleship *Maine* in 1898 in Havana Harbor, supposedly by a Spanish mine, could have as easily been caused by an accidental fire in the coal bunker. But because the Spanish were blamed, the destruction of the *Maine* launched the Spanish-American War, which lasted for 10 months.

ENIAC, UNVEILED IN 1946, TOOK UP 1,800 SQUARE FEET OF FLOOR SPACE.

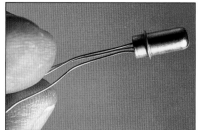

TRANSISTORS CAME ON THE SCENE IN 1947.

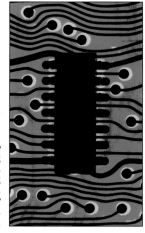

A MICROCHIP MADE THE APPLE II POSSIBLE, THE FIRST MASS-MARKET MICRO-COMPUTER.

## THE BAD WITH THE GOOD?

Of course, along with all these wondrous achievements the computer has brought new societal problems as well. The computer and, more recently, the Internet have brought on questions of privacy and governmental regulation into the previously private realms of life. Arguments prevail on the role of society in policing the behavior of the individual in a digitized world. What is more, hackers have wrought havoc in major networks, proving that individuals with unsavory agendas can wield power with an ease heretofore unseen. And more than one person in this newly wired society has wondered whether our increasing reliance on artificial intelligence will someday make us pay an incalculably heavy price.

That said, few can argue against the quality-of-life improvements the invention of the computer has brought. From computer dating to video games to a tool augmenting human intelligence, computers have pervaded human life in too many ways to list. But if the human mind is a device for processing information, then the computer can be considered a powerful mechanism for improving and expanding it.

# WOMEN PIONEERS

Though names like Aiken and Jobs and Wozniak and Gates all belong to men, many computer pioneers were women. In fact, the first computer "compiler" was invented by Grace Murray Hopper in 1952. Her revolutionary software facilitated the first automatic programming of computer language. Each time the computer needed instructions that were common to all programs, the compiler would have the computer refer to codes in its own memory. The compiler was a time- and error-saving breakthrough for the computer world, and yet Hopper didn't

**THAT NAME AGAIN?** ▼

stop there. She also invented COBOL, the first user-friendly business software program, which is still in use today.

A decade later, Evelyn Boyd Granville, one of the first African-American female computer scientists, developed computer programs that were used for trajectory analysis in the Mercury Project (the first U.S. manned mission in space) and in the Apollo Project, which sent America's astronauts to the moon.

Another woman predated these pioneers by well over a century—the daughter of the great romantic poet Lord Byron. In 1833 an English mathematician named Charles Babbage designed a steam-powered "analytical engine" that contained many of the operating principles in use in today's computers—data storage, printouts, even decision-making functions.

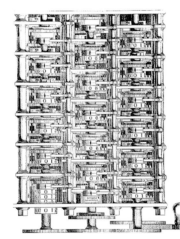

Babbage was never able to complete his machine, mainly because metal technology could not meet his unique demands. His assistant in his labors was Augusta Ada Byron, Lady Lovelace, who became, as author of the "code" to run Babbage's machine, history's first computer programmer. In 1979, a high-level computer language, Ada, was named in her honor.

**CHARLES BABBAGE RELIED ON THE EXPERTISE OF ADA BYRON, LADY LOVELACE (ABOVE), TO RUN HIS ANALYTICAL ENGINE (LEFT).**

**STEVE JOBS, CO-FOUNDER OF APPLE, WITH THE NEW APPLE II.**

**BILL GATES (ABOVE) TOOK MICROSOFT TO THE ZENITH OF THE COMPUTER INDUSTRY.**

**THE INTERNET IS CHANGING THE WAY TEACHERS TEACH—AND STUDENTS LEARN.**

# A Virus Named "Good Times"

ALMOST IN THE BLINK OF AN EYE, COMPUTERS AND THE Internet have become a fact of our daily lives. Yet the majority of people who use them have only a very basic grasp of how the machine they are using works, and what its potential dangers are. Proponents of the Internet often celebrate its ability to "interconnect" our lives. But this very same interconnectedness that is the glory of the Internet can, at times, be the source of its most severe disasters. When a sophisticated computer virus is introduced into the world of the Internet, it can spread by vast and lightning-quick proportions.

## THE REAL THING

Numerous viruses struck computer systems worldwide during the 1990s. One of the most famous was named Melissa. This dangerous dame with an innocent name was easy to create and preyed on operating systems present in more than 70 percent of the world's computers; it was transmitted by simply downloading an attachment from an e-mail. Once present in the computer, the virus could automatically send itself to the first 50 names on the user's e-mail address list. By the time the virus was reined in, 1.2 million computers were affected in North American businesses alone, and systems throughout the world had been disrupted. The virus had been launched by a 30-year-old named David L. Smith, from his apartment in Aberdeen, New Jersey. It was named Melissa after a topless dancer favored by Smith. On December 9, 1999, Smith pled guilty to charges that he had created the virus and was sentenced to five years in prison.

## HOAXES AND MYTHS

Viruses themselves are only a fraction of the virus problem. Far more virulent than actual encrypted viruses are the countless virus hoaxes and myths spread every day on the Internet. Preying on the fear of hypochondriac computer users who know very little about their operating systems, pranksters the world over have originated more baseless panic attacks than can be listed.

Virus myths generally take the form of e-mail warnings about a savage bug on the loose. Sent with good intentions from friend to friend, they can be almost as annoying as an actual virus, clogging inboxes and dominating newsgroups. Most of these hoaxes are dismissed before they can disrupt too many lives, but several have proven to be true epidemics, racing round the world.

One of the best-known virus myths of the 1990s was the "Good Times" hoax of 1994. According to this story, a virus by that name was being transmitted by e-mail. Simply reading a message with the fun-promising Good Times entered in the subject line would erase your entire hard drive, or even destroy your computer's processor, the myth warned. The original message ended with instructions to forward the warning to "all your friends." Many people did, and the Good Times warning entered the hallowed halls of popular mythology. To this day, it still floats around the Internet.

There have been many other hoaxes of this sort. Though of a slightly different variety, the Y2K bug was in many senses a virus myth. It is safe to say that as long as individuals and businesses entrust their lives to machines that they know very little about, we will continue to see outbreaks of both types of disease—the computer virus and the computer virus hoax.

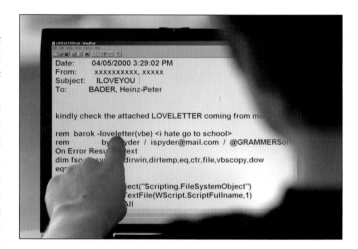

REAL VIRUSES ARE NO JOKE. A PC USER IN VIENNA (ABOVE) READS AN E-MAIL CARRYING THE "LOVE BUG" IN APRIL 2000. THE VIRUS, SENT BY E-MAIL BEARING THE SUBJECT LINE "I LOVE YOU," STRUCK SYSTEMS AROUND THE WORLD. AT RIGHT, IN THE PHILIPPINES, REOMEL RAMONES (CENTER) IS DETAINED FOR QUESTIONING ABOUT THE VIRUS.

# PRIEST: THREAT TO THE SECRET SERVICE?

One of the first computer viruses to achieve serious results was the infamous "Satan Bug," which attacked computers in the fall of 1993. The bug was the work of a 16-year-old computer hacker from San Diego who was known around the Internet as Priest. It worked its way into some U.S. government systems and caused widespread panic. The State Department issued an alarm, and government employees on the Compuserve network posted terrified messages, claiming that the virus was capable of "eating" all the data on a computer. Most dramatically, the bug knocked out the computer system of the Secret Service for three days. When agents tracked down Priest, they found themselves face-to-face with a troublemaker of a new variety. The 16-year-old did not work for anyone (least of all a hostile foreign government, a theory advanced by the media), and he had not targeted the Secret Service network at all.

In fact, Priest seemed to have no devious plans at all. When asked about the origins of his career as a virus writer, he blithely said, "It was something to do besides blasting furballs in [the video game] Wing Commander."

**PRESIDENT CLINTON MET LEADERS OF THE COMPUTER INDUSTRY AT THE WHITE HOUSE IN FEBRUARY 2000 TO DISCUSS SECURITY IN THE INTERNET AGE.**

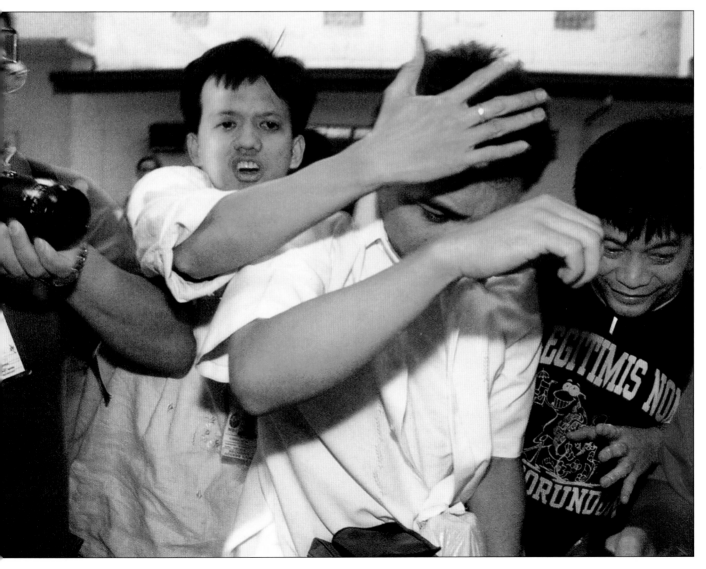

# Will We Ever Travel to Other Planets?

**The idea of space travel has pervaded our culture through science fiction and popular movies.**

"OUR PASSIONATE PREOCCUPATION WITH THE SKY, the stars, and a God somewhere in outer space is a homing impulse," said Eric Hoffer, a U.S. philosopher, after man's first moon landing in 1969. "We are drawn back to where we came from." Will that homing impulse prove strong enough to carry human beings to other planets, both within and outside of our solar system? In science fiction, races that haven't traveled far beyond their own planet are seen as terribly backward. But will the human race decide there are more important things to spend money on than sending people into deep space? And will we ever have both the technology and the desire to send people there?

The odds are fair that before too long, humankind will have at least stepped on our nearest planetary neighbor, Mars. We are already close to having the technology. The National Aeronautics and Space Administration (NASA) began its first unmanned missions to the "red planet" in 1964 and has since launched orbiters and landers that have gathered a wealth of information about both the planet's surface and its atmosphere.

The most exhilarating of these missions was that of the Mars *Pathfinder* in the summer of 1997, which dropped a tiny rover called the *Sojourner* on the surface. The world was thrilled as it watched the rover "sniff" rocks and take dramatic pictures of Martian vistas.

## NO SMALL PROBLEM

Getting a lightweight unmanned rover to Mars is a complex and challenging task, but it is decidedly less daunting than the chore of sending humans there and back. In the case of unmanned missions, rocket engineers do not have to concern themselves with a return flight—which becomes a major consideration when planning any human mission (only in the

realm of science fiction is a crew of astronauts likely to volunteer for a one-way death mission to Mars). Given current technology, no rocket can carry the weight of the equipment and fuel required for the round-trip, which would take about one year each way. And building a ship bit by bit in space would be too costly.

## SURMOUNTABLE CHALLENGES?

There has been no shortage of ideas, however, to get around the problem of traveling to Mars. Aeronautic engineers Robert Zubrin and Larry Clark have made a prototype of a machine that could potentially use the carbon dioxide in the Martian atmosphere and combine it with hydrogen brought from home to create rocket fuel—specifically, methane—on Mars.

Zubrin's proposal calls for two separate launches per mission, one for the "personnel ship" and another for the "earth return vehicle." He says his plan could carry out a manned Mars mission with a relatively cheap price tag: $2 billion per year for at least a decade.

Not surprisingly, there remain some kinks regarding physics and life support that need to be ironed out before we can strike out to explore our solar system (or any other). A major problem posed by extended space travel is its adverse effect on human health. Russian cosmonauts who set records for time spent in space have suffered a number of health problems because of extended weightlessness—among them, the loss of bone density and the atrophy of the heart and other muscles.

Astronauts would also be exposed to high volumes of radiation in outer space, despite their protective gear. At the moment, space flights are scheduled to avoid periods of heightened solar-flare activity, but an extended mission to Mars might not have that luxury.

Then there is the difficulty of providing food and water to the astronauts. A problem indeed, but recent research suggests that once the astronauts got there they could probably drill for water that lies beneath the Martian surface.

## 21 YEARS TO PLUTO!

Physics as yet has failed to provide an easy way to replicate those fast-as-the-speed-of-light space machines that are the stuff of *Star Trek* and *Star Wars* films. Even if such a machine could be built, it would be subject to incalculable damage as it neared the speed of light. At

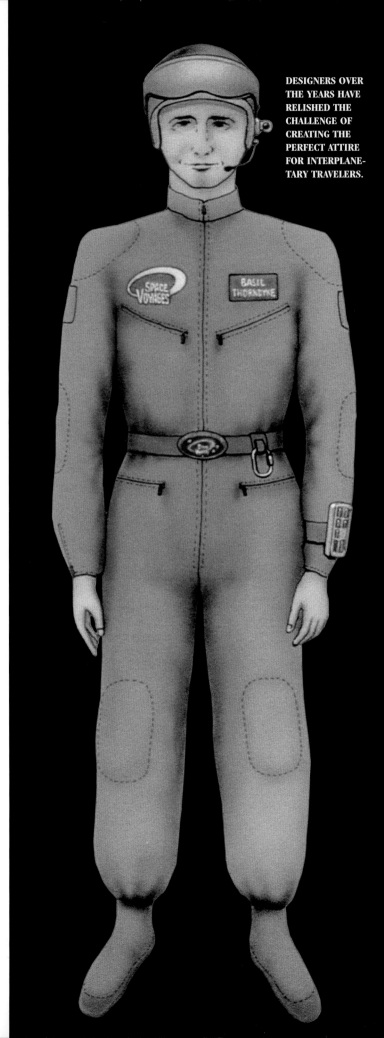

DESIGNERS OVER THE YEARS HAVE RELISHED THE CHALLENGE OF CREATING THE PERFECT ATTIRE FOR INTERPLANETARY TRAVELERS.

HIBERNATION MAY BE NECESSARY FOR CREWS ON SPACE VOYAGES, AS SHOWN HERE IN A SCENE FROM *2001: A SPACE ODYSSEY*.

this speed, the tiniest speck of dust in the medium of interstellar space would assume the destructive force of something weighing thousands of tons—a "hailstorm" to end all hailstorms.

True, rockets of the future may be aided by new research into ion propulsion. But scientists see no way now to create a machine that could remain intact and travel anywhere near the speeds that would make human travel to planets besides Mars expedient or safe.

Some science-fiction writers imagine that the energy from black holes could be used to propel a spaceship through the immensity of the universe, but the nearest black hole to earth is about 3,000 light-years away. At present speeds, a one-way trip to Pluto, the most distant planet in our solar system, would take more than 21 years. Going outside the solar system seems more daunting. "Why should human society pay trillions of dollars so that we can send a few dozen travelers on a virtually one-way, decades-long journey to the nearest star?" asks NASA's Dr. Sten Odenwald.

## LOOKING TO THE FUTURE

Whether we ever have a good answer for that question may prove to be the defining point as to whether the human race ever extends its reach beyond Mars and the moon. There is no biological imperative, at least in the foreseeable future, for us to colonize other planets, and the planets available to us in our solar system are not exactly welcoming to human life.

Since 1995, however, more than 20 planets have been discovered outside our solar system, and astronomers now suggest that stars everywhere could be surrounded by planets. One can only imagine the reaction if scientists discover a planet that has a circular orbit (like the earth's) and is at a safe-enough distance from its star to make life there hospitable. If our own planet were threatened or its resources exhausted, would there be people of the future willing to risk a generations-long journey on a Noah's Ark or Mayflower of Space?

It is a question that we are currently unable to answer. But the naysayers would do well to remember the admonition of Robert Goddard, the American physicist who developed and launched the first liquid-fuel rocket in the mid-1920s: "It is difficult to say what is impossible, for the dream of yesterday is the hope of today and the reality of tomorrow."

# Is Print Dead?

### As our society moves further and further into the digital age, will it mean the end of the printed word?

**MOST READERS REMAIN ATTACHED TO NEWSPRINT, AND VEHEMENTLY SO. BUT FUTURISTS PREDICT THAT DEVICES LIKE THE ROCKET eBOOK, A PORTABLE SCREEN THAT DISPLAYS ONE PAGE AT A TIME, SOMEDAY WILL REPLACE THE PRINTED WORD ALTOGETHER.**

FUTURE ANTIQUARIANS SORTING THE EFFECTS OF the 20th and 21st centuries, trying to determine how the printed word of ink and paper came to be largely replaced by pixelated letters on glowing screens, might stumble with interest upon an article by Vannevar Bush in the July 1945 edition of *The Atlantic Monthly* magazine. The article, titled "As We May Think," spoke of the increasing difficulty for anyone who attempted to gain information in a way

Bush considered archaic—print. "Professionally our methods of transmitting and reviewing the results of research are generations old and by now are totally inadequate for their purpose," Bush wrote. "The difficulty seems to be, not so much that we publish unduly in view of the extent and variety of present-day interests, but rather that publication has been extended far beyond our present ability to make real use of the record." Bush insisted that humans needed a new way to thread through the abundance of information available—a method that would not use paper and ink.

He proposed a machine called a "memex," which would create links of associations that the user could follow as his or her interests see fit. "Wholly new forms of encyclopedias will appear, ready-made with a mesh of associative trails running through them . . .," Bush postulated. "The lawyer has at his touch the associated opinions and decisions of his whole experience, and of the experience of friends and authorities. The patent attorney has on call the millions of issued patents, with familiar trails to every point of his client's interest."

Here, almost 30 years before its launch, lies the idea behind the World Wide Web, which now includes almost 100 million people around the globe in its virtual community. People not only can conduct research online but send mail to each other, chat with instant messaging services, and create Web communities that are no longer bound by physical geography.

## COMPUTER DRAWBACKS

Will the names of Vannevar Bush and J.C.R. Licklider (who wrote a 1968 paper proposing an "intergalactic computer network") be as revered in the 24th or 25th century as Johannes Gutenberg—the German inventor who opened the way for the democratization of knowledge with the 1436 creation of the movable-type printing press—is to us today? Will computer networks, with their speed and their vast resources of information and video, make pen and ink, books and paper obsolete?

The rise of computers does have its detractors. The French philosopher Jean Baudrillard argues that the Internet may, by its excess of information, do little to solve the problem of information glut. "Computer science only indicates the retrospective omnipotence of our technologies," Baudrillard says. "In other words, it has an infinite capacity to process data (but only data—i.e., the already given) and in no sense a new vision. With that science, we are entering an era of exhaustivity, which is also an era of exhaustion."

Those who make the argument that the digital medium will never trump the written word also point out the inherent unreliability of electronic hookups, faulty computer equipment, and information that is scattered across several servers. Pen on paper is more concrete, solid, trustworthy. "To err is human," said a participant in a BBC radio program in 1982, "but to really foul things up requires a computer."

## ALL HAIL THE E-BOOK?

Still, many people argue for the great advantages of the digital medium over the printed word: the ability to follow links quickly in a fashion that more closely resembles the associative nature of the human brain; the power to share information in the fields of medicine and science (and facilitate quicker development of research through the process of collaboration); and the capacity to pinpoint information in several minutes that might have taken days or weeks in the stacks of a library.

For those feeling a little nostalgic about the days when you could curl up by the fire with book in hand, Franklin Electronic Publishers released the Rocket e-Book in 1999. With the help of three scrolling buttons and four icons on this handheld device, users can download up to 10 novels at a time from the Internet and scroll through them at their leisure.

It is hard to tell whether a classroom in the year 2100 will consist of students who need only come to class with stylus and e-book in hand. Books and newspapers of paper and ink have proven to be remarkably resilient through six centuries. Even with the rise of the digital age, bookstores have continued to vend their commodity at a brisk pace—and that's not even to mention online sellers of books like Amazon.com and Barnes & Noble. It is also likely that people will still read books on paper in another 100 years for the sense of authenticity that only a book with dog-eared pages and a history of individual readers can confer.

Then again, some point out that the printed book is the text's container, not its essence. Moreover, e-books will cost little, never go out of print, and will always be at the ready online.

# Is ESP Real?

**Without the use of the five traditional senses, can we glimpse the unknown or look into the future?**

**IN MOST SENSORY PERCEPTION, SOME SIGNALS ARE EXTREMELY SUBTLE AND LIE OUTSIDE CONSCIOUS AWARENESS. HOW MUCH COMMUNICATION OF THIS KIND ACCOUNTS FOR INSTANCES OF "EXTRA-SENSORY" PERCEPTION IS STILL THE FOCUS OF MUCH DEBATE.**

EXTRASENSORY PERCEPTION (ESP) IS DEFINED AS any sort of premonition or foreknowledge via telepathy or clairvoyance. Most of the evidence for ESP is anecdotal and is dismissed by skeptics as trickery—that is to say, the result of selective thinking, wishful thinking, gullibility, ignorance, fraud, or a poor grasp of probabilities and of the law of truly large numbers.

But some parapsychologists who study this phenomenon in laboratories have occasionally come up with seeming evidence of the paranormal: psychics capable of discerning the content of sealed envelopes, predicting the roll of a die or the draw of a card, and drawing pictures that describe exactly the view as observed by someone at a remote location.

Most reported extrasensory experiences, however, occur not on command but when they are least expected. Reports of dreams of impending disasters and of mothers certain that some accident has befallen their children are rampant. Subjecting these experiences to scientific verification is tricky and far from conclusive. Shakespeare's Hamlet famously lectures Horatio that "there are more things in heaven and earth than are dreamt of in your philosophy." This is true for all of us. As critical thinkers, we may have trouble accepting the phenomenon of ESP, yet knowing that our understanding of nature and the human mind is incomplete, there is room for doubt.

Despite continued skepticism in the scientific establishment, many respected schools and organizations have kept an open mind. A chair of parapsychology was established in 1984 at Edinburgh University. In 1927, a parapsychological laboratory was set up at Duke University, North Carolina. In 1953, the first European professorial chair of parapsychology was founded at the University of Utrecht, the Netherlands. Students are studying psychical research at Trinity College, Cambridge, and at New College, Oxford. In New York, the Parapsychology Foundation is a center for publication and for the awarding of research grants.

## SKEPTICS STEP IN

Though these particular fields have been established as academic disciplines, skeptics are concerned that these areas of "pseudoscience" taint the significance of science as a discipline. The experimental problem for ESP research is that even its proponents concede there is no clear and affirmative evidence for its existence.

When scientists or academics have conducted tests in support of ESP, the results were often clouded and never proven. The Rhine Experiments were performed at Duke University by Joseph Banks Rhine, who conducted ESP experiments in the 1930s. In his book

*Extra-Sensory Perception*, he claimed to have found solid evidence of ESP. He also made "ESP cards" famous by using them in successful guessing experiments. Other psychologists were unable to mimic his results, and it is now known that Rhine's experiments were poorly designed. It was also discovered that information was released between subject and tester.

In a series of experiments in the 1970s at SRI International, physicists Harold Puthoff and Russell Targ claimed that certain subjects could "see" a distant place through the eyes of another person. The target team would visit places such as a shopping center, while the experimenter would ask the subject to describe his or her impressions of that particular place. Clearly, the process of deciding whether the subject's interpretations matched the ideal "place" was somewhat subjective. Methodological errors also tainted the research, and other experimenters were unable to imitate the

results. The National Research Council has said of the SRI experiments, "By both scientific and parapsychological standards, then, the case for remote viewing is not just very weak, but virtually nonexistent."

Another series of tests, called the Ganzfeld (German for "whole field") experiments, are named after the term used by Gestalt psychologists to designate the complete visual field. In these experiments, the test subjects wore halves of Ping-Pong balls over their eyes, while white noise was piped in through headphones. In this state of sensory deprivation, a sender, usually in an acoustically shielded room, would attempt to psychically communicate a visual stimulus—an image—to the subject. The subject was later asked to match his or her perceptions to the image. The Ganzfeld tests have been probably the most meticulously administered and the most carefully scrutinized. Still, in the end, the tests failed to produce results that convince psychologists that ESP really exists. ESP, of course, is only one arm of the paranormal, or supernatural. Spiritualists who claim contact with spirits go back to the beginning of time. Spiritualism was virtually a hobby in 19th-century England, with seances almost a form of entertainment. And the universal fascination with ghosts and haunted houses has never flagged.

## THIRST FOR THE UNKNOWN

Interest in the supernatural had a significant revival in the 1960s, foreshadowing New Age interests. In the 1970s, Uri Geller had people convinced that he could bend spoons by sheer mental effort. "Channelers," who supposedly give voice to ancient spirits, came out of the woodwork in the 1980s. And in the 1990s, the overabundance of psychic hotlines advertised on television suggested that millions of people were willing to let a complete stranger tell them what the future had in store.

## THE FOUNDING OF CSICOP

Pseudoscience—the label skeptics give ESP and other paranormal phenomena—is not defined as erroneous science but as science that doesn't stand up to the rigorous testing on which the scientific method is based. Worried by media coverage of ESP, UFOs, crop circles, and levitating gurus, philosopher Paul Kurtz founded the Committee for the Scientific Investigation of Claims of the Paranormal (CSICOP) in 1976, an organization of sci-entists, academics, magicians, and others dedicated to scrutinizing the pseudosciences. One of its purposes? To tell the media the other side of the story. After launching a magazine dedicated to debunking the pseudosciences, *The Skeptical Inquirer*, CSICOP established a Web site that stands as a vigilant voice of scientific (and common) sense in an age of psychic hotlines, horoscopes, exorcisms, haunted houses, and purported alien abductions.

**PIECES OF THE PUZZLE** ▼

But back to ESP. If tests were to support its reality, it wouldn't be the first time scientists were proved wrong. Science's purpose is, in fact, to test and test again. And for sure, researchers will never stop trying to plumb the more mysterious workings of the human mind.

TO PREDICT THE FUTURE, PEOPLE USE PARANORMAL TECHNIQUES. CANADIAN PRIME MINISTER MACKENZIE KING (ABOVE LEFT) USED SEANCES TO SEEK POLITICAL DIRECTION FROM THE SPIRITS OF THE DEPARTED. LEFT, URI GELLER BENT SPOONS BY SHEER WILL. HIS ABILITIES HAVE OFTEN BEEN SHOWN TO RELY ON MAGICIAN'S TRICKS AND THEATRICS, BUT SOME OF HIS TESTS AND PERFORMANCES ASTOUNDED AND INTRIGUED EVEN THE MOST SKEPTICAL OBSERVERS.

# Who Really Runs Things?

 As a member of Congress I'm deeply offended...

 ...by those who claim lobbyists...

 ...tell us what to do.

**SOME LOBBIES ARE ABLE TO WIELD SO MUCH POWER THAT A QUESTION IS RAISED: WHO IS REALLY IN CHARGE WHEN DECISIONS ABOUT GOVERNMENTAL POLICY ARE MADE?**

A QUICK INTERNET SEARCH UNEARTHS conspiracy theories from every side of the political spectrum. These mixtures of fact, fancy, and speculation all have one thing in common: be it the United Nations, the Masons, or a Pentagon program hiding UFOs, there's almost always a secret "shadow government" thought to be pulling the world's strings. According to a Gallup Poll, half of all Americans believe that the government is actually run by a handful of huge interests. Our novels, movies, and television shows reflect this; the popular TV program *The X Files* has as its slogan, "The Truth Is Out There." But just what truth might that be?

The truth is indeed out there—and it's not all that hard to get, either. The United States enjoys a level of freedom unprecedented in

**Who's in charge of our democracy— a select few, or a complex, elaborate system?**

human history, and thanks to the Freedom of Information Act, American citizens can obtain all but the most classified government documents. And yet, in this most open and democratic of countries, the average citizen feels powerless and distrustful of government. To understand why (and why they may be right), it is necessary to note the historical relationship between power and democracy.

## A NEW KIND OF POWER

From the ancient Greek city-state of Athens to Shays' Rebellion in 1786, the history of democracy has always been one of struggle, its main enemy being corruption. But it was not until the turn of the 20th century that democracy's biggest challenges emerged: mass media and the corporation. Spurred by technology, these immensely powerful institutions transformed American democracy in ways the nation's founders could scarcely have imagined.

The corporation created a centralized power of the type the Founding Fathers viewed with suspicion. The interests of corporations and the public are often in conflict. In the century between the Industrial Revolution and World War II, corporations and the public became so at odds that, by the time of the Great Depression, many thought democracy had no future. Worldwide, democracy was falling to Communism on the left and Fascism on the right.

Yet America is still a free country, with a free press. Although, as the Founders knew, one of the main functions of power is to hold on to and expand its power, no large organization could change the Constitution. Instead, business interests sought to use the media to manipulate public opinion. And a new industry was born: public relations.

## THE PUBLIC RELATIONS ANGLE

Some believe that the public relations industry is merely an extension of democracy. Edward Bernays, who is considered by many to be the father of American business public relations, believed that the effort to persuade others is the essence of democracy. In the 1920s, political scientist Walter Lippmann saw public relations as "a revolution in the art of democracy." He said that the nation should be run by a specialized class of managers who would then try to sell their policies to the American public.

This trend continued under both Democratic and Republican presidents. In 1975, the Trilateral Commission, a think-tank of intellectuals from the U.S., Europe, and Japan, released a report called "The Crisis of Democ-

racy," which stated that the greatest threat to democracy was, of all things, democracy itself. Why? Because of its tolerance of special interests. Today, many complain that government is increasingly run by and for special interests. Whether it's the Iran-Contra scandal, fundraising scandals, or scripted, poll-driven campaigns, money and power continue to exert considerable influence on American politics.

Even voters' referendums, thought to more directly reflect the voice of the people, are manipulated by massive advertising campaigns, media spin, and the reduction of complex issues to "yes or no" questions. But a clamoring for reform that transcends ideological lines has begun to emerge. In 1992, The Reform Party scored 19 percent of the popular vote for president. In the 2000 presidential primaries, both political parties were stormed from within by John McCain and Bill Bradley, insurgents with a message of reform.

So who really runs things? We still do. But these days the issues are so couched in spin, public relations, and doubletalk that often even the most well informed of us can't be sure what exactly those issues are.

**CARTOONS OF THE POLITICAL KIND HAVE SATIRIZED THE HYPOCRACIES OF GOVERNMENT AND THE RULING CLASSES FOR CENTURIES. AT BOTTOM LEFT, UNCLE SAM IS STAKED OUT MUCH LIKE GULLIVER, AT THE PLEASURE OF MYRIAD SPECIAL INTEREST GROUPS.**

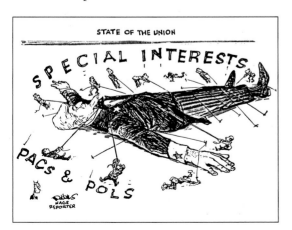

## MAYBE THEY DO?

Some believe that the real "shadow government" is the leadership of the Federal Reserve, chaired as of 2000 by Alan Greenspan, who regularly appears on front pages across the U.S. The Reserve determines U.S. monetary **PIECES OF THE PUZZLE** policy, and can create economic booms and busts at will. Americans usually vote their pocketbooks, and some analysts think that by meddling with the economy, past chairmen determined presidential elections in 1960 and 1980.

# The Urban Legend

A NOCTURNAL
INSECT, THE EARWIG
IS SAID IN LEGEND
TO SEEK OUT EARS
AND TO CRAWL
INTO THE HEAD.

FANTASTIC OR EERIE EVENTS THAT MAY OR MAY NOT HAVE happened have come to be called urban legends. They are almost always transmitted orally, and thus acquire numerous regional variations. They generally have a point, whether moral, cautionary, or instructive.

Such stories serve another purpose: Recounting a potential traumatic event releases some of the collective anxiety surrounding it. This idea is borne out by the topics taken up in many folktales, including the kidnapping of children (think the Brothers Grimm). For the most part, the tales deal with fears. Fears feature even more in contemporary urban legends, perhaps because there is so much to be anxious about in modern life. Stories abound about drunken driving, murder, frightening telephone calls, horrific baby-sitting episodes, airplane travel, and other modern concerns. Many urban legends feature cars.

A staple of modern urban legends is that they are carefully presented to appear truthful. Nearly all are traced to a "friend of a friend," and the teller often remains convinced the story truly happened. The aim of folktales—

be it to purge or to instruct—is more readily achieved if the tellers can claim some grain of truth for their stories. But is there really any truth behind them?

### EARWIGS ET CETERA

One of the oldest legends is the tale of an earwig (or ants or other insects) that crawls into someone's ear and wreaks havoc on the brain. A version of this story has been told since at least as far back as the year 1000.

The most common modern telling has a woman sunbathing at a beach when an earwig crawls unnoticed into her ear. Days later she goes to the doctor, complaining of terrible earaches. After discovering the bug, the doctor tells the patient that it is too far inside to do anything but wait until it crawls out the other ear. When it does, several weeks later, the doctor ruefully explains that the earwig is a female and has laid eggs in the patient's head, which, upon hatching, will produce brain-devouring baby earwigs. In fact, in 1971 a Boise, Idaho newspaper reported that an earwig had crawled into a local woman's ear—but her doctor removed the insect without trouble. It is in the occasional real ear attack like this one, along with the great fear of a bug crawling into the head, that keeps some long-standing myths in currency.

In 1986, Ann Landers fell for a legend, recounting in her column the grisly story of a drunk driver who returns home at 2 A.M., immediately falls asleep, and wakes to find the lifeless body of an eight-year-old girl stuck to the grille of his car. Landers used the item to warn her readers about the perils of drunk driving. Several versions of this story exist; some have the man's wife discovering the body. But urban legend aficionados have turned up no factual basis for the tale, which seems most likely to

**LONELY ROADS ARE AN URBAN LEGEND STAPLE. ONE TALE IS OF A HITCHHIKER IN A PROM DRESS WHO IS PICKED UP, VANISHES INTO THIN AIR, AND TURNS OUT TO BE A GIRL WHO HAD BEEN KILLED IN AN AUTO ACCIDENT AT THE SAME SPOT SEVERAL YEARS BEFORE.**

# MANIAC! WITH HOOK!

Perhaps no home-grown urban legend is more widespread than "The Hook," which oftentimes goes like this:

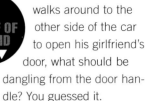
THE STUFF OF LEGEND ▼

Two teenage lovers are necking in a car parked on a country road, their radio tuned to a pop station. "Bulletin!" yells the announcer. "A homicidal maniac has escaped from the insane asylum. And his right hand is a *metal hook!*" Frantic, the boy revs up the engine and drives into town. When he walks around to the other side of the car to open his girlfriend's door, what should be dangling from the door handle? You guessed it.

One of the more implausible variations on this fable of narrow escape has the boy driving straight to the police station. When he emerges from the car, he's shocked to see the maniac atop the car, hoisting an axe in a metal-to-flesh grip and ready to chop through the car's roof.

**CARS FIGURE LARGE IN URBAN LEGENDS, FROM THE HOOK-ON-THE-DOOR-HANDLE TO THE BODY-IN-THE-GRILLE. PSYCHOLOGISTS SAY URBAN LEGENDS ARE A WAY OF RELEASING UNIVERSAL ANXIETY.**

have come from either a 1950s comic book strip relating a similar accident or, once again, the fear of being either the driver or the victim in such a careless mishap.

### THE HEEL IN THE GRATE

Sometimes, urban legends actually do have a factual basis. Such is the case with the well-known heel-in-the-grate story. According to the legend, during a wedding one of the bridesmaids catches her heel in a ventilation grate. Unable to dislodge the shoe, she walks ahead, shoeless. Behind her, an usher sees the shoe and picks it up, accidentally pulling up the whole grate. Hoping to avoid a scene, he walks on, shoe and grate in hand. Following the usher is the bride, who falls into the uncovered shaft. In some versions of the tale, she perishes.

This story can actually be traced back to a 1949 incident at the Hanover Presbyterian Church in Hanover, Indiana. The true story is almost identical, except that it happened during regular church services, while the choir was marching down the aisle singing. A baritone fell in the open shaft. Again, anxiety—this time of a ruined wedding—plays a major role in the creation of the legend.

# What Happens
# When We Die?

**Countless people claim to have glimpsed
the afterlife in brief near-death experiences.
But could the vision be illusory?**

"WHAT TIME HAS BEEN WASTED DURING MAN'S destiny in the struggle to decide what man's next world will be like!" said the Irish dramatist Sean O'Casey in 1954. "The keener the effort to find out, the less he knew about the present one he lived in." Despite O'Casey's disapproval, one cannot help but be a little curious. What will our next world look like? Or is there anything beyond the grave?

The good news is that those who have almost been there and faced death often come back with glowing reviews. In his 729 AD *The Ecclesiastical History of the English People,* the Venerable Bede, a theologian, relates the story of a Northumbrian man whose relatives took him for dead: "He came back to life and suddenly sat up—those who were weeping around the body were very upset and ran away. 'I was

guided by a handsome man in a shining robe,' he said. 'When we reached the top of a wall, there was a wide and pleasant meadow, with light flooding in that seemed brighter than daylight or the midday sun. I was very reluctant to leave, for I was enraptured by the place's pleasantness and beauty and by the company I saw there. From now on I must live in a completely different way.'" The man soon abandoned all of his worldly ties and entered a monastery.

## "THE BRILLIANT WHITE LIGHT"

Not everyone who survives what has come to be called a near-death experience, or NDE, enters a monastery. But judging from the blossoming of current literature on NDEs, the story that the Bede related is hardly unique. Raymond Moody's 1975 bestseller *Life After Life*

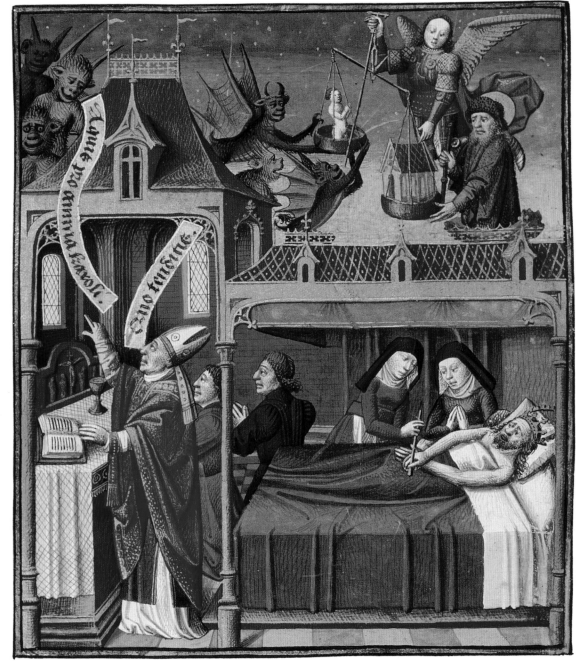

RELIGION HAS USED THE AFTERLIFE AS A MEANS OF GIVING A UNIVERSAL MEANING TO AN INDIVIDUAL'S LIFE AND ACCOMPLISHMENTS. "THE DEATH OF CHARLEMAGNE," BY VINCENT DE BEAUVAIS, IS FROM *LE MIROIR HISTORIAL*, A 15TH-CENTURY ILLUMINATED MANUSCRIPT. ANGELS WEIGH THE DYING KING'S DEEDS BEFORE DECIDING WHETHER HE SHOULD ENTER PARADISE.

tells of the fifteen most frequent experiences among 150 people surveyed who had come back from the brink of death. Among these were feelings of peace and quiet and the awareness of a being of light that the person was drawn toward—a light that often represented love and knowledge in its purest form.

"This white light began to infiltrate my consciousness," says Jayne Smith in her video *A Moment of Truth*. "It came into me. It seemed I went out into it. I expanded into it as it came into my field of consciousness. There was nothing I was aware of except the brilliant white light. The light brought with it the most incred-ible feeling of total love, total safety, total protection." Recent bestsellers, including Betty Eadie's *Embraced by the Light* (1992), tell a similar story, and mention a new awareness of the beauty of life after returning from a head-on encounter with death. Eadie and others also maintain that they no longer feared death after returning from their experience.

The fascination with near-death experiences is understandable, given that NDEs are only one embodiment of the human need to confront and make sense of the inevitability of death. Another, reincarnation, has been a part of cultures and religions since time immemorial. Modern preoccupations with reincarnation have been rekindled by highly publicized hypnotic regressions to past lives, starting with the Bridey Murphy case of the 1950s. (In hypnosis sessions over the course of a year, a young Wisconsin woman, Virginia Tighe, revealed that in a previous life she had been an Irish girl named Bridey Murphy. A number of extremely obscure facts that she could not have known from normal sources were proved accurate.) More recently, the famous have not shied away from professing a belief in reincarnation—most notably, the actress Shirley MacLaine, author of *Dancing in the Light* and other books that tell of her past lives. The books of James Van Praagh, who claims to be able to communicate with the dead, are a more recent addition to the bestseller lists; one bears the hopeful title, *Talking to Heaven.* The huge sales of such books speak to the deep need humanity has to believe that we exist in some form after death.

## THE SKEPTICS' VIEWS

Despite all these reassuring visions of the life to come, some critics deny that the near-death experience has any spiritual reality. The British psychologist Dr. Susan Blackmore, of the Brain and Perception Laboratory at Bristol University in England, has argued in her book *Dying to Live: Near-Death Experiences* (1993) that the long tunnel with the bright light at the end is nothing more than the natural result of the brain being denied oxygen at death, causing nerve cells to fire randomly in the eye and providing the illusion of a bright white light. Other researchers insist that the blissful feelings of an NDE are produced by nothing more than a quick jolt of the body's natural, chemical defense mechanism against pain—endorphins.

The one sure thing about life after death is that we probably will never know what it is like

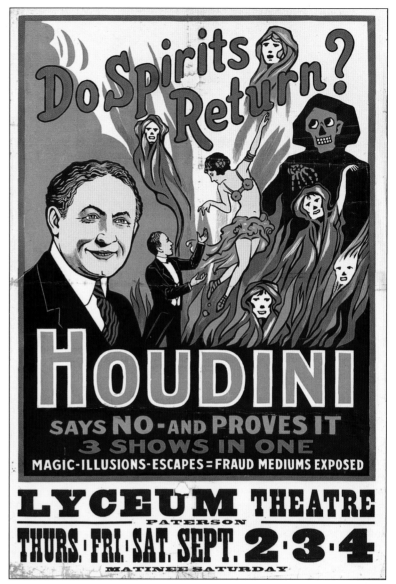

on this side of the grave. Those fearful should take comfort that in the last century, all religions seem to be moving gently away from the concept of eternal hellfire and brimstone for the unrepentant sinner. There are still honest differences of opinion, though, between Eastern and Western visions of the afterlife. Eastern religions tend to believe in reincarnation until one reaches the state of Nirvana, or nonbeing; Western Christianity tends to argue for a single existence, with one's chances for life afterward based on one's behavior here on earth.

Then there are those who have tried to put a less somber face on our earthly end—among them, transcendentalist Henry David Thoreau. While on his deathbed, Thoreau was asked by the abolitionist Parker Pillsbury whether he believed in an afterlife—to which Thoreau exclaimed, "Oh, one world at a time!"

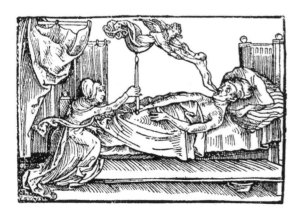

APART FROM HIS CAREER AS A CELEBRATED MAGICIAN, HARRY HOUDINI RESEARCHED THE POSSIBILITY OF AN AFTERLIFE WITH A SERIOUSNESS FEW OTHER MODERN INVESTIGATORS COULD MATCH. LEFT: IN A 16TH-CENTURY GERMAN WOODCUT, A SOUL DEPARTS AS A CHILD IS TAKEN BY THE ANGEL OF DEATH.

# How Will the
# Earth End?

**There are billions of years to go before the earth ends,
but will human beings hasten the process?**

MANY PEOPLE—FROM SCIENCE-FICTION WRITERS to religious prophets—have speculated about the Earth's final days, but perhaps only astronomers have provided an end-date that is inescapable. Our sun has been converting hydrogen into helium in its core for about 4.65 billion years. It has enough hydrogen left for another 4.5 billion before the outer layers will expand to have a circumference that extends to the orbit of the earth or farther. This new "red giant" star will one day swallow up the earth.

But there is good reason to suspect the end of humankind will come before 4.5 billion years. The most difficult question to answer is whether humans will be the cause of their own undoing or whether they will be the subject of forces outside of their control.

In the 1980s, scientists began to note with alarm that carbon dioxide levels in the atmosphere had increased by more than 25 percent from their level a century before. While some believe this rise is a natural fluctuation, others say the increase is attributable to man's excessive burning of fossil fuels. Not only does the level of carbon dioxide make the air smell and create smog, but it also runs the larger danger of enhancing the "greenhouse effect" and raising world temperatures. When sunlight bounces off the earth, gases like carbon dioxide are responsible for "catching," or reflecting, some of the radiation before it bounces back into space.

## EFFECTS OF $CO_2$

With too much carbon dioxide in the atmosphere, we risk creating a pressure cooker that could in time endanger plant life—and plants are our only means of converting carbon dioxide into oxygen. The warmer temperatures could also potentially melt the two polar ice caps, producing a water level that could slowly submerge coastal cities and make less land habitable. If human and plant life died this way, it would be a death of slow attrition.

Wars, plagues, malnutrition, and immunity disorders like AIDS have weakened population growth in the past, but as societies become more interconnected and science has learned to tackle disease, the large populations of the future may find themselves in contentious struggles for natural resources if they do not create sustainable alternatives for energy and food production. Direct attempts at controlling the population, like China's one-child policy, are admirable in some ways, but they have also revealed potentially dangerous side effects: there are 115 males to 100 females in China, largely because of selective abortion.

Contrasted to the more protracted ways for mankind to destroy itself, there are also the quicker alternatives, like nuclear holocaust. "Every man, woman, and child lives under a nuclear sword of Damocles," said President John F. Kennedy in a September 1961 speech to the United Nations General Assembly, "hanging by the slenderest of threads, capable of being cut at any moment by accident or miscalculation or madness."

## THREATS FROM SPACE

Another possible danger comes from space debris—comets and asteroids—which may present the most tangible threat to earth as we know it. It was most likely the impact of an asteroid that led to the extinction of dinosaurs 65 million years ago; another asteroid or comet striking the earth could lead to a similar climatic shift that changes the face of the planet. On May 19, 1996, an asteroid that measured one-third of a mile wide came within 275,000 miles of earth, just a hair in astronomical distances.

Astronomers have said that it would require an asteroid larger than one kilometer wide to create a global disaster. An estimated 2,000 asteroids larger than one kilometer intersect earth's orbit; one may strike its surface before 4.5 billion years, but the question is how long we can continue to play dodgeball. It should be cheering to know that studies are in the offing that might allow us to use nuclear technology to deflect a comet or asteroid.

So is man's hope for survival, as depicted by the cold lens of science, fairly bleak? Maybe. For all of our best scientific guesses, there are just as many works, including the Bible's Book of Revelation and Nostradamus's writings, which offer cryptic predictions of what is to come. Trying to match biblical or prophetic forecasts with modern correlatives has proven tricky, however. For centuries, cult after doomsday cult has predicted a time for Armageddon, only to be disillusioned.

Despite our curiosity and our best educated guesses, only those humans who are alive at the time will know the story of our planet's endgame; the true story of what happens may catch even them by surprise. At this point, the question of whether the earth will end with a bang or in a whimper stays unanswered.

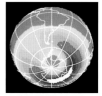

**OCTOBER 1979**

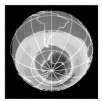

**OCTOBER 1994**

THESE IMAGES (ABOVE) SHOW THE TOTAL MONTHLY OZONE AVERAGE IN THE EARTH'S ATMOSPHERE. HUMAN ACTIVITY HAS CONTRIBUTED TO THE EROSION OF THE OZONE LAYER, WHICH MAY IN TIME LEAD TO HIGHER TEMPERATURES ON EARTH. THAT, IN TURN, COULD RESULT IN A MELTING OF THE POLAR ICE CAPS (LEFT), WHICH WOULD CAUSE THE OCEANS TO RISE AND COULD FLOOD COASTAL REGIONS WORLDWIDE.

# Utopia?
## Or the new
# Dark Ages?

**Will the 21st century bring about a perfected paradise, or the ravaged wasteland of science fiction?**

BIG BROTHER IS WATCHING YOU

1984 A Novel by GEORGE ORWELL
A SIGNET BOOK
Complete and Unabridged

**IN HIS CLASSIC NOVEL *1984*, PUBLISHED IN 1949, GEORGE ORWELL ENVISIONED A SOCIETY IN WHICH GOVERNMENT POLICED PEOPLE'S THOUGHTS. ORWELL WAS NOT THE ONLY WRITER OF HIS TIME TO PREDICT A LESS-THAN-ROSY FUTURE FOR HUMANKIND.**

PERHAPS IT IS A SIGN OF JUST HOW PERVASIVE skepticism toward the future has become that many people might take issue while reading the works of the 17th-century German philosopher and mathematician Gottfried Wilhelm Leibniz, who argued that everything bad that happens ultimately leads to a greater good, and that ours is "the best of all possible worlds."

In the early 21st century, we fear political terrorism and the potential for chemical warfare. Our televisions bring us contemporary images of slaughter in Rwanda and Burundi and starvation in Ethiopia. Yet, on the positive side, we have the capability to improve the health and life expectancy of virtually everyone on earth, and a movement toward human rights seems inevitable in the world's dictatorships. Another plus: Unlike in the past, we are making

efforts to care for the planet. So what will happen to future generations? Could the world move toward a greater good and a utopian—or ideal—society? Or are our best days behind us?

Skepticism that "everything is for the best in the best of all possible worlds" began as far back as Leibniz's contemporaries—perhaps most notably with the great French writer François Voltaire, in his fictional work *Candide* (1759). Voltaire had recently seen the death of his mistress, had read of the terrible suffering of victims of the 1755 Lisbon earthquake, and had become increasingly alienated from King Frederick the Great. *Candide* is the brilliant tale of a man, his mistress, and a wayward philosopher who naively try to cling to the notion that everything is for the best, even as incredible disasters befall them.

## ATTEMPTED UTOPIAS

Present hope about the possibility of a future utopian society has been somewhat tarnished by the history of past attempts to create such societies in miniature, schemes often ending quickly in failure. Transcendentalists in New England created the cooperative farming community called Brook Farm in 1841, abolishing money and assuming the goodwill of all involved. The community only lasted until 1847, however, unable to recover after its main building burned down. Socialist Robert Owen purchased 20,000 acres of land in Illinois and Indiana in 1825 and tried to create a utopian communal village called New Harmony, but the residents often proved to be an unruly bunch. By 1828, the community had become anything but harmonious, and it dispersed.

Attempted utopian societies of the past have often required that their members abandon

personal will for what is perhaps one man or woman's vision of a great time; these communities also require the abolishment of dissent. Adolf Hitler had a utopian vision for Germany, but his plan involved Aryan supremacy that led to the murder of millions of people.

With the Third Reich often serving as a precedent, many 20th-century writers conjured specters of future dystopias (dystopia being the opposite of utopia), where an agency or authority has complete power over its people. George Orwell's *1984*, published in 1949, describes a government that is so far-reaching that it polices people's thoughts. Ray Bradbury's *Fahrenheit 451* (1953), named after the temperature at which paper catches fire, imagines the life of a fireman of the future whose society assigns him the task of burning books and punishing book readers and owners.

But perhaps the most prescient portrait of a dystopia comes from Aldous Huxley's 1932

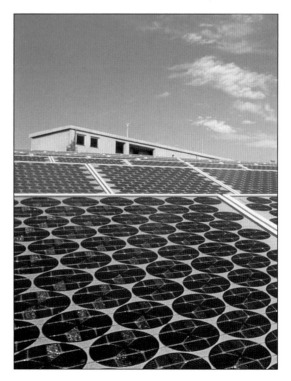

CLEAN ENERGY IS KEY TO A BRIGHT FUTURE. ENERGY-EFFICIENT HOMES (ABOVE) AND SOLAR PANELS (LEFT) THAT CONVERT SOLAR RADIATION INTO ELECTRICITY ARE BECOMING MORE WIDESPREAD. A REVOLUTIONARY NEW DEVICE IS THE FUEL CELL, WHICH GENERATES ELECTRICAL CURRENT BY MEANS OF CHEMICAL REACTIONS.

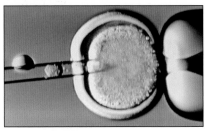

RECENT ADVANCES IN GENETICS HAVE ALLOWED HUMANS TO CLONE ANIMALS LIKE DOLLY, TOP. ABOVE, A SHEEP EGG WITH ITS OWN DNA REMOVED IS INJECTED WITH AN EMBRYONIC CELL DURING THE CLONING PROCESS.

*Brave New World*, which imagines the future world of 632 AF ("After [Henry] Ford," or about 2535 AD on the Gregorian calendar). In this world, universal human happiness supposedly has been achieved. Science has taken reproduction from the womb to the assembly line, where workers fiddle with embryos to produce human beings that range from the phenomenally bright Alpha Pluses to the short and dim-witted Epsilons, with each class of citizen preprogrammed to love its kind of work. Mass consumption of goods is celebrated, and a drug called "Soma" allows people to experience pleasure all the time.

Huxley's vision has eerie echoes both in consumer-driven, pill-popping cultures and in advances in genetic manipulation, which have resulted in the cloning of five piglets and a sheep named Dolly. The mapping of the human genome has permitted us to know more than ever before how genes help create a human being. Gene conditioning appears to be a viable technology in the not-too-distant future, and whether it is to be feared or will work toward the greater good remains to be seen.

Could something like Huxley's *Brave New World* come into being? It is hard to say. But it's also important to remember that *Brave New World*, *Fahrenheit 451,* and *1984* all feature main characters who rebel against the totalitarian nature of their respective "utopias." The trouble with imagining a happy future society in which no one dissents is that true happiness is often predicated on the very ability to dissent—that is, to think for oneself.

Another kind of potential dystopia is the New Dark Ages scenario, in which our natural resources are wholly ruined, and society has broken down completely. In this dark view, the few remnants of society would be wandering the barren earth searching for sustenance. Environmentalists and nuclear alarmists fear such a world. "If the Third World War is fought with nuclear weapons," wrote British admiral Lord Louis Mountbatten in 1975, "the fourth will be fought with bows and arrows."

**REASONS FOR HOPE**

Still, there are reasons to hope that the future will bring welcome changes, though no one can guarantee that the world will ever see perfect peace or happiness. On the environmental front, the auto industry, acknowledging our

AT CALIFORNIA'S TEHACHAPI WIND FARMS, WIND POWER IS USED TO DRIVE TURBINES AND GENERATE ELECTRICITY. SUCH CLEAN METHODS ARE BEGINNING TO RIVAL COAL-FIRED POWER PLANTS, BODING WELL FOR THE PLANET AND ITS PEOPLE.

limited supply of fossil fuels, will soon have figured out how to make a viable electric car; if all automobiles go electric, future generations will be breathing cleaner air. And the hole in the ozone layer? Human ingenuity is more than likely to come to the rescue and mend it; already, more than 120 governments have eliminated the use of chlorofluorocarbons. Wind-generated electricity is finally being produced at a cost that rivals coal-fired power plants, and solar energy and energy-efficient homes are more widespread. We are also figuring out efficient ways to clean up the disease-ridden water supplies of economically suffering countries, a development that could lead to a sharp drop in infant mortality, ultimately lowering birth rates and slowing population growth.

Likewise, medical advances are proceeding in leaps and bounds. Within a generation, it is possible that we will see cures for major diseases like cancer and AIDS, especially now that the human genome has been mapped.

Clean air, good health, peace, and the pursuit of happiness: There are obstacles to surmount before we achieve them, but humanity has plenty of reasons to hope for better tomorrows.

## A "CONFORMING SUBURB OF THE SOUL"?

To be truthful, human beings might not want to wish for a future in which the temperature is perpetually 72 degrees, the skies are clear, everyone is adequately fed, whoever we love most loves us, and all conflict and strife have vanished. Why? Because of the possibility we all could die of boredom! "I would sum up my

**WILL IT EVER HAPPEN?** ▼

fear about the future in one word: boring," said the British author J.G. Ballard in a 1982 interview. "And that's my one fear. . . [that] the future is just going to be a vast, conforming suburb of the soul." The American psychologist Erich Fromm adds in his 1955 book, *The Sane Society,* that "the danger

of the past was that men became slaves. The danger of the future is that men may become robots. True enough, robots do not rebel. But given man's nature, robots cannot live and remain sane . . . they will destroy their world and themselves because they cannot stand any longer the boredom of a meaningless life."

# Index *Boldface indicates illustration*

# Picture Credits

**Cover:** Top band L to R: Popperfoto/ Archive, Corbis, Archive, Photri, Photodisc; Bottom band L to R: Archive, Bettman/ Corbis, Corbis, Bridgeman Art Library

**10** Corbis **11** Goddard Space Center/ NASA **12** NASA/SPL/Photo Researchers **13** Bettmann/Corbis **14** Goddard Space Center/NASA **15** Nitin Vaduku **16** top left, The Granger Collection; top right, Science Source/Photo Researchers; bottom, Sinclair Stammers/SPL/Photo Researchers **17** top, The Granger Collection; center, SPL/Photo Researchers; bottom, SuperStock **18** top, The Granger Collection; bottom, SPL/Photo Researchers **19** top, NASA/Science Source/Photo Researchers; bottom, Julian Baum/SPL/Photo Researchers **20** NASA/SPL/Photo Researchers **21** top, NASA/SPL/Photo Researchers; center left & center right, JPL/NASA; bottom, Planetary Society/Phototake **22** Julian Baum/SPL/Photo Researchers **23** D. Van Ravensway/SPL/ Photo Researchers **24** top, Tom McHugh/ Photo Researchers; bottom, D. Van Ravenswaay/SPL/Photo Researchers **25** both, Louis O. Mazzatenta/National Geographic Society **26** Louis O. Mazzatenta/National Geographic Society **26-27** James Amos/Photo Researchers **28-29** David Gifford/SPL/Photo Researchers **29** bottom, NASA; **30** top, Robert Sisson/National Geographic Society; bottom, The Granger Collection **31-33** all, John Reader/SPL/Photo Researchers **34** John Reader/SPL/Photo Researchers **35** top, John Reader/SPL/Photo Researchers; bottom, American Museum of Natural History/ Photo Researchers **36** The Iraq Museum, Baghdad/Art Resource **37** both, Pierre Boulat/Life Magazine ©Time Inc. **38** top, H.M. Herget/National Geographic Society; center, The Pierpont Morgan Library/Art Resource; bottom, Lynn Abercrombie/ National Geographic Society **40** both, The Granger Collection **41** John Reader/SPL/ Photo Researchers **44** top, George Gerster/Photo Researchers; bottom, Adam Woolfit/Corbis **45** Archive Photos **46-47** Werner Forman/Art Resource **48** Erich Lessing/Art Resource **49** top, Robert Frerck/ Odyssey Productions; bottom left, Boltin Picture Library; bottom right, Culver Pictures **50** top, Louvre/Erich Lessing/Art Resource; bottom, The Granger Collection **51** left, Museo Archeologico, Florence/Scala/Art Resource; top, National Museum, Athens/ Kurt Scholz/SuperStock; bottom, Corbis **52** top left & bottom, The Granger Collection; top right, Roger Wood/Corbis **53** top left, Vanni Archive/Corbis; top right, The Granger Collection; right center, Galleria Spada, Rome/Alinari/Art Resource; bottom, Nationale Museum, Athens/Werner Forman/ Corbis **54** Museo Civico, Padua, Italy/Scala/ Art Resource **55** top left, AKG London; top right, Corbis; bottom, Museo della Scienze e Tecnica, Milan/Scala/Art Resource **56** Wood Ronsaville Harlin **57** Museo Capitolini, Rome/Art Resource **58** The Granger Collection **59** Fred Maroon/Photo Researchers **60** all, Vatican/Scala/Art Resource **61** top,

Archive Photos; bottom, Vatican/Scala/Art Resource **62** Corbis **63** both, Erich Lessing/Art Resource **64** top, Kunsthistorisches Museum, Vienna/Scala/Art Resource **65** top, The Granger Collection; bottom, George Gerster/Photo Researchers **66** Vatican/Scala/Art Resource **67** top, Historical Picture Archive/Corbis; bottom, Dave Bartruff/Corbis **68** British Library, London/Art Resource **69** The Pierpont Morgan Library, New York/Art Resource **70** top left, The Granger Collection; top right, The Pierpont Morgan Library, New York/Art Resource; bottom, Nationale Museum, Prague/Erich Lessing/Art Resource **71** The Pierpont Morgan Library, New York/Art Resource **72** NASA/SPL/Photo Researchers **73** top, Alinari/Art Resource; center all, Mark Evans **74** Archive Photos **74-75** The Granger Collection **75** left, Richard Nowitz/Photo Researchers; right, Charles Mayer/Photo Researchers **76** top, The Granger Collection; bottom, Museo Nazionale Romano, Rome/Art Resource **77** top, The Granger Collection; bottom, Museum of Roman Civilization, Rome/Art Resource **78** top left, Macmillan/McGraw-Hill/Art Resource; top right, Bettmann/Corbis; bottom, North Carolina Museum of Art/Corbis **79** top, Musee des Beaux-Arts, Beziers/Giraudon/Art Resource; bottom left & center, Archive Photos; bottom right, Bettman/Corbis **80** top, Eric Lessing/Art Resource; center, Museo Nazionale Napoli/Art Resource; bottom, The Granger Collection **81** left, The Granger Collection; right, Musee des Beaux-Arts, Lille, France/Giraudon/Art Resource **82** top, The Granger Collection; bottom, American Numismatic Society/Laurie Platt-Winfrey Inc. **83** Brian Brake/Photo Researchers **84** top, SuperStock; bottom left, Ancient Art & Architecture Collection; bottom right, Acme Design Company **85** left, The Granger Collection; right, Historical Museum Moscow/SuperStock **86** Alte Pinakothek/Art Resource **87** top, AKG London; bottom, Museo Archeologico Florence/Art Resource **88** Private Collection, Paris/Art Resource **89** left, Vatican/Scala/Art Resource; right, Werner Forman/Art Resource **90** Georg Gerster/ Photo Researchers **91** Museum of Mankind/ e.t.archive/SuperStock **92** Culver Pictures **93** both, The Granger Collection **96** Bettmann/ Corbis **97** top, SuperStock; bottom, The Granger Collection **98** British Library/e.t. archive **99** top left, Bibliotheque Nationale, Paris/Art Resource; top right, The Granger Collection; bottom, The Pierpont Morgan Library/Art Resource **100** Capitoline Museum/Canali Photobank/SuperStock **100-101** Alinari/Art Resource **102** both, e.t.archive **103** top left, Accademia di S. Fernando, Madrid/Art Resource; top right, The Granger Collection; bottom, Archivo de Simancas/Index/Bridgeman Art Library **104** left, The Granger Collecton; center, AKG London/SuperStock; bottom, AFP/Corbis **105** top, Scala/Art Resource; bottom, British Museum/e.t.archive **106** Mary Evans Picture Library/Photo Researchers **107** top, Private

Collection/Bridgeman Library; bottom, Brown Brothers **108** Private Collection AKG Berlin/SuperStock **109** top, Herbert Art Gallery & Museum, Coventry, UK/Bridgeman Library; bottom, Culver Pictures **110** The Granger Collection **111** left, Private Collection/Bridgeman Library; right, The Granger Collection **112** Bibliotheque Nationale, Paris/Bridgeman Library **113** top, Bibliotheque Nationale Paris/Laurie Platt-Winfrey Inc.; bottom, Victoria & Albert Museum/SuperStock **114** top, Bibliotheque Nationale, Paris/Art Resource; bottom, e.t.archive **115** left, The Granger Collection; right, Bibliotheque Nationale, Paris/e.t. archive **116** Jean-Loup Charmet/SPL/Photo Researchers **117** top, The Granger Collection; bottom, Museum Pomorskie, Danzig/AKG London **118** Sipa Press/Art Resource **119** SuperStock **120** The Granger Collection **121** top, The Granger Collection; bottom, Susan McCarthey/Photo Researchers **122** left, e.t.archive; right, Giraudon/Art Resource **123** top, Centre Jeanne d'Arc, Orleans, France/Giraudon/Art Resource; bottom, Bibliotheque Nationale, Paris, France/Giraudon/Art Resource **124** top, Gutenberg Museum, Mainz, Germany/Erich Lessing/Art Resource; bottom, The Pierpont Morgan Library, New York/Art Resource **125** both, Ancient Art & Architecture Collection **128** top, The Granger Collection; bottom, Naval Museum, Pegli/Scala/Art Resource **129** Karen Stickler/The Smithsonian Institution **130** top, National Gallery, Oslo; bottom, Sigrid Kaland/University of Bergen, Norway **131** Beinecke Rare Book and Manuscript Library, Yale University **132** The Granger Collection **133** top, North Dakota Historical Society; bottom, Wisconsin Historical Society **134** SuperStock **135** Tate Gallery, London/Art Resource **136** Corbis **137** top, New York Public Library; bottom, B. & C. Alexander/Photo Researchers **138** top, The Granger Collection; bottom, British Library/Bridgeman Library **139** both, The Granger Collection **140** National Portrait Gallery/Smithsonian Institution/Art Resource **141** top, American Heritage; bottom, The Granger Collection, **142** top, Bibliotheque Nationale, Paris/Bridgeman Library **142-143** The Granger Collection **143** top, Tate Gallery, London/Art Resource; center, The Granger Collection **144-147** The Granger Collection **148** Private Collection/Bridgeman Library **149** Culver Pictures **150** top, Art Resource; bottom, National Portrait Gallery, London/SuperStock **151** British Library/Bridgeman Library **152** top, Erich Lessing/Art Resource; bottom, The Granger Collection **153** Academie des Sciences, Paris/Giraudon/Art Resource **154** Culver Pictures **155** top, Brown Brothers; bottom left, The Smithsonian Institution; bottom right, Culver Pictures **156** The Granger Collection **157** left, Private Collection; top right, Staatsbibliothek, Munich/ Foto Marburg/Art Resource; center right, The Granger Collection **158** both, The Granger Collection **159** top, Metropolitan Museum of Art, Arthur Hoppock Hearn

Fund, 1950; bottom, The Granger Collection **160** top, Washington & Lee University; bottom, Mount Vernon Ladies' Association **161** The Granger Collection **162** top, Chicago Historical Society; bottom, National Gallery of Art **163** Amon Carter Museum, Fort Worth **164** top, The Granger Collection; bottom, Eric Lessing/Art Resource **165** Mozart House, Salzburg/Scala/Art Resource **166** Giraudon/Art Resource **167** Musee de Versailles/Laurie Platt-Winfrey Inc. **168** Musee des Beaux-Arts, Valenciennes/Giraudon/Art Resource **169** top, The Granger Collection; bottom, Museo del Risorgimento/Scala/Art Resource **170** Musee de l'Armee, Paris/Giraudon/Art Resource **171** Museo Lazaro Galdiano, Madrid/Giraudon/Art Resource **172** top, SPL/Photo Researchers; bottom, Jean-Loup Charmet/SPL/Photo Researchers **173** top & center, Archive Photos; bottom left, The Granger Collection; bottom right, Culver Pictures **174** top, Texas State Capitol, Austin; center, The Granger Collection; bottom, The Alamo Museum, San Antonio **175** top, The Granger Collection; center, SuperStock; bottom, New York Public Library **176** SuperStock **177** National Archives, American Heritage **178** top, Southwest Museum, Los Angeles; bottom, New York Public Library **179** left, Northern Pacific Railroad; right, The Granger Collection **180** The Granger Collection **181** top, Archive Photos; bottom, The Granger Collection **182** Fall River Library, Massachusetts **183** top, Fall River Historical Society; middle, Culver Pictures; bottom, Fall River Historical Society **184** top, National Portrait Gallery, Smithsonian Institution/Art Resource; bottom, Brown Brothers **185** top left, Archive Photos; top right, The Granger Collection; center & bottom, The Granger Collection **186** Library of Congress, American Heritage **187** both, Culver Pictures **188** Bettmann/Corbis **189** Hulton-Deutsch Collection/Corbis **190** top, British Library; bottom, The Granger Collection **191** Hulton-Deutsch Collection/Corbis **194** top right, Science Museum, London/Bridgeman Library; left and middle, The Granger Collection **194-195** bottom, Culver Pictures **195** top left, The Granger Collection **196** top, The Granger Collection; bottom, Library of Congress/American Heritage **197** top, Edison National Historic Site/National Park Service; bottom, Corbis **198-199**, Library of Congress **199** top, The Smithsonian Institution/American Heritage; bottom, U.S. Air Force/American Heritage **200** top, Underwood & Underwood/Corbis **200-201** Library of Congress/American Heritage **201** The Smithsonian Institution **202** David Parker/SPL/Photo Researchers **203** both, Sovfoto **204** top, Christie's Images/Corbis; bottom, Culver Pictures **205** top, National Baseball Hall of Fame Library, Cooperstown; bottom, New York Public Library/Culver Pictures **206** Brown Brothers **207** top, The Granger Collection; bottom all, John Frost Newspaper Archive **208** top, Brown Brothers; bottom, The Granger Collection **209** top, SuperStock; bottom, Culver Pictures

**210** top, Brown Brothers **210-211** The Granger Collection **211** top, Denis Cochrane Collection/e.t.archive **212-213** Brown Brothers **213** top, Archive Photos; center, The Granger Collection; bottom, CulverPictures **214** top, The Granger Collection; bottom, Culver Pictures **215** left, The Granger Collection; right, Stock Montage/SuperStock **216** top, Culver Pictures; bottom, Bettmann/Corbis **217** Archive Photos **218** Culver Pictures **219** top, Archive Photos; bottom, Popperfoto/Archive Photos **220** The Granger Collection **221** Brown Brothers **222** Culver Pictures **223** top, Bettmann/Corbis; bottom, 20th Century Fox/Harper Collins **224** Culver Pictures **225** top, Bancroft Library, University of California, Berkeley; bottom, The Granger Collection **226** Mount Everest Foundation **226-227** Jake Norton **227** The Granger Collection **228-229** all, Jim Fagiolo/Liaison Agency **230-231** both, New York Times/Archive Photos **232** Archive Photos **233** top, Bettmann/Corbis; bottom, The Granger Collection **234** Bettmann/Corbis **235** New York Times/Archive Photos **236** top, The Granger Collection **236-237** Corbis **237** Bettmann/Corbis **238** top, The Granger Collection; bottom, Corbis **239** top, Culver Pictures; bottom, AP Wide World Photos **240** top left, The Granger Collection; top center, The Granger Collection; top right, SuperStock; bottom, The Granger Collection **241** Culver Pictures **242** bottom, Archive Photos; top, Culver Pictures **243** SuperStock **244** bottom, AP Wide World Photos; top, Corbis **245** The Granger Collection **246-247** Culver Pictures **248** top, Corbis; bottom, Culver Pictures **249** left, AKG London; right, Corbis **250** Brown Brothers **251** Pictorial Parade **252-253** United Nations/American Heritage **253** Culver Pictures **254** bottom, AKG London; top, Yad Vashem Archives courtesy U.S. Holocaust Museum **255** KZ Gedenkstatte Dachau courtesy U.S. Holocaust Museum **256** Cartoon-Caricature-Contor **257** left, AKG London; center & right, Stern-Syndication **258-259** U.S. Air Force/American Heritage **259** top, AKG London; center, Brian Brake/Photo Researchers **260** top, Culver Pictures; bottom left, SuperStock; bottom right, Library of Congress/American Heritage **261** top, AP Wide World Photos; bottom, Bettmann/Corbis **264** Bettmann/Corbis **265** both, Bettmann/Corbis **266-267** Michael O'Neill **268** both, Cecil Stoughton/John F. Kennedy Library **269** bottom, AP Wide World Photos; top & center, Corbis **270** both, Bettmann/Corbis **271** top, AP Wide World Photos; bottom, Bettmann/Corbis **272** both, Photofest **272-273** all, Photofest **274** Dick Strobel/AP Wide World Photos **275** Bill Eppridge/Life Magazine ©Time Inc. **276-277** both, Bettmann/Corbis **278-279** Ernest C. Withers courtesy Panopticon Gallery **279** bottom, AP Wide World Photos **280** Joseph Louw, Life Magazine ©Time, Inc. **281** top, Bettman/Corbis; bottom, Corbis **282** Corbis **283** bottom, Archive Photos; middle, Bettmann/Corbis; top, Corbis **284** SuperStock **285** both, AP Wide World Photos **286** Corbis **287**

Hulton Getty/Liaison Agency **288** top, Corbis; bottom, Photofest **289** Hulton Getty/Liaison Agency **290** top, Bettmann/Corbis; bottom, Sovfoto **291** right, Sovfoto; left, Roger Ressmeyer/Corbis **292** top center, Bettmann/Corbis; bottom, Win McNamee/Archive Photos **293** top, Archive Photos; bottom, SuperStock **294-295** Archive Photos **295** SuperStock **296** top, Sovfoto; center, John Frost Newspaper Archive; bottom, AP Wide World Photos **297** Roberto Koch/Contrasto/SABA **298** Archive Photos **299** AP Wide World Photos **300** AP Wide World Photos **301** top, Jerry Wachter/Photo Researchers; bottom, Luc Novovitch/Archive Photos **302** Ian Waldie/Archive Photos **303** top, John Frost Newspaper Archive; bottom, AP Wide World Photos **304** left, John Frost Newspaper Archive; right, Bettmann/Corbis **305** Photofest **306** top left, Archive photos; top right, Corbis; bottom, John Frost Picture Archive **307** top, Archive Photos; center, Archive Photos; bottom, SuperStock **310** Roger Ressmeyer/Corbis **311** top, Roger Ressmeyer/Corbis; bottom, Lynette Cook/SPL/Photo Researchers **312-313** Harvard University Archives **313** Owen Franken/Corbis **314** top, James King-Holme/SPL/Photo Researchers; bottom left, Bettmann/Corbis; bottom center, Tony Craddock/SPL/Photo Researchers; bottom right, Charles O'Rear/Corbis **315** top, SPL/Photo Researchers; center, SPL/Photo Researchers; bottom left, Owen Franken/Corbis; bottom center left, AP Wide World Photos; bottom center right, Gregory Heisler/Corbis/Outline; bottom right, SuperStock **316** top, Corbis; bottom, AP Wide World Photos **317** top, Win McNamee/Archive Photos; bottom, AP Wide World Photos **318** left, Kobal Collection right, Julian Baum/SPL/Photo Researchers **319** David Hardy/SPL/Photo Researchers **320** Liaison Agency **321** Photofest **322** top, Richard Smith/Corbis; bottom, AP Wide World Photos **324** Bruce Stromberg/Graphistock **325** Christopher Wray-McCann/Graphistock **326** AP Wide World Photos **327** top, AP Wide World Photos; bottom, Corbis **328** Clay Bennet courtesy St. Petersburg Times **329** top, Ed Gamble courtesy Florida Times-Union; bottom, Jim Dobbins courtesy N.A.G.E. Reporter **330** Andrew Syred/SPL/Photo Researchers **331** both, SuperStock **332** Castel Capuano, Naples/SuperStock **333** SuperStock **334** Musee Conde, Chantilly/Giraudon/Art Resource; **335** top, SuperStock; bottom, The Granger Collection **336** top, D. VanRavenswaay/SPL/Photo Researchers; bottom, Photofest **337** left, Galen Rowell/Corbis; right, NASA **338** left, Library of Congress/American Heritage; right, Laurie Platt-Winfrey Inc. **339** Tommaso Guicciard/SPL/Photo Researchers **340** top, Remi Benali & Stephen Ferry/Life Magazine/Liaison Agency; bottom, James King-Holmes/SPL/Photo Researchers **341** top, John Mead/SPL/Photo Researchers; bottom, Hopkins/Baumann

PICTURE RESEARCH Carousel Research, Inc.